The Southern Debate over Slavery

VOLUME 1

The Southern Debate over Slavery

VOLUME 1: PETITIONS TO SOUTHERN LEGISLATURES, 1778–1864

EDITED BY

LOREN SCHWENINGER

UNIVERSITY OF ILLINOIS PRESS

URBANA AND CHICAGO

Publication of this book was supported by a grant from the National Historical Publications and Records Commission.

Manufactured in the United States of America
The paper in this book meets the guidelines for permanence and durability of the Committee on Production Guidelines for Book Longevity of the Council on Library Resources. ♾

Library of Congress Cataloging-in-Publication Data
The Southern debate over slavery / edited by Loren Schweninger.
p. cm.
Includes bibliographical references and index.
ISBN 0-252-02632-2 (v. 1 : acid-free paper)
1. Slavery—Political aspects—Southern States—History—Sources.
2. Slavery—Social aspects—Southern States—History—Sources.
3. Slavery—Government policy—Southern States—History—Sources.
4. Slaves—Legal status, laws, etc.—Southern States—History—Sources. 5. Afro-Americans—Legal status, laws, etc.—Southern States—History—Sources. 6. Southern States—Race relations—Sources. 7. Southern States—Politics and government—To 1775—Sources. 8. Southern States—Politics and government—1775–1865—Sources. I. Schweninger, Loren.
E446.S7 2001
326'.0975—dc21 00-010790

C 5 4 3 2 1

FOR LUTHER PORTER JACKSON
AND JAMES HUGO JOHNSTON,
PIONEER SCHOLARS

Citizens shall freely communicate their Wants or Wishes, pointout their Wrongs or Injuries, that their Representitives, whom they look up to, as Guardians & Promoters of public Justice will be not only ready to hear, but willing to extend Redress, as far as sound Policy & equal Justice, will dictate the Propriety of doing.

— Citizens of Gloucester County to the Virginia General Assembly, 15 November 1787

CONTENTS

ACKNOWLEDGMENTS

Many archivists and librarians have assisted in locating and photocopying documents for this volume. They include Edwin Bridges and Norwood A. Kerr at the Alabama Department of Archives and History; Joanne Mattern and Randy Goss at the Delaware State Archives; Kenneth H. Winn and Patsy Luebbert at the Missouri State Archives; Jeffrey Crow, Russell Koonts, Dennis Daniels, and William Brown at the North Carolina Division of Archives and History; Steven Tuttle, Robert MacIntosh, Caroline McDonnell, and Marion Chandler at the South Carolina Department of Archives and History; Ann Alley and Wayne Moore at the Tennessee State Library and Archives; Carol Kaplan of the Public Library of Nashville and Davidson County; Conley Edwards, Minor Weisiger, Chris Kolbe, Gwynne Tayloe, and John Hopewell at the Virginia State Archives; and Suzanne Levy and Edith Sprouse of the Virginia Room, Fairfax County Public Library. I am very grateful for their generous and patient assistance.

Graduate research assistants on the Race and Slavery Petitions Project at the University of North Carolina at Greensboro who have assisted in this volume include Duane Galloway, Doug Bristol, Katie Knight, David Herr, Michael Huber, Denise Ettenger, Jim Giesen, and Jeff Winstead. Staff assistant Adrienne Middlebrooks and undergraduates Jeanette Jennings and Tania Taylor helped in various ways, as did Charles Holden, Denise Kohn, and Robert Shelton. Assistant editors Chad Bowser and Lisa Maxwell perused the entire manuscript, making a number of improvements. Members of the Race and Slavery Petitions Project's advisory board offered encouragement and helpful advice at crucial junctures. Funding for research assistants, travel, staff, photocopying, release time, and computer hardware was provided by grants from the National Historical Publications and Records Commission, the National Endowment for the Humanities, and the Charles Stewart Mott Foundation. Their generosity has made this volume possible. Technical assistance was provided by James Clotfelter, Gary Grandon, Marlene Pratto, John Major, Leroy Bell, and Soraya Trolinger at the Department of Instructional and Research Services at the University of North Carolina at Greensboro. Very special thanks go to Ira Berlin, who recommended many helpful revisions; to Marguerite Ross Howell, who proofread several drafts and helped in a variety of other ways; and to the editor's wife, Patricia Schweninger, who sustained the Race and Slavery Petitions Project during its first three years as an unpaid editorial assistant.

PREFACE AND EDITORIAL METHOD

In the years following the American Revolution, growing numbers of southerners petitioned their legislatures for redress of grievances. They communicated "their Wants or Wishes," as one group wrote in 1787, so "that their Representitives, whom they look up to, as Guardians & Promoters of public Justice will be not only ready to hear, but willing to extend Redress."[1] Just as their forebears could petition King George III and the British Parliament, they had the right to petition state governments to redress wrongs, a right guaranteed in the First Amendment to the U.S. Constitution.

The range of their grievances seemed almost endless. Petitioners demanded new county seats, new courthouses, new roads, new canals, and new bridges; they sought charters for banks, academies, towns, and schools; they asked for private acts to secure boat, ferry, and liquor licenses; and they demanded laws to eliminate poll taxes, expand the suffrage, and protect citizenship rights. Among their many requests, perhaps none seemed more urgent or weighed more heavily on their minds than matters involving race and slavery.

Only three thousand petitions concerning slavery have escaped the ravages of time, but the surviving documents—coming from the Upper and Lower South, eastern and western states, and across the decades from the late eighteenth century to the mid-nineteenth—provide a geographical and chronological cross section. They also offer material on a great variety of subjects, including slaves who were obedient and faithful to their owners, interracial sex, free people of color, the black family, and attitudes among various groups of blacks and whites. The petitions come mainly from seven states—Delaware, Virginia, North Carolina, South Carolina, Tennessee, Mississippi, and Texas—with only a scattering from Florida, Alabama, Maryland, and Missouri, and only one each from Georgia and Louisiana. No legislative petitions from Kentucky and Arkansas have apparently survived.[2]

This volume contains 160 selected documents, chosen mainly to illustrate the chronological, geographical, and topical diversity of the larger collection but also to illuminate how slavery penetrated nearly every aspect of southern life and how various groups of southerners—black and white—responded to some of the most difficult problems they confronted as a result of living in a slave society. The smaller number of documents concerning Africa, the domestic slave trade, quasi-free slaves, southern sectionalism, and religion reflects a smaller number in the larger collection. Of course, any selection process is subjective, but every effort has been made to pick documents that are representative of the larger body of evidence.

The petitions are organized chronologically. This method was chosen because the documents often defy simple categorization. Nearly every petition contains discussions of matters only tangentially related to the main purpose of the plea. Indeed, this is one of the great strengths of these documents.

The documents remain virtually unchanged except for being transcribed. Spelling, capitalization, punctuation, phraseology, and sentence structure remain the same as in the original. Only when the meaning is unclear has *sic* been used, and only when the document was damaged or the writing illegible have ellipses been used, followed by a brief explanation of the ellipses in brackets. Doubtful transcriptions have been placed in brackets with a question mark. The few minor changes that have been made include indenting paragraphs in a standard manner, deleting repeated words, eliminating the underlining of a few letters in a word, and lowering raised letters or inserted words and phrases to their normal positions. In the text, underlined words and phrases appear in italics, and double underlined words and phrases appear in underlined italics. In short, every effort has been made to maintain the integrity of the original documents and allow petitioners to speak for themselves.

Besides the few barely legible petitions, one of the most vexing editorial problems involved long signature lists. The scribbled names not only were difficult and sometimes impossible to decipher but also went on for pages in some cases. When there were many petitioners, only the first ten signatures were transcribed, and the total number was included in brackets. Occasionally, a name could not be deciphered or found in the census or other contemporary records. Following such a signature is either the word *undecipherable* or a probable spelling in brackets with a question mark. To conserve space, single signature lists have been broken into two columns.

A microfilm edition of the petitions in this volume (with the exception of document 95, misfiled and later found) as well as virtually all other extant legislative petitions has been published by University Publications of America, complete with a guide and index.[3] Each petition in the microfilm edition is preceded by a computer-generated Petition Analysis Record (PAR), containing an abstract as well as other pertinent information. The PAR number at the end of each petition cited in this volume can be used for finding the item in the microfilm edition. In addition, with the editorial guidance of Paul Finkelman, University Publications of America published a microfiche edition entitled *State*

Slavery Statutes, which contains the laws and private acts passed in response to many of the petitions. Researchers and others interested in complete signature lists and other information relating to legislatures and laws should consult these editions.[4]

Some mention should be made about the annotation. To identify even a small number of petitioners—who ranged from illiterate slaves to prominent politicians—would be intrusive and burdensome to readers. In some instances, there would be more annotation than text. The same would be true for any attempt to discuss the differing views of historians on a given topic. The documents therefore contain few biographical sketches and no historical debate. Besides an occasional explanation about geography, population size, or the British antislavery crusade, almost all of the annotations concern the changing nature of the laws governing free blacks and slaves and the legislative response to individual petitions. Every attempt has been made to keep these as brief as possible, but in a few cases—for example, groups of slaves suing for their freedom—it became necessary to include more detailed information.

NOTES

1. Petition of Citizens of Gloucester County to the Virginia General Assembly, 15 November 1787, Legislative Petitions, Gloucester County, VSA.

2. For more on the original three thousand documents, see Loren Schweninger, ed., *Race, Slavery, and Free Blacks: Series 1, Petitions to Southern Legislatures, 1777–1867* (Bethesda, Md.: University Publications of America, 1998), microfilm edition, 23 reels; and Loren Schweninger, *A Guide to the Microfilm Edition of Race, Slavery, and Free Blacks: Series 1, Petitions to Southern Legislatures, 1777–1867* (Bethesda, Md.: University Publications of America, 1999). The 450–page *Guide* contains abstracts of all the petitions in the collection as well as a subject, name, and geographic location index.

3. Ibid.

4. Paul Finkelman, editorial adviser, *State Slavery Statutes* (Frederick, Md.: University Publications of America, 1989), microfiche edition; Paul Finkelman, editorial adviser, *State Slavery Statutes: Guide to State Slavery Statutes* (Frederick, Md.: University Publications of America, 1989).

INTRODUCTION

Over the years, historians have relied on a variety of sources to analyze race and slavery in the South. Ulrich Bonnell Phillips, in his pioneer study *American Negro Slavery: A Survey of the Supply, Employment and Control of Negro Labor as Determined by the Plantation Regime* (1918), quoted extensively from contemporary newspapers and travel accounts as well as various pre–Civil War tracts, diaries, correspondence, and government records.[1] Kenneth Stampp, in his classic revisionist study *The Peculiar Institution: Slavery in the Ante-Bellum South* (1956), used many of the same sources, although he relied more heavily on diaries, journals, and a few slave narratives. Stampp also utilized an important source not available to Phillips: Helen Catterall's five-volume summary of appellate court cases on slavery.[2]

Both scholars were aware of petitions as a primary source for studying slavery. In his two-volume *Documentary History of American Industrial Society* (1910), Phillips included several legislative petitions; and in his study, Stampp quoted from a South Carolina petition in discussing slave literacy and cited petitions from eleven Virginia counties in his bibliography.[3] But neither Phillips nor Stampp paid more than passing attention to this type of evidence.

Although not widely read at the time, the books and articles of two pioneer black scholars, Luther Porter Jackson and James Hugo Johnston, did cite a number of petitions. In their studies of black property ownership, race relations, and miscegenation in Virginia and the South, both used petitions to analyze the attitudes of slaveowners, the struggles of free people of color, and the quest of slaves for freedom. "Such petitions as these, reflecting the opinion of the great mass of Virginia people," Jackson wrote in *Free Negro Labor and Property Holding in Virginia, 1830–1860* (1942), "clearly indicate that in a proslavery society, such as Virginia developed after 1830, free Negroes were in an anomalous position."[4] Johnston, in his 1937 University of Chicago doctoral dissertation, "Race Relations in Virginia and Miscegenation in the South," later published as a book, was even more reliant on legislative petitions in his analysis of interracial sex, master-slave relations, and the plight of mulattoes in a society that equated even small amounts of "Negro blood" with slavery.[5]

Sixteen years after Stampp's study appeared, John Blassingame published *The Slave Community: Plantation Life in the Antebellum South* (1972), a significant reexamination of slave community life. Blassingame not only focused on neglected topics—acculturation, African survivals, black culture, the slave family—but also relied on previously unused primary sources, including slave narratives and slave autobiographies. Two out of five citations in the book, excluding secondary works, came from seventy-eight volumes written or narrated by former slaves.[6]

During the 1970s and 1980s, the literature on slavery grew enormously, with studies on the black family, slave religion, slave music and folklore, urban and industrial slavery, rice culture, and many other subjects. While continuing to rely on traditional sources, historians increasingly turned to a new body of evidence: *The American Slave: A Composite Autobiography* (1972–79), a thirty-nine-volume set of Depression-era interviews of former slaves by Works Progress Administration employees. The lure of quoting the words of ex-slaves was powerful. Few scholars dealing with the subject failed to utilize *The American Slave,* and some quoted extensively from the well-indexed collection. Perhaps no other primary source has had such a profound impact on the study of slavery.[7]

The scholarship on slavery continues to rely heavily on the testimony of prominent whites and the autobiographies and reminiscences of former slaves. Even the recent interest in women's history has uncovered diaries of elite white women or produced monographs about black women based mainly on recollections. As a consequence, people who inhabit the pages of recent books and articles are sometimes far removed in time and place from the South they describe or, due to conventions or the purpose of a diary, are less than candid in their observations. In addition, some of the best recently published editions, including *The Black Abolitionist Papers* (1985–92) and the prizewinning *Freedom: A Documentary History of Emancipation, 1861–1867* (1982–), focus on events outside the South or at the end of slavery.[8]

In contrast, legislative petitions offer immediate testimony on a broad range of subjects by a variety of southerners—black and white, slave and free, slaveowner and nonslaveowner, women and men—for nearly a century. Moreover, responding to a specific event, situation, or danger, petitioners realized that it behooved them to be as forthright and candid as possible. Female petitioners, for example, knew that they would gain little by pretense or deception because most people in their communities knew their situations. They therefore discussed their circumstances with remarkable candor and accuracy. Of course, all sources are biased, but the primary source has a high degree of credibility when it is in the interest of individuals or groups to state their case as clearly and truthfully as possible and to secure corroborating testimony.

In some areas, legislative petitions flesh out, enrich, and supplement material available from other sources. Beginning in 1913, with the publication of John H. Russell's *Free Negro in Virginia, 1619–1865,* three generations of scholars have examined free blacks in the South. James Wright, Charles Syndor, Luther Porter Jackson, E. Horace Fitchett, and John Hope Franklin created an important body of early literature, while Ira Berlin and others added to it in subsequent years.[9] They analyzed the social, religious, and economic strivings of this anomalous group in different settings during different time periods. They also examined how free blacks coped with legal restrictions, the hostility of whites, and racial violence.

Legislative petitions illuminate the changing status of free blacks over the years by documenting how they achieved their freedom, how they struggled against onerous laws, and how they sustained themselves and their families. Free blacks entered a wide range of occupations, as blacksmiths, masons, carpenters, shoemakers, barbers, draymen, tailors, seamstresses, laundresses, and cooks, among others; and some, especially in the Lower South, became farm owners, planters, and slaveholders. They also attempted to form independent schools, churches, and mutual benefit societies; obtain equal treatment and citizenship rights; and purchase family members out of slavery.

The documents also complement the historical literature concerning white racial attitudes and southern sectionalism. As early as 1804, a group of Virginia slaveowners called for new laws to punish northern boat captains who violated the "Laws of Hospitality, of social Intercourse and moral rectitude" of the slaveholding class.[10] Other southerners discussed how outsiders from the North were corrupting the minds of slaves. Not all outsiders were white. No greater evil existed, a group of South Carolina slaveholders asserted, than the "constant intercourse, which is maintained between the blacks of the North and the South." Slaves learned "pernicious principles and opinions," methods of resistance, and ideas about rebellion. The same group of South Carolinians petitioned the legislature to prohibit any person of color from entering the state or returning to it after traveling above the Potomac and Susquehanna rivers.[11]

Some of these petitions lend support to what some historians have called the clandestine slave economy. Under this system, slaves, free blacks, and whites bought, sold, and bartered goods and commodities with one another. Petitions reveal the widespread nature of such market activities among slaves. Even though the clandestine economy was illegal—slaves were not permitted to trade goods without their masters' permission—it grew from one decade to the next. Slaves cultivated rice, tobacco, and sugar; raised horses, cattle, hogs, and sheep; and owned wagons, carriages, and boats. They used their crops, livestock, and other property, a group of North Carolina residents said, "to sell, buy, traffick."[12] Echoing requests in other parts of the South, a group of planters in South Carolina's Orangeburg District asked the legislature to prohibit slaves from cultivating their own cotton. Cotton was subject "to the depredations of the night walking thief," they said, "& when lost, it would be the height of folly to attempt finding it among negroes who all have cotton of their own: It would be like looking for a drop of water lost in a river."[13]

Petitions also supplement our knowledge of what contemporaries called "virtually free" or "quasi-free" slaves. These bondsmen and bondswomen hired out their own time, earned their own livelihoods, and paid their owners for the privilege of freedom. The most famous self-hired slave was Frederick Douglass, who worked as a Baltimore ship's caulker, but historians have examined other privileged slaves in a variety of different settings and occupations. Petitions not only add valuable details about individuals already cited in the literature but also provide unique evidence about the lives of previously unknown slaves who acted as free persons. Stephen Lytle of Nashville, for example, hired out his own time, purchased himself and his wife, and, while still in bondage, acquired real estate. He was, according to whites who knew him, an honest, industrious, and dependable man.[14] While rare, such autonomy was greatly valued by slaves. Other petitions reveal how previously nameless self-hired slaves struggled, often for many years, to free themselves or members of their families.

The evolution of slave societies can also be traced in legislative petitions. With the decline of African- and West Indian–born blacks in the slave population during the late eighteenth century and early nineteenth, distinct slave societies emerged in the South. These included the growing black urban artisan class in Baltimore, Richmond, Charleston, Savannah, New Orleans, and other cities; the increasing numbers of unskilled term-slaves (destined to be freed at a future date) in Delaware, Maryland, and the District of Columbia; Chesapeake slaves who planted, cultivated, and harvested tobacco, grains, and cotton; Sea Island blacks in South Carolina and Georgia who labored in the rice and cotton fields and maintained many cultural ties with West Africa and the Caribbean; and slaves in the lower Mississippi River valley who toiled on sugar plantations. Glimpses of these and other slave societies, including their different customs, attitudes, work routines, languages, and dialects, can be found in petitions.

Information on the distinct and evolving patterns of race relations can also be uncovered in petitions. In the aftermath of the American Revolution, the ideals espoused in the struggle against Great Britain, especially in states in the Upper South, spilled over into white-black relations. Some white southerners expressed sympathy for bondspeople and even espoused antislavery sentiments. Of course, some of this sympathy came as a result of the belief that slavery was becoming less profitable, especially during the 1790s. But race relations seemed less rigid, more flexible, as revealed in large-scale manumissions and less rigid laws. Even in the Lower South, white-black relations, drawing on French and Spanish traditions, remained more pliant in the early years than in the decades leading up to the Civil War. This could be seen in the large percentage of persons of mixed racial origin among free persons of color.

Legislative petitions provide supplemental information in a number of other areas as well, including colonization, divorce, miscegenation, plantation management, politics, religion, and the domestic slave trade. With regard to the domestic slave trade, petitions show how various states sought to regulate the interregional transportation and sale of slaves. In the Upper South, slaveholders worked to rid themselves of what they termed "obdurate," "ungovernable," and "rebellious" slaves; in the Lower South, they sought to erect barriers against what a group of South Carolina slaveholders called the "importation of vicious or criminal slaves from other States."[15] The discussions about buying and selling slaves in the different sections of the South complement the literature on the domestic slave trade.

In a number of areas, however, legislative petitions offer new insights about race and slavery in the South. Perhaps the most important of these is the picture they present of the disparity between the legal codes—enacted and revised over several generations—and the effectiveness of these laws in practice.[16] In virtually every state in the South, whites complained about the inadequacy of the laws regulating slaves and free blacks. When South Carolina whites despaired in 1797 that the existing law prohibiting the importation of French West Indian Negroes met with "continual infraction," they were articulating what future generations would say again and again.[17] In 1835, a group in the same state asserted that the law prohibiting slaves from learning to read the Bible was "a *dead letter.*"[18] It was not unusual, they said, to hear prudent men declare they were "'prepared to disrespect such a law.'"[19] About 1852, slaveholders in Wilkinson County, Mississippi, told of "riots, routs, and unlawful assemblies," of "crowds of negroes, drinking, fiddling, dancing, singing, cursing, swearing, whooping and yelling," and of "every violation of the penal laws."[20] Although various studies have examined slavery and the law, legislative petitions show better than any other primary source what it meant for a society to have its laws violated and what it meant to have "prudent men" disregard the law.

There is also new material about petitioning as a legal and political process. How people communicated their wishes, the problems they confronted during various political crises, and the complex nature of the legislative process are all revealed in this body of evidence. Each petition, for example, might be read, amended, tabled, postponed, referred to committee, rejected, or drawn into a bill.[21] Even if a bill became a law or a private act, it might include only part of the petitioner's original request. During any of these stages, legislators could offer amendments, debate the specifics, demand roll calls, offer substitutes, or request a vote. When, where, and why certain petitions were granted and others rejected provide details for a better understanding of the legal and political systems of the Old South.[22]

Among the most significant questions these documents shed light on are how and when illiterate slaves or semiliterate free blacks could bring their cases before legislatures. It is perhaps not surprising that most of their remonstrances, primarily concerned with manumission and anti–free black residency laws, were rejected. What is surprising is that their petitions made it to the halls of statehouses. Those who were successful often were directly related to whites, who either wrote petitions in their behalf or hired lawyers to do so. Even those who failed in their requests, however, were often persons of mixed racial ancestry who could seek assistance from white relatives or from locally prominent whites who knew about their backgrounds. It was extremely rare for a black person without white assistance to send a request to the legislature and even rarer for a private act to be passed in his or her behalf.

It might be expected that legislative petitions would cast new light on the law and politics. What is remarkable are other areas where petitions point to new interpretations. This is particularly the case with manumission. As noted earlier, there are a number of books and articles about free blacks. Far less is known, however, about how and when blacks achieved their freedom and how many actually did so, especially since they were required by law to leave their family and friends. In the same vein, the petitions provide a clear picture of the pressures—legal, economic, and political—pushing manumitted slaves backward toward slavery. Heirs of slaveowners were often reluctant to give up large numbers of manumitted slaves and struggled to maintain ownership following the death of an owner. The tenuous nature of freedom and the precarious balance tipping backward toward slavery can be clearly seen in these documents.

The symbiotic relationship between former slaves and former owners can also be observed in the petitions. The fear of being returned to slavery forced manumitted blacks to seek the protection of prominent whites, often their former masters. Indeed, as the doors of manumission closed during the early decades of the nineteenth century, freed slaves sought such protection as a matter of necessity. They asked whites for certificates of recommendation, travel passes, guardianship papers, and reference letters. In many aspects of free black life—economic well-being, occupational status, class attitudes, color consciousness—there were profound differences between the Upper and Lower South, but among manumitted slaves there were striking similarities in the need for white "protectors." The impact on those who sought such assistance, as well as the attitudes of slaveowners who offered it, is nowhere more clearly revealed than in legislative petitions.

The documents also illuminate the unique role of free women of color.[23] Manumitted in larger numbers than their male counterparts and constituting a larger portion of the free black population, free black women struggled to protect themselves and their families.[24] "Tis with anxious and trembling forebodings then that your Petitioner presents herself before the Legislature to supplicate of their liberality and clemency," Elvira Jones, a former slave, wrote the

Virginia General Assembly in 1823; she asked for permission for "herself and children to live and die in the Land of their nativity."[25] Jones's dilemma was shared by other women who confronted increasingly restrictive laws, faced wrenching decisions about their families, and struggled against economic, political, and legal barriers.[26] How they responded, as well as how, in the end, many of them failed, is captured in legislative petitions perhaps better than in any other primary source.

Perhaps the most striking feature about legislative petitions is the picture they paint of slave resistance. In 1943, Herbert Aptheker published *American Negro Slave Revolts,* a book criticized by some scholars as unrepresentative and anecdotal.[27] Legislative petitions bear out many of his contentions and provide substantial documentation to show that the South was a place of fear, anger, hostility, and violence. It is difficult to read the more than five hundred petitions concerning slaves who died or were executed without being struck by the amount of interracial violence. Owners sought compensation for slaves killed by patrols, executed for robbery or murder, and murdered by white "outsiders." Others sought compensation for services rendered at slave executions.[28] In 1802, William Simmons, a Charleston resident, asked for payment of more than ten pounds, explaining that he had stood guard over Smart, a slave sentenced to be hanged, and had purchased wood, tar, chains, and a post for Davy, "Sentenced to be burnt for Robbery & Murder."[29]

Other petitions deal with the efforts of slaveowners to control outlying and rebellious slaves. The story of Sambo in Goochland County, Virginia, in 1778, was repeated with various scenarios in different sections during subsequent decades. Arrested and jailed for preparing "poisonous medicens," Sambo escaped with a fellow slave, assembled "in Rebellion" deep in the woods, and committed "many Hostilitys, Break.g open Houses, kill.g Hoggs &c, Whereupon diffr sirches was made after them the sd. Slaves, who was at Length routed at or near their cave in the Ground wch. they the sd. Slaves to all appearance had us'd for their place of residence & safty for some time." Despite repeated entreaties to surrender, Sambo refused and was shot "dead on the spott."[30]

How pervasive these problems became was revealed in a petition from a group of planters in Christ Church Parish, South Carolina, in 1829. They wrote about "great irregularity and disorder" among their slaves, "a state of insubordination and danger affecting the lives of individuals and the security of property," and "the great evil of absconding slaves and their ruinous depredations." The "insubordination and danger" existed in every section of the "lower and middle divisions of the State." The planters cited two causes for these problems: the ideas of liberty infused into the minds of servants by free blacks and "worthless white people"; and an 1821 law making it a capital offense to murder a slave.[31]

It is doubtful that slaves needed to discuss their plight with free blacks or poor whites before becoming defiant or that they became mutinous because they learned that if they were killed the murderer might face a death penalty. Southern whites' frantic search to explain "great irregularity and disorder" among their slaves was less important than their admission of widespread unrest. If only a few petitions were in this vein, they might be dismissed as aberrations, but many documents point to slave unrest, while others reveal the continual, often violent confrontations between slaves and their owners and overseers.

It was during periods of heightened anxiety that slaveowners and others submitted the largest number of petitions. In North Carolina, for example, residents submitted more petitions following rumors of revolt in 1800 and 1802 than during any other period. During the 1820s, after the Denmark Vesey plot in South Carolina, petitioners sent nearly twice as many petitions to the general assembly as during any other decade. During the 1830s, following the Nat Turner revolt in Virginia, whites directed more petitions to the assembly than during any other decade. As the following table and graph indicate, it was during periods of greatest fear that southerners submitted the largest number of petitions (at least from our knowledge of extant documents) to their legislatures.

Thus, while legislative petitions augment our knowledge in many ways, they also provide an opportunity to see slavery in a new and different light. This is especially the case for slavery and the law, manumission, race relations, free women of color, and slave resistance. But what sets these documents apart is not merely the opportunity to revise old interpretations. Unlike reminiscences and autobiographies, written long after events, petitions provide immediate observations. Moreover, unlike many contemporary sources, including diaries and personal correspondence, petitions were scrutinized by many observers for accuracy, and it was to the benefit of petitioners to set forth their case as succinctly and truthfully as possible. As a result, legislative petitions provide a remarkably clear view of the institution of slavery, one not diluted by conventional mores or the passage of time.

Table 1. Petitions to Southern Legislatures by States and Decades, 1777–1867

Decade	Dela.	Miss.	N.C.	S.C.	Tenn.	Tex.	Va.	Other	Totals
1777–1779			2				12		14
1780–1789	9		25	25			35		94
1790–1799	30		77	85	2		26		220
1800–1809	21	2	80	67	15		75		260
1810–1819	82	10	51	96	80		174	3	496
1820–1829	140	32	55	170	70		100	10	577
1830–1839	49	27	50	62	114	23	198	6	529
1840–1849	77		30	43	81	39	95	6	371
1850–1859	10	33	55	51	46	43	46	7	291
1860–1867		23	16	10	7	8	21	5	90
undated		24		5					29
Totals	418	151	441	614	415	113	782	37	2,971

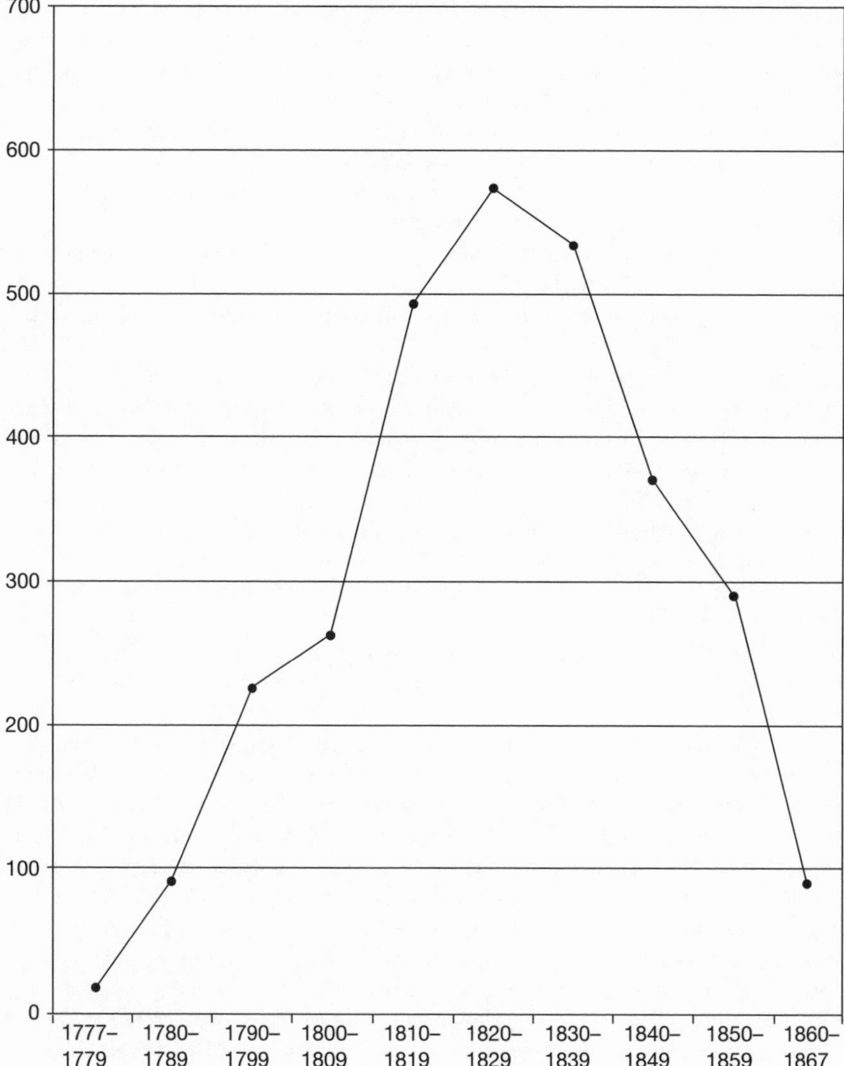

Figure 1. Petitions to Southern Legislatures by Decades

NOTES

1. Based on an analysis of approximately 1,100 footnoted sources cited in Ulrich B. Phillips, *American Negro Slavery: A Survey of the Supply, Employment and Control of Negro Labor as Determined by the Plantation Regime* (New York: D. Appleton, 1918). For similar use of sources, see Ulrich B. Phillips, *Life and Labor in the Old South* (Boston: Little, Brown, 1929), which won the Pulitzer Prize.

2. Based on an analysis of approximately 1,375 footnoted sources cited in Kenneth Stampp,

The Peculiar Institution: Slavery in the Ante-Bellum South (New York: Alfred P. Knopf, 1956). Excluding secondary sources, Stampp cited Helen T. Catterall, ed., *Judicial Cases concerning American Slavery and the Negro,* 5 vols. (Washington, D.C.: W. F. Roberts, 1932; reprint, New York: Octagon Books, 1968), in about 8 percent of his citations.

3. Ulrich B. Phillips, ed., *Documentary History of American Industrial Society,* 2 vols. (Cleveland: Arthur H. Clark, 1910), 2:151–64; Stampp, *The Peculiar Institution,* 211–12, 436.

4. Luther Porter Jackson, *Free Negro Labor and Property Holding in Virginia, 1830–1860* (Washington, D.C.: American Historical Association, 1942), 19.

5. James Hugo Johnston, "Race Relations in Virginia and Miscegenation in the South, 1776–1860" (Ph.D. diss., University of Chicago, 1937); James Hugo Johnston, *Race Relations in Virginia and Miscegenation in the South, 1776–1860* (Amherst: University of Massachusetts Press, 1970), 105–13.

6. Based on an analysis of approximately 1,600 footnoted sources cited one or more times in John W. Blassingame, *The Slave Community: Plantation Life in the Antebellum South* (New York: Oxford University Press, 1972). Slave narratives were written by runaway slaves who made it to freedom and wrote about their experiences. They were published during the antebellum and Civil War periods.

7. George P. Rawick, ed., *The American Slave: A Composite Autobiography,* 39 vols. (Westport, Conn.: Greenwood, 1972–79). See also David Thomas Bailey, "A Divided Prism: Two Sources of Black Testimony on Slavery," *Journal of Southern History* 46 (August 1980): 381–404.

8. C. Peter Ripley et al., eds., *The Black Abolitionist Papers,* 5 vols. (Chapel Hill: University of North Carolina Press, 1985–92); Ira Berlin et al., eds., *Freedom: A Documentary History of Emancipation, 1861–1867* (New York: Cambridge University Press, 1982–).

9. John H. Russell, *The Free Negro in Virginia, 1619–1865* (Baltimore: Johns Hopkins University Press, 1913); James Wright, *The Free Negro in Maryland, 1634–1860* (New York: Columbia University Press 1921); Charles Syndor, "The Free Negro in Mississippi before the Civil War," *American Historical Review* 32 (July 1927): 769–88; Jackson, *Free Negro Labor;* E. Horace Fitchett, "The Origin and Growth of the Free Negro Population of Charleston, South Carolina," *Journal of Negro History* 26 (October 1941): 421–37; John Hope Franklin, *The Free Negro in North Carolina, 1790–1860* (1943; reprint, Chapel Hill: University of North Carolina Press, 1995); Ira Berlin, *Slaves without Masters: The Free Negro in the Antebellum South* (New York: Pantheon Books, 1974); Leonard Curry, *The Free Black in Urban America, 1800–1850: The Shadow of the Dream* (Chicago: University of Chicago Press, 1981); Larry Koger, *Black Slaveowners: Free Black Slave Masters in South Carolina, 1790–1860* (Jefferson, N.C.: McFarland, 1985; reprint, Columbia: University of South Carolina Press, 1995); Christopher Phillips, *Freedom's Port: The African American Community of Baltimore, 1790–1860* (Urbana: University of Illinois Press, 1997); Tommy L. Bogger, *Free Blacks in Norfolk, Virginia, 1790–1860: The Darker Side of Freedom* (Charlottesville: University Press of Virginia, 1997).

10. Petition of Benjamin Duval et al. to the Virginia Assembly, 20 December 1804, Legislative Petitions, Richmond City, VSA.

11. Petition of the South Carolina Association to the Senate, ca. December 1823, Records of the General Assembly, #1415, SCDAH.

12. Petition of Inhabitants of Craven County to the North Carolina Assembly, 19 December 1831, Records of the General Assembly, Sessions Records, NCDAH.

13. Petition of Sanders Glover et al. to the South Carolina Senate and House of Representatives, 4 December 1816, Records of the General Assembly, #95, SCDAH.

14. Petition of Stephen Lytle to the Tennessee Assembly, ca. 1832, Legislative Petitions, #140-1833-1-3, reel 13, TSLA; Certificate, Will Lytle et al., 28 June 1832, ibid.

15. Petition of S. T. Robinson et al. to the South Carolina Senate and House of Representatives, ca. 1843, Records of the General Assembly, #2824, SCDAH. The Upper South includes Delaware, Maryland, Virginia, North Carolina, Kentucky, Tennessee, and Missouri; the Lower South includes South Carolina, Georgia, Florida, Alabama, Mississippi, Arkansas, Louisiana, and Texas.

16. For recent studies on the subject, see Thomas D. Morris, *Southern Slavery and the Law, 1619–1860* (Chapel Hill: University of North Carolina Press, 1996); Philip J. Schwarz, *Twice Condemned: Slaves and the Criminal Laws of Virginia, 1705–1865* (Baton Rouge: Louisiana State University Press, 1988); Philip J. Schwarz, *Slave Laws in Virginia* (Athens: University of Georgia Press, 1996); Edward L. Ayers, *Vengeance and Justice: Crime and Punishment in the Nineteenth Century South* (New York: Oxford University Press, 1984); Judith Kelleher Schafer, *Slavery, the Civil Law, and the Supreme Court of Louisiana* (Baton Rouge: Louisiana State University Press, 1994); Mark Tushnet, *The American Law of Slavery, 1810–1860: Considerations of Humanity and Interest* (Princeton, N.J.: Princeton University Press, 1981); Andrew Fede, "Legitimized Violent Slave Abuse in the American South, 1619–1865: A Case Study of Laws and Social Change in Six Southern States," *American Journal of Legal History* 29 (April 1985): 93–150; and Jenny Bourne Wahl, "The Bondsman's Burden: An Economic Analysis of the Jurisprudence of Slaves and Common Carriers," *Journal of Economic History* 53 (September 1993): 495–526.

17. Petition of Sundry Citizens of Charleston to the South Carolina Senate, 11 December 1797, Records of the General Assembly, #87, SCDAH.

18. Petition of David Hemphill et al. to the South Carolina Legislature, 1835, Records of the General Assembly, #1812, SCDAH.

19. Ibid.; *Acts and Resolutions of the General Assembly, of the State of South Carolina, Passed in December, 1834* (Columbia: E. F. Branthwaite, 1834), 13–15; John Codman Hurd, *The Law of Freedom and Bondage in the United States,* 2 vols. (Boston: Little, Brown, 1858–62; reprint, New York: Negro Universities Press, 1968), 2:98.

20. Petition of Citizens of Wilkinson County to the Mississippi Senate and House of Representatives, ca. 1852, Records of the Legislature, vol. 27, Petitions and Memorials, 1850–59, RG 47, MDAH.

21. In North Carolina, for example, names of committees dealing with race and slavery included Propositions and Grievances, Claims, Judiciary, Private Bills, House Select Committee, Joint Select Committee of the House and Senate, Finance, and Divorce; in South Carolina, they included, among others, Accounts, Public Accounts, Religion, Roads, Judiciary, and Colored Population.

22. Petitions are, of course, the beginning of the process. Occasionally, the result of the request can be found on the docket page of the petition itself, but most often what happened can be traced only in published house and senate reports or in published acts and laws of the state.

23. With a few exceptions, historians have neglected the plight of free women of color. The exceptions include Cheryl Fish, "Voices of Restless (Dis)continuity: the Significance of Travel for Free Black Women in the Antebellum Americas," *Women's Studies* 26 (October 1997): 475–95; Whittington B. Johnson, "Free African-American Women in Savannah, 1800–1860: Affluence and Autonomy amid Adversity," *Georgia Historical Quarterly* 76 (Summer 1992):

260–83; Suzanne Lebsock, *The Free Women of Petersburg: Status and Culture in a Southern Town, 1784–1860* (New York: W. W. Norton, 1984); Adele Logan Alexander, *Ambiguous Lives: Free Women of Color in Rural Georgia, 1789–1879* (Fayetteville: University of Arkansas Press, 1991); Kent Anderson Leslie, *Woman of Color, Daughter of Privilege: Amanda America Dickson, 1849–1893* (Athens: University of Georgia Press, 1995); Judith Kelleher Schafer, "'Open and Notorious Concubinage': The Emancipation of Slave Mistresses by Will and the Supreme Court in Antebellum Louisiana," *Louisiana History* 27 (Spring 1987): 165–82; and Loren Schweninger, "Property Owning Free African-American Women in the South, 1800–1870," *Journal of Women's History* 1 (Winter 1990): 13–44.

Much more attention has been devoted to female slaves. Among the numerous works on slave women are John Campbell, "Work, Pregnancy, and Infant Mortality among Southern Slaves," *Journal of Interdisciplinary History* 14 (Spring 1984): 793–812; Elizabeth Clark, "Matrimonial Bonds: Slavery and Divorce in Nineteenth-Century America," *Law and History Review* 8 (Spring 1990): 25–54; Mary Ellison, "Resistance to Oppression: Black Women's Response to Slavery in the United States," *Slavery and Abolition* 4 (March 1983): 56–63; Elizabeth Fox-Genovese, *Within the Plantation Household: Black and White Women of the Old South* (Chapel Hill: University of North Carolina Press, 1988); Paul Finkelman, ed., *Women and the Family in a Slave Society* (New York: Garland, 1989); Darlene Clark Hine and David Barry Gaspar, eds., *More Than Chattel: Black Women and Slavery in the Americas* (Bloomington: Indiana University Press, 1996); Herbert Gutman, *The Black Family in Slavery and Freedom, 1750–1925* (New York: Pantheon Books, 1976); Thelma Jennings, "'Us Colored Women Had to Go Through a Plenty': Sexual Exploitation of African-American Slave Women," *Journal of Women's History* 1 (Winter 1990): 45–74; Sally G. McMillen, *Southern Women: Black and White in the Old South* (Arlington Heights, Ill.: Harlan Davidson, 1992); Ann Patton Malone, *Sweet Chariot: Slave Family and Household Structure in Nineteenth-Century Louisiana* (Chapel Hill: University of North Carolina Press, 1992); Leslie A. Schwalm, *A Hard Fight for We: Women's Transition from Slavery to Freedom in South Carolina* (Urbana: University of Illinois Press, 1997); Marli F. Weiner, *Mistresses and Slaves: Plantation Women in South Carolina, 1830–1880* (Urbana: University of Illinois Press, 1998); Carole Shammas, "Black Women's Work and the Evolution of Plantation Society in Virginia," *Labor History* 26 (Winter 1985): 5–28; Deborah Gray White, "Female Slaves: Sex Roles and Status in the Antebellum Plantation South," *Journal of Family History* 9 (Fall 1983): 248–61; Deborah Gray White, *Ar'n't I a Woman? Female Slaves in the Plantation South* (New York: W. W. Norton, 1985); Betty Wood, *Women's Work, Men's Work: The Informal Slave Economies of Low Country Georgia* (Athens: University of Georgia Press, 1995); and Wilma King, *Stolen Childhood: Slave Youth in Nineteenth-Century America* (Bloomington: Indiana University Press, 1995).

24. Among the 414 petitions submitted by blacks, 94, or 23 percent, were submitted by women.

25. Petition of Elvira Jones to the Virginia General Assembly, 5 December 1823, Legislative Petitions, Henrico County, VSA.

26. Following Virginia's example, most Upper South states required manumitted slaves to leave the state or face reenslavement; by the 1820s and 1830s, most Lower South states prohibited manumission except by a special act of the legislature. Peter Kolchin, *American Slavery, 1619–1877* (New York: Hill and Wang, 1993), 89–90, 128; *A Collection of All Such Acts of the General Assembly of Virginia of a Public and Permanent Nature as Have Passed since the Session of 1801* (Richmond: Samuel Pleasants Jr., 1808), 97. Even earlier, South Carolina had

put severe restrictions on manumission. In 1800, for example, lawmakers stipulated that slave-owners who wanted to free their slaves were required to notify a magistrate and summon five freeholders to judge the worthiness of the slave to be freed. *Acts and Resolutions of the General Assembly, of the State of South-Carolina, Passed in December, 1800* (Columbia: Daniel and J. J. Faust, 1801), 39–41; *Acts and Resolutions of the General Assembly of the State of South-Carolina, Passed in December, 1820* (Columbia: D. Faust, 1821), 22–24.

27. Herbert Aptheker, *American Negro Slave Revolts* (New York: Columbia University Press, 1943).

28. Most states compensated owners who lost slaves while working on public roads, canals, or bridges.

29. Petition of William Simmons to the South Carolina House of Representatives, November 1802, Records of the General Assembly, #180, SCDAH; Certificate, John Johnson, Justice of the Peace, 8 November 1802, ibid.

30. Petition of Archer Payne to the Virginia House of Delegates, 13 November 1778, Legislative Petitions, Goochland County, VSA.

31. Petition of John Jonah Murrell et al. to the Speaker and Members of the South Carolina House of Representatives, 1829, Records of the General Assembly, #90, SCDAH.

ABBREVIATIONS

ADAH	Alabama Department of Archives and History, Montgomery, Alabama
DSA	Delaware State Archives, Dover, Delaware
FSA	Florida State Archives, Tallahassee, Florida
MDAH	Mississippi Department of Archives and History, Jackson, Mississippi
MoSA	Missouri State Archives, Jefferson City, Missouri
NCDAH	North Carolina Division of Archives and History, Raleigh, North Carolina
PAR	Petition Analysis Record
RG	Record Group
SCDAH	South Carolina Department of Archives and History, Columbia, South Carolina
TSLA	Tennessee State Library and Archives, Nashville, Tennessee
TSL-AD	Texas State Library–Archives Division, Austin, Texas
VSA	Virginia State Archives, Richmond, Virginia

PETITIONS TO SOUTHERN LEGISLATURES, 1778–1864

1. Archer Payne, Goochland County, to Virginia House of Delegates, 1778

To the Honourable Mr. Speaker & Gent. of the House Deligates now Seting.

The petition of Archer Payne of Goochld County Humbly Sheweth, that whereas Sambo a negroe man Slave the property of the sd. petitioner was on or abt. the 20th. August 1777 taken ~~up~~ by a justices Warrant out of the Service & custody of his master the petitioner & was thereby commited to the Goal of the said County on suspicion of preparg poisonous medicens And did actily administer part thereof to a negroe Man Slave the property of Thos. F. Bales Genl., but on a night or two before the said Sambo was to have had his Tryal for the sd. Offence, he in company with another negroe man Slave the property of James Bullock who was then in the sd. Prison did both break out the Goal and assemble themselves in Rebellion together in a thick part of Woods, or large Slash in the neighbourhood of the sd. Bullock & then & thereabouts commit many Hostilitys, Break.g open Houses, kill.g Hoggs &c, Whereupon diffr sirches was made after them the sd. Slaves, who was at Length routed at or near their cave in the Ground wch. they the sd. Slaves to all appearance had us'd for their place of residence & safty for some time, who was repeatedly called upon to stand & surrender but they refusing—Edwin Gibson who was one the Company in pursuit of the sd. Slaves, did shoot the sd. Petitioners negroe Sambo dead on the spott. Whereupon he the sd. Payne prays such relief in the premises as you in yr. great Wisdom shall think most just & reasonable & he in Duty bound shall pray &c

[no signature]

SOURCE: Petition of Archer Payne to the Virginia House of Delegates, 13 November 1778, Legislative Petitions, Goochland County, VSA. PAR #11677805.

2. Jacob Alford et al., Bladen County, to North Carolina Assembly, 1779

Bladden County, January 23d Day 1779

Unto The Honourable Gentleman of Both Houses of Assembly

The petition of Jacob Alford Captin & The Inhabitants of the Upper part of Bladden County. Humbly Sheweth. That Your petitioners are in Constant dread & Fear of Being Robbed and Murdered by A Set of Robbers And Horse Thiefs, Which have been among us this week to the number of About Forty, Who have Commited A Great deal of Mischief Already, & we Understand by Some of them, They Soon Intend to Ruin us Altogether In the Borders of our District and Anson County, Some have had their Houses Broke and All Their Cloaths Taken from Them, Even Their Babes and Infants were Stripped naked, Women were knocked down with stakes & Tommyhakes in their Husband's Absence, Many had All Their Cattle taken Away from them, & Their Corn Robbd out of Their Cribs, By Which many of Them are entirely undone & Ruined, The most part of The Robbers Are Molattoes, And Chiefly Came from the south province when the Vagrant Act Came Among Them, We lay our Distress and our unhappy Case before Your Honourable Assembly. And Hopes Youl take our Unfortunate Situation Unto Your humain Consideration—And Grant us such Relief As Your Goodness may Think proper Whether you may Allow us to Get Arms to Defend Ourselves, Or Youl Order Some Oyrs. to protect us. The Orders Must be Speedy Otherwise We are Outerly undone.

And your petitioners As in Duty Bound Shall Ever pray &c, &c.

[no signatures]

SOURCE: Petition of Jacob Alford and Inhabitants of the Upper Bladen County to the North Carolina General Assembly, 30 January 1779, Records of the General Assembly, Session Records, NCDAH. PAR #11277901.

3. Anne Bennet to Virginia House of Delegates, 1780

To the Honourable the Speaker and other members of the house of delegates of the Commonwealth of Virginia,

The Petition of Anne Bennet, an Infant under the age of twenty one years, by William Alvey, her guardian, humbly,—Sheweth, that Ann Colvin, deceased a woman in low circumstance and Possessed only of one Slave, made her last will & testament, in Writing on the twenty fifth day of Nov.r in the year of OUR Lord one thousand seven hundred, and seventy six, wherein she bequeathed the same slave, who is named will, and a horse, to Elizabeth Bennet your Petitioner's Cousin, and directed that the remaining part of Her Estate should be sold, and divided in certain proportions ~~for~~ Between the said Elizabeth, and your Petitioner (who were her Grand Children & her only descendants) making them at the Same time Reciprocally heiresses to one another; Soon after, Elizabeth Bennet Died, without Issue, and on the twenty Second day of July, In the year of our Lord, one thousand, seven hundred, and Seventy Nine, the said Ann made a Codicil to her said Will, whereby She did will, and ordain, the said Slave Will, to be free, and not Subject to Slavery in Consideration of the long and faithful Service, done to her, by him, and moreover, bequeathed the Said Horse & a lone yearling to the Said Will; before the making of this Codicil, no Meritorious Service was proved before the Governor And Council, to have been done by the Said Slave, and Consequently No Judgment was given by them, that he deserved his freedom, And no licence Issued for the purpose of setting him free, nor Indeed Has any of those things happen'd Untill this day. these things However your Petitioner has understood are required by Law, Before any Slave can be set free; and that She has the greatest Veneration for the memory of her deceased grandmother, yet, She Cannot help Suggesting to this Honourable house, that She Believes that the Codicil to her Grandmother's will was made, on account of the fear which she Entertained of receiving some Personal Injury from him, rather than on account of any gratitude for his past Services, as an Evidence that this Suggestion is well founded, your Petitioner believes that She can prove that the Slave Will, after having often threatened, and once attempted to take away his own life in order to revenge himself of his Former Master for giving him a Slight Correction, has made an attempt upon the life of your Petitioner's Grandmother, who was to him a most indulgent mistress, and Constantly told her that he would never Serve any person to whom She should Leave him. From hence it will appear, that instead of meriting freedom, or being a proper person to become a Member of the Civil State as a free man, he Stands in Need of the watchful eye of a Master Constantly over him, to prevent him of Executing his Horrid purposes. Your petitioner therefore prays that this honourable house will reject a petition of the Said Will for his freedom now lying before it And abstain from exercising the power of Suspending the operation of the laws, lodged in their hands, in such a Manner as to bestow Liberty on an undeserving man And deprive her of the Only Slave to whom She is Entitled And your Petitioner as in Duty bound, shall Ever Pray, &c.

[no signature]

SOURCE: Petition of Anne Bennet [also spelled Bennett] to the Virginia House of Delegates, 11 December 1780, Legislative Petitions, Miscellaneous Petitions, VSA. Tabled. PAR #11678002.

4. Citizens of Henrico County to Virginia House of Delegates, 1782

To the Honourable the Speaker and Gentlemen of the House of Delegates

The petition of sundry of the Inhabitants of the County of Henerico & others humbly sheweth:

That whereas many persons have suffer'd their Slaves to go about to hire themselves and pay their masters for their hire and others under pretence of puting them free set them out to live for themselves and allow their masters such hire as they can agree on by which means the said Slaves live in a very Idle and disorderly manner and in order to pay their masters their due hire are frequently Stealing in the Neighbourhood in which they reside or which tends to a worse Consequence encourage the Neighbouring Slaves to steal from their masters and others, and they become the receivers and Traders of those Goods, haveing time to go at large, and allso gives great discontent to other Slaves who are not allow,d such Indulgencies; it being generally beleiev,d that those Slaves do not labour [su]fficient to pay their masters their hire and clothe themselves in an Honest manner—Now We your Petitioners pray that this Honourable House will take this matter under your serious consideration and pass an Act to put a Stop to such pernicious practices; and your petitioners as in duty bound shall ever pray &c.—

[signed]	John Mayo Junr.	Thomas Owen
	Wm. Gaithright	D Trueheart
	Hobson Owen	Robt. Goode
	Tho. Prosser	Jno. Williamson
	Adam Craig	Jno McKean
		[23 additional signatures]

SOURCE: Petition of Citizens of Henrico County to the Virginia House of Delegates, 8 June 1782, Legislative Petitions, Henrico County, VSA. Referred to the Committee on Propositions. PAR #11678201.

5. Daniel Cannon et al., Charleston, to South Carolina House, 1783

To The Honourable Hugh Rutledge Esq. Speaker, and the other Members of the Honourable House of Representatives of the State of South Carolina in General Assembly Convened.

The Petition of the House-Carpenters and Bricklayers of Charleston,
Humbly Sheweth,

That your Petitioners have laboured under very great Inconveniences in their respective Occupations ever since the Commencement of the present War, having scarce had sufficient Employment to support their Families, owing, they apprehend, in a great Measure, to a Number of Jobbing Negroe Tradesmen, who undervalue Work by undertaking it for very little more than the Materials would cost, by which it is evident the Stuff they work with cannot be honestly acquired. Your Honourable House will be sensible that this Practice must be prejudicial, not only to the Proprietors of Materials for building, but highly detrimental to your Petitioners, Who are thereby deprived of the Means of gaining a Livelihood by their Industry.

Your Petitioners therefore humbly request your Honourable House to take their distressed Case into your serious Consideration, and to enact such a Law as may prohibit Negroes from undertaking Work on their own Account, and to adopt and salutary Measures for the Redress of said Grievance, and for the Encouragement of Industry as to your Wisdom shall seem meet, and your Petitioners as in Duty bound shall pray, &c, &c,

Charlestown
19th Feby 1783.

[signed]	Daniel Cannon	Benjamin Wish
	Stephen Shrewsbury	Benjn Russell
	John Clement	John Calvert Junr
	John Lesesne	John Lewis Poyas
	Jno Muncrief	Jas Brown
		[26 additional signatures]

SOURCE: Petition of Daniel Cannon et al. to South Carolina House of Representatives, 19 February 1783, Records of the General Assembly, #159, SCDAH. PAR #11378304.

6. Sarah Greene, Fairfax County, to Virginia House of Delegates, 1784

To the honourable the Speaker and Members of the house of Delegates of Virginia

The Petition of Sarah Greene humbly sheweth That your petitioner tho born in Slavery has never felt the hardships of that miserable State, it having been her Lott to fall into the hands of one of the best of Masters, the Reverend Charles Greene, late of the County of Fairfax deceased. That having had the good fortune to recommend herself to the favour of her said Master by many years of faithful service he had determined to reward your petitioner with Liberty to herself and Children. your petitioner is informed that the laws of this Country at that time would not admit of her masters liberating her by Will. and Death prevented him from putting in execution (by legal means) his benevolent Intentions towards your petitioner and her two Children. but that in his last Illness he exacted a promise from his Lady that she would fulfill those intentions after his death. Your petitioner further begs leave to show to your honble House that her said Master left his whole fortune in this Country to his Widow Mrs Sarah Greene who in the year 1767 intermarried with Doctor William Savage lately deceased, that previous to the said marriage Doctor Savage executed a Bond to George Washington and Bryan Fairfax Esquires obliging himself to pay a certain sum annually for the use of the said Mrs Greene during her life. That when the Bond was prepared and before it's execution Mrs Greene insisted that a clause should be inserted enabling her to set free your petitioner and Children. that Doctor Savage agreed that your petitioner and Children should be set free, but to save the trouble of drawing the bond over again promised that he would after the marriage execute an Instrument of writing empowering and enabling his said intended wife to emancipate your petitioner and her two Children, and called upon Witnesses to take notice of his said promise and your petitioner has been informed that he actually executed an Instrument of Writing for that purpose. Some unhappy Differances having arisen between Doctor Savage and his Lady he carried her to Ireland about the year 1769 and left her he returning to Virginia. after this time your petitioner and her Children were suffered to enjoy their Liberty for many Years. When a Mr Rice said to be a Relation of Doctor Savage took by force from your petitioner her two Children and carried them to Carolina, and has lately attempted to carry off your petitioner and two other Children since born, and still threatens to take the first opportunity of forcing them into Slavery, which your petitioner fears he will do unless your honble House will be pleased to interpose in their favour   And as it was the intention of their Master to give them freedom and as Doctor Savage assented to his Lady's having that power. it is presumable that Mrs Savage (who your petitioner is informed died in obscurity and great poverty in Ireland without leaving any Relations) did direct them to be set free by her last Will. Tho even if she did not your petitioner humbly hopes that your honble house will pass an act to confirm to herself and Children that Freedom which it was the wish and intention of their Master that they should enjoy. and to which Doctor Savage had himself assented as part of his marriage Contract.

And your petitioner as in duty bound will ever pray &c

[signed] Sarah Greene

SOURCE: Petition of Sarah Greene to the Virginia House of Delegates, 3 December 1784, Legislative Petitions, Fairfax County, VSA. Tabled. PAR #11678403.

7. James, New Kent County, to Virginia Assembly, 1786

To the honorable the Speaker & Gentlemen of the Genl. Assembly,

The petition of James (a slave belonging to Will Armistead of New Kent county) humbly sheweth: That your petitioner persuaded of the just right which all mankind have to Freedom, notwithstanding his own state of bondage, with an honest desire to serve this country in its defence thereof, did, during the ravages of Lord Cornwallis thro' this state, by the permission of his master, enter into the service of the Marquis Lafayette: That during the time of his serving the Marquis he often at the peril of his life found means to frequent the British Camp, by which means he kept open a channel of the most useful communications to the army of the State. That at different times your petitioner conveyed inclosures from the Marquis in to the Enemies lines of the most secret & important kind; the possession of which if discovered on him would have most certainly endangered the life of your petitioner: That he undertook & performed all commands with chearfulness & fidelity in opposition to the persuasion & example of many thousands of his unfortunate condition. For proof of the above your petitioner begs leave to refer to certificate of the Marquis Lafayette hereto annexed, & after taking his case as here stated into consideration he humbly intreats that he may be granted that Freedom, which he flatters himself he has in some degree contributed to establish; & which he hopes always to prove himself worthy of: nor does he desire even this inestimable favor, unless his present master from whom he has experienced everything which can make tolerable the state of slavery, shall be made adequate compensation for the loss of a valuable workman, which your petitioner ~~prays~~ humbly requests may be done & your petitioner shall ever pray &c

[no signature]

SOURCE: Petition of James to the Virginia General Assembly, 30 November 1786, Legislative Petitions, New Kent County, VSA. Granted. PAR #11678601.

8. James Wimbish, Halifax County, to Virginia Assembly, 1789

To the Honble the Speaker and Gentlemen of the General Assembly of Virginia.

The Petition of James Wimbish humbly Sheweth. That some time in the Month of July 1773 a Negro man Slave, named Toby, the Property of your Petitioner made his elopement, and afterwards to wit: on the 14th day of February 1778 enterd into the Service of the United States as a Soldier in the 14 Virg.a Regiment under the fictitious name of William Ferguson, and Serv'd, till legally dischargd from thence by Colo. William Davies; as by several Certificates and

This is to Certify that The Bearer By the Name of James
Has done Essential Services to Me While I Had the Honour to
Command in this State. His Intelligence from the Enemy's
Camp were Industriously Collected and More faithfully Delivered
He perfectly Acquitted Himself With Some Important Commissions
I Gave Him and Appears to me Entitled to Every Reward his
Situation Can Admit of. done Under My Hand, Richmond
November 21st 1784.

Lafayette

A portrait of the slave James, owned by Will Armistead of New Kent County in Virginia, and a statement signed by General Marquis de Lafayette on 21 November 1784 attesting that James served as a spy during the American Revolution. With General Lafayette's assistance, James acquired his freedom. (Courtesy of the Valentine Museum, Richmond, Virginia) a Discharge from the Officers under whom the said William Ferguson Alias Toby servd; which vouchers your Petitioner now has and begs leave of referrence to them—That your Petitioner was depriv'd of the Service of the said Slave from the day of July 1773 until the 10th day of Septem'r 1785, when your Petitioner discover'd that his said Slave had been in the Service of the United States, and upon his retiring from the said Service had married a white Woman, by whom he had several children—Your Petitioner compassionating the case of his said Slave, in consequence of his faithful and meritorious Services to the Public, Subscrib'd a considerable sum towards obtaining his freedom; which was affected by Several Gentlemen who subscrib'd and bore apart of the loss with your Petitioner in Emancipating the said Slave

That the pay and Depreciation due the said William Ferguson alias Toby, has not been drawn or Settled either by himself or your Petitioner—Wherefore your Petitioner humbly begs that your Honble House will take into tender consideration his said case, and pass such a Resolution therein, as may enable him to obtain a Settlement with the Auditor of Public accts for whatever may be Justly due the said William Ferguson, alias Toby for his Services renderd the United States—

And your Petitioner as in duty bound shall ever pray &c

[signed] James Wimbish

SOURCE: Petition of James Wimbish to the Virginia General Assembly, 22 October 1789, Legislative Records, Halifax County, VSA. No act was passed. PAR #11678901.

9. Thomas Cole, Peter Bassnett Mathewes, and Matthew Webb to South Carolina Senate, 1791

To the Honorable David Ramsay Esquire President and to the rest of Honorable New Members of the Senate of the State of South Carolina

The Memorial of Thomas Cole Bricklayer P: B: Mathews and Mathew Webb Butchers on behalf of themselves & others Free Men of Colour.

Humbly Sheweth

That in the Enumeration of Free Citizens by the Constitution of the United States for the purpose of Representation of the Southern States in Congress, Your Memorialist have been considered under that description as part of the Citizens of this State. Although by the Fourteenth and Twenty ninth [sections] in the Act of Assembly made in the Year 1740 and intitled an Act for the better ordering and Governing Negroes and other Slaves in this Province commonly called The Negroe Act[1] now in force. Your Memorialist are deprived of the Rights and Privileges of Citizens by not having it in their power to give Testimony on Oath in prosecutions on behalf of the State from which cause many Culprits have escaped the punishment due to their atrocious Crimes nor can they give their Testimony in recovering Debts due to them, or in establishing Agreements made by them within the meaning of the Statutes of Frauds and Perjuries in force in this State except in cases where Persons of Colour are concerned, whereby they are subject to great losses and repeated Injuries without any means of redress.

That by the said Clauses in the said Act, they are debarred of the Rights of Free Citizens by being subject to a Trial without the benefit of a Jury and subject to Prosecution by Testimony of Slaves without Oath by which they are placed on the same footing.

Your Memorialist shew that they have at all times since the Independence of the United States contributed and do now contribute to the support of Government by chearfully paying their Taxes proportionable to their property with others who have been during such period and now are in full enjoyment of The Rights and Immunities of Citizens Inhabitants of a Free-Independent State.

That as your Memorialist have been and are considered as Free-Citizens of this State they hope to be treated as such, they are ready and willing to take and subscribe to such Oath of Allegiance to the States as shall be prescribed by this Honorable House and are also willing to take upon them any duty for the preservation of the Peace in the City or any other occasion if called on.

Your Memorialist do not presume to hope that they shall be put on one equal footing with the [white population in] general they only humbly solicit such indulgence as the Wisdom and Humanity of this Honorable House shall dictate . . . [ink spot] by repealing the clauses the Act beforementioned, and substituting such a Clause as will efectually Redress the grivences which your Memorialists humbly submit in this their Memorial but under such restrictions as to your Honorable House shall seem proper.

May it therefore please your Honors to take your Memorialists case into tender consideration and make such Acts or insert such Clauses for the purpose of relieving your Memorialists from the unmeritted grivance they now Labour under as in your Wisdom shall seem meet.

And as in duty bound your Memorialists will ever pray

Signed 1t Jany 1791 Thos. Cole
Peter Bassnett Mathewes
Matthew Webb

SOURCE: Petition of Thomas Cole, Peter Bassnett Mathewes, and Matthew Webb to the South Carolina Senate, 1 January 1791, Records of the General Assembly, #181, SCDAH. Rejected. PAR #11379109.

1. In the aftermath of the Stono Rebellion, the South Carolina General Assembly passed a detailed statute restraining the activities of slaves and free blacks. Peter Wood, *Black Majority: Negroes in Colonial South Carolina from 1670 through the Stono Rebellion* (New York: W. W. Norton, 1974), 324.

10. John Holman to South Carolina House, 1791

To the Honorable the Speaker and the Members of the House of Representatives of South Carolina the Petition of John Holman

Most respectfully sheweth.

That your Petitioner has resided for upwards of twenty five years on the Coast of Africa where he was engaged in commercial transactions the exports of which chiefly entered in South Carolina.

Soon after the late war was ended your Petitioner formed a scheme of removing to South Carolina with seventy slaves which he had long possessed in Africa. In prosecution of this scheme your Petitioner visited Carolina in 1787, and having made arrangements for purchasing land therein returned to Africa with an intention of bringing out his slaves in order to a fixed settlement. Previous to the departure of your Petitioner for Africa he went in conjunction with his friend the Honorable Henry Laurens to the Custom House and informed the Collector Mr George Abbot Hall of his intentions to come with his slaves to settle in South Carolina and enquired whether by so doing he would offend against the laws of the State and was assured that he would not, and that he might freely bring his slaves with him. Your Petitioner reposing confidently in these assurances and in the stability of the laws of the land sailed for Africa in February 1788, and embarked with his Slaves in June 1790 for Charleston and had ordered Insurance only for that port. When your Petitioner arrived off this coast, he was informed that the moment his Negroes were landed, they were liable to seizure and himself to a fine of a hundred pounds for each Negro so imported. Your Petitioner then learned that the clause of the three years instalment law passed in 1787 which permitted bonafide settlers to come with their slaves and reside in this State, though of force when he left this State viz: in February 1788 was repealed after he had left it viz: in November 1788. and in room thereof was substituted the present instalment law which prohibits the importation of all Negroes, but such as at the time of the passing of the law belonged to the Citizens of the United States and were at the same time within the United States. The slaves of your Petitioner were not at that time within the limits of the United States and of course by the change of the law in his absence he was liable to be reduced to beggary, though he was so far from any intention of contravening the laws of the State, that he intended to bring all his property and live under them. Your Petitioner in this distressing situation was obliged to seek a temporary residence in Georgia where for several months he has been subject to the inconveniences of wanting a home, friends, money and credit, all of which he could have commanded in South Carolina, for your Petitioner has his resources of supply so connected with the inhabitants of the State of South Carolina that he has not the means of establishing himself in any other of the United States. Your Petitioner therefore humbly hopes that your honorable House will take his peculiar and very hard case into consideration and permit him to come with his slaves and settle in Carolina, in which case your Petitioner promises obedience to all your laws and to demean himself as a good citizen, and your Petitioner as in duty bound shall ever pray.

[signed] J Holman

I certify that the Enquiry attended to the foregoing Petition was made to me, and the answer given as therein expressed, agreable to the Law of the State then existing—Custom house Charleston 23rd Decemr 1790

[signed] Geo. Abbott Hall Cmr

I Certify that the principal facts stated in the foregoing Petition are to my knowledge substantially true.

23d. Decem 1790

[signed] Henry Laurens

SOURCE: Petition of John Holman to the Speaker and Members of the South Carolina House of Representatives, 13 January 1791, Records of the General Assembly, #123, SCDAH; Certificate, George Abbott Hall, 23 December 1790, ibid.; Certificate, Henry Laurens, 23 December 1790, ibid. Granted.[1] PAR #11379102.

1. See Report of the Committee on the Petition of John Holman, 13 January 1791, Records of the General Assembly, #125, SCDAH; and *Acts of the General Assembly of the State of South-Carolina, from February, 1791, to December, 1794, Both Inclusive,* vol. 1 (Columbia: D. and J. J. Faust, 1808), 135–36.

11. Samuel Jasper to North Carolina Assembly, 1792

Unto the Honorable the General Assembly of the State of North Carolina

The Petition of Saml Jasper Executor of Caleb White deceased Humbly Sheweth

That his Brother Caleb White by his last Will and Testament liberated his Negroe Slave Jack upon condition that the said Jack would pay the sum of £100 to his Executor.

Sheweth that the services performed by the said Jack were such as did great honor to the name of humanity and highly merited much greater reward than that of Emancipation—A Service no less than that of taking prisoners the whole Crew of a British pri[v]ateer & releasing his Master and a number of others who were at that time captured by the said British Cruiser together with making the said British privateer a Capture to the United States—Sheweth that the said Negroe Jack at Annapolis in the year of received the thanks of the Congress of the United States then siting for the said service & a recommendation to his

Master to liberate him therefore; Sheweth that the said Jack hath paid the sum of £100 as directed by the Will of your Petitioner's Testator.

And your Petitioner prays that the said Jack may be liberated by Law and your Petitioner as in duty bound shall ever pray.

[signed] Saml Jasper, Extor of
Caleb White

Indian Town, 17 Novr. 1792
Sir,

I Promised you an act. of our Ingagemt. at sea which Happend as Follows—

On board Schooner Polly Comd. by Caleb White & Navigated by three Men one of which was Jack a Negro, the Property of Henry White, Part owner of sd Schooner, Loaded with Corn Pease and Pork. bd. to Ws. Ind. & saild from Curituck 14 Feby 1780 on 16th Inst. was boarded and Taken by a British Privateer Calld Fame—of N. York, Comd. by John Adkinson, Latt. 37n, Long. 73s. we were Imediately Confined in Irons and allowanced on one Gill of raw Pease and one Gill of water per day. on the 19th we attempted to retake the Schooner by first getting Jack out of Irons but was discoverd before we cd. Prosecute our design by some of the Crew. They const of a Prize Master and 4 hands—They Immediately confined us below deck and Sasht. the feet of Jack to a Stantion on the quarter deck, his hands being Irond whire he lay 24 hours in a gale of wind or Snow Storm every sea Making a breach over us. however he survived that afterward was—Loosed and Permited below with us—The reason of his usage was because he never wd. Consent to Join them and attempting to get out of Irons—However we Orderd him to Turn himself a Enemy of America this had the effect we wishd. They Loosed him from his Irons and he soon become their Right hand Man with Promise of freedom and Many Rewards after arriving at York but when ever he got an opportunity of Speaking to us continued to Tell us he was ready to assist us any Moment in the recapture on the 22 the gale abating they were abt. making sail. My Brother who was the Master got out of Irons gave the watch word and Engaged the Prize Master. Jack Imediately Contrary to their Expectations Engaged two of them which he soon worsted having no Weapon but a Marlin Spike In the Intrim I got out of Irons having Procured a Cullash but was much beaten before I got out after Bloodshed on both sides we Conqd. them which we confind and carried in to Anapolis & delivered to Congress, but by the wounds & frost Jack received he Never walkd a step for five weeks—after we returned home his Master: abused him somewhat Jack Applyd to us for redress upon which My Brother Bought him and in his last Will Sold sd. Jack his freedom [by] his Paying his Exet. £100. The said fellow behaves himself well, Honest and Industrous is Very Manerly to all and has Comanded a schooner for Me five years, is Intrusted by Mr Daughty with Many Hundred Pound every year.

Time Fails
adieu
Your friend
[signed] Sam Jasper

SOURCE: Petition of Samuel Jasper, Executor of Caleb White, to the North Carolina General Assembly, 14 December 1792, Records of the General Assembly, Session Records, NCDAH. No act was passed. PAR #11279202.

12. William Giles, Rowan County, to North Carolina Assembly, 1794

The Memorial of William Giles to the General Assembly Now setting at Raleigh

Respectfully sheweth, that your memorialist is a Citizen of this State, and has resided in Rowan County upwards of thirty years, in which time by the efforts of Industry and the blessing of providence he hath obtained a Comfortable eastate Both Real and personal. That his estate is free from the incumberances of debts or the Lawfull claims of any individual—That among a considerable number of valuable slaves which your memorialist possesses there are two negro Men One of the Name of Anthony about the age of Twenty seven the Other of the name of Cumbey of the age of Thirty two y[ear]s, who have always distinguished themselves by the Strictest attention to their masters Interest, and the Most dutifull obediance to all his Orders—That these Two slaves were born the property of your memorialist, and brought up in his family, where no pains was spared to instruct them in the principles of Morality, and the knowledge of farming in all its Branches—

For these Considerations, and in order to reward the Said slaves for their uncommon fidelity, and good behaviour, your memorialist is induced to Solicit your honorable body, to pass a Law in the present session to emancipate them by the Names of Anthony Giles and Cumbey Giles in as full and compleat a manner as if they had both been born free—

And your Memorialist as in duty bound will ever pray &c
[signed] Wm Giles

SOURCE: Petition of William Giles of Rowan County to the North Carolina General Assembly, 1794, Records of the General Assembly, Session Records, NCDAH. Referred to the Committee on Emancipation in House of Commons. No act was passed. PAR #11279501.

13. John Carruthers Stanly, Craven County, to North Carolina Assembly, 1798

To the Honorable the General Assembly of the State of North Carolina

The Petition of John Caruthers Stanly,[1] a man of mixed blood, humbly sheweth That in consideration of the long, faithfull & meritorious services of your petitioner, heretofore the Slave of Alexander Stewart & Lydia his wife, the said Alexander & Lydia petitioned the County Court of Craven for permission to emancipate & sett your petitioner free, and in pursuance of a licence so obtained, did execute to your Petitioner a deed, whereby they give, grant & confirm unto your Petitioner his freedom, liberty & emancipation, which said deed, together with the licence from the County Court of Craven, your petitioner has hereto annexed & prays may be received as part of his petition. Your petitioner further shews your Honbl. body, that by honest & persevering industry, he has acquired a considerable real & personal estate, and being apprehensive that some accident may deprive him of the evidence of his emancipation & thereby of the fruits of his honest industry, Humbly prays your Honble. body taking his case into your consideration will by a Law, confirm, establish, and Secure to your petitioner his Fredom, with the rights & privelidges attendant thereon—And your Petitioner as in duty bound shall ever pray—

Craven County, Novr. 19, 1798

[no signature]

SOURCE: Petition of John Carruthers Stanly to the North Carolina General Assembly, 19 November 1798, Records of the General Assembly, Session Records, NCDAH. Granted.[2] PAR #11279805.

1. Although the petition spelled his name Caruthers, the correct spelling is Carruthers. For further information on John Carruthers Stanly (1774–ca. 1845), the son of an African Ibo woman and a white merchant shipper, see Loren Schweninger, "John Carruthers Stanly and the Anomaly of Black Slaveholding," *North Carolina Historical Review* 67 (April 1990), 159–92.

2. *Laws of North-Carolina. At a General Assembly, Begun and Held at the City of Raleigh, on Monday the Nineteenth Day of November, in the Year of Our Lord One Thousand Seven Hundred and Ninety-Eight, and of the Independence of the United States of America the Twenty-Third: It Being First Session of This Assembly* (n.p., 1799), 49.

14. Inhabitants of Nashville to Tennessee Assembly, 1799

The Honole The General Assembly of the State of Tennessee—

The petition of the Inhabitants of Nashville and its Vicinity—Humbley Sheweth—

Your petitioners, Conceive that considerable Inconven[ie]nces Arises from divers Negroes Now in Nashville keeping Houses of Entertainment by Trading with other Negroes in the County, as well as a Disgrace to the Town—We therefore pray that a Law may be passed to prohibit any Negro or negroes keeping a house in said Town, to Effect which we think it will be advisable to pass a law to prevent Masters of Slaves from allowing their Slaves any such Liberties—

Your Petitioners are bound and ever pray &c.

[signed]	Thos Masterson	Patrick Lyons
	A. Hooper Junr	Ezekiel Able
	Absalom Hall	Moses Mitchell
	D Dupree	David Robinson
	James McAllister	Giles Harding
		[20 additional signatures]

SOURCE: Petition of Inhabitants of Nashville to the Tennessee General Assembly, 19 September 1799, Legislative Petitions, #1-2-1799, reel 1, TSLA. Read and referred to the Committee on Propositions and Grievances in both the House and Senate. Granted.[1] PAR #11479901.

1. In 1799, the Tennessee General Assembly passed a law forbidding slaves from moving about to conduct any type of business without "a pass from his or her master, mistress, or overseer, expressing the time when, and the business for which they go." Persons trading with slaves without permission were subject to a ten dollar fine for each offense. *Acts Passed at the First Session of the Third General Assembly State of Tennessee, Begun and Held at Knoxville, on Monday the Sixteenth Day of September, One Thousand Seven Hundred and Ninety Nine* (Knoxville: Roulstone and Wilson, 1799), 70–71; see also John Codman Hurd, *The Law of Freedom and Bondage in the United States,* 2 vols. (Boston: Little, Brown, 1858–62; reprint, New York: Negro Universities Press, 1968), 2:90.

15. Gurdon Deming, Cumberland County, to North Carolina Assembly, 1800

To the Honorable the General Assembly of the State of North Carolina

The Petition of Gurdon Deming a citizen of the county of Cumberland Humbly sheweth, that he is the owner of a Certain woman named Lucy and her child Laura Who were represented to be slaves and as such purchased by your petitioner—

That he has reason to believe and doth believe from diligent inquiries made, that the Said Lucy ought not to be held longer in bondage. Your petitioner is aware that legal proof cannot be made of the fact, yet your petitioner is fully satisfied, that the Said Lucy is the daughter of a free white Woman—that to conceal this circumstance, so as to protect the reputation of the real mother, Lucy at her birth was placed in charge of a woman a slave of one John Selph—Your petitioner learns from a number of the most respectable citizens of Fayetteville, that it was always the intention of Mr Selph to manumit the Said Lucy at his death—but the death of Mr Selph being sudden and his estate proving insolvent, his intentions were frustrated—Lucy was sold by his administrator and she was purchased at a mere nominal Sum by Several Gentlemen with the View to Carry out the wishes of Mr Selph; Owing however to the insolvency of the person delegated to bid her off, occurring soon after, She was again Sold and has subsequently fallen ~~with~~ into the hands of your petitioner—

The History of Lucy is a romantic one, and if your petitioner could detail it without giving offence and bringing to light, what has long been forgotten and thereby do injury perhaps to persons now residents of a distant state, he is certain your honorable body would not hesitate a moment in assisting him in doing simple justice to this injured Girl, by authorising her immediate Emancipation—

Lucy in colour is perfectly White, and cannot be distinguished from the purest of the race, her associations have been distinct from the coloured population, and her whole demeanor that of the whites to which class she evidently belongs.

In consideration of these things your petitioner humbly prays your honorable body to pass a law authorising the Emancipation of the Said Lucy, and her child Laura, And as in duty bound, your peititioner will ever pray.

[signed] Gurdon Deming

SOURCE: Petition of Gurdon Deming to the North Carolina General Assembly, December 1800, Records of the General Assembly, Session Records, NCDAH. No act was passed. PAR #11280005.

16. James Huske et al., Fayetteville, to North Carolina Assembly, 1800

To the Honorable the General Assembly of the State of North Carolina

The Petition of the Undersigned Citizens of the town of Fayetteville and of the county of Cumberland Humbly Sheweth

That they are personally Acquainted with Gurdon Deming Esquire a citizen and Magistrate of this county They represent to your honorable body that he is a Gentleman of intelligence and character that the Statement made in a petition to your honorable body praying for the Emancipation of his Woman Lucy and her child Laura is entitled to your Serious Consideration—Many of your petitioners have every reason to believe that the facts disclosed relative to the parentage of Lucy is true Such has been the general reputation for many years in this community where Lucy was born and raised—

Others of your petitioners Who have known Lucy more recently have no hesitation in saying that from her general appearance they verily believe that She is of pure White blood too White to be a Slave and ought to be manumitted.

Your petitioners therefore cheerfully join in the application of Mr Deming and respectfully ask your honorable body to pass an act Emancipating Lucy and her child Laura believing that in doing so, you will do an act of Justice to an unfortunate woman illegally held in bondage, Who for more than Eighteen Years has faithfully performed the Menial duties of a Servant without Murmuring—tho often importuned to assert her freedom

And as in duty bound your petitioners will every pray

[signed]	James Huske	R M Orrell
	P. Taylor	Benj. Robinson
	D G MacRae	B W Robinson
	James Kyle	W.T. Mallett
	James Gibson	J.G. Shepherd
		[29 additional signatures]

SOURCE: Petition of James Huske et al. to the North Carolina General Assembly, 5 December 1800, Records of the General Assembly, Session Records, NCDAH. No act was passed. PAR #11280006.

17. Inhabitants of Davidson County to Tennessee Assembly, ca. 1801

To the honorable the General Assembly of the State of Tennessee

The petition of Sundry the inhabitants of Davidson County Sheweth that A negro man called Bob who now is & has for a number of years been an inhabitant of ~~Davidson C~~ The Town of Nashville, has by his industry and economy raised money & purchased himself but cannot enjoy that freedom which through ~~by~~ his labour & perservance he has become intitled too [*sic*], unless by act of the General assembly.

Your petitioners therefore hope you will by act of your Honorable body emancipate Said negro Bob. Giving him all the privileges that is usually Given to persons in a Similar situation and your petitioners will ever pray.

[signed]	Richard Cross	James King
	B J Bradford	Tho, Childress
	John Deatherage	J A Parker
	Thos Deatherage	William Lytle Jr.
	Jno Anderson	Geo. B. Curtis
		[37 additional signatures]

SOURCE: Petition of Inhabitants of Davidson County to the Tennessee General Assembly, ca. 1801, Legislative Petitions, #20-1-1801, reel 1, TSLA. Granted.[1] PAR #11480101.

1. In 1794, while still in bondage, "Black Bob" was given permission by the Davidson County Court to "sell Liquor and Victuals on his Good Behavior." Anita Shafer Goodstein, *Nashville, 1780–1860: From Frontier to City* (Gainesville: University of Florida Press, 1989), 81 (quote); Anita Shafer Goodstein, "Black History on the Nashville Frontier, 1780–1810," *Tennessee Historical Quarterly* 30 (Winter 1979): 412–13; *Acts Passed at the First Session of the Fourth General Assembly of the State of Tennessee, Begun and Held at Knoxville, on Monday the Twenty-First Day of September, One Thousand Eight Hundred and One* (Knoxville: George Roulstone, 1801), 198.

18. Richard Furman et al., Amelia Township, to South Carolina House, 1801

To the Honorable, the House of Representatives of the State of South Carolina: The Memorial and Petition of the Charleston Baptist Association, consisting of the Ministers and other Representatives of Thirty religious Congregations of Citizens of the State aforesaid, met at Amelia Township, the thirty-first day of October, 1801,

Sheweth,

That however necessary or important it was to enact the Law passed at the last Session of the Legislature, for the better Governing of Negroes and other Persons of Colour; yet your Memorialists consider this Law as infringing in some Respects, on the Religious Rights and Privileges of Churches and Citizens of this State, whose Principles and Conduct are most friendly to its civil, political and domestic Interests; by laying on them Restrictions, respecting the Time and Manner of giving religious Instruction to the Persons whose Situation is contemplated in the Act; and by exposing said Churches to the Danger of Interruption and Insult, from the Rudeness of Persons who move in the lowest spheres of Authority, whenever they choose to appear as the Enforcers of Law:[1]

That the Act complained of appears to look with an unfavorable Aspect on religious Instruction, as though it tended to inspire the Minds of Domestics with Sentiments unfriendly to subordination and Peace, whereas it is certain that the plain Doctrines and positive Precepts of Christianity, as professed and supported by the Body of our Citizens, have a direct, contrary Tendency, and do actually produce contrary Effects:

That many of your Memorialists having, as Ministers of the Gospel, been long in the habit of giving religious Instruction to Negroes, as being a part of their ministerial Duty, and having enjoined on them, with a View to the public peace and Security of the State, their Duty of being subject to Authority, as a Test of their Sincerity in Religion; can with the strictest Truth declare, that from the most careful Observation, they have obtained very satisfactory Evidence that the Principles so inculcated, have been conscientiously imbibed by the Body of those Negroes who have attended on their Ministry, and have governed their Conduct in the Manner stated in the [illegible] Article; even in the Time of the Revolutionary War, when Temptations to a contrary Conduct were numerous and powerful:

That there is great Reason to fear, that by the aforesaid severe Restrictions, imposed in this Act, it will have a strong indirect Tendency to produce the Evil it was designed to prevent; by making that Class, of the religious Negroes, who value religious Privileges, feel unhappy, and consider themselves oppressed; by tending to take away that Security which the Citizens have in the Fidelity and Attachment of Such, which Fidelity and Attachment are greatly secured by their being encouraged in truly virtuous and religious Pursuits; by preventing the beneficial Effects which their Influence is known to have on the other Classes; and by exposing themselves, finally, to the Danger of Seduction, from the Acts of those who plan Schemes of Mischief:

That you Memorialists are sensible, that this Subject, as it applies to the Citizens of this State, in their existing Circumstances, is delicate; and they are far from thinking that legislative Authority should not be employed in guarding against the Dissemination of Sentiments, though done under the Pretense of Religion, which in their operation would destroy the Foundations of Peace and social Order; but they must think that Policy, as well as Justice, requires that a proper Discrimination should be made between the Innocent and those of an opposite Character; of which Discrimination, known Principle and Conduct form the true Criterion.

Your Memorialists therefore Pray,

That the aforesaid Act may be revised, and such Alterations made therein as may relieve the virtuous Citizens from the Embarrassment complained of, and have their religious Liberties unimpaired.

[signed] Richard Furman — Robt Bradley
Joseph B, Cook — James Brown
John M. Roberts — George Whitley
Frame Woods

SOURCE: Petition of Richard Furman et al. to the South Carolina House of Representatives, 31 October 1801, Records of the General Assembly, #123, SCDAH. Granted.[2] PAR #11380108.

1. The statute made it unlawful "for any number of slaves, free negroes, mulattoes, or mestizoes, even in company with white persons, to meet together and assemble, for the purpose of mental instruction, or religious worship, either before the rising of the sun, or after the going down of the same." Whites who dispersed such meetings were exempt from prosecution. *Acts and Resolutions of the General Assembly of the State of South-Carolina, Passed in December 1800* (Columbia: Daniel and J. J. Faust, 1801), 37–38.

2. "Whereas certain religious societies in this state, have petitioned the legislature to alter

part of an act," the preamble of the new law read, it would henceforth be unlawful for any person to disrupt a religious gathering before nine o'clock at night unless the person first obtained a warrant from a magistrate stationed within three miles of the meeting place. *The Statutes at Large of South Carolina* (Columbia: A. S. Johnston, 1840), 448–49.

19. John Carruthers Stanly, Craven County, to North Carolina Assembly, 1802

The Honourable the General Assembly of the state of North Carolina

The Petition of John Caruthers Stanly humbly complaining, Sheweth unto your honourable body, your petitioner John C Stanly of the Town of New Bern in the County of Craven and state aforesaid, having he presumes, ever conducted [himself] as a good and peaceable citizen, and industrious by every laudable endeavour in the acquisition of wealth, fame and reputation, and successful he hopes in the attainment of the two last; concerning the truth of which representations should it in any wise affect the prayer of this petition, your petitioner, would humbly refer your honourable body to Edward Harris, Esquire, of the Town of New Bern, and William Blackledge and William Bryan, Esquires, of the County of Craven, who have it in their power more fully and particularly, to inform your honourable body, of and concerning, your petitioners situation and conduct, than would be meet in him to detail in this his petition;—In tender consideration whereof; your petitioner submits that on the 20th of May 1800, he purchased from Godernan Reverchon,[1] a mulatto boy named John, known and distinguished in the bill of sale (which your petitioner prays may be taken and considered as part of this petition) as a negro male child of the age of two years, named John, whom he considers his child;—And your Petitioner humbly suggests, that as in his opinion it is inconsistent with nature, for the parent to wish his child in a state of vassalage, either to another or himself, he therefore prays that the said John may be emancipated and known in future by the name of James Florence.—

Your Petitioner further respectfully submits that on the 12th day of May 1801 he purchased from Richard Green of the County of New Hanover a mulatto child named John, who is the result of a matrimonial connection between your Petitioner and Kitty, who is known and described in the said bill of sale (which is prayed may be taken and considered as part of this petition) as a certain young mulatto child named John my property said child John being a son of Kitty.— for which child your Petitioner feels all that interest and affection, which the tender ties and mutual good offices and kindnesses, which the matrimonial State begets in the bosom of its notaries, is susceptible And your Petitioner prays your honourable body taking into consideration the demeanour of your petitioner, the connection between father and son, to manumit the said John and permit him hereafter to be known & distinguished by the name of John Stewart Stanly.

And your Petitioner as in duty bound will ever pray.

[no signature]

SOURCE: Petition of John Carruthers Stanly of Craven County to the North Carolina General Assembly, 1802, Records of the General Assembly, Session Records, NCDAH. Granted.[2] PAR #11280205.

1. The deed, signed by Godernan Reverchon, indicated that Charles G. Reverchon sold Stanly's son to him for sixty dollars. Copy of Deed of Sale, Charles G. Reverchon to John C. Stanly, 20 May 1800, with Petition of John C. Stanly to the North Carolina General Assembly, 1802, Records of the General Assembly, Session Records, NCDAH.

2. See *The Laws of the State of North-Carolina Passed in 1802* (n.p., 180[2]), 43.

20. William Simmons, Charleston, to South Carolina House, 1802

So. Carolina

To the Honorable the Speaker and the Honorable the members of the House of Representatives of the State aforesaid

The Petition of William Simmons, of the City of Charleston in the State aforesaid,

Humbly Sheweth

That he rendered the several services mentioned in the foregoing account as is therein particularly stated & hath not yet received any compensation for the Same—

Your petitioner therefore humbly prays that relief be afforded to him in the premises—And your Petitioner will pray &cc

[signed] Wm. Simmons

The State of So Carolina

1800	To William Simmons Dr.	
Decemb 4th	To Materials viz. Wood, tar, post & Chains &cet: furnished for the Execution of a Negro fellow named Davy found Guilty of & Sentenced to	
ded. 6/10	be burnt for Robbery & Murder	
		£ 7.6.10
5	To attending the Execution of the Negro Smart at the 13 Mile Bouse, Armed to prevent a rescue, by	
ded. 30/	Order of a Magistrate—	3.0.0
		£ 10.6.8 [*sic*]

I Certify that William Simmons Did, at my request, as a Justice of the Peace who had presided at the trials of the above Negroes, Furnish the Materials for the Execution of Davy above mentioned, and did also attend, armed under the apprehension of a rescue, at the Execution of Smart as aforesaid—And I further Certify, That in my opinion the Several charges above mentioned are reasonable & justly demandable by the said William Simmons

Charleston 8 Novemb. 1802.

[signed] John Johnson J.P

SOURCE: Petition of William Simmons to the South Carolina House of Representatives, November 1802, Records of the General Assembly, #180, SCDAH; Certificate, John Johnson, Justice of the Peace, 8 November 1802, ibid. Granted. PAR #11380206.

21. Petition of the Incorporated Mechanical Society of Wilmington to North Carolina Assembly, 1802

To the Honorable the General Assembly of the State of N. Carolina

The Memorial and Petition of the Incorporated Mechanical Society, and other Inhabitants, of the Town of Wilmington in the State aforesaid, Respectfully Sheweth,

That notwithstanding the Acts of Assembly for the especial purpose made and provided it has been the practice of many Owners of Slaves in this Town, to hire to them their own time; that the major part of those Slaves being Mechanics undertake work on their own account, at, sometimes less, than one half the rate that a regular bred white Mechanic could afford to do it—; that those Slaves so hired, again hire other Slaves to work under them, and take apprentices also—that tho' laws are made to restrain this practice, still the due execution and enforcing those laws not being the particular province of any person they lie neglected, and of no avail:

Your Memorialists are conscious that Your honorable Body, will see the evil tendency of practices of the nature above set forth, in many shapes; but they beg leave to point out and bring to your view more immediately many ways by which, those practices are, and may be still more hurtful, as well to individuals, as the Country at large viz: the discouragement to population; for while Slaves can work at one half the price a White Man can, white Mechanics will never settle in the country; Also the real injury these transactions, have done and still will continue to do (if not timely suppressed) to the white Mechanics and their families, already settled in Wilmington; for it is a well known fact that a number of old and respectable Mechanics from being underworked and deprived of bread in the manner, and from the causes aforesaid, have been obliged to relinquish the trades they were regularly brought up to, and follow other occupations to procure sustenance for themselves and families—Again, that most of those Negroes whose time is hired to themselves, employ on work to their own benefit and advantage, gangs of from eight to twelve negroes; that those gangs are consequently entirely dependent on, and at the disposal of their employers, and by having so much time to themselves and consorting daily and nightly together, insurrections, and plans against the lives and property of the citizens may be formed, matured, and carried into execution with unanimity, secrecy, and dispatch.

Your Memorialists also consider as an additional and grievous hardship that while they are compelled to perform military duty, serve upon Juries, and pay taxes the bread should be taken out of the mouths of themselves and families by persons, who circumstanced as they are, are the irreconcilable enemies of the Whites.

Your Memorialists therefore humbly Petition Your honorable body to enact, that it shall be the duty of some one, particular civil Officer, to adopt and pursue such vigorous measures for prevention of abuses of the nature they complain of, as in your wisdom shall seem meet.

And Your Memorialists shall &c. &c.

[signed] John Allan, William Keddie, Normand MacLeod, Peter Harris, James Telfair, John Simpson, Jacob Hartman, Saml Morgan, Anthy B. Toomer, Andrew Ure [11 additional signatures]

SOURCE: Petition and Memorial of the Incorporated Mechanical Society of Wilmington to the North Carolina General Assembly, 29 November 1802, Records of the General Assembly, Session Records, NCDAH. No act was passed.[1] PAR #11280206.

1. In 1794, the North Carolina General Assembly passed an act to prevent slaveholders from allowing their slaves to hire out their own time. "WHEREAS great mischiefs have arisen from slaves being permitted to hire their own time," the preamble read, "it shall not be lawful, under any pretense whatever, for any person or persons to allow his, her or their slave, or any slave under his, her or their command or direction, to hire his, her or their time." A fine of twenty pounds for each offense would be levied upon conviction. Nonetheless, self-hire remained an owner's prerogative, and few whites were prosecuted for disobeying the law. In 1800, a bill was introduced requiring masters to obtain a license from the county court if they wished to permit a slave such freedom, but the bill was rejected. *Laws of North-Carolina. At a General Assembly, Begun and Held at the City of Raleigh, on the Thirteenth Day of December, in the Year of Our Lord One Thousand Seven Hundred and Ninety-Four, and in the Nineteenth Year of the Independence of the Said State: Being the First Session of the Said Assembly* (n.p., 1795), 3–4; Guion Griffis Johnson, *Ante-Bellum North Carolina: A Social History* (Chapel Hill: University of North Carolina Press, 1937), 499–500.

22. Inhabitants of Stokes County to North Carolina Assembly, 1803

To the honorable the General Assembly of the State of North Carolina in the year One Thousand Eight hundred three

The Petition of the Subscribers inhabitants of Stokes County respectfully sheweth—That the Owners of a Negro man named Aaron have applied to them for assistance to petition your honorable body for the emancipation of said Aaron, if they thought him deserving of freedom.—

They do therefore in the first place certify that during a long time that the said Aaron lived in Salem he conducted in all respects well, and worthy of better Fate than to be for life a Slave; Submissive, humble, faithful, Industrious, sober and devout was his conduct and such the Virtues he exercised, by which he proved, that,—rare as it is—yet there are Men of Black colour who deserve to be free—If therefore your honorable body ever intend to give Liberty to any human being your memorialists humbly conceive that the said Aaron is an Object deserving it, and such a one who will be an Example to his race; They do there fore freely assist his present owner in praying that the said Aaron may be emancipated from Slavery & be called Aaron Moses—and your petitioners as in duty bound shall pray—

[signed] Lewis Meinung, Samuel Stols, John Gambold, Benjamin Vierling, C. L. Benzun, Charles Holder, Rudolph Christ, Charles Gotthold Reichel, George Biwighauss, John Herbst, Conrad Kreuses, Adam Elrod, John Rights

SOURCE: Petition of Inhabitants of Stokes County to the North Carolina General Assembly, 1803, Records of the General Assembly, Session Records, NCDAH. No act was passed. PAR #11280304.

23. Citizens of Guilford and Stokes Counties to North Carolina Assembly, 1803

To the honourable General Assembly of the State of North Carolina
Session 1803

The petition of the undersigned Citizens of your Counties of Guilford and Stokes respectfully Sheweth,

1. That James Love Sen.r late of the County of Stokes deceased was in his lifetime and at his death possessed of a Negro man named Aaron and a negro

Woman named Magg who by their industry and good management with little or no direction or assistance maintained him their Aged and infirm Master in a decent and Creditable manner, were Steady to his interest and tender to him in the latter part of his life he being very weak and infirm and needing much assistance and nursing which they promptly performed. And particularly distinguished themselves by their Sympathetic kindness and gentle treatment in his last long and afflicting illness, behaving towards him as became good Obedient Slaves towards a generous, aged, debilitated and dying Master—

2. That the Said James Love who was a quiet orderly Citizen in Consideration of their uncommon Services was desirous that after his death they should be liberated with a promise whereof he frequently encouraged them to continue in their duty, and with that intention did by his last will and testament (a copy whereof is herewith laid before your honourable body) bequeath them unto Seven persons therein named verbally enjoining on them to use Such lawful measures as they might think proper to procure their liberation

3. That with the Same view and in Conformity to the Said Will James Love Jun.r Administrator thereof did on the 29th day of September 1800 formally and Actually deliver the said Aaron and Magg unto the Said Legatees, in whose peaceable possession they have Since remained and now are and have behaved and do behave themselves in a Sober, quiet, orderly, and industrious manner—

We therefore the Surviving Legatees (Edmond Jean being dead) do most earnestly pray your honourable Body, to take the subject under Consideration and if it should appear to your Wisdom expedient to carry the intention of the Said James Love into effect, that you would liberate the Said Aaron by the name of Aaron Moses and Magg by that of Mary Magdalene and your petitioners as in duty bound will ever pray &c.

[signed] George McKinny
Reuben McDaniel
Travis Jones
William Jean
James Campbell
Seth Coffin

SOURCE: Petition of Citizens of Guilford and Stokes Counties to the North Carolina General Assembly, 1803, Records of the General Assembly, Session Records, NCDAH. No act was passed. PAR #11280303.

24. Benjamin Duval et al., Richmond, to Virginia Assembly, 1804

To The Honble the General Assembly of the Commonwealth of Virginia.

The petition of sundry Inhabitants of the City of Richmond sheweth—That the most nefarious practices have for some time prevailed in many parts of this Commonwealth but particularly in this place, which appear to require legislative interference, and are now about to be explaind.

Many Captains of the Northern trading vessels which frequent the Rivers and inlets of this Commonwealth, have established a clandestine and marauding intercourse and trafic with the slaves whose morals they corrupt—in many Instances they inculcate in their weak minds a spirit of discontent, tending to insurrection. In others they beguile them to commit Robberies on their masters and others, of and every portable article of value, which they receive in barter for spirits or baubles—and in others, decoy them away in expectation of obtaining their Liberty—and after being thus beguiled they employ them as slaves, and convey them to ports where slavery is tolerated, and there sell them as such.—

There are many neighbourhoods in the lower parts of this Commonwealth which severely feel and loudly complain of these fraudulent practices.—and altho former legislatures appear to have taken the subject under consideration, yet Experience proves that the several acts which have been passed to prevent and punish these Evils are not sufficiently penal or terrefic, nor sufficiently extensive to prevent the daily commission of crimes, which a reference to the sections will explain.

Revisd. Code page 190. Sec: XXIX

"If any person or persons shall steal any negro or mulatto whatsoever out of, or from the possession of the owner or overseer of such slave, the person or persons so offending, shall be, and are hereby declared to be felons, and shall suffer death without benefit of Clergy."

Altho the punishment of the offence is great, yet it is not sufficiently rigorous, and the Evil which it is intended to guard against is not prevented. Besides The law as it is, contemplates the punishment after the fact has been fully committed and proved, which can hardly ever happen, because a knowledge or even suspicion of the Guilt seldom occurs until the vessel which has received the slave has gone to sea—and even tho the Captain should return, he will take care to bring with him none of the former Crew, who might be used as Witnesses.—and even then it would be worth more than the value of the slave to carry on a prosecution. Hence owners of slaves generally find it most prudent to abandon their claims altogether.

Page 192. Sec:II.

"No master of any ship or any other vessel, shall transport or carry away any servant whatsoever, or any negro, mulatto, or other slave out of this Commonwealth, without the Consent or permission of the person or persons to whom such servant or slave doth of rights belong, upon penalty of forfeiting and paying one hundred and fifty dollars for every servant, and three hundred dollars for every slave transported or carried hence, contrary to this act; one moiety to the Commonwealth, and the other moiety to the owner of such servant or slave, to be recovered with costs, by action of debt or information in any court of record of this Commonwealth; and moreover, such master shall be liable to the suit of the party grieved, at the common law, for his or her damages."[1]

The same or similar objections lay against this Section also—no suit can be supported against a master of a vessel for the recovery of the penalty, who shall be about to commit, or having partially committed the offence.—Hence therefore, tho a slave should be apprehended at the Capes and taken out of the possession of a master of a Vessel, yet the penalty would not be incurred, because the Apprehension took place before the slave had been carried out of the Commonwealth—and the master of a vessel having shewn all the Intentions of fraud, would escape the punishment which he merited, because the penalties could not be inflicted until he had gone without the Jurisdiction of the Commonwealth.

In the Session of 1802 and 1803, the Legislature offered some further relief, as follows—"That any master or skipper of a vessel, who shall permit any slave to come on board his vessel without the leave or consent of the master or overseer, given in writing, or shall buy, sell, or receive of, to, or from a slave, any commodity whatsoever, without the leave or consent of the master or overseer given in writing as aforesaid, shall forfeit and pay for every such offence, in addition to the penalties now imposed by law, the sum of twenty dols."

Here again it is evident that the punishment or penalty is not equal to the offence—it will hardly ever happen that a slave, who is about to put him self under the protection of a master of a vessel for the purpose of absconding, has not made previous arrangements, so as to indemnify the master by the spoils which he has plundered from his master. The detection therefore, in as much as it subjects the Capt. of the vessel to the penalty of twenty dollars and no more is no Bar to his conduct, because to that extent he will take care to be previously indemnified by deposits from the slave, either in money or other value before he will be allowed to go on board.

Your Petitioners have most respectfully submitted these several Sections of the law, and remarks which are subjoined to the consideration of the Legislature without pretending to recommend any Specific alterations. They humbly pray for themselves and fellow citizens in general, that new modifications will be established and other penalties will be ordained which will tend to prevent these nefarious practices, or will hold out such immediate and severe punishments which will deter these marauders and depredators from such flagrant violations of the Laws of Hospitality, of social Intercourse and moral rectitude—And your Petitioners in duty bound will pray &c—

[signed]	Benj'n DuVal	H Y Dabney
	John Leslie	Saml White
	Wm Prichard	Thomas Cowles
	Henry Harris	Benjn Hooper
	Harry Tompkins	Patk McMara
		[44 additional signatures]

SOURCE: Petition of Benjamin Duval et al. to the Virginia General Assembly, 20 December 1804, Legislative Petitions, Richmond City, VSA. Referred to the Select Committee. Granted.[2] PAR #11680403.

1. See "An Act to Reduce into One, the Several Acts concerning Slaves, Free Negroes and Mulattoes," passed 17 December 1792, in *A Collection of All Such Acts of the General Assembly of Virginia, of a Public and Permanent Nature, as Are Now in Force* (Richmond: Samuel Pleasants Jr. and Henry Pace, 1803), 186–92.

2. In January 1805, the assembly passed a law to expand the definition of slave stealing. It included not only those who "willingly and designedly" took slaves from their owners but also masters of sailing vessels who, with evil intent, allowed slaves to board their vessels. The penalties included a fine of not less than one hundred or more than five hundred dollars and a prison term of not less than two or more than four years. *Acts Passed at a General Assembly of the Commonwealth of Virginia, Begun and Held at the Capitol in the City of Richmond, on Monday, the Third Day of December, One Thousand Eight Hundred and Four* (Richmond: Samuel Pleasants Jr., 180[5]), 9.

25. William Odom et al., Robeson County, to North Carolina Assembly, 1805

To the Honorable the General Assembly of the State of North Carolina

The petition of Major William Odom, William Townsend, John Barnes, Charles Pate, Jacob Blount, Joseph Blount & Job Baxley, of the County of Robeson in the State aforesaid, respectfully Sheweth:

That at the last October Term of the Superior Court of Fayette Ville District, your Petitioners was try'd for a Riot; prosecuted by a Mullattoe, by the name of Elisha Cumboe, which your petitioners beg leave to state to your Honorable Body originated in the following manner—In the Neighborhood where your petitioners lives, there also lives a family of these Mullattoes, who are well known to be of Infamous Characters, who have been for a great number of Years continually in the practice of Villanous Transactions; they have been prosecuted, Convicted & punished, both for Grand & petit-Larceny, as can be made appear by the records of the Superior Court of Fayette Ville District, & the County Court of Robeson—Exclusive of this your petitioners can assure your Honorable Body that these men are envious Malicious & dangerous persons, having a Villanous Clan about them, so dissipated in their Morals & depraved in Character, are ready & willing to come forward at all times & Counteract any evidence that can be brought to bring these Villains to Just punishment; and by these means are almost in defiance of the Laws of their Country.—The particular transactions which led to the circumstance which was deemed a riot, originated in the following manners: William Townsend, one of your petitioners prosecuted & Convicted a Brother of said Elisha Cumboe for Larceny;—Out of revenge for which, said Elisha Cumboe a few nights afterwards went several Miles to the plantation of Mr. Townsend, shot & kill.d a Valuable Horse of his, though there has been no positive proof of it; yet the circumstance is so plain & the presumption so great, that no person acquainted with the circumstances, has the least doubt of his guilt.—For this Offence your petitioners proceeded to apprehend said Cumboe, perhaps without the Legal process of Law; for which he preferred a Bill of Indictment and succeeded so far as to get the above named Major William Odom fined in the Sum of Fifteen Pounds, & each of your other petitioners in the Sum of Ten pounds.—Now as your petitioners will prove to your Honorable Body by Affidavits & Certificates of respectable Characters, that these Cumboes are of Infamous characters, & Notorious Villains, and that the whole of the conduct of your petitioners was Instigated by an ardent wish to procure order & good Neighborhood.—

Your Petitioners pray that your Honorable Body will take our Case into Consideration, & grant us relief by remitting the fine as above-mentioned,[1] or otherwise as You in Your wisdom may deem proper.—

By granting the prayer of this petition, your petitioners as in duty bound, will ever pray. ~~&c~~ this 15th November 1805

[signed] William Odom
Jacob Blount
John Barnes
Charles Pate
William Townsand
Joseph Blount Jun
Jobe Baxly

SOURCE: Petition of William Odom et al. to the North Carolina General Assembly, 30 November 1805, Records of the General Assembly, Session Records, Joint Committee Reports, Propositions and Grievances–1, November–December 1805, folder 2, NCDAH. Rejected. PAR #11280513.

1. Despite testimony from a number of witnesses that members of the Cumboe family were of "Infamous Character" and carried on "illicit trade," the Committee of Propositions and Grievances in the House of Commons ruled that the evidence was not sufficient to grant the request. Certificate, Thomas Barnes et al., 15 November 1805, and Report of Committee of Propositions and Grievances, 10 December 1805, with Petition of William Odom et al. to the General Assembly, 30 November 1805, Records of the General Assembly, Session Records, Joint Committee Reports, Propositions and Grievances–1, November–December 1805, folder 2, NCDAH.

26. Christian Limbaugh to North Carolina Assembly, 1805

Nov.r 27 1805
Gentlemen of the Senate & of the House of Representatives.
Your Petitioner Christian Limbaugh, now Orderly Sargeant of Capt McCauls company in the 2d United States Regiment, humbly complaining respectfully Sheweth That some time in the year 1796 it was my misfortune to marry a certain Catharina Hess, daughter of John Hess of Rowan County with whom I lived but a short time & that short time in a state of the most poignant misery, owing to her rude ungovernable temper, & particularly her incontinency; for I frequently had reason to believe, that her immoral & indecent turn of mind led her to be connected with other men than myself. These circumstances weighing heavily on my mind forced me to leave her on the 24th of Aprile 1799; from which time we have never been together. Your Petitioner further states, that the said Catherina [*sic*] Hess shortly after removed to the county of Lincoln, that there she was looked upon as infamous by all with whom she was acquainted; it being the current report & general belief, & it is the firm belief of Your petitioner that she was delivered of one or more Mulatto children. Your petitioner States that at March term 1804 of Salisbury Supr court, the said Catharina was convicted of having barbarously murdered her infant child, which was generally believed in the neighbourhood to have been a mulatto.[1] That afterwards through the clemency of our Governor She was pardoned under the gallows.[2] For the truth of the above facts, your petitioner referrs you the General Mumford [*sic*] Stokes,[3] to the Governor himself & to all the members from the County of Rowan. And for the truth of the circumstances relative to her general character, I have hereto annexed the signatures of several respectable persons who are willing & have hereby attested the correctness of the above statement.

With the foregoing few, but serious facts Your petitioner submits his unhappy situation to be acted upon as You in Your wisdom may think fit, firmly believing that a bill of Divorce will be passed in his favour.

[signed] Christian Limbaugh

SOURCE: Petition of Christian Limbaugh to the Senate and House of Representatives of North Carolina, 3 December 1805, Records of the General Assembly, Session Records, Divorce Petitions, November–December 1805, box 3, NCDAH. Rejected. PAR #11280515.

1. Pleading for mercy, Ed Jones wrote Governor James Turner from Salisbury, "She was convicted on clear full testimony but she is a woman—was left unprotected desolate and in poverty by her vagabond husband, it is said she expected his return and that her crime was caused by such expectation." In any event, the murder was "not an example so dangerous to society as most others." Ed Jones to James Turner, 28 March 1804, Papers of Governor James Turner (G.P. 27), 202, NCDAH.

2. Governor Turner (1766–1824) granted the pardon on 12 April 1804. Papers of Governor James Turner (G.P. 27), 202, NCDAH.

3. Montford Stokes (1762–1842), a longtime Salisbury resident, was appointed a major general in the state militia in 1804, and he served as governor during the early 1830s. Robert Sobel and John Raimo, eds., *Biographical Directory of the Governors of the United States, 1789–1978*, 4 vols. (Westport, Conn.: Meckler Books, 1978), 3:1125–26.

27. Thomas Reekes, Mecklenburg County, to Virginia House of Delegates, 1805

To the Honourable, the speaker of the House of Representatives the petition of Thomas Reekes Humbly Sheweth,

That in the Year of our lord one thousand eight Hundred & two a certain Henry Ashton a magistrate of this County, duly issued his warrant, directed to an Authorized officer of the County for the purpose of apprehending Several Negroe slaves suspected and charged with plotting and Conspiring the Murder of some ~~Certain~~ Citizens of this County by mixing a Certain Mortal poison with their food,[1] that the said warrant being executed by the officer aforesaid, the said slaves were apprehended, and duly examined by the Magistrate aforesaid upon the result of which, three were deem,d Guilty and accordingly Committed to the Custody of the sheriff or goaler of this County for the purpose of being arraign,d and tryed before a Court of Oyer and Terminer, which were legally summoned for their arraignment and tryal aforesaid, that one of the slaves so Committed was the property of your petitioner and named Frank, for the Verification of which fact, your petitioner, hath Annexed the Copy of the Mittimus as duly Authenticated by the Clerk of the County, that the day on which said Frank was to be tryed he was suddenly taken ill, and departed this life, an~~d~~ event which your petitioner firmly believes was produced by the Cruel rigour of his Confinement, for the Verification of which fact, your petitioner her[e]to subjoins the Certificate of the sheriff of the County made Out on the day of said slaves death & Recorded by Clerk of the County From a review of all which Circumstances your petitioner thinks it highly reasonable the Commonwealth should make him a Compensation for his slave, A valuable one to him indeed, being the only male one he posses,d and his labour being absolutely nesasary for the support of your petitioners family, Your petitioner Cannot on this Occasion forbear to state, that Among the Various rights which appertain to the Citizens of this Commonwealth, there is none which The legislature has ever regarded in a more sacred manner than the right of personal property, on no Occasion ever permitting them to be infringed but always guarding them by the Severest sanctions, that even when the Interest of society required, that a certain portion of private personal property shall be given up or taken for the General good an equivalent for the property so taken has always been made to the proprietor, Actuated by principels of this Nature, the legislature of this

Country enacted the law Making Compensation to masters, for slaves, which the good of society requir,d should be executed, Your petitioner Humbly Conceives that the Case which he has Submitted for your Consideration Comes within the reason of those principels which gave birth to the law aforesaid for the slave was the property of your petitioner the law required he should be given up, in order to be tryed for those Crimes with which he was charged, The general good required it, and surely as he was arrested for that purpose Your petitioner is entitled to be paid his Value by those for whose good he was taken from him, To wit the Community, from all which Circumstances & reasons Your petitioner prays that a law may be pass,d making him a Compensation for the slave aforesaid and your petitioner will ever pray

[signed] Thos Reekes . . . [supporting certificate and signatures]

Mecklenburg County 29th. Nov: 1805

In the month February 1802 (at which time I acted as Deputy Sheriff of Mecklenburg County) the[re] were several negroes in said County accused with ploting together, some to poison their Masters & some to do other unlawful acts which made it necessary to arrest fifteen or twenty for the purpose of investigating and examining into their Conduct It appeared that Dick the Property of John Gregory had made a plot with Frank the property of Thomas Reeks [*sic*], to poison the said Gregory, from the evidence the said Frank was the person whom Dick obtained his poison from, and was the instructor in the way of administration. Several negroes seem'd to have a Knowledge of the conspiracy, But Frank the property of Reeks was a very artful fellow, and appeared to have been the foundation of the evil designs of the rest, relative to the poisoning Dick the property of John Gregory ~~Good~~ was examined by the Court of Mecklenburg County & was condem[n]ed & executed, and Frank the property of Thomas Reeks on his way from the jailers died a very sudden death, That the cause of his death was attributed to be, either the confinement in a waggon or his taking poison before he started from the jailors which was about Seven miles from this Court house & he died the morning before his examination was to take place from the cause aforesaid as was supposed—The negroe was a well Healthy looking person & appea[re]d to be of a very vicious disposition proud & Malignant, with great impudence—I believe it was the General oppinion, That Frank the property of Thomas Reeks was ~~the~~ the instigator of the ploting, and deserved death by the law of the land,—and I think the oppinion was quite correct

[signed] Richard Apperson

SOURCE: Petition of Thomas Reekes to the Speaker of the Virginia House of Representatives, 11 December 1805, Legislative Petitions, Mecklenburg County, VSA; Affidavit, Richard Apperson, 29 November 1805, ibid. Rejected. PAR #11680508.

1. Between 1740 and 1784, with the exception of burglary, poisonings and illegal administration of medicines were the most common capital cases prosecuted against slaves. By the early nineteenth century, violent murder, conspiracy, and insurrection took precedence, but fear of being poisoned remained strong among whites. Philip J. Schwarz, *Slave Laws in Virginia* (Athens: University of Georgia Press, 1996), 7.

28. Charlotte Ball, Culpeper County, to Virginia House of Delegates, 1806

To the Honorable the Speaker and Gentlemen of the House of Delegates of the Commonwealth of Virginia: The petition of Charlotte Ball of the County of Culpeper respectfully represents;

That in the month of May in the year 1800 she intermarried with a certain William Ball of the same County, who being nearly of her own age and possessing a property, very adequate with care and industry to their decent support, she had every reason to hope for as great a portion of happiness as most people enjoy in a married state. a very few weeks however had elapsed before his treatment of her became so extremely cruel and oppressive, as to be almost insupportable; but determined most scrupulously to observe the vows which her solemn engagement had imposed, as long as it was possible, she conducted herself on all occasions towards him with humble duty, fidelity, and affection: the humility of her deportment and her anxious cares to win his good will and affections, far from producing any change in his conduct favorable to her happiness, appeared to increase the outrages he practised on her person. In a short time after their marriage he transported her far from her family and friends, and after a circuitous journey of some hundreds of miles, during which no day passed without his inflicting on her blows and other ill-usage, they took up a temporary residence in the County Frederick. In this situation after he had wasted his substance to the last farthing in profligacy and debaucheries, she bore her miseries with patience, untill her life was more than once attempted by him, and her feelings tortured with his frequent criminal connections with the most abandoned of the human species which he took no pains to conceal either from her knowledge or her sight. Injuries so intolerable excited the commisseration of some of her neighbours who with much persuasion and difficulty induced him to suffer her return to her father. She has now with unremitted industry for more than four years supported herself and her children, without receiving from her husband the smallest aid, or even seeing him; but having been well informed that he has of late threatened, and really designs to despoil her of the little property she has accumulated, the hard earnings of her assiduous industry, and again to leave her and her children destitute on the world, she is induced to implore the interposition of your honorable body, and to pray if, she shall substantiate the allegations contained in her petition, which she is now ready to do, by the depositions of many respectable persons, that a law may pass releasing her from the bonds of matrimony: or that some court may take cognisance of her case, with authority on sufficient cause being shown to pronounce a decree of divorce—or that such other relief may be extended to her as may appear meet to the legislature; and she will as in duty bound pray &c.—

[no signature] . . . [depositions]

The affidavit of Travers Barns taken before us the Subscribers two of the Commonwealths Justice of the peace for the said County of Shenandoah County and State of Virginia at the house of Travers Barns on Mill Creek in said County on the first day of November 1806 Respecting a certain Controversy between Charlottee [*sic*] Ball and her Husband William Ball the said Travers Barns being first being duly sworn and of lawful age deposeth & saith that some time in the last of February 1801 being in Company with William Ball and his wife as they were moveing from Shenandoah County to Frederick County I saw W Ball ~~out of~~ in anger strike at his wife but I do not know whether he hit her or not but I suppose if I had not interfeard he would Continued to treat her ill and being Very well acquainted with W Ball and to my knowledg he was much subjected to strong drink and when drunk would treat his family very ill being frequently at W Balls House I always Saw Mrs Ball civil and I believe an Industrious discreet woman—

I have reason to believe that the sd William Ball was Remarkable fond of other women from his own Confession to me he told me that Mrs Ball saw himself Coppulating with a negro woman named Filis belonging to said Balls Mother the said Ball did frequently tell me that he had Carnal knowledg of different women after he was married to his wife both white and black Some short time after the Sd Ball was married to his wife Charlottee Ball he became possesed of a handsome fortune Sufficent to Support a family very decently and in a few years by neglegence and bad management he was reduced to poverty and—his family to want

Sworne to before us—
Jno Huss
Samuel Walton
[signed] Travers Barns

SOURCE: Petition of Charlotte Ball to the Virginia House of Delegates, 14 December 1806, Legislative Petitions, Culpeper County, VSA; Affidavit of Travers Barns, 1 November 1806, ibid. Rejected. PAR #11680606.

29. Samuel Kerfott, Frederick County, to Virginia Assembly, 1808

To The Honble The General Assembly of Virginia

The Petition of Samuel Kerfott of Frederick County Respectfully states that on the 1st day of December in the year 1807 a court of Oyer & Terminer was held in Frederick County for the Trial of Negroe Joseph a slave the property of your petitioner on a charge of having attempted to Commit a Rape on the body of Nancy Mitchell a free white Woman by which Court he was Convicted of the charge and ordered to be Castrated as appears by a Copy of the Record of said Court here unto annexed[1] Your petitioner further states that the castration was performed by Dr. Robert Mackay whose high standing and ~~long~~ long practise as a Physician & Surgeon is well known and altho' every possible care was bestowed on said Negroe Joseph he died on the 13.th December 1807 no human means was left untried to save him & the greatest professional skill exerted, the negroe was about 26 years of age strong & sound & about one week before his Commitment on this charge your petitioner gave £110 for him Thus situated your petitioner has lost a valuable Slave ever obedient to the Law he immediately gave him up to meet its fullest inquiry and hopes the General Assembly will allow him Compensation for the Serious Loss he has sustained to that honorable body he now appeals no existing Law embracing his case leaves no other remedy, that a man whose Slave is executed should be paid his value is founded on principles of Justice & Sound policy which are believed to apply equally to a case where in Consequence of a Corporal punishment Death has ensued to a Slave various Reasons Could I would [*sic*] be used to prove the propriety of this Claim but to the Superior Intelligence and wisdom of the General Assembly he Submits his case, what he omits will be Supplied he prays that the value of the Slave which is established by a Document here unto annexed may be allowed him and he will pray &c

[signed] Samuel Kerfott

25th Nov. 1808 . . . [supporting certificate and signatures]

On the 4th day of Decr 1807, In obedience to an order of th[e] County Court of Frederick to me directed, I castrated a Negro Slave, (named Joe) the property of Mr. Samuel Carfoot [*sic*] of said County, who appeared to be in a state of recovery till the morning of th[e] 11th ensuing, when he was seized with a Tetanus of which he expired on the night of the thirteenth following, notwithstanding every attention a[nd] Medical aid was given him, whether this was produced by cold received during his confinement or taken the night previous to his being attacked with the Symptoms (part of which he informed me he lay without covering) I cannot determine given under my hand at Winchester 25th. Nov.r 1808

[signed] Robt. Mackey

SOURCE: Petition of Samuel Kerfott to the Virginia General Assembly, 9 December 1808, Legislative Petitions, Frederick County, VSA; Certificate, Robert Mackey, 25 November 1808, ibid. Granted.[2] PAR #11680803.

1. In 1792, the general assembly enacted a law stating, "It shall not be lawful for any county or corporation court to order and direct castration of any slave, except such slave shall be convicted of an attempt to ravish a white woman, in which case they may inflict such punishment." *A Collection of All Such Acts of the General Assembly of Virginia, of a Public and Permanent Nature, as Are Now in Force* (Richmond: Samuel Pleasants, 1814), 265.

2. The assembly authorized the auditor of public accounts to pay Kerfott $366 for the loss of his slave. *Acts Passed at a General Assembly of the Commonwealth of Virginia, Begun and Held at the Capitol, in the City of Richmond, on Monday the Fifth Day of December, in the Year of Our Lord One Thousand Eight Hundred and Eight . . .* (Richmond: Samuel Pleasants Jr., 1809), 51.

30. Petition of Quakers, Guilford County, to North Carolina Assembly, 1809

From our yearly meeting of Friends, held in Guilford County, North Carolina,

To the ensuing General Assembly of North Carolina;

Friends, We desire not to weary your attention, by repeated solicitation; but the clemency with which our former applications have been received, encourages us again to take the liberty of addressing you on the interesting, and important subject of Slavery.

Believing, as we do, that Liberty is the unalienable, and incontrovertible Right of all the Human Species, and that the God of the Universe, hath made of one blood all Nations of men, for to dwell on all the face of the Earth, we again solicit your candid; and impartial attention to the investigation of this momentous concern.

With candor, and gratitude may we acknowledge our intire satisfaction with the result of your deliberations, as relates to ourselves; but the indispensible obligation of doing to others, as we would they should do unto us, induces us to "open our mouths in the cause of those who may, with emphasis, be said to be 'dumb.'"

To set this matter in a clearer Point of view Permit us for a moment, to call your attention to the case of any American Citizen when captured by the algerines, and subjugated to Slavery, with what Pathos! with what energetic Zeal are his Brethren Stimulated to procure his enlargement, and restoration! Then, to be consistent, let us go the whole length of our Principles, and not refuse the extension, and application of these Rights to others, which we so pertinently, and strenuously assume, and apply to our selves.

And, whilst we would not be understood as favoring, or desiring an immediate emancipation, yet we believe that every Principle of Justice, and humanity, calls for the gradual extension of the inestimable blessing of Liberty to the unhappy, and long-injured African race in our Land, as far, and as fully, as may be consistent with the Peace, and conservation of the State.

And, although we desire you may not lose sight of the general Principles of this serious matter; yet should you deem it inadmissible to enter on it in a general way, we earnestly desire that some wise Provision may take place in such as to extend the Privileges, and immunities of freedom to those who have been, or may, hereafter be liberated by those who are conscientiously scrupulous of Perpetuating their Slavery.

[signed] Barnabas Coffin
Clk to the meeting this year

SOURCE: Petition of Quakers to the North Carolina General Assembly, 1809, Records of the General Assembly, Session Records, Miscellaneous Petitions, November–December 1809, box 3, NCDAH. No act was passed. PAR #11280904.

31. Alexander Smith, Ashe County, to North Carolina Assembly, 1809

To the Honorable the General Assembly of the State of North Carolina N[o]w in Session

Humbly petitioning your Petitioner Alex. Smith Esq of Ashe County begs Leave to Lay before this Honorable Assembly a statement of f[a]cts and atrue ac't of his—situation. In the year 1784 he married a Miss Sarah Dickson and took her as the companion of his choice with whom he Lived many years in domastic peace and pleasure had no reason of suspition against the virtue or Chist [chaste] conduct of the said Sarah his wife—she had during the time they lived together Five children all Girls and he never had the most distant thought they were not his own he made use of Every means in his power to make them happy in Life but in the year 1800 the said Sarah his wife became base in her conduct on the 14th day of April 1801 She Eloped from your petitioners Bed and Board not regarding the situation or safety of her children which your petitioner has carefully provided for ever since. And as it is your Petitioners wish to secure his property and put it out of the powers of a person of such baseness as his wife Sarah is and has been ever since when she eloped she went off with a Mullatoe man nearly as Black as an Negro and has lived without the Bounds of this State with said man of mixt Collur ever since time now as your Petitioner cannot be relieved from his present disagreeble situation without the aid and assistance of this Honorable Assembly who are the Guardein of the peoples Rights and Secures the Safety of the Citizen against Baseness and insult of this kind as above Stated-

That your Petitioner may secure his property and dispose of it as he thinks proper at his own pleasure for the good of his children and obtain relief from his unhappy situation he claims the attention and compation [compassion] of the Honorable Assembly to divorce him from his wife Sarah and for ever to prevent her in Law or in Equity to Claim any right Title or interest to any part of your Petitioners Estate or property real or personal and your Petitioner as in Duty bound will ever pray—

Novr 23d 1809

[signed] Alex smith

SOURCE: Petition of Alexander Smith to the North Carolina General Assembly, 27 November 1809, Records of the General Assembly, Session Records, Divorce Petitions, November–December 1809, box 3, NCDAH. Granted.[1] PAR #11280902.

1. Notations on the docket page of the petition indicate that the petition was referred to the Committee on Divorce and Alimony, read in the House and Senate, and granted.

32. Benjamin Edwards Browne, Surry County, to Virginia Assembly, 1809

To the Honourable the General Assembly of Virginia,

The petition of Benjamin Edwards Browne Humbly sheweth, that on succeeding to the office of High Sheriff for the County of Surry he found in the Jail of the said County the following negroes towit Pleasants, Billey, Catey, & Joe, & James

That the said negroes had been apprehended & committed as runaways—Your petitioner here annexes the warrant of commitment under the hand & seal of one of the commonwealths justices of the peace for the said County of Surry & prays that it may be taken as a part of this petition. That as the said negroes were found in Jail & appeared to have been regularly committed your petitioner deemed it his duty to continue them.[1] He states that they were in every respect dealt with as the law required—That they were regularly advertised & at the proper period offered for hire. That the said negroes from their ages & sex were expensive & that no person would take them except on condition of being paid for their support.

Under these circumstances your petitioner deemed it his indispensible duty to continue them in custody on the Jail allowance untill by due course of Law they should be discharged. They remained in Jail untill the prison fees amounted to the sum of Four hundred twenty two dollars and thirty seven cents as the accompanying documents will distinctly shew.

The said negroes were taken proper care of & received whilst in jail clothes & blankets which their naked condition rendered indispensible. Pleasants the only adult, whilst in jail, was delivered of a child, consequently gave much trouble

& additional Expense to the keeper. Your Petitioner further represents that at a Court held for Surry County December 27 1807 a certain Wm. Rowlett appeared before the Court & made oath that the aforesaid slaves were the property of a certain Henry Daniel whereupon the Court ordered that the said slaves should be retained in the custody of the officer for the said Henry Daniel till legally claimed by him or his representative—& that the said slaves should not be sold as is prescribed by law in cases where they are not claimed—A copy of the said order attested by the Clerk is here annexed—That at a Court held for the said County of Surry on the 24th day of January 1809 the Court made an order that the said slaves should be delivered to the said William Rowlett in right of Henry Daniel and that neither the said William Rowlett or Henry Daniel should be bound to pay prison fees or any other expense incurred by the commitment & confinement of the said slaves. An attested Copy of which order is here annexed.[2]

Your petitioner being the immediate officer of the Court, his office being one of great responsibility he felt bound to pay respect to the orders & decrees of the Court—He resolved to take some legal step to get rid of an order which opperated so injuriously on his interests:—To effect which purpose he consulted several members of the bar who after some conference unanimously concurred in recommending an application to the Chancellor of the District—In conformity to this advice an application was made for an injunction to prevent the removal of the said slaves untill the relief sought could be obtained or untill the fees were paid or secured The Chancellor refused to interpose as will appear from his certificate at the foot of the bill—which is here annexed. When Your petitioner could not suspend the operation of the judgmt. or order he considered it his duty to yield to the decision whether right or wrong & accordingly delivered the slaves as will appear from one of the documents above referred to—

Thus situated your petitioner presented his case again before the Court of his County praying them to afford him some relief—He expected that from a levy on the County, he should be reimbursed the expenses he had incurred by supporting its magistracy. The Court after some time certified the claim to the Auditor of Public accounts for the state of Virginia—The claim has been presented & rejected as will appear from the annexed document marked A.

Your petitioner approaches with great deference & respect the Legislature of his Country. He is well convinced that it is only on important occasions that applicants should present themselves before that Honourable body for relief.—He believes that he shall stand justified in the opinion of those to whom he now appeals.

When a case is without relief in the tribunals constituted to administer justice between the Citizens of the state resort can alone be had to the Legislative body. Your petitioner without the slightest fault or shade of negligence on his part has been deprived of a sum large in amt. & to which he has every claim which justice & equity can give. He feels conscious of having discharged legally & diligently the duties imposed on him by his office. His is an office which imposes on him the necessity of inforcing obedience to the law. Shall he then suffer for doing his duty and bowing to the judgment of that very Court whose process he is bound to execute.

He conceives & humbly hopes that the Legislature of his Country will say he shall not. Hoping that his case will meet the attention of the Genl. Assembly of Virga. & that he shall finally receive that relief which heretofore he has sought in vain—He remains ~~their~~ its Humble petitioner and as in duty bound shall every pray &c.

[signed] Benjamin E. Browne
Sheriff of Surry County

SOURCE: Petition of Benjamin Edwards Browne to the Virginia General Assembly, 16 December 1809, Legislative Petitions, Surry County, VSA. Rejected. PAR #11680925.

1. In 1785, the law governing runaway slaves permitted their apprehension by any person. A reward would be paid to the apprehender. If the owners were not found, then the runaways were hired out with iron collars around their necks. After one year, if the owners still could not be determined, the slaves, after being advertised in the *Virginia Gazette,* were sold. June Purcell Guild, comp., *Black Laws of Virginia: A Summary of the Legislative Acts of Virginia concerning Negroes from the Earliest Times to the Present* (Richmond: Whittet and Shepperson, 1936; reprint, New York: Negro Universities Press, 1969), 63.

2. On 6 February 1810, a member of the general assembly "Recd the documts accompanying B. E. Brown's peto leave havg been given to withdraw them." They were never returned. Receipt of William Randolph, 6 February 1810, with Petition of Benjamin Edwards Browne to the Virginia General Assembly, 16 December 1809, Legislative Petitions, Surry County, VSA.

33. Samuel Templeman, Westmoreland County, to Virginia Assembly, 1809

To the honourable the Speaker & House of Delegates of the Commonwealth of Virginia, your petitioner, Samuel Templeman, sheweth:

That William Hutt, by his last will & testament, bearing date the day of appointed your petitioner his executor, who qualified as such in the county court of Westmoreland, on the day of : that the testator died considerably indebted, and that the principal part of his personal estate consisted in negroes; from the sale of which negroes alone did your petitioner expect ever to satisfy the just demands of the creditors of the deceased: that Joe, a young, large, and likely negro man, was one of the slaves belonging to the said Hutt's estate, whom, your petitioner believes, he might have sold for at least £100: that this negro had been a runaway for some time previous to the orders from the executive of this commonwealth dated the day of December last, which issued in consequence of the alarming intelligence, that, on the day preceding Christmas, a massacre of ourselves & of those most dear to us was intended by the negroes: that, on the receipt of this intelligence & these orders, the citizens of Westmoreland armed, as one man, in defence of themselves & the community, & with promptness obeyed the commands of their respective officers; which were, to search every negro cabin, to apprehend such negroes & mulattoes as were found traveling, or from home, particularly in the night, & to put to death such as resisted, or ran & could not otherwise be stopped: that on the evening of the 24th. of December, orders were first given for a general patrol, and that on this night, the said negro man was found in a cabin where his wife was: that, on hearing the voices & enquiries of the patrollers, he was alarmed, and attempted to escape by flight that he was commanded to stop, but continued to run when a gun was fired at him, and he died of the wound which he received.

Your petitioner further represents, that he has applied to counsel learned in the law, to know whether he can obtain satisfaction for the said loss by application to the judicial courts of this commonwealth; & that he has been advised by them, that his only redress therefor must be expected from the determination of your honourable body.

Now, your petitioner conceives, that, as the patrollers acted in conformity to orders which were dictated by a regard to the welfare of the state; if any particular loss accrued under these orders to individuals, this loss ought to be reimbursed by the public. He has always thought that the burdens of a civil society ought not to be borne by particular persons, & that if any individual member of a State should be deprived of his property for the benefit of the ~~benefit of the~~ commonwealth, the collective body of the citizens should make him a compensation for the loss. This seems to have been the opinion of a former legislature of Virginia; when they enacted that "the value of a slave condemned to die, who shall suffer accordingly, shall be paid by the public to the owner":[1] and your petitioner cannot imagine any cause why the reason of this law will not apply to the case above submitted to your consideration, as well as to that which is mentioned in the clause just cited.—Hard, indeed, it would be, if the creditors of William Hutt deceased should suffer by a loss which has been unavoidably sustained for the advantage of the community.

Impressed with these sentiments, & confiding in the justness of his claim, your petitioner prays, that your honourable body will direct that the value of the said negro be recompensed to him from the public treasury; especially since he is driven to this request by the impossibility which exists of obtaining a compensation, by applying to the judicial courts of this state; as has been before observed.—

And your petitioner will ever pray, &c.

[signed] Samuel Templeman

Having been requested by Mr. Samuel Templeman to declare the circumstances attending the death of the negro man Joe, who was killed on the 24th of December last; in compliance with his request, I do hereby certify, that, on that day, in the evening, I was summoned by a messenger (from Capt. Gerard McKenney, I believe) to attend immediately at a certain Gerard Hutt's, to receive orders for opposing a conspiracy which, he said, was on foot among the negroes. I attended accordingly, and was told by the said McKenney that I must patrol the neighbourhood, during the night, under arms; for that he was empowered, under the executive authority, to give these commands. I armed myself, & was associated with two others, James Robinson & William McKenney. If I misremember not, the orders given us by capt. McKenney were, to search the negro cabins, & take every thing which we found in them, which bore a hostile aspect, such as powder, shot &c. into our possession; to apprehend every negro whom we found from his home; & if he made any resistance, or ran from us, to fire on him immediately, unless he could be stopped by other means. After having been on patrol for about four or five hours, we came to Mr. Solomon Redman's, where the above-named Robinson resided; & the latter, hearing a strange voice in one of the huts to which we went, demanded who was there. Some evasive answer was made by a woman (as I thought), & a negro man came out at the door. McKenney & Robinson made an effort to stop him; but he pushed by. We commanded him to stop, but he continued his flight, and Robinson, finding there was no other means of bringing him to, fired. The man still ran, & it was imagined by us that he had made his escape. After a short time, however, we heard his cries, & had him carried to Redman's kitchen. Upon examination, he was found wounded in the knee & foot, He lived for a day or two, & then died of the wound he had received.—

It is my opinion that Mr. Robinson acted perfictly in consistence with the orders which were given him.

Mr. Templeman asks what I suppose to have been the negroe's reason for running.

I was impressed with a belief, from every circumstance to which I was a witness on the night this unfortunate accident happened, that if a conspiracy were brewing, intelligence of it had not reached the negroes here; and I am told that this was the general opinion throughout the county: I therefore suppose he thought us common patrolers, & ran to prevent us from delivering him to his master.

[signed] [Foxhall][2] Sturman

SOURCE: Petition of Samuel Templeman to the Virginia General Assembly, 21 December 1809, Legislative Petitions, Westmoreland County, VSA; Certificate, Foxhall Sturman, ca. 1809, ibid. Rejected. PAR #11680924.

1. Consolidating statutes passed in 1786 and 1790, a 1792 law stated that slaveowners should be compensated by the state for a slave condemned to die "who shall suffer accordingly, or before execution of the sentence perish." The value of the slave was to be determined by three trial justices. *A Collection of All Such Acts of the General Assembly of Virginia, of a Public and Permanent Nature, as Are Now in Force* (Richmond: Samuel Pleasants, 1814), 267.

2. For his given name, Sturman used a highly stylized abbreviation.

34. Christopher MacPherson, Richmond, to Virginia Assembly, 1810

To the Honorable General Assembly of the State of Virginia—

The Petition of Christopher MacPherson Humbly Sheweth—That by an Ordinance for the corporation of the City of Richmond passed on the 18th June 1810 entitled an ordinance to amend an ordinance for regulating Waggons Drays and Carts and for other purposes, it is provided that no person shall keep for hire, any Gig chair or other carriage, without causing the same to be registered and taking out a license therefor and it is provided, that previously to registering and granting such license, bond and security in the penalty of Two hundred dollars shall be given with condition, that no Negro or mulatto shall be permitted to use the same, except in the Capacity of Maid or Servant to some Lady or Gentleman, hiring and riding therein.—

Your Petitioner further sheweth, that he is a free person and a Native of Virginia and has a family—That being a mulatto he and his family come within the provision of the said ordinance and a House keeper and owner of real property of considerable value in the said City, acquired by a life of long and laborious industry.—

He further begs leave humbly to represent, that during the revolutionary War he was employed as Clerk for the Commercial Agent for the State of Virginia and Clerk of one of the Commissary Generals at the Siege of York Town—That he afterwards was employed by the Clerk of Congress as an enrolling Clerk and has since been employed as a Clerk in different publick Offices both under the General & State Governments—and by Merchants & others in examining & settling accounts and other business of that nature, which requires fidelity, industry and a knowledge of accounts—

That your Petitioner is now employed in this business, by means whereof, he is enabled to Earn a decent support for his family—

Your Petitioner trusts he may say, without fear of Contradiction, that he has given general satisfaction to his Employers and that he has uniformly sustained and deserved the character of an honest and industrious man—

That your Petitioner and his wife being both advanced in life and occasionally subject to disease—it has happened and may again happen, that the occasional use of a carriage when they are unable to walk, may be necessary not only for their comfort but their health and for the carrying on of the business of your petitioner, which lays in various parts of the said City—

Your Petitioner submits without a murmur, to those Laws of the Commonwealth, which impose disabilities on that class of people to which he belongs and he is not disposed to deny, that there may be persons with respect to whom, the ordinance aforesaid might properly apply, but he humbly concieves that the said ordinance is unjust as it respects himself and family and that it deprives him of rights to which he is entitled under the laws and Constitution of this Commonwealth.—

Your petitioner humbly begs leave to state, that he has represented his case to a Number of the members of the corporation of Richmond by letter, requesting that his case might be laid before the Common Hall and that he might be excepted from the provisions of the said Ordinance but hath not been able to obtain a decision thereon. Your Petitioner is and always has been disposed, to conform to all such laws and rules as the publick good might be thought to require by those placed in authority, nor would he now complain, did he not sustain real inconvenience from the said ordinance and were he not apprehensive, that as he and his wife grow older and more infirm, this inconvenience will be greatly heightened. Wherefore your petitioner humbly prays, that your Honorable Body will be pleased to take his case into consideration and that he may be protected in the enjoyment of such rights as are given him by the General Laws of this Commonwealth and that your Honorable Body will be pleased to enact such regulations as will prevent those rights from being infringed—

And your Petitioner, as in duty bound will Ever pray &c—

[no signature]

SOURCE: Petition of Christopher MacPherson to the Virginia General Assembly, 10 December 1810, Legislative Records, Richmond City, VSA. Deemed reasonable and reported out of committee, but no act was passed. PAR #11681021.

35. James Carmichael et al. to South Carolina House, 1812

The Honorable the Speaker and Members of the House of Representatives of the State of South Carolina now in Session in Columbia—

The Petition of the Subscribers

Humbly Sheweth

That they have witnessed with satisfaction for years past the general disposition of the people of this State to emeliorate the condition of Slaves and have felt pleasure in observing the favorable changes which have been made in their condition without making them less useful to their owners or more dangerous to society. But they have lately observed with regret and concern that one of the consequences of softening their condition as slaves has been their forgetting that they were such and their attempting to exercise among some of the lower classes of white people freedoms and familiarities which are degrading to them and dangerous to society. We allude to the attempts which are made and some of them with success at sexual intercourse with white females, an offence to which our existing laws annex no adequate punishment; because as we presume their former humble condition and conduct forbid the belief that such presumption would have been found in the one or such degradation in the other. But so the fact is that instances do now occur in which not merely the dregs of society are concerned but some reputable families are disgraced and covered with infamy by the presumptuous advances of a slave or free Negro to their weak and perhaps desolate child. The want of an adequate penalty for such an offence has in some instances induced an incensed and indignant neighborhood to errect a tribunal of their own and to measure out justice to the offender with their own hand. The necessity of such a resort ought in the opinion of your petitioners to be guarded against by the passage of a law annexing to such criminal conduct a penalty commensurate to the offence. Your petitioners therefore submit the case to your consideration hoping that you will adopt such measures as wisdom and sound policy shall direct and as in duty bound &c.

[signed] James Carmichael, V.D.V. Jamison, David Rumph, Sam P Jones, Sanders Glover Jur, Donald Rowe, Stephen Moss, Martin Friday, Wm Rowe, G. Jennings [30 additional signatures]

SOURCE: Petition of James Carmichael et al. to the South Carolina House of Representatives, 12 December 1812, Records of the General Assembly, #111, SCDAH. Referred to the Judiciary Committee. No act was passed. PAR #11381203.

36. Citizens of Tennessee to Tennessee Assembly, 1813

To the Honorable the General Assembly, of the State of Tennessee

Your Memorialists beg leave to represent to your Honorable Body, that Many of the good Citizens of this State labour under great inconvenience and disadvantage, from the numerous Tipling Shops erected on the high way, and in our Towns, by free Negroes and others to such an extent that Our Servants cannot with safety be sent on Our Ordinary business Owing to the trafic and intoxication encouraged and carried on, at those Links of Corruption, that our holy Sabbath days are regularly Violated and profaned by the Numerous crowd of Slaves collected for the propose of drinking and bartering for Whiskey, the stolen property of their Owners and others, We have in vain attempted to Suppress this dangerous, and growing evil but find the present Laws too feable to accomplish the end. Your memorialists therefore pray your honorable Body (seeing the times are precarious) to take the Subject under your wise consideration, and make Such provision to remedy the evil as you in your wisdom may deem proper, and we as in duty bound will ever pray—

[signed] James Whitsill, Joseph Seales, Caleb Hewitt, Wm Howlet

D Moore	Jonathan, H. Rains
Jessey Wharton	Jno Nelson
N. A. McNairy	Robert Boyd
	[70 additional signatures]

SOURCE: Petition of Citizens of Tennessee to the General Assembly, 8 October 1813, Legislative Petitions, #15-3-1813, reel 4, TSLA. Granted.[1] PAR #11481305.

1. See "An Act to Supress Tipling [*sic*] Shops and for Other Purposes." A fine of five to ten dollars was the penalty for anyone who sold "spirituous liquors or other drink capable of producing intoxication" to a slave without an owner's permission. Half the fine would go to the informant and half to the owner. *[Acts Passed at the] General Assembly of the State of Tennessee, Begun and Held at Nashville* . . . (Nashville: T. S. Bradford, 181[3]), 183–84.

37. Lucinda, King George County, to Virginia Legislature, 1813

To the Legislature of the Commonwealth of Virginia,

The petition of Lucinda, lately a slave belonging to Mary Matthews of King George county respectfully sheweth.

That the said Mary Matthews, by her last will and testament, among other things, emancipated all her slaves, and directed that they should be removed by her executor to some place where they could enjoy their freedom by the laws there in force. That all the slaves so emancipated (except your petitioner) were removed this year to the State of Tennessee; but your petitioner declined going with them, as she had a husband belonging to Capt. William Hooe in King George county, from whom the benefits and privileges to be derived from freedom, dear and flattering as they are, could not induce her to be separated: that, in consequence of this determination on her part, a year has elapsed since the death of her late mistress Mary Matthews, and your petitioner, is informed that the forfeiture of her freedom has taken place under the law prohibiting emancipated slaves from remaining in this State;[1] and that the Overseers of the Poor might now proceed to sell her for the benefit of the Poor of the county: Your petitioner, still anxious to remain with her husband, for whom she has relinquished all the advantages of freedom, is apprehensive that, in case of a sale of her by the Overseers of the Poor, she may be purchased by some person, who will remove her to a place remote from the residence of her husband: to guard against such a heart rending circumstance, she would prefer, and hereby declares her consent, to become a slave to the owner of her husband, if your honorable body will permit it; and for that purpose she prays that you will pass a law vesting the title to her in the said William H. Hooe and directing that all proceedings on the part of the Overseers of the Poor for King George county to effect the sale of her may be perpetually staid;

And your petitioner will pray &c

Nov: 27th 1813—
[signed] Lucinda

SOURCE: Petition of Lucinda to the Legislature of Virginia, 27 November 1813, Legislative Petitions, King George County, VSA. Tabled. PAR #11681303.

1. Any slave emancipated after 1 May 1806 who remained in the commonwealth more than twelve months could be seized and sold back into slavery. *A Collection of All Such Acts of the General Assembly of Virginia of a Public and Permanent Nature as Have Passed since the Session of 1801* (Richmond: Samuel Pleasants Jr., 1808), 97.

38. Hezekiah Mosby, Powhatan County, to Virginia Assembly, 1815

To the Honourable The Speakers and Members of both Houses of the General Assembly of Virginia

Your Petitioner Hezekiah Mosby of the County of Powhatan begs leave humbly to represent That in the year he intermarried with Betsy Merriman of Cumberland; expecting to enjoy that happiness which the married state affords to those who are actuated by proper motives when entering into it, and pursue a correct moral conduct afterwards—That your petitioner has endeavoured as far as his judgment directed, to perform *his* part of the solemn contract in which, before the eyes of God & Man he voluntarily engaged—But with deep felt sorrow he is constrained to declare that such has not been the demeanour of that person to whom he once gave his hand and heart—On the contrary your petitioner has had cause often to suspect that she was not *only, not* faithful to the marriage bed, but moreover, that she bestowed her favours on men of a different colour from herself—so thoroughly impressed was he with this belief, that in the month of July last when his wife was about to be delivered of a child, he sent for several highly respectable ladies of the neighbourhood that they might see & judge when the child was brought into the world, before any accident could happen to it—These ladies did come, & have given their affidavits to the fact of the child's being one of colour and to which affidavits I beg leave to refer your honorable body—Indeed the circumstance is notorious in the neighbourhood, & has been substantially admitted by my wife as will appear by the affidavit of Mr. Thomas Miller, also forwarded herewith—Your Petitioner therefore humbly prays that he may be divorced from his wife Betsy aforesaid, and (as far as any earthly Tribunal can affect it) restored to that condition which he occupied before marriage—Your petitioner cannot presume it necessary to urge to your honorable body any additional reasons in order to induce you to comply with his request—He only solicits each member to place himself for a moment in his situation, & then call to mind the divine precept "Do unto others as you would they should do unto you"

Powhatan Novr the 27th 1815

his
Hezekiah X Mosby
mark

SOURCE: Petition of Hezekiah Mosby to the Virginia General Assembly, 6 December 1815, Legislative Petitions, Powhatan County, VSA. Bill drawn. Granted.[1] PAR #11681530.

1. The Act of Divorce stipulated that Betsy "shall be wholly precluded from the right to intermarry with any other person during the life of said Hezekiah." If she did marry she would be liable to "all the pains and penalties imposed by law upon the offence of bigamy." Also, if it was later discovered that Hezekiah had not performed his duties as a husband, he would be "precluded from intermarrying with any other person" notwithstanding the divorce decree. *Acts Passed at a General Assembly of the Commonwealth of Virginia, Begun and Held at the Capitol in the City of Richmond, on Monday the Fourth Day of December, in the Year of Our Lord, One Thousand Eight Hundred and Fifteen* (Richmond: Thomas Ritchie, 1816), 246–47.

39. Richard Dawson Sr. et al., Beaufort District, to South Carolina Assembly, ca. 1816

State of South Carolina Beaufort District

To the Honorable the president and Members of the Senate & House of Representatives of the State of South Carolina.

That your Memorialists are considerably aggrieved from the want of a Law, by means of which, the Slaves of this district could be restrained from the mischievous practice of Killing up the stock and otherwise injuring the peaceable and well disposed citizens of this district. That there are a great number of large Plantations without any white person living thereon, the Negroes belonging thereto not being restrained are in the constant habits of Killing the stock of Cattle and Hogs of the Neighbors adjoining them, and also of the taking their Corn from their fields before it could with safety be housed. That on some few plantations the owners or overseers remain until the Month of June, but are then absent until some time in October during which period the stocks and crops of the greater part of the inhabitants especially on the Sea Coast are materially injured. That in consequence of no white persons residing on those plantations, the Citizens of the Neighborhood are inadequate to the duties required by Law as a Patrol That your Memorialists are aware of the act of assembly of Eighteen hundred and Twelve the sixty fifth section where of imposes a penalty on those having a Plantation with Thirty slaves without also residing on, or having a person to reside thereon, capable of performing Patrol duty, but beg leave to suggests to your Honorable body, that the number of Slaves allowed on a plantation are so great and the penalty is so small that it is almost invariably disregarded and as the above act does not make it the duty of any persons particularly to inform against the violators of that Law the same is of little effect. Your Memorialists therefore humbly pray that your Honorable body would pass a Law imposing a severe penalty on the owners of [such] Plantations who do not reside thereon or keep some white person on the same during the year and also to point out some officer of this district whose duty it shall be to give information of all those who violate the said Law And Your Memorialists as in duty bound will ever pray and so forth

[signed]	Richd Dawson Senr.	John A. Corley
	Wm B Buckner	John X Mew
	Philip J. Besselleu	G, B, Cheny
	Isaac Taylor	Wm Humbert
	B. Corley	William Rivers
		[81 additional signatures]

SOURCE: Petition of Richard Dawson Sr. et al. to the South Carolina Senate and House of Representatives, ca. 1816, Records of the General Assembly, #1862, SCDAH. Referred to the Judiciary Committee. Rejected. PAR #11381613.

40. Robert Wright, Campbell County, to Virginia Assembly, 1816

To the Honorable General Assembly of Virginia,

The Petition of Robert Wright a free man of Color resident in the County of Campbell respectfully sheweth:

That your petitioner in the year 1806 in pursuance of a licence obtained for that purpose from the Clerk of Campbell County was married by a certain William Heath, a regularly licensed Minister of the Gospel, to a certain Mary Godsey, a free white woman—That since the said Intermarriage your petitioner hath allways demeaned himself towards the Said Mary as a kind and affectionate Husband—and for several years enjoyed great domestic comfort, and felicity in her society—That sometime in the year 1814 the said Mary became acquainted with a certain William Arthur a free white man who by his artful and insidious attentions entirely supplanted your petitioner in her affections—That on the 14th day of January 1815 the said Mary unknown to your petitioner secretly eloped with the said William Arthur carrying with her a negro girl and other property belonging to your petitioner—That on their route as is believed to the western country they were overtaken in the Town of Liberty, your petitioners property recovered, and the said Mary prevailed upon to return to the Home, and the Husband she had so ungratefully and cruelly abandoned—That notwithstanding this infidelity on the part of the said Mary, your petitioner after her return still continued to her that affection and protection which she had of right forfeited, and hoped that time, and a course of affectionate [care] on his part would reconcile her to her Situation and restore her to Happiness—But in this just expectation your petitioner was disappointed. That the Said Mary on the 30th day of November 1815 again Secretly, and unknown to your petitioner eloped with the said William Arthur, and as your petitioner is credibly informed and verily beleives is now living in a state of adultery with the Said Arthur in the Town of Nashville, & State of Tennessee—That your petitioner is advised that although the Law inflicts a penalty on the minister of the Gospel who shall marry a white person with a negro or mulatto, and subjects the white person so married to fine, and imprisonment, yet such marriage is to all intents and purposes valid and bindin between the parties—Your Petitioner under the circumstances herein allready set forth prays your Honorable Body for the passage of an act divorcing him from his said Wife Mary and as in duty bound &c &c

[signed] Stephen Perrow
Chas Gilliam
Lewis Franklin

SOURCE: Petition of Robert Wright to the Virginia General Assembly, 16 November 1816, Legislative Petitions, Campbell County, VSA. Rejected. PAR #11681603.

41. Harry Jackson Jr., Norfolk Borough, to Virginia Assembly, 1816

To the Honorable the Speaker & Members of Both Houses of the General Assembly of Virginia

The Petition of Harry Jackson a Free man of Colour residing in the Borough of Norfolk, Most respectfully Setteth forth,

That your Petitioner is the son of Harry Jackson the Elder, who is now, and has been for a Long time past, a Regular Branch Pilot of the First Class, for the Chesapeake Bay and its waters within the State of Virginia—That at the time, that the father of your Petioner, obtained his Branch as aforesaid, it was lawful for a Negro or man of Colour as well as any other person to obtain a Branch & to perform the duties of Pilot—That his said father by virtue of his Branch as aforesaid & under the authority of an act of Assembly passed in the year 1792, kept a Pilot-Boat of the lawful size & complied with all the stipulations imposed upon Pilots, by the then Existing Laws—That about the year 1797 your petitioner being then about Fifteen years of age was taken by his said father as an apprentice on board of his Pilot Boat, to learn the Art & Mystery of a Pilot—Your Petitioner was taught to read & write, and his Father, (whose Reputation as a Pilot has been long established) took the utmost pains to instruct him, as well in the duties & obligations of a Pilot, as in the Knowledge of the Waters, they were in the habit of Navigating, under the belief & persuasion, that after he had gone through a Regular apprenticeship and servitude for seven years, that he would be able under the Existing laws of the Commonwealth to obtain a Branch & to perform the duties of a Pilot in Virginia. Influenced by these prospects & encouraged by this Hope Your Petitioner proceeded under the care of his father, to learn the Art, and to practice the duties of a Pilot; with the design & intention, to apply for a Branch, as soon as he should have been Twenty one years old—on the 23d day of January 1802 however when you Petitioner was not quite 20 years of age, and when he had been serving as an apprentice for nearly five years, an act was passed by this Honorable House—Entitled an act to amend & reduce into one, the several acts Concerning Pilots & regulating their fees—By which Statute it was Enacted, among other things, That no Negro or Mulatto should thereafter obtain a Branch as a Pilot—with a Proviso however, that the Prohibition should not Extend to, or affect, any such person then having a Branch—This Honorable House will at once perceive that there was no reservation provided in this Law, for the Rights of those who were at that time serving as apprentices to the business, and who had reason to calculate upon obtaining a Branch within a very short time. This Law therefore, which, cut off all the rights of People of Colour to obtain a Branch in future, fell with particular weight and severity upon your petitioner.

The law of 1792 had wisely provided, that every applicant for a Branch as a Pilot should Exhibit satisfactory Proof to the Examiners of his having served as an apprentice, to some Branch Pilot within the state for five years at least—The Profession of a Pilot is one of Great Trust & importance to the Public, requiring great skill, long practice & Experience, When therefore your Petitioner was induced under the promise of the Existing Laws to become an Apprentice to the business, and to qualify himself as the Law required, to Enjoy the rights of a Pilot—He humbly submits to your honorable Body, whether it is right, that he should have been thus suddenly & unexpectedly precluded from those rights—

He is well assured that it was not the design of the Legislature of that day to abridge or curtail the Existing rights of any Individual, acquired under the former Law, and that if his case had been then made known to the House, it would have been Embraced within the Proviso, before recited protecting the rights of those, who had been induced by the priviledges of the Law of 1792, to devote them selves to this Profession & who had then obtained a Branch Your Petitioner therefore humbly prays That this Honorable assembly will now Extend to him the benefit of such a proviso, as ought to have been granted to him in the first Instance—His character & skill as a Pilot is well supported by the annexed Certificate of a number of the most respectable Merchants & Gentlemen of Norfolk—He therefore prays, that a Special Law may be passed, to permit him to be Examined by the Examiners appointed by Law and upon his complying with all the requirements thereof He may be permitted to obtain a Regular Branch as a Pilot of the Chesapeak Bay & its waters in such degree or class as the Examiners may think him properly entitled to—

And your Petitioner as in duty bound, will ever pray &c
[signed] Harry Jackson jr-
~~By B Polla~~

We the Subscribers, understanding that Harry Jackson junr, intends making application to the Legislature of Virginia for permission to obtain a Branch & to act as a Pilot of the waters of the Chesapeak in this state Do hereby certify that we have been long & well acquainted with the said Harry Jackson, That we believe him to be a person of Honesty, Probity & good demeanor, That his skill as a Pilot is as good as that of almost any man and that we believe him to be fairly & properly entitled to the Benefit, for which he intends to petition

[signed] Tristrim Butler
Jno Cox
H Allmand
Geo. Rowland
Alex Wilson
George Raincock—
A Maclure
Wilson Borish
Wm Seymour
Rob Jennings
[25 additional signatures]

SOURCE: Petition of Harry Jackson Jr. to the Virginia General Assembly, 20 November 1816, Legislative Records, Norfolk Borough, VSA; Certificate, Tristrim Butler et al., ca. 1816, ibid. A bill was drawn, but no act was passed. PAR #11681605.

42. Sanders Glover et al., Amelia Township, to South Carolina Assembly, 1816

Amelia Township December 4th 1816.

A petition of sundry inhabitants, of Orangeburgh district, to the honorable members of the legislature of South Carolina

Honorable Speaker of the house of representatives & Honorable President of the Senate

Gentlemen

We your humble petitioners would esteem it as a fortunate circumstance if our domestic economy was under no necessity, of legislative intervention: but this is not the case. For in many parts of this district, there are Several citizens, (good meaning respectable people) ~~too~~ but actuated by a false or a mistaken humanity, have extended ~~have extended~~ the privileges of their negroes so far, as to be injurious to themselves, & in many cases a nuisance to the public, & may ultimately prove fatal to many of the negroes themselves.

Every measure that may lessen the dependence of a Slave on his master ought to be opposed, as tending to dangerous consequences. The more privileges a Slave obtains, the less depending he is on his master, & the greater nuisance he is likely to be to the public. In many parts of this district negroes have every other

Saturday, keep horses, raise hogs, cultivate for themselves every thing for home consumption, & for market, that their masters do; But of all their privileges that of their making *Cotton* is the most objectionable.

Cotton, not like many other valuable comodities, that can be Secured by the turning of a key, but in the field, on the Scaffold, & even in the gin house; Cotton is Subject to the depredations of the night walking thief, & when lost, it would be the height of folly to attempt finding it among negroes who all have cotton of their own: It would be like looking for a drop of water lost in a river. The privilege of the rascal covers the clandestine property, so as to preclude discovery.

To authorize a slave to make cotton for himself is encouraging him to be a thief, by putting him in the way of Secreting what he Steals. What can be a greater temptation to theft than Securing the thief from detection? Could there any plan be devised to corrupt more completely the morals of the most honest?

Some may tell us that we are at liberty to grant no such privileges to our negroes and let others do as they please, But this would be no alleviation of the grievance, a man may not allow his negroes the privilege, & yet suffer as much or more than those that do. The negroes that make cotton for themselves, may act as factors, for those that do not.

A master may make what improvement he pleases in the lodging, clothing, & food of his slaves, in short there are many ways to encourage their industry, without granting them privileges that would enable them to Steal with impunity.

It is therefore gentlemen our humble opinion, that it is highly necessary a law Should be enacted this Session prohibiting negroes making cotton for themselves—And that there may be such a law made in such a manner as Your Superior wisdom may suggest, is the sincere Prayer of Your humble Petitioners.

[signed]	Sanders Glover	Sam P. Jones
	Edward Dudley	James Daniels
	Timothy Barton	Jno T McCord
	Jonathan Nichols	Andw Heatly
	Jacob Hare	James Lovell
		James Stuart

SOURCE: Petition of Sanders Glover et al. to the South Carolina Senate and House of Representatives, 4 December 1816, Records of the General Assembly, #95, SCDAH. Referred to the Judiciary Committee. Granted.[1] PAR #11381601.

1. In 1817, South Carolina lawmakers passed an act to "increase the penalties which are now by Law inflicted on persons who deal or trade with negro slaves, without a license or ticket from their master or owner or the person having charge of them." The penalties now included a fine of up to a thousand dollars and imprisonment up to one year. Among the trading items listed were rice, tobacco, indigo, and cotton. *Acts and Resolutions of the General Assembly of the State of South-Carolina. Passed in December, 1817* (Columbia: Daniel and J. J. Faust, 1818), 25–26.

43. Harriet Laspeyre, New Hanover County, to North Carolina Assembly, 1816

To the Honorable the General Assembly of the State of North Carolina.

The memorial of Harriet Laspeyre of the County of New Hanover humbly complaining, sheweth unto your honorable body, that your memorialist was married to a certain Bernard Laspeyre late of the Island Hispaniola in the year of 1795. That her friends more prudent than herself caused to be secured to her the much greater part of her little property by a marriage settlement bearing date the day of May 1795.—

That not many weeks had elapsed, subsequent to their union when your Memorialist discovered to her infinite mortification that her property, trifling as it was had been the primary object of his warmest affection

That he would urge in the most pressing manner, for her consent to sell the Negroes secured to her by said settlement, upon her refusal he would fall in to the most violent poroxysms of rage, and abuse her in the most virulent language the vulgarity of his mind could possibly suggest in language too gross and indecent to be repeated

Your Memorialist at length wearied out by his reiterated importunit~~y~~ sies, intimidated by his ~~violence~~ threats and fondly, hoping that a compliance with his wishes, might purchase her kinder treatment, consented three different times to his selling three of the said Negroes and joind him in making titles thereto

This acquiescence on the part of your Memorialist persuaded him that her consension had been only procured from a dread of his resentment; and had no other effect but that of exposing her to new and aggravated insults.—a peremptory and menacing requisition was made of a surrender of her whole property with denounciations of his vengeance in case of her non compliance—Your Memorialist was too soon made sensible of his fixed determination to compell her by every diabolical scheme the brutality of his manners and the malignity of his heart could devise to a surrender of every thing she held in her own right—Your Memorialist was at length stripped of the right that every woman claims and is so very tenacious of the direction and superintendance of her house hold affairs divested of her keys, deprived of the authority of a mistress her negroes forbidden to obey her orders under penalty of the severest punishment, exposed to contumely and want and every attempt made to render her an object of detestation to her own Children.—The profits arising from the labor of her Slaves, which ought to have been appropriated, to the support and education of her Children, she had the ~~mortification~~ extreme vexation to see wantonly lavished on his black and mulatto mistresses—The natural temper of the said Bernard Laspeyre is both capricious and tyranic, rendering every person he has the power of commanding wretched and unhappy—Your Memorialist has while subject to his authority, suffered the most degrading and humiliating treatement, abused in the dirtiest language such as a welbred man would blush to apply to the worst of Servants, actually threatened with manual chastisement, and frequently order'd to leave his House—That the said Bernard Laspeyre in violation of every law human or divine and setting publick opinion at defiance has lived for a long time in the Town of Wilmington in open adultery with a negro wench taken her in to his House and permitting her to exercise all the rights and authorities of a Wife—The atrocity of his character has been recently developed by his absconding and bearing off the greatest part, and most valuable of her Negroes

Your Memorialist no longer capable of enduring such accumulated wrongs in hourly expectation of violence to her person and seriously apprehensive of an attempt upon her life she left his House, with a fixed and immutable determination never again to subject herself to his tyranny.

Your Memorialist therefore humbly prays your Honorable body in tender consideration of her wretched and desolate situation, to pass an act to sepparate her from her said husband, and to secure to her the residue of her little property and what she may hereafter acquire, by her own industry or by inheritance &c—And your Memorialist as in duty bound shall pray &c.

[signed] Harriet Laspeyre

SOURCE: Petition of Harriet Laspeyre to the North Carolina General Assembly, 18 December 1816, Records of the General Assembly, Session Records, Petitions for Divorce and Alimony, November–December 1816, box 2, NCDAH. Rejected.[1] PAR #11281601.

1. According to the docket page, the Senate rejected the request for divorce but apparently accepted Harriet Laspeyre's request to control any property she might acquire in the future.

44. Jonathan Bacon et al. to Tennessee Assembly, ca. 1817

To the Honorable senate & House of Representatives of the State of Tennessee Assembled—

We your humble petitioners hereunto subscribed, feeling Solicitous to promote the rights of man, As acknowledged and held forth, in the constitution of the United States of America & Declaration of Independence; Are induced to petition your Honorable body to take into consideration the deplorable situation of the people of colour who are held in bondage in this our highly favoured, and high professing Country; And in your wisdom devise some plan & pass it into a law, for their relief; such as allowing Masters who are, or may be convinced of the impropriety of holding them in slavery, to Emancipate them, on terms which will not involve them nor their Estates for their Maintainance &c provided That the court shall be of oppion th[at] the slave ~~so~~ to be Emancipated Shall in all probability be capable of Maintaing themselves—

And further we would suggest to you the propriety, the Justice, and good policy &c of your Honorable body passing a law; declaring agreeable to the purport of Our Federal Constitution; Our declaration of Independence; and the laws of Nature; that all Men, are, and Shall be free. (But Notwithstanding the laws which have hither to been in force, have involved a considerable part of our population in slavery)—That All the descendants of slaves which may be born after the passing of such a law shall be free; ~~after~~ at some Age that your Honorable body (doing as you would be done by) may fix upon. Meanwhile enjoining it on those who may have the raising of such: To teach them some occupation by which they may get an Honest living—& Teach them at least to read the Holy Scriptures And give them reasonable priviledge for attending Divine Worship—And Further more we would not Solicit you—Knowing your entire capability of Digesting this our petition & passing it into a Law—for which we humbly pray the Author of Justice & willer of rights to influence your minds thereunto &

	Petitioners Names	Petitioners Names
[signed]	Isaac [Mumsey?]	Jonathan Bacon
	George Sqibb	Marshall Hartman
	Joseph Archer	Henry Hartman
	[too faint to read]	John Warren
	George Cox	

SOURCE: Petition of Jonathan Bacon et al. to the Tennessee General Assembly, ca. 1817, Legislative Petitions, #90-1817-6, reel 6, TSLA. Rejected. PAR #11481706.

45. Joseph Holleman et al., Isle of Wight County, to Virginia Assembly, 1817

To the Honble the Speaker & Members of both Houses of the General Assembly of Virginia.

The Humble Petition of sundry inhabitants freeholders & Citizens of Isles of Wight County sheweth that great and serious evils have resulted to the peaceable & orderly inhabitants of this section of the state, from the black population. that these evils are encreaseing to the great annoyance, & disturbance of the peace & tranquility of society—That neither the persons, or the property, of the Citizens, can be considered in a state of safety. Within the last year several Murders have been committed in this County, by persons of that colour. Among the victims, your petitioners have to lament the loss of one of their most valuable & respectable Citizens. Your petitioners beg leave most respectfully, to invite the attention of the General Assembly to the subject—The number of slaves & free persons of colour, in this part of the state is so great—as to render it a subject of deepest solicitude to your petitioners that the most efficient laws for the restraint & controul of those persons should exist—Your petitioners are impressed with the opinion, that the laws on the subject of slaves freenegroes

& Mulattoes are susceptible of many very salutary amendments, They believe the sum at present allowed by law for the apprehending of out lying & runaway slaves is entirely two [*sic*] low. That it might be advantageously encresed or augmented to fifteen or twenty Dollars.

That the penalty on freepersons for harbouring runaway slaves, ought to be rendered as severe as would comport with the genious & principles of the Government—They most respectfully submit to your honorable body whither, free white persons, who are so forgetful of their own honor as to harbour runaway slaves ought not to be deemed guilty of a misdemeanor or Crime punishable by confinement in the Jail or penetentiary House & whither free persons of colour who are guilty of the offence of harbouring runaway slaves, ought not to be deemed felons & punished by Death.[1] Your petitioners are well aware that the penalties they propose are very severe, & that severe penalties sometimes defeat the object of the legislature, Yet they believe that the evils of which they complain can be arrested by the most severe & exemplary punishments only—They have long witnessed with the deepest regret the facilities furnished by base & immorral white persons & freepersons of colour, to the slaves, to deprive their owners of their services & to plunder them of their property with impunity. That such intercourse between slaves and free persons is calculated to produce crimes of the most serious and dreadful consequences, to promote insubordination & a spirit of disobedience among the slaves, & finally to lead to insurrection & blood. Your petitioners are fully satisfied that the peace & tranquility & happiness of the people, will always receive from the General Assembly of Virginia every security within the reach of its constitutional powers—

Your petitioners fully convinced of the truth of the last proposition most respectfully submit to the wisdom of the legislature, the propriety of passing laws on the subject above refered to. Your petitioners Humbly pray that their situation may be taken into consideration by the Honble. the General Assembly. That the penalty for Harbouring outlying & runaway slaves by freepersons—may be greatly encreased. That the penalty on free white persons & free persons of Colour for dealing with slaves, be augmented, and that a larger sum be allowed for apprehending runaways.

And that such other & further amendments be made to the laws on the subject as shall be deemed best calculated to promote the welfare, felicity & happiness of the Citizens of Virginia—

And your petitioners as in duty bound will ever pray &c

[signed]	Joseph Holleman	Bartha Lightfoot
	Chs. Wrenn	Wm Holleman
	Arthur Smith	Bailey Davis
	Joseph W Ballard	Nath P. Phillips
	Dawson Delk	Merit D. Stringfield
		[39 additional signatures]

SOURCE: Petition of Joseph Holleman et al. to the Virginia General Assembly, 12 December 1817, Legislative Petitions, Isle of Wight, VSA. Rejected. PAR #11681712.

1. Free persons of color who harbored runaways were subject to corporal punishment of up to thirty-nine lashes if they could not afford the ten dollar payment to the informant. *Acts Passed at a General Assembly of the Commonwealth of Virginia: Begun and Held at the Capitol, in the City of Richmond, on Monday, the Fourth Day of December, One Thousand Seven Hundred and Ninety-Seven* (Richmond: Augustine Davis, 1798), 4–5.

46. William Johnson to Mississippi Assembly, 1820

To the Honorable the Senate and House of Representatives of the State of Mississippi in General Assembly convened—

The Petition of William Johnson respectfully represents, that your Petitioner being possessed of a mulattoe woman named Amey was induced from her good conduct and fedelity, to have her emancipated according to the Laws of Louisiana. Your Petitioner at the time he emancipated the said Amey, was desirous of emancipating her Child named William, but was prevented on account of his minority, and consequent incapacity to execute a Bond as required by the existing Laws.

Your Petitioner has long resided in the St[ate] of Mississippi, and has here fixed his perm[anent] residence—He is not indebted to anyone, whic[h] would render the act of emancipation imprope[r] or unjust. Your Petitioner humbly prays your Honorable Body to permit him to make that disposition of his property most agreeable to his feelings & consonant to humanity—the act will give that Liberty to a human being which all are entitled to as a Birth right, & extend the hand of humanity to a rational Creature, on whom unfortunately Complexion, Custom, & even Law in this Land of freedom, has conspired to rivet the fetters of Slavery. Your petitioner prays, that your Honorable Body will pass a Law emancipa[ting] the Boy William, and your Petitioner as in duty bound will ever pray &c.

January 21 1820
[signed] William Johnson

SOURCE: Petition of William Johnson to the Senate and House of Representatives of Mississippi, 21 January 1820, Records of the Legislature, Petitions and Memorials, 1820, RG 47, MDAH. Granted.[1] PAR #11082002.

1. On 22 January 1820, Lewis Winston, a representative from Adams County, presented the petition to the House of Representatives. It was referred to a special committee, and a bill granting the request passed both houses and was signed into law by the governor on 10 February 1820. The act required Johnson to post a one thousand dollar bond "made payable to the governor for the time being" and to educate and maintain the mulatto boy William until he reached the age of twenty-one. *[Acts] of the State of Mississippi, Passed by the General*

Assembly, at their Third Session, Which Commenced the Third of January, and Ended the Twelfth of February, 1820 in the City of Natchez (Natchez: Richard C. Langdon, 1820), 38.

47. Micah Jenkins et al., Charleston, to South Carolina Assembly, 1820

South Carolina
To the honorable the Speaker and
Members of the house of Representatives,
The humble petition of the Undersigned
Respectfully sheweth,
that,

Your petitioners have seen with anxious concern the number of Free Negroes and coloured people, who have migrated into this State from various quarters, and when the late Legislative Acts of Virginia and Georgia, are duly considered as relates to these people, Your petitioners have every reason to apprehend a daily increase of this alarming evil, to prevent which Your petitioners pray Your honorable body to interdict by the most energetick Laws all free Negroes and coloured people from migrating into this State, hereafter from any neighbouring State or elsewhere, insomuch as such as have already migrated into this State from any neighbouring State whatever, or elsewhere within the last five years may be Banished. And Your petitioners further pray Your honorable Body to prohibit all persons whatever, hereafter, from emancipating his or her slave or slaves, unless such emancipated slave or slaves, shall within twelve months after such emancipation, leave the State.

Your petitioners beg leave to invite the attention of the Legislature to other existing evils, in communicating which they have first to state, that a spacious Building has lately been erected in the immediate neighbourhood of Charleston for the *exclusive* worship of Negroes and coloured people, from means supplied them by Abolition Societies in the Eastern and Northern States, as Your petitioner's are credibly informed, this Establishment is no less impolitick than unnecessary in as much as ample accommodation is, and has always been provided and afforded the Negroes and coloured people in the numerous Churches and places of Publick worship in the City of Charleston and its ~~neighbor~~ neighbourhood.—Another evil equally impolitick, is that of permitting our free Negroes and coloured people, to visit the Eastern States for *Ordination* and other religious pretences and again returning, Your petitioners pray Your honorable Body, that all free Negroes and coloured persons (seamen and Servants excepted) who shall hereafter leave this State shall be prohibited by Law, from ever returning.

Another evil, and one of the greatest magnitude, is that of suffering schools or assemblages of Negroes slaves to be taught reading and writing, organized and conducted not only by Negroes and coloured people and in some instances by white persons of this State, But it is well known, during the last Winter, that several *Missionary School-Master's* or teachers arrived in Charleston from Philadelphia amply furnished with pecuniary means by Abolition societies of that State, for the avowed purpose of educating our Negroes. Your petitioners are [aware] that there is an Act of the Legislature of this state forbidding Negroes being taught to write, but the act is silent as to their being taught to read, which is easier attained, equally mischevious and impolitick and at variance with slavery. In communicating these serious evils, Your petitioners forbear from accompanying them with observations which would be no less injudicious than unnecessary, as they cause reflections that cannot escape Your honorable Body, they are briefly narrated in the confident expectation that the remedy will be no less prompt than ample.

And Your petitioners as in duty bound will ever pray

Charleston 16– October 1820.

[signed]	Micah Jenkins	Thomas B. Seabrook
	Jas Lowndes	B. D. Roper
	W. Dawson	Thos Wigfall
	Charles P. Dawson	J. J. Darrell
	B. Elliott	Benjn Seabrook
		[95 additional signatures]

SOURCE: Petition of Micah Jenkins et al. to the South Carolina House of Representatives, 16 October 1820, Records of the General Assembly, #143, SCDAH. Referred to the Judiciary Committee. Granted.[1] PAR #11382019.

1. On 20 December 1820, the assembly passed a law prohibiting future emancipations except by the legislature and forbidding the entry of free Negroes or mulattoes into the state after 1 March 1821. Free persons of color who disobeyed the law were given fifteen days to leave and afterwards were subject to a twenty dollar fine. Those who could not pay the fine would be "publicly sold" for a period of up to five years. In 1822, the assembly prohibited free blacks who left the state from returning. *Acts and Resolutions of the General Assembly of the State of South-Carolina, Passed in December, 1820* (Columbia: D. Faust, 1821), 22–24; *Acts and Resolutions of the General Assembly of the State of South-Carolina, Passed in December, 1822* (Columbia: Daniel Faust, 1823), 11–14; *The Statutes at Large of South Carolina* (Columbia: A. S. Johnston, 1840), 461–62.

48. John Winston, Pennsylvania, to Virginia Assembly, 1820

To the Honorable the Speaker and members of the Legislature of the State of Virginia—The petition of John Winston a free man of colour, most humbly sheweth, that your petitioner was emancipated sometime in the year 1815, by the

Will of Izard Bacon Esqr late of the County of Henrico, and was compeled under the Act of Assembly in such cases made & provided, to leave this State, or forfeit his claim to freedom, that he was induced from the love of Liberty (the predominant passion of man) to make a sacrifice of his domestic happiness, by quiting his Wife & two children whom he most ardently and tenderly loves—without whose society, he finds it impossible for him to be happy, & removed to the State of ~~Maryland~~ Pennsylvania, where he has resided the last twelve months—that Your petitioner was induced to adopt this course, under a hope that this Honorable body, when fully informed of his Character and good conduct through life, would feel some degree of sympathy for him, and permit him again to return to the bosom of his family—Your petitioner begs leave to refer to the annexed certificate subscribed by more than Gentlemen, as evidence of his orderly behaviour and good fame—Yr. Petitioner therefore, relying on the Humanity & Liberality of yr. honorable body, confidently hopes, & humbly prays that a Law may pass, permitting him to reside (with his family) in the State of Virginia—And yr. petitioner as in duty bound will ever pray &c

[signed] John Winston a
free Man of Colour . . . [docket page]

We the subscribers do hereby certify, that we have known John Winston, a free man of colour, many years; that he has uniformly conducted himself in such a way, as to meet our approbation—We know him to be orderly and industrious, and believe him to be strictly honest—and We have understood that His late Master Capt Izard Bacon, always spoke of him, as the most meritorious slave he had—In short, from our knowledge of the man we do not hesitate to declare that we should be pleased, if the Legislature would pass a Law, permitting him to reside in this State with his family—Given under our hands this day of in the year one thousand Eight hundred and twenty—

[signed]

Richd Gregory	Chris Branch
Miles Ball	Thomas Ladd
Bev. Smith	Thomas M Ladd
Fred. Clarke	Ben Sheppard
Danl Weisigers	Wm Young
	[9 additional signatures]

SOURCE: Petition of John Winston to the Virginia General Assembly, 11 December 1820, Legislative Petitions, Henrico County, VSA; Certificate, Richard Gregory et al., 1820, ibid. Rejected. PAR #11682001.

49. Samuel Johnston, Fauquier County, to Virginia Assembly, 1820

To the Honorable General Assembly of the Commonwealth of Virginia.

Your petitioner Samuel Johnston a free man of Colour Humbly Sheweth, that in the year upon the recommendation of divers respectable Citizens of this Commonwealth & in Consideration of faithful services and singular good Conduct; an act of your honourable body was passed authorizing the emancipation of your petitioner. That Subsequent to the passage of said act, the deportment of your petitioner, has been uniformly upright, industrious, & moral, that by honest exertions, he has accumilated, a tolerable estate, Consisting of real, and personal property; that he has acquired the ownership of three slaves to wit his wife Patty, aged , his daughter Lucy, aged , & his son Samuel, aged , That the Conduct of said slaves, and the management of your petitioner, towards them, has merited and met with the approbation of all the most sober and prudent part of the Community.

Your petitioner, farther sheweth, that from feelings incidental to all men, and peculiar to those individuals who have led the harmless and unexceptionable life of your petitioner; he is desirous and anxious to Set free, the said Slaves & would long ago have executed a Deed of emancipation had he not been intimidated by the penalties of the Statute which requires their speedy departure from the Commonwealth.

Your petitioner therefore humbly seeks from your honourable body, the passage of an act whereby the said Slaves, when emancipated, will be permitted to Continue inhabitants of this Commonwealth; by which your petitioner in his declining years will be secured in the enjoyment of those natural blessings; and domestic Comforts; to which, from his long, and faithful services, as well as his Virtuous course of life he trusts he is entitled.

And your petitioner will ever pray &c.

November 1820

[signed] Samuel Johnston[1]

We the undersigned Subscribers Inhabitants of the Town of Warrenton and its vicinity believe that the facts stated in the foregoing petition are true; and we join in soliciting the passage of the act prayed for in the petition.

[signed]	F. W. Brooke	Wm Smith
	David Rodes	J W Ford
	William Payne	Thos L. Moore
	Wm Thompson	H B Powell
	Stephen McCormick	John W. Tyler
		[28 additional signatures]

Warrenton Fauquier County Virginia—
We the undersigned Having been Called upon by Saml. Johnson a freeman of Collour living in this place to make a correct estimate of his property both real & Personal, do hereby certify that we believe it to be worth Three Thousand Six hundred dollars given under our hands & Seals this Twenty Seventh day of October 1820

[signed] Nelson S Hutchinson
William H. Digges
Wm. W. McNeale

SOURCE: Petition of Samuel Johnston to the Virginia General Assembly, 14 December 1820, Legislative Records, Fauquier County, VSA; Certificate, F. W. Brooke et al., ca. 1820, ibid.; Certificate, Nelson S. Hutchinson, William H. Digges, and Wm. W. McNeale, 27 October 1820, ibid. Bill drawn. No act was passed. PAR #11682004.

1. In 1811, Samuel Johnston petitioned the Virginia General Assembly for an act of emancipation and permission to remain in the state with his slave wife and children. The petition was granted. Later, he unsuccessfully petitioned the assembly to free his wife, Patty, and children, Lucy and Samuel. *Acts Passed at a General Assembly of the Commonwealth of Virginia, Begun and Held at the Capitol in the City of Richmond, on Monday the Second Day of December, in the Year of Our Lord, One Thousand Eight Hundred and Eleven . . .* (Richmond: Samuel Pleasants, 1812), 137; Petitions of Samuel Johnston to the Virginia General Assembly, 12 January 1812, 16 December 1815, 17 December 1822, 4 December 1823, 25 January 1834, 19 January 1835, Legislative Petitions, Fauquier County, VSA.

50. Robert Johnston, Davidson County, to Tennessee Assembly, ca. 1821

To the Honourable the General assembly of the State of Tennessee, the Petition of Robert Johnston Executor of David Beaty late of Davidson County, humbly Sheweth, that Some time in the year 1815 David Beaty made his will and testament, & Shortly thereafter departed this life, by Said will he appointed your petitioner one of his executors. Who alone qualified, and also directed amoung other things that his Slaves then in his possession Should be emancipated by your petitioner, & made also provision for the Support and maintainance of Said Negroes, all which will better appear by a certified copy of Said Will, which will be shown to this honourable body—Shortly after the death of Said testator one Ann Hope, the Sister & only h[e]ir of Said testator contested the executor of Said will, which contest was finally determined in favour of the Will in the Circuit Court for Davidson County at November Term 1816—Imidiately after the termination of this suit your petitioner was proceeding to execute the Will agreable to thee [*sic*] wishes of his deceased friend, when on the 5th day of Febuary 1817 Ann Hope filed a bill in Equity against your petitioner alledging that the provisions of Said Will were against Law & Void, and alledging that your petitioner was preparing to take the Slaves as directed by the Said will to the State of Indianne where they would be free & praying an injunction to prevent the removal of Said Negroes or any other Steps to procure their emancipation, and also that Said Slaves Should be delivered on to her [&] not of him which injunction was granted and your petioner further, professes [that] after much delay & great trouble to your petitioner, the question upon the disolution of Said inju[n]ction Came in to be heard before the Supreme Court at September Term 1821 (Sept. 4) an inter locutory[1] order was made allowing to your petitioner one year from that time to use evry legal means to procure the emancipation of the Negroes, a copy of which properly certified is ready to be Shown to the—legislature, For Several months after Said order was made your petitioners health was Such as prevented his carrying it into execution but at lenth he had prepared evry thing, & was ready to remove those unfortunate Persons to Indianna, and that [fervent] hope which they had So long indulged in, but which had been so long depresed seemed about to be consumated—they were yet doomed to further disapointment a day or two before your petitioner was to Start, the Son of Mrs Ann Hope came in the night time to where the Negros were (except two or three) and forcibly & Secretly tooke them a way, carried them off and concealed them from your petitioner—

Some time elapsed before possession of them could be regained, and not untill your petitioner had ~~ins~~tituted a criminal proceeding against the persons who had been guilty of this outrage—

After possession of the negroes was thus obtained Your Petitioner['s] private affairs & Situation of his family made it all most impossible for him to leave home within time to execute Said inter locutory decree, as your petitioner has bin informed that the laws of Indiana require a residence of Some time perhaps three months, before the Said Slaves wo[u]ld be come free, besids all what Said Ann Hope friends have Strongly protested against as well as openly resisted, a removal of Said Negroes, and threaten that if by Such means your petitioner Should procure the freedom of Said slaves they will make him responsible out of his own estate to [pay] for the value of them; and this threat has to your petitioner carried more force as in making said decree the Court of appeals was divided in opinion, and one of the Judges who was favourable to the emancipation of Said Slaves having since resigned his Seat, if his Sucessor on [the bench] Should join the opposing Judge in opinion, the Situation of your petitioner might be extremely perileous—His fortune is such that if he ware Compeld to pay the value of Said negreos out of his own estate, he would be uterly ruined Your Petitioner has applied to the County Court of Davidson who have refused to emancipate the Said Negroes. Thus your Petitioner having engaged at the request of his deceased friend Mr. Beaty in the execution of his Will, and also indu[c]ed from motives of [humanity] to undertake the emancipation of the Slav[e]s in the will mentioned, has been for Several years invo[l]ved in a continual [stream] of litigation, which to him has been to the utmost degree harrasing & Injurious, his attention and his time have been diverted from his own business; & his pe[a]ce of mind has been broken in upon, and finally his health has become So very much impaired as to put it out of his power to Sustain the contest any longer,

Now as a last effort, on the part of those poor and allmost [defenseless] persons, he has come on their part and as the representative of David Beaty decd h[um]bly to submit this case under the Statements of facts, to the humanity and to the Justice of the legislature of Tennessee.

This I do with the more confidance when I perceive the intelligance & charcter of the man to whome this address is made, & whome I reflect on the strong reasons which call on you in this case to exercise the powers you possess,—

The owner of these persons has declared their freedom by his last Solemn act of his life, he has provided for their support, they have been redy at all times to give Security as requird by law, or to remove to the State of Indiana in the will of Mr Beaty What principl then Stands opposed to their emancipation no principl of Justice be cause the owner has expressed his wish that it Should be So; nor of humanity for she has been pleading with resistless eloquence the cause of the captive & the Slave in all places & in all ages, to loose the Sh[a]ckels of the Slave, to bring up the captive out of captivity, and to . . . [unclear] restore Liberty to the bonds man[.] . . . [unclear] I trust She [humanity] will be seen Walking in the midst of you upon this occasion, pleading & operating in behalf of those now applying at your bar.

Nothing Stands opposed to the just Claimants of these Slaves to their freedom but avarice, that dark lust of gain which would sacrifice the liberty & the happiness of these persons your poor supplicat[o]rs, to its unholy gratification Into your hands I commit them, hopping that you will mete unto them that measure of Justice which you would have others measurd unto you

[no signature]

SOURCE: Petition of Robert Johnston to the Tennessee General Assembly, ca. 1821, Records of the Tennessee Supreme Court, Middle District, Johnston vs. Hope, 1815, box 7, TSLA. Granted.[2] PAR #11482204.

1. An interlocutory decree is pronounced during the course of a suit, pending a final decision.

2. Following the Davidson County Court's refusal to hear the case, the legislature permitted Johnston to file a freedom suit in any adjacent county. He was required, however, to give Ann Hope five days notice, and, if the court ruled that the slaves were free, Johnston was responsible for removing them from Tennessee within six months. *Acts Passed at the Second Session of the Fourteenth General Assembly of the State of Tennessee* (Knoxville: G. Wilson and Heiskell and Brown, 1822), 156–57.

51. Catharine Smith, Williamson County, to Tennessee Assembly, 1821

To the honourable the General Assembly of the state of Tennessee now in session at Murfreesborough

The Petition of Catharine S. Smith respectfully sheweth that on the twenty-second Day of April in the year eighteen hundred and ninete[e]n she was duly and legally married to John P. Smith, that shortly after her marriage with Mr. Smith her situation was rendered incompatable and disagreeable to an excess by the conduct of her husband which has continually been of the most abandoned dissolute & dissipated description—

Your Petitioner states that from the time that she left the family of her father and commenced living alone with her husband, her habitation was opened to the worst of company who resorted there for the purpose of engaging in the most extrav[a]gant scenes of lewdness, drunkenness and debauchery; that he has often treated your Petitioner in an inhuman and intolerable manner by inflicting violence on her person; and that in direct violation of his matrimonial vow, he has been repeatedly engaged in illegal intimacies with other women and even with the slaves that were subject to his controll—

As a reason why your petitioner does not make application to court, she states that after the commission of such acts by Mr. Smith, as would there entitle her to redress, she was induced by his promises and solicitations to live with him again with a hope that he might reform, whereby, as your Petitioner is informed, she is entirely excluded from that relief which she might once have obtained in court—

In consideration of the facts above stated, all of which are sufficiently authenticated by the accompanying documents—your Petitioner prays that she may be divorced from her husband and that the bands of matrimony be entirely dissolved

And your Petitioner &c
[signed] Catharine S. Smith
Oct 6th 1821

State of Tennessee } this being the 4th day of
Williamson County } October 1821

Levi H Reader personaly came before me and made oath that John P Smith acknowledged to him that he had been G[u]ilty of fornication with his own negro Girl Some time since he was married to his wife & the said Reader further makes oath that he has lived in the house of the said Smith and has seen him treat his wife in a verry harsh manner & that he do[es] not think She woud be safe ~~living~~ continuing with him

Sworn to & Subscribed
before me the day & date
first above written
Test J Farrington JP

his
Levi X H. Reader
mark

SOURCE: Petition of Catharine Smith to the Tennessee General Assembly, 9 October 1821, Legislative Petitions, #49-1821, reel 7, TSLA; Certificate, Levi H. Reader, 4 October 1821, ibid. Granted.[1] PAR #11482106.

1. See Gale W. Bamman and Debbie W. Spero, eds., *Tennessee Divorces, 1797–1858; Taken from 750 Legislative Petitions and Acts* (Nashville: Gale Bamman, 1985), 87.

52. Colored People of Hertford County to North Carolina Assembly, ca. 1822

To the Honorable the General Assembly of the State of North Carolina.

Your petitioners coloured persons citizens of this State would approach your Honorable Body with all the defferece & respect due to the Character of representatives of the People

They beg leave to state that some of them whose names are assigned to this petition bore an honorable part in the Seven years War which established the Liberties of their Common Country. That during that eventful period they were taught to believe that all men are by nature free & equal, and that the enjoyment of life, liberty, and property aught to be secured alike to every Citizen without exception & without distinction.

With these views they need not attempt to express to your Honorable Body the deep concern with which they learned of the passage of a Law at the last Session of the Legislature by which their lives & liberties are virtually placed at the mercy of Slaves. They would ask of your Honorable Body whether their situation even before the Revolution was not preferable to one in which their dearest rights are held by so slight a tenure as the favour of slaves and the will & caprice of their vindictive masters for it cannot escape the notice of your Honorable Body that persons of this description are bound to a blind obedience, and know no Law, but the will of their masters.

Your petitioners will not believe that Your Honorable Body will hesitate to lend a compassionate ear to their well-grounded complaints, and to redress a grievance so oppressive to them, and so wholly incongenial with the spirit of Republican Government

They therefore humbly pray your Honorable Body that the Act of the last Session of the Legislature making slaves competent witnesses against them in criminal cases may be repealed.

[signed] Allen Brown Deanel Garnes
John X Runiel Moses Manly

William Brown Senr	Dempsy X Flood
William Smith	John X Sears
James Smith	Buton X Read
	[42 additional signatures]

SOURCE: Petition of Colored People of Hertford County to the North Carolina Assembly, ca. 1822, Records of the General Assembly, Session Records, November–December 1822, NCDAH. Rejected.[1] PAR #11282201.

1. In 1821, the North Carolina General Assembly passed a law to eliminate the "various and contradictory" interpretations about the testimony of slaves and free blacks in court. Henceforth, persons of Negro, Indian, mulatto, or mixed ancestry—defined as "descended from negro or Indian ancestors, to the fourth generation inclusive, (though one ancestor of each generation may have been a white person)"—whether slave or free, could bear witness only against one another. *The Laws of the State of North-Carolina, Enacted in the Year 1821* (Raleigh: Thomas Henderson, 1822), 41–42.

53. J. E. Holmes, Charleston, to South Carolina Senate, ca. 1822

Charleston SC

To The Honble the President and Members of the Senate—

The respectful memorial of J E Holmes—

Sheweth—

That he was appointed by the Court of Common Pleas, Guardian of a Negroe wench, named Catherine who claims her freedom. A bill was filed in the Court of Equity for Charleston in the So Circuit—Feby 16th—1820—which Bill sets forth that the wench Catherine was the property of Peter Cat[a]net, Merchant of Charleston, and that the sd wench was purchased from sd Catanet by Dr Plumeau—with the avowed object of enabling the Wench to purchase her freedom.[1] the Wench was a valuable and favourite Servt of Mr Catanet—and he sold her for the sum of 300 Dlls to Dr Plumeau (a sum far below her value) for the purpose of conferring on the Wench a Benefit—and enabling the Sd Dr Plumea [*sic*] to carry into effect his charitable intention—a Contract was then entered into between Dr. Plumea and the Wench Catherine, in presence of Mr Catanet and his Wife—That the Wench Catherine shd pay to Dr Plumeau (300) Dlls the amt of purchase money pd by Dr Plumeau to Catanet and that when the sd sum shd be paid by Catherine to Dr Plumea—Dr Plumeau would execute Papers—emancipating the Sd Wench Catherine. Dr Plumeau is since dead, and the legatees, have taken possession of the Wench Catherine under the Will of sd Dr Plumeau— the Bill further states that the Wench Catherine paid to Dr Plumeau before his death—300 Dlls—the sum agreed on as the price of Emancipation. The answer to this Bill was filed—Feby 15—1821—denying any knowledge of the Transaction—and stating that the owner or person claiming sd Wench—is a native of France, and possesses no knowledge of the Contract entered into between Dr Plumeau and the Wench Catherine—two Witnesses were examined before the Honble Court of Equity—who proved that Dr Plumeau was capable of so despicable a transaction as defrauding this Negro of her rights—*nay,* it was proved he had been in the habit of inducing masters of slaves to sell them for a less price than the value—under pretense of emancipating them—and then defrauding the Slaves themselves—

Mr Catanet proved the Agreement between the Parties and also that the Wench was sold at a price far below her value—which wd not have been the case—if the fullest reliance had not been placed on the promise of Dr. Plumeau to emancipate the Wench whenever the Wench shd pay to Dr Plumeau 300 Dlls—it was further proved that the Wench had been working out and carrying in Wages—for a period sufficiently long to have pd double the sum—Mrs Catanet also proved, that Dr. Plumeau had confessed to her that the Wench Catherine had paid to him the sum of 300 Dlls—but remarked that he was entitled to interest on that sum—it was then proved by the Executor Dr. Plumeau that the Interest had been paid—on the Argument it was, contended that the Doctrines relative to Slaves were drawn from the Civil Law—and that the Civil Law must govern the Case—so far as the acts of Assembly did not affect it—That by the Civil law a Slave could not contract because he might affect the rights of his master—but when this reason failed he cd contract—namely—he could contract with the leave & by permission of his master—(Authorities were produced in support of this position) therefore a Slave could contract with his master who gave him leave to do so, several cases were produced to shew that this had actually happd—the Judges of the Appeal Court of Equity then declined, deciding the Case, and recommended, a Petition to the State Legislature as by a late law they were constituted the proper Tribunal to decide upon Cases of this Nature—Stating at the same time that they would cheerfully give all the Information to that Honble Body—respecting the facts as they came out in Evidence before the Court of Equity—

Your Memorialist therefore prays your honourable House to pass an act—whereby the sd Wench Catherine may be emancipated and enjoy all the rights & privileges of a free Negroe in the State of So Carolina—

[signed] J E Holmes
Guardian of Catherine—

SOURCE: Petition of J. E. Holmes to the South Carolina Senate, ca. 1822, Records of the General Assembly, #1751, SCDAH. No act was passed. PAR #11382227.

1. In 1800, the emancipation law stipulated that slaveowners who wanted to free their slaves were required to notify a magistrate and summon five freeholders to judge the worthiness of the slave to be freed. The owner was required to testify about the slave's moral character, and the magistrate and freeholders were required to sign an oath that the slave had good habits and could earn a living. The owner would then sign a deed of emancipation and register it

with the clerk of court. In 1820, shortly after Catherine brought her case, the South Carolina General Assembly banned emancipations except by an act of the legislature. *Acts and Resolutions of the General Assembly, of the State of South-Carolina, Passed in December 1800* (Columbia: Daniel and J. J. Faust, 1801), 39–41; *Acts and Resolutions of the General Assembly of the State of South-Carolina, Passed in December, 1820* (Columbia: D. Faust, 1821), 22–24.

54. John Carmille, Charleston, to South Carolina Senate, ca. 1823

To the Honourable the President & Members of the *Senate of the State of South Carolina*—

The Petition of John Carmille respectfully sheweth: That he is a resident in the city of Charleston in the said state & that for many years past has endeavored to conduct himself as an upright & useful citizen—That some years ago it was his fortune to form a domestic connection with a female named Henrietta & he has had by her three children to wit: Charlotte, Francis & Nancy. That the said Henrietta & her children are of the following ages to wit: Henrietta, Twenty Six Charlotte, Eleven, Francis five, and Nancy three years of age all of the class called Mulattoes, & according to the Laws of this state in the condition of absolute Slaves, the property of your petitioner—Your Petitioner is aware that in making the above statement, he is open to censure as infringing the rules of propriety & decorum—He has however no alternative but to make the present application or to remain indifferent to the present melancholy situation of his family, who excluded as they are from the blessing of society, are still dear to your Petitioner & dependent on him for those comforts which the Policy of our Laws may afford to that class of the community—The object of the Petitioner is to solicit that you would Kindly interpose & adopt such measures as may effect the emancipation of the said slaves and as an inducement to a result which would be so grateful to the feelings of your Petitioner he begs leave to state, that it had always been his intention to adopt the legal means for the accomplishment of the above object until he was unexpectedly disabled by the act of the last Session—He therefore indulges the fond hope that a proceeding of the Legislature so unforeseen will not be permitted to have the deplorable effect of rivetting on his partner & children the bonds of perpetual & remediless slavery—As a further consideration which he trusts will be duly regarded by your honorable Body—Your Petitioner has been blessed with a Sufficient Estate to insure the Comfortable maintenance of his said family, so that no apprehensions can be entertained that they will ever become a charge on the Public—That on the contrary his constant efforts will be employed to support them decently & make them useful members of society—

And your Petitioner will ever pray &c—

[signed] John Carmille

We the Subscribers hereby certify that we are acquainted with the within Petitioner Mr. John Carmille & believe him to be an upright & honest citizen & that he has a sufficient Estate to maintain his family within refered to—

[signed] Robt. R. Gibbes
Jno. Schutz
Jas. Lowndes
Chas. E. Rowand
John Hume

SOURCE: Petition of John Carmille to the Members of the South Carolina Senate, ca. 1823, Records of the General Assembly, #1807, SCDAH; Certificate, Robert R. Gibbes et al., ca. 1823, ibid. Rejected.[1] PAR #11382123.

1. Later attempts of Carmille to protect Henrietta and her mulatto children resulted in a state supreme court case. In 1830, a few days before marrying a white woman, Carmille drew up a deed of trust to permit Henrietta and the children "to work out for their own maintenance" and to keep any money they might earn after paying the trustees one dollar per year. After Carmille and his wife died in the early 1830s, one of his daughters sought to have Henrietta's trust nullified. After years of litigation, the case reached the state supreme court. In 1842, the court ruled that the deed should be honored. Henrietta and her children would be permitted to possess personal property, and nothing in the laws of South Carolina prevented quasi-emancipation. The master-slave relationship was a matter for *meum et tuum*—a matter for the owner to decide. Helen T. Catterall, ed., *Judicial Cases concerning American Slavery and the Negro,* 5 vols. (Washington, D.C.: W. F. Roberts, 1932; reprint, New York: Octagon Books, 1968), 2:381–83; Thomas D. Morris, *Southern Slavery and the Law, 1619–1860* (Chapel Hill: University of North Carolina Press, 1996), 403.

55. Thomas D. Bailey, Somerset County, to Delaware Assembly, 1823

To The Honbl.

The Senate and House of Representatives of the State of Delaware in General Assembly met

The petition of Thomas D. Bailey of Somerset County in the State of Maryland

Your petitioner, most Humbly Represents to your Honors that he has lately moved from Sussex County in the State of Delaware into Somerset County in the State of Maryland leaving, (at the time of said Removal) his Slave a Negroe Girl named Alsey aged Now about Ten years, with a Certain James Nichols in the County of Sussex in the State of Delaware, to be a Nurse for Children in his family, with whom she has lived ever since, and lived with him. Two years previous to the Removal of your petitioner, without hire, compensation or profit to your said petitioner for her services, but was permitted to remain, purely for the Benefit & Convenience of the said Nichols on account of family connection.

Your petitioner further Represents to your Honors that the said Negroe Girl Alsey was born in his family his Slave, and raised to the age of about five years, at which age she was permitted by your said petitioner to be carried into the family of the said Nichols. That your petitioner wishes to take the said Girl into his family, in the State of Maryland where he now resides, And further he is informed that there are existing Laws of the State of Delaware prohibiting the carrying out such property, into another State, unless the same be authorized by an act of the General Assembly for that purpose.

Your petitioner therefore Humbly begs that your Honbl. Body will take the aforesaid premises into consideration, and pass a Law Authorizing your said petitioner to Carry the said Negroe Girl Alsey from Sussex County, State of Delaware, into Somerset County in the state of Maryland providing thereby that in Case she should at any time after elope from Maryland to Delaware, she shall not be entitled to the Benefit of the Laws of the State of Delaware about petitioners for freedom, but that your petitioner may hold her as a Slave. And your petitioner as in Duty bound will ever pray &c.

January 1823
[signed] Thomas D. Bailey

SOURCE: Petition Thomas D. Bailey to the Senate and House of Representatives of Delaware, 16 January 1823, General Assembly, Legislative Papers, DSA. Granted.[1] PAR #10382305.

1. *Laws of the State of Delaware [Passed at a Session of the General Assembly in 1825]* (Dover: n.p., [1826]), 483.

56. Free People of Color of St. Augustine to Florida Legislative Council, 1823

[To His Excellency the Governor and the Legislative Council] of the Tirritory of East and West Florida

The petition of the Free colured people of St. Augustine, humbly shewith.

That your petitioners confiding in the wisdom and justice of your Excellency, implore that they may be permitted to enjoy the privelages of Citizens of the United States, which they at present are deprived of by certain ordinances issued by the Corporation of this City, prohibiting them from the liberty of walking the Streets, or assemblying among themselves for the purpose of amusement after the hour of nine oClock. Your petitioners have always heretofore been in the habit of enjoying the same privelages as the white inhabitants and no instance can be produced of their having in any way abused such indulgence. Therefore your petitioners have taken the liberty of soliciting your friendly interference in their behalf. and as in duty bound will ever pray.

St. Augustine 31st May 1823.—

[signed]	Antonio Williams	Peter Duvigneau
	John Fish	[torn top of page]
	Antonio Asolonia	Saul Write
	William Hodgson	Adam Write
	Peter Sebell	Abraham Write
	Louis Balentine	Stephen Write

SOURCE: Petition of Free People of Color of St. Augustine to Florida Legislative Council, 31 May 1823, Territorial Legislative Council [Unicameral], box 1, folder 6, RG 910, Series 876, FSA. No act was passed. PAR #10582301.

57. Officers of the Edisto Island Auxiliary Association to South Carolina House, 1823

To the Honorable, the Speaker, and Members of the House of Representatives

The Petition of William Seabrook, Senr. Benjamin Bailey, John R. Mathewes, William Edings, and Whitemarsh B Seabrook, Officers of the Edisto Island[1] auxiliary association—

Respectfully sheweth,

That a sacred regard for the safety of their property, and the welfare of the State, have forcibly induced them to establish a Society in aid of the constituted authorities, with respect to the regulation of the Coloured Population. Altho' it is their peculiar boast and pride, that they do live under a government of laws, yet, it must be conceded that in the execution of an edict, the assistance of individuals is oft times not only required, but imperiously demanded. Experience has clearly demonstrated the fact, that notwithstanding the activity and vigilance of our Police officers, the mid-night incendiary has escaped with impunity and the assassin perfected his schemes of horror. The history of the times too warrants the conclusion, that the period is rapidly approaching, when the sober dictates of reason ~~must yeild~~ on the subject of slavery must yield to the hypocritical feelings of a mis-guided philanthropy. To avert so serious a calamity—to remove the misty veil which obscures the light of truth and justice, and forever to crush the spirit of insubordination and revolt, it is not necessary only that the civil authorities should display their customary alertness and devotion to the public weal, but that the zealous aid of every patriotic citizen should be freely offered. If our constitutional rights are in imminent peril of being forever lost; if the tenure by which our most valuable privileges are held, is dubious and uncertain; surely, the laws of God and Man invoke us not to behold a scene so dear to the human heart, unconcerned and free from serious apprehensions.

The crisis is indeed assuming a critical and an imposing aspect. The ties of consanguinity and interest are insufficient to prevent even our neighbours from publicly thundering their anathemas against the holders of Slaves; neither moral considerations, or political motives can restrain their demagogues from infusing into the bosoms of our credulous and superstitious ~~population~~ coloured people, the most dangerous and revolting doctrines.

With our mixed and peculiar population, it is vitally important, not only that the provisions of the Legislature relative to the government of our Slaves, should be strictly and rigidly enforced, but that no aberrations from the line of policy marked out by the State should ever be permitted. To effectuate so laudable a purpose, and to *inform and assist* the legal powers, are the sole motives which induce your petitioners now to beg the countenance and support of your Honorable Body. Independently of the other general arguments which could be advanced, your petitioners would call the attention of the House to one consideration peculiarly local. The white population of Edisto Island is to the Black, as 200 to 3000, or as 1 to 15. This fact speaks volumes. It exhibits the urgent necessity of extreme circumspection on the part of the constituted authorities, and shews clearly what might be effected if our police regulations are permitted to be infringed with impunity. Your Petitioners therefore respectfully beg, that the "Edisto Island Auxiliary association" may be incorporated as a Body Politic, with the usual rights and privileges, and as in duty bound, they will ever pray.

Edisto Island
November 18th 1823.

[signed]	Wm Seabrook Senr.	Prest
	Benj. Bailey	V.P.
	John R Mathewes	V P
	William Edings	Trear
	Whitemarsh B. Seabrook, Sec.	

SOURCE: Petition of the Officers of the Edisto Island Auxiliary Association to the South Carolina House of Representatives, 18 November 1823, Records of the General Assembly, #151, SCDAH. Granted. PAR #11382317.

1. Edisto Island, about twenty-five miles southwest of Charleston, was in Colleton District. It was about twelve miles long and between one and five miles wide and was located between two branches of the Edisto River as the river entered the Atlantic Ocean. Daniel Haskel and J. Calvin Smith, *A Complete Descriptive and Statistical Gazetteer of the United States* (New York: Sherman and Smith, 1847), 193.

58. South Carolina Association to Senate, ca. 1823

To the HONOURABLE the Members of the SENATE of the State of SOUTH-CAROLINA;

THE MEMORIAL

Of the Officers and Members of the South-Carolina Association;

SHEWETH,

That a complaint amongst our citizens, being of late years very prevalent, that the laws enacted against free persons of colour, were not executed; your Memorialists have recently formed themselves into an Association, for the purpose of aiding in their enforcement, by giving to the constituted authorities, the earliest information of their infraction. The fundamental principle of their Society, being, OBEDIENCE TO THE LAWS, and reverence for the civil magistrate, and their labours being felt, to be evidently beneficial to the State at large, they have had the good wishes of their fellow-citizens generally, and their Association has increased, in numbers and respectability, beyond their most sanguine expectations.

In the prosecution of their object, your Memorialists have had ample opportunities, from the personal experience of their Standing Committee, of perceiving the defects in some of the these laws: and they have thought it their duty, with the utmost deference to the Legislature, to notice a few of the most prominent, and to petition for redress.

In the first place, there can scarcely exist in our southern community, an evil of greater magnitude, to the country at large, than the constant intercourse, which is maintained between the blacks of the North and the South. The means of communications has been confined, principally to the City of Charleston: and hence it is, that in the interior, there is not the same knowledge of the danger to the State at large, from this intercourse. Not only are the greatest facilities afforded, to such as would inveigle away our slaves, by the employment of blacks on board of the passage vessels and packets, whereby this evil has increased of late to an alarming degree; but abundant opportunities are offered these people, for introducing among our slaves, the moral contagion of their pernicious principles and opinions. These evils are the more to be dreaded, because, there appears every prospect of this intercourse increasing. The difficulty on the part of the free negroes at the North, in procuring employments suited to their habits and inclinations, and the consequent low wages at which they may be procured, has induced many ship owners there, to employ them, in preference to whites. In one instance the Liverpool Line Ship *Canada* arrived here from New-York (in June last) with her whole crew, fifteen in number, all black, and the Brig *Maine* from Boston, has also since come into this port, with her crew also black. There is scarcely a vessel which arrives in our port from the North, which has not two or three, or more black persons employed, as stewards, cooks, or mariners; and the belief is general, that were it not for the obstacles, offered by the informations and prosecutions of your Memorialists, most of the vessels coastwise, would, in a few years, be manned principally by free negroes and persons of colour from the Northern and Eastern States. The consequence of this, to our slave property, and to the peace and quiet of the State, must be obvious to all. Now too, that so many different lines of packets are established, between this port and New-York, and the opportunities for embarking are occurring almost every day in the year, there can be no security, that our slaves, will not be seduced from the service of their masters, in greater numbers than heretofore, and that the Abolition Societies of the North, will not be encouraged to persevere in their designs, to intrigue, through this class of persons, with our slave population. Heretofore the societies there, have confined their views, to the abolition of slavery in the particular State, or section of the Union, in which they originated. But of late, their views have been greatly extended,—To permit a free intercourse to exist, under such circumstances, between *our* slaves and *their* free persons of colour, would be, to invite new attempts at insurrection. To your Memorialists, who, from the agents which they employ, have the best knowledge of the proceedings of the blacks at the North, and of the projects of their adherents and friends there, the evil presents itself, in a form truly appalling, to every owner of lands and negroes.

But it is not from North alone, that we are threatened with doctrines subversive of our peace. In all the British West-India Islands, with scarcely an exception, there is, at this moment, considerable inquietude, in consequence of the desire of a strong party in the British Parliament, to interfere with the regulations of their slaves. In the Island of *Grenada,* a memorial was presented by the free persons of colour, setting forth, "that as loyal and dutiful subjects, they ought to be admitted into a participation, in the rights and privileges to which every Englishman is entitled, under the British Constitution." The Committee to whom the House of Assembly referred this memorial, have reported, "that a bill should be brought into the House, to repeal an existing law in that colony, so far as the rights and privileges of the free coloured inhabitants are affected thereby, and also that the elective franchise ought to be extended, to free persons of colour, possessing the qualification required by law."[1] In *Antigua* and *St. Christophers,* similar petitions have been presented to their Colonial Assemblies, the fate of which is not known. In the Island of *Jamaica,* a similar question was intended to be made, and such has been the uneasiness in some of the Islands, that some persons, it is said, have actually removed into the United States with their families. But, in *Demerary,* as appears by the Governor's proclamation of the 19th August, the United Colony of *Demerary and Essquebo,* was put under martial law, in consequence of a very serious attempt, at a general insurrection. From official documents, it appears, that on the East coast of Demerary, near one thousand armed negroes were embodied, but afterwards defeated and dispersed by the military, with the loss of about one hundred and fifty negroes; and by the Royal Gazette of that Colony of the 28th August, it also appears that the convictions were numerous, and the examples prompt and terrible. In the Island of *Barbadoes*, the Governor in August last, was obliged to issue his proclamation, to contradict a report, that the slaves were to be emancipated; and later accounts represent, that they were then in alarm, in the expectation of an insurrection.[2] From other Islands, other reports on the same subject, entitled to great credit, have from time to time reached different parts of the United States; but, as they come to your Memorialists in no official form, they forbear to mention particulars. Your Memorialists, however, repeat with the utmost confidence, that at no period of the history of the West-Indies, has there been such uneasiness and excitement, and angry feeling on the part of the whites, and such insubordination amongst the slaves, as has been experienced of late in that quarter, attributable altogether to the proceedings of the African Associations in London, and to the influence of Mr. Wilberforce in Parliament, whose object is now open and avowed, that the work of abolishing slavery in the Colonies, ought immediately to be commenced.[3] The conductors of the public journals in all the Islands, unhesitatingly charge the intemperate enthusiasts in and out of the British Parliament, as the sole, and immediate cause of all the disturbances, and from several of the Colonial Assemblies, remonstrances and addresses have been forwarded to the Mother Country, in spirit and feeling, not greatly inferior to a Declaration of Independence.

With such proceedings in these Islands, and with the known habits and sentiments, of the coloured people of the North, aided and encouraged as they are, by a portion of their white population, your Memorialists cannot conceive a measure, which can give greater security to the State in general, than to prevent ANY FREE COLOURED PERSON FROM ANY PART OF THE WORLD *ever entering again into the limits of the State of South-Carolina,* by LAND OR BY WATER.

It has been the most anxious desire of your Memorialists, to avail themselves of the existing laws for the purpose of stopping an intercourse, which they feel to be so ruinous to the country; and defective as the laws are, by reason of the mildness of their penalties, your Memorialists have, nevertheless, at considerable expense to their Society, greatly succeeded. Many masters of vessels begin to bring white seamen into our port, and with a little aid from the Legislature, your Memorialists are confident, that by the excellence of their organization, and by means of their incessant informations, and prosecutions, it would be in their power, to bring to justice all violators of these laws, and to suppress the intercourse *for ever hereafter.* They confidently hope, that every man who has a family, or property to protect, would rejoice at such an event.

That the Legislative body may be apprized, of the extent, to which this intercourse may be maintained, your Memorialists beg leave to submit, that since the organization of their Society, which is not much more than two months, they have on one subject alone, caused the Act of the Legislature to be executed against *one hundred and fifty-four* coloured persons, who have entered the State, in defiance of its enactments. Of these, there were

From Northern Ports,	118
the West-Indies,	15
Europe,	21
	154

If in so short a time, and principally during a season, when there is little or no trade, so many have arrived here, some idea may be formed, of the number which must enter into our limits, in the course of the year.

In entering upon their important duties, your Memorialists have had to struggle, with a great and an increasing difficulty. This arises from the inadequacy of the law, to prevent its re-iterated infraction, by some who have already been subjected to its penalties. Amongst those who have entered the State contrary to law, some have been confined in jail *twice,* and some *thrice* for the same offence. The penalty of mere confinement during the stay of the vessel in port, which in the case of Northern vessels, generally does not exceed a few days, seems to be disregarded by many, who would cheerfully submit to this temporary deprivation of liberty, rather than forego the irresistible temptation which these people have to come to a Southern country. As the act now stands, there is no penalty upon the captain, who brings into the State a person of colour. The penalty only occurs if the master refuses or neglects to carry him away; your Memorialists would, therefore, respectfully suggest, that an adequate fine be imposed upon the master of the vessel in the first instance; and that, for the *first* offence, the seaman should be confined in jail, during which confinement he should receive regular notice from a magistrate, never to enter again into the State; and that if he shall ever return to the State, after being regularly warned and sent away, that he should be liable to corporal punishment, or to be sold for a term of years. With these alterations in the law and by extending the act to all the descendants of negroes, whether on the father's or mother's side, your Memorialists believe, the evil would be at once suppressed, whilst as the law stands at present, it can never be enforced, so as to be productive of the good, contemplated by the Legislature.

The intercourse being so far stopped, that no person of colour from abroad shall ever again land on our shores; your Memorialists would pray to have the law revised, which prohibits free persons of colour from visiting the Northern and Eastern States; nor is it less essential to extend the provisions of the act, so as to prevent slaves who are carried out of the State by their masters, from being returned again into it, if at any time during their absence, they have been in the West-Indies, or in any part of Europe, or within the limits of States North, of the Potomac, or the Susquehanah.

Your Memorialists lastly, most respectfully pray your honourable body, that you would give your earliest attention, to the state of our laws, respecting slaves and free persons of colour generally. Most of these laws were passed, prior to the adoption of our State Constitution, and when we were a Colony of Great

Britain. Some of their provisions are useless, some obsolete, and many require modification. To adapt them to the present state of society, and to the new relations in which we stand to the rest of the world, would be productive of great public good. Passing from the dependency of a Colony, to the rank of a sovereign State, and at liberty to resort to any measures which may be necessary for our own security, Your Memorialists cannot but hope, that the dangers which menace our prosperity as a Slave-holding-State, will be met by a corresponding energy in the laws. Your Memorialists, without presuming to point out the alterations which may be necessary and proper, most respectfully suggest and pray your honourable body, that a general revision of these laws should take place, with all the assistance, that time, deliberation and research, and experience and talents can give to the subject; so that our magistrates and citizens hereafter, instead of being compelled to look into hundreds of acts and parts of acts passed in the course of a century, may be presented by the Legislature, with one CONSOLIDATED NEGRO ACT, or code, for the government of this class of people; embracing the provisions of every previous act, which may heretofore have been enacted, and which policy requires to be continued, and repealing, at the same time, every other act or part of an act, in relation to the subject which is to be found on the Statute Book. An act of this nature and character, drawn up with great care and with the subject well distributed and arranged, and in which the framers of it, shall avail themselves, as well "of the reproaches of our enemies, as the suggestions of our friends," and having in view at the same time, every regulation or plan of discipline, which is essential to our own preservation, will give security to the master, without taking away from the protection of the slave; and whilst it shall enable every planter and citizen, at one glance to see his rights and his duties, and thus be a public convenience, it will, in the humble opinion of your Memorialists, give more confidence to the capitalist, and more permanency to the quiet and good order of our slave population, than can be expected, under our present system. And your Memorialists, as in duty bound, will ever pray.

[signed] Keat Simons, President

On behalf of the Officers and Members of the South-Carolina Association.
[334 names were printed on the next page of this typeset petition]

SOURCE: Petition of the South Carolina Association to the Senate, ca. 1823, Records of the General Assembly, #1415, SCDAH. Granted.[4] PAR #11382224.

1. In their petition, free coloreds of Grenada argued that as property owners, loyal citizens, and law-abiding residents, they deserved the right to vote and serve as members of the assembly. They asserted that they had a greater vested interest in the colony than white foreigners did. Edward L. Cox, *Free Coloreds in the Slave Societies of St. Kitts and Grenada, 1763–1833* (Knoxville: University of Tennessee Press, 1984), 101–2.

2. In June 1823, Sir Henry Warde, governor of Barbados, issued a proclamation denying

rumors that slaves were soon to be freed. He warned slaves to ignore such rumors. In August 1823, slaves in Demerara, or British Guiana, rose in revolt, but the insurrection was quickly suppressed. Within twelve days of the declaration of martial law in Demerara, word of the revolt reached Barbados. Robert H. Schomburgk, *The History of Barbados Comprising a Geographical and Statistical Description of the Island* (London: Longman, Brown, Green and Longman's, 1848; reprint, London: Frank Cass, 1971), 416.

3. In March 1823, William Wilberforce (1759–1833), British statesman and humanitarian, presented to Parliament a Quaker petition against slavery. In May 1823, Sir Thomas Buxton (1786–1845) offered a resolution in the House of Commons that "the state of slavery is repugnant to the principles of the British Constitution and of the Christian religion." The institution ought to be abolished "with as much expedition as may be found consistent with a due regard to the well-being of the parties concerned." W. L. Burn, *Emancipation and Apprenticeship in the British West Indies* (London: Jonathan Cape, 1937), 81.

4. This law prescribed corporal punishment for free people of color who violated the nonentry law and stipulated that "any master or captain of any vessel" or anyone else who illegally brought a person of color into the state was subject to a one hundred dollar fine for the first offense and a one thousand dollar fine and a prison term of up to six months for a second offense. *Acts and Resolutions of the General Assembly of the State of South-Carolina, Passed in December, 1823* (Columbia: D. and J. M. Faust, 1824), 59–63.

59. Inhabitants of Claremont, Clarendon, St. John, St. Stevens, and Richland Districts to South Carolina Senate, ca. 1824

To the Honourable, The President And The Senate of the Legislature of the State of South Carolina

We the subscribed Petitioners inhabitants of Claremont, Clarendon, St. Johns, St. Stevens and Richland Districts beg leave to offer to your honourable and enlightened Body, the following narrative as Containing the grounds of their most reasonable petition. It is now some years since Mr—[George] Ford a highly worthy and respectable Citizen of our State was murdered some where not far from Georgetown So. Ca—by a Negroe belonging to Mr. Carroll of Richland District named Joe (or Forest) We believe that unhappy occurrence happened under the Executive administration of the honourable Thomas Bennett. The relatives of Mr.—Ford offered liberal rewards for the apprehension of this out lawed fellow.[1] The Executive offered an appropriate reward also, but neither the temptation of the private reward, nor the public reward of the Governor, nor both combined could lead to his capture. He was so cunning and artful as to elude pursuit and so daring and bold at particular times when no force was at hand as to put every thing at defiance.[2] Emboldened by his successes and his seeming good fortune he plunged deeper and deeper into Crime until neither fear nor danger could deter him first from threatening and then from executing a train of mischief we believe quite without a parrellel in this Country.

Most of the runaways flew to his Camp and he soon became their head and their life. He had the art and the address to inspire his followers with the most Wild and dangerous enthusiasm Such was his Cunning that but few of the enterprises for mischief planned by himself fail'd of success. We believe that nearly four years have now elapsed since the murder of Mr.—Ford, the whole of which time until [Joe's] merited death was marked by crimes, by mischiefs and by the desemination of notions the most dangerous among the blacks in ~~of~~ our Sections of the Country.[3] (Such as were calculated in the end to produce insubordination and insurrections with all the hideous train of evils that usually follow.[)] Such at length began as we believed to be the danger arising from the power and influence of this example and such we believed were the indications given of approaching insurrection, that we deemed it ~~propper~~ expedient to call on the propper Military department to send an adequate force either to capture or destroy a species of enemy that kept our families and neighbourhoods in a constant state of uneasiness and alarm. This propper and justifiable application for assistance being disregarded, We made direct application to the Commander-in-Chief who taking no notice of our appeal to him we were compelled as we conceived from the necessity of the case to associate together for the purposes of domestic safety and for the object of impressing our blacks with propper fears by the power of wholesome example We cannot but think that the state Authorities as well Civil as Military were bound not only to have aided and assisted in car[r]ying into effect these most laudable views but that they were bound also without delay to have attended to the peace and protection of an important and interesting section of the State of South Carolina, for it is held as a just and fundamental maxim of government that States are bound to give to their Citizens as adequate protection as possible in Cases of alarm and danger. We organised several companies as Infantry, from among our association, and being prepared for some days active service under persons Chosen to Command We or many of us scoured Santee River Swamp from the Confluence of the two rivers that form it to Munys Ferry a distance even by land of sixty miles. Notwithstanding however the zeal and alacrity with which we continued pursuit We should at length, oppressed by the sultry sun of August October 1823, wearied down by excessive fatigue and rendered dispirited by the number, extent and character of their places of retreat and Concealment should have abandoned our their enterprise as being likely to yield nothing but disappointment to ourselves and triumph to the objects of our pursuit, but for the fidelity of a slave belonging to *Mrs Perrin* of Richland District *named Royal.* He in perfect good faith conducted a select party of your Petitioners to the Camp of Joe and his followers, and having the Command of a boat, being its Patroon he with considerable judgment and address managed to decoy those whom we had long sought towards the Boat, where were stationed, a party expressly detailed for this duty. Soon perceiving their mistake and the danger full before them, they instantly attempted to defend themselves with well charged musquets but at a single well directed fire from the party of whites in the Boat Joe with three of his party fell dead. The rest of the gang of runaways were subsequently either killed in pursuit, hung for attempts to murder or were frightened to their respective homes. Now therefore we your most humble and respectful Petitioners concieving that we particularly and that the State generally ~~are~~ are deeply indebted to this Slave Royal for his fidelity and good conduct in making himself the immediate instrument in bringing to merited punishment an offender, against the laws of the land, ______________________________

____

pray that in due consideration of these things will award to him such compensation as may be fully adequate and as your honourable and enlightened Body may think most compatible with the best interests of the State and with its dignity and character in rewarding those that have rendered services to it—The good faith and honour of your Petitioners are implicated so far towards this Slave on account of his good Conduct and faithfulness that they are bound most earnestly to pray your honourable Body to grant their prayer in which event they shall as in duty bound ever pray—

[signed]	William D. Wilder	Isaac Norton
	John Mayrant Jr.	A. P. Johnston
	Richd Moore	James H. Hext
	Warner Mason	T. N. Johnston
	John China Jun	L. M. Brunson
		[70 additional signatures]

SOURCE: Petition of Inhabitants of Claremont, Clarendon, St. John, St. Stevens, and Richland Districts to the Senate of South Carolina, ca. 1824, Records of the General Assembly, #1874, SCDAH. Granted.[4] PAR #11382410.

1. The reward was for one thousand dollars, an extraordinary sum at the time. *Acts and Resolutions of the General Assembly of the State of South Carolina, Passed in December, 1825* (Columbia: D. and J. M. Faust, 1826), 102.

2. In 1822, the Committee on Claims of the South Carolina General Assembly awarded Meshack Williams $160.62 for the supplies he furnished the militia while they were searching for Joe. *Acts and Resolutions of the General Assembly of the State of South-Carolina, Passed in December, 1822* (Columbia: Daniel Faust, 1823), 89.

3. The Senate Committee on Claims said that Joe's reign of terror along the lower Santee River was "unparalleled in this State." *Acts and Resolutions of the General Assembly of the State of South Carolina, Passed in December, 1825* (Columbia: D. and J. M. Faust, 1826), 102.

4. The assembly granted Mrs. Perrin seven hundred dollars to manumit Royal within the next three years. Ibid.

60. Andrew Barland, Jefferson County, to Mississippi Assembly, ca. 1824

The petition of Andrew Barland of Jefferson County

To the Honble the Senate and House of Representatives of the State of Mississippi;

Your petitioner Humbly Sheweth That he is the offspring of a white man by a mulatto woman[1]—That he was born in Adams County and is now about thirty nine years of age, that his father gave him a decent education and property enough to be independant, that he intermarried with a respectable white family, by which said wife he has two children, that he has resided about sixteen years in the County of Jefferson and is well known to the most respectable Citizens of said County, that he has almost in every case & by every means, been treated and received as well as tho he had been a white man and of fair character; that he has been summoned as a juror very often and served as Grand & Petit Juror and often given testimony in open court as a Legal witness—that his vote at elections has often been taken & for many years your petitioner has enjoyed all the priviledges of a free white Citizen, but a controversy with a bad man of the name of Joseph Hawk caused an exception to be taken to your petitioners testimony on account of his blood, but with pride your petitioner can state, that altho his oath was refused the jury who tried the cause gave a verdict in favor of the word of your petitioner altho opposed by the oath of his adversary, a white man—

Your petitioner further sheweth to your Honble bodies that his education, his habits, his principles and his society are all identified with your views, that he holds slaves and can Know no other interest than that which is common to the white population, that his sisters have all married white men of fair and respectable standing and have always recd. the same respect shewn to white women of the same station in society—

Your petitioner prays your Honble. bodies, to extend to your petitioner such priviledgs as his Count[r]y men may think him worthy to possess, ~~and them~~ and to their recommendation your petitioner most confidently refers your Hon. bodies & your petitioner will ever pray.

[signed] Andrew Barland

We whose names are hereto subscribed have know[n] Andrew Barland for many years, some have known him from his childhood others as long as they have lived in the County, and view him as a most excellant man honest, moral, industrious and worthy the granting of priviledges of a free man, and recommend him for that purpose, ~~but should the~~

[signed] P. B. Harrison R. Dunbar Jun.
Tho. Hinds Philip Dixon

B. M. Bullen
Jas. G. Wood
James Dunbar
Filmer W. Green
Wm Harper
K.H. Holmes
Wm M. Green
Jacob Stampley-Se[n]ior
Abner Pipes

SOURCE: Petition of Andrew Barland to the Mississippi General Assembly, ca. 1824, Records of the Legislature, RG 47, MDAH; Certificate, P. B. Harrison et al., ca 1824, ibid. No act was passed. PAR #11082401.

1. His mother, Elizabeth, was owned by his father, William Barland, who in 1814 freed Andrew (and his eleven brothers and sisters) by petitioning the territorial assembly. *Acts Passed at the Second Session of the Eighth General Assembly of the Mississippi Territory Begun and Held at the Town of Washington, on the Seventh Day of November, One Thousand Eight Hundred and Fourteen* (Natchez: P. Isler and McCurdy, 1814), 40–41; William Ransom Hogan and Edwin Adams Davis, eds., *William Johnson's Natchez: The Ante-Bellum Diary of a Free Negro* (Baton Rouge: Louisiana State University Press, 1951), 334, note 9.

61. John L. Wilson for Jehu Jones, Charleston, to South Carolina Senate, ca. 1824

The State of South Carolina

To the Honorable President and members of the Senate,

The petition of John L Wilson Guardian at Law of Jehu Jones a free person of color of Charleston, shews to your Honorable body, that the acts of the Legislature passed in 1821 and 1822 restraining the free ingress & egress of persons of color into & from the State of South Carolina have been peculiarly oppressive to the said Jehu Jones, inasmuch, as he was preparing to leave the State as soon as he could make sale of his valuable estates in Charleston. That a great part of his family had already removed, & he intended to follow. From the great [amount] of property in Charleston, your petitioners ward has not been able to effect a sale of his estates, & have been cut off from his family untill the present time—Your petitioner represents that his ward is a man of good moral character, attached to the Laws & Government of this State, & prays your honorable Body that the said Jehu Jones may be permitted to leave the state & return to the same as his interests may demand—

[signed] John L. Wilson
for Jehu Jones—

SOURCE: Petition of John L. Wilson, Guardian of Jehu Jones, to the South Carolina Senate, ca. 1824, Records of the General Assembly, #1871, SCDAH. No act was passed. PAR #11382414.

62. Malachi Hagins, Jefferson County, to Mississippi Assembly, ca. 1824

The Petition of Malachi Hagins, of Jefferson County State of Mississippi

Humbly Sheweth, that he is a black man or as is commonly called a coloured man, that he is descended from a free parents for several generations, that his grand mother was a white woman—He further saith that during the Revolutionary War, his father entered the service of the Revolted Colonies, and was Killed at Coosa[s]hatchie Bridge, fighting under Colonel [John] Laurens; That about twenty two years [ago] your petitioner emigrated to this State, that he resided a little while & from thence moved to Jefferson County, where he has resided ever since—Your petitioner has become proprietor of a tract of land, stock of cattle, and nine negro slaves—It is with great satisfaction your petitioner can say to your Honble bodies that in South Carolina & in this State, he has so conducted himself as to acquire the good will and respect of the most respectable Citizens of the neighborhood in which he resides, that his wife by whom he had nine children was a white woman—With this exposition your Honble Bodies, will discover the very deplorable situation of your petitioner, subject to be driven from his Country, his property taken or robbed, and even his life always in Jeopardy, for the want of the guardian protection of the laws of the land—Your petitioner most humbly prays your Honble. Bodies to take his case into their Kind consideration, and by law to give him, that security & protection, such rights and liberties, as they in their wisdom may deem humane, politick and right. And your petitioner as in duty bound will ever pray.

[signed] Malachi Hagins

To the Hon. Senate and }
House of Reps. of the }
State of Mississippi, }
in General Assembly }
convened }

We whose names are hereto affixed have been long acquainted with the petitioner Malachi Hagins, and recommend him and his Petition to the attention of the Legislature of the State, believing him worthy to enjoy every right compatable with the condition of his unfortunate colour—

[signed]	Thomas Hinds	William Montgomery
	Felix Hughes	Dugal Torry
	John Burch	Robt McCray
	R Harrison	John Snodgrass
	Jacob Stamply	Bailey E. Chaney
	Hiram Baldwin	P B Harrison

source: Petition of Malachi Hagins to the Mississippi General Assembly, ca. 1824, Records of the Legislature, Petitions and Memorials, 1817–39, RG 47, MDAH; Certificate, Thomas Hinds et al., ca. 1824, ibid. Granted. PAR #11000016.

63. Washington Darden et al., Jefferson County, to Mississippi Assembly, ca. 1824

To the Honble. the Senate & House of Representatives of the State of Mississippi, in General Assembly Convened.

The petition of Sundry Citizens of Jefferson County Humbly Sheweth That Malachi Hagins, has been long a Resident in this County, for and about twenty years, that his late wife was a white woman, by whom he had ten children, viz Sally, John, Mary, Malachi, Elizabeth, Angelina, Susannah, David, Rhode[s] & Gideon, all now alive, that he has acquired both real & personal property, and that on all occasions he has conducted himself with great propriety of Conduct as an honest and upright man, that he has been long a close member of the Babtist [*sic*] Church, in which, he has demeaned himself as becomes a christian of that order to the entire approbation of his pastors and brethren—with his fair and excellent character we are prefectly assured that he will never injure society by extending his priviledges so far as to authorise him by law to sue and be sued as a free white citizen of this State—We your petitioners, therefore pray your Honble Bodies to extend to the said Malachi Hagins and to his children the rights of free citizens of this state so far as to enable them to sue and be sued, to be allowed the benefit of their oaths in all cases, and in all suits of law exercise and enjoy all the rights priviledges and immunities of a free white person of this State And your petitioners as in duty bound will ever pray—

[signed] Washington Darden, Lewis Cabel
P. B. Harrison, Theos Marble
James Dunbar, Buckner Darden
Tho Hinds, William Montgomery
E Duggan, Dugal Torry
James R. Marsh, John Burch

source: Petition of Washington Darden et al. to Mississippi Assembly, ca. 1824, Records of the Legislature, Legislative Papers, 1817–39, RG 47, MDAH. Granted.[1] PAR #11000024.

1. The act noted that Hagins had descended from free parents and had comported himself "in an upright and orderly manner." He was therefore granted the right to reside in the state of Mississippi, as a freeman of color, to possess property, real and personal, and to sue and be sued, in the same manner as a free white man. *Laws of the State of Mississippi* (n.p., 182[4]), 14–15.

64. Charleston Wharf Owners to South Carolina Senate, ca. 1825

To the Honorable the President and Members of the Senate of the State of South Carolina—

The Memorial of Sundry Wharf owners and Merchants of the City of Charleston, Humbly Sheweth, That your Memorialists have long suffered under the inefficiency of the Laws for the protection of the Cotton and Rice lying upon the Wharves of Charleston. Cotton especially, from the immense quantities received, and the little injury it sustains from exposure to the weather, is frequently not Stored, and is always in large quantities lying upon the wharves; and consequently, liable to continual depredations by Slaves and free persons of Colour who frequent them. Unfortunately, there are men in our community, whom no principles deter from any traffic which may offer a prospect of gain; and the Laws as they exist against trafficking with Slaves, admit of Such easy expedients for evading their application, that they are equivalent to no laws at all. This traffic is rendered legal by the production of written permit; and this is easily obtained, not only from white persons without property or Character, but from Slaves and free persons of Colour, who being able to write, readily Manufacture tickets in the name of the owner or employer or any other person, and frequently in the name of a fictitious person. It is true, the law requires the Shopkeeper to prove the authenticity of the permit, but the evidence offered for this purpose by the accused can Seldom be rebutted by the State, The ticket is produced only at the trial, when it is too late to bring evidence to disprove its authenticity. And independently of this difficulty, should the permit be proved to be not authentic, the Jury will always be slow to convict one who can shew *the appearance* of being deceived himself, and plead the absence of Criminal intention. Nor is there any remedy against those who forge these permits. The law of Forgery will not apply, because it can seldom or never be proved, that any particular individual has sustain'd injury by the Forgery. Altho' the property is stolen, it is impossible to determine to whom it belongs, and thus shew the injury sustain'd, by which the forgery could be establish'd. Hence, the guard which the Law intended to afford, by requiring a ticket to legalise trafficking with slaves is utterly inefficacious. It is also required by the Laws, as they now exist, that the actual trade and barter shall be proved to have taken place,—that the article was received, and the equivalent paid.—Prosecutions are easily defeated, by ostensibly not completing the barter at the time the article is received. The article is received at one time and paid for at another; or an account is Kept, and a settlement is made Some time after the article is received. But a still greater defeat of the Laws on this Subject, if possible, is in requiring distinct proof that the illicit traffic of the Clerk of the Shopkeeper is sanctioned or authorised by the employer. It is vain to prosecute the Clerk for he is totally irresponsible, and if convicted, will only throw expense upon the State: And to attempt to make him a witness against his employer, experience has proved to be equally futile. He whom poverty or a want of principle, has driven to a habitual violation of the laws, cannot be trusted as a witness to support them; and a Law which rests upon a contrary presumption, will ever prove in practice a nullity. By these and many other artifices, most easily resorted to, the Laws are made to afford no protection against illicit traffic with Slaves and free persons of colour; and Rice, and Cotton especially, to an immense amount, are plundered upon our wharves, without the possibility of bringing the chief offenders and instigators to justice, or of protecting ourselves, As Startling as the fact may appear, Your Memorialists confidently believe that in the article of Cotton alone, not less than *Five Hundred Bales* are purchased in illicit traffic by the Shops in Charleston from Slaves and free persons of colour. The evil has at length gone so far, that Your Memorialists, after repeatedly endeavouring to right themselves by the Laws as they Stand, are now induced to come before your Honourable Body for relief and protection. The Legislature of the State have thought proper, contrary to the great principles of free trade, arbitrarily to fix the rates of landing and Storage upon the wharves in Charleston. However injurious and unjust these regulations might have been when first establish'd,—yet Your Memorialists, are not now disposed to Complain of them; the value of the wharves having been in some degree graduated by these rates. But upon every principle of justice and equal rights we respectfully submit, that the Legislature ought to do one of two things, either protect by efficacious laws, the wharf owners from depredations upon the planters property, which now fall exclusively on them,—or leave them to protect themselves, by abolishing all legislative regulations of the rates of wharfage—If the latter alternative is preferred, Your Memorialists will be content. It will then be their duty as well as interest to put the rates of wharfage at such a point, as shall indemnify them for the thefts committed. The loss will then fall where it ought to fall, upon him who is plundered. It is with honest pride, that Your Memorialists are enabled to say that hitherto the Characters of the Merchants of Charleston have been so high in foreign parts, that the weights of an Invoice have been frequently taken for what it calls upon its face, without re-weighing or examination But latterly in consequence of the depredations upon their wharves after the Cotton is weighed and before it is shipped the weights have fallen short so repeatedly, that not only do our pecuniary interests Suffer, but what is of far more importance to an honest mind our characters at home and abroad are in danger of imputation Your Memorialists are indeed but a small portion of the People of the State, but we trust that we may not be deemed guilty of self exaltation in Submitting that the character of a people for honor and honesty with foreign nations depends more upon its merchants than any other class of its citisens. All the pecuniary transactions of a State with foreign powers are carried on through them and them alone. The character of the State is therefore deeply implicated in common with ours in these abuses.—Your Memorialists, cannot anticipate the remedies for the evils of which they complain that your Honourable Body in its enlighten'd wisdom, may apply. They however trust that it will not be deemed indecorous to suggest to the Legislature what it appears to them will be adequate to the evil. First, let the formality of a ticket be dispensed with in all trafficking with Slaves in the two great articles of Cotton and Rice, and the penalties now existing against trafficking illegally with Slaves, be made to apply to all trading with Slaves or free persons of colour *either with or without a ticket*—The master of a Slave or the Guardian of a free person of Colour can with but little inconvenience accomplish any legal traffick for them in these two commodities—In Law,—nothing that a Slave is in possession of, is his; it is his masters; and this principle as regards these articles, should be carried out in all traffick with Slaves, Experience has proved, that to concede the privilege of trafficking with Slaves is to license and encourage plundering No Slaves or free persons of color, at least with us, raise these commodities, and when they sell them the presumption is in fact, and ought to be in law, that they are Stolen. We would in the *Second place* respectfully suggest for the reasons we have already assigned, that all those who *receive* these commodities from slaves or free persons of color should be put upon the Same footing as those who trade for them. The evasion now so common of receiving the article at one time and paying for it at another, would then be defeated; and the presumption, which will then exist in Law will only be that which now exists in fact,—No one receives these commodities from Slaves but those who trade for them. *Thirdly,* We think, that in all trading or receiving in these commodities, the acts of the clerk of a shopkeeper should be considered as the acts of his employer who should be indictable therefor. This presumption however, should be liable to be disproved by any other person than the Clerk himself. *Fourthly* we would Submit That the forgery of tickets for trading should be suppressed, by additional penalties, it should be rendered penal for any other person than the owner, protector or Employer of a Slave to give a ticket to a Slave—

All which is respectfully Submitted to Your Honorable Body

[signed] ChsEdmund Hart
Jno Crawford
Geo: Chisolm Jr
Kiddell Uhay
pr Wm. Marsh
Chs H Bryant
for Clarksons Whrf

Patterson & Maywood
Jno Fraser & Co
for Prices Wharf
James Adger
A W Campbell
[43 additional signatures]

SOURCE: Petition of Charleston Wharf Owners to the South Carolina Senate, ca. 1825, Records of the General Assembly, #1895, SCDAH. Referred to the Judiciary Committee. No act was passed. PAR #11300005.

65. Citizens of Rutherford County to Tennessee Assembly, ca. 1825

To the Honorable the General Assembly of the State of Tennessee now in Session The petition of the undersigned, citizens of Rutherford county, beg leave humbly to represent that from twenty to thirty families of free negroes reside in one neighborhood in this county, that it is believed they influence slaves to steal, and instill into their minds views of liberty injurious to the interests of their owners—that in elections for militia officers, they are in the habit of uniting upon some favorite candidate and thusly controal as they please all elections where they have a vote.[1] that they are rude and insolent in their behaviour, and in every respect bad neighbours and bad members of society—

Your petitioners therefore pray that your honorable body, will be pleased [in] your wisdom, to pass a law compelling all free persons of colour forthwith to leave the county of Rutherford and take up their abode in some State beyond the Ohio where slavery is not tolerated And your petitioners as in duty bound will ever pray.

	Subscribers names	Subscribers names
[signed]	William Johnson	~~Jno Glaze~~
	B [F.?] White	F P, Crockett
	Squire Crews	John K henry
	Moses Ashbrook	Francis Hancock
	Robt Walker	[84 additional signatures]
	Wm C Emmit	

SOURCE: Petition of Citizens of Rutherford County to the Tennessee General Assembly, ca. 1825, Legislative Petitions, #144-1825, reel 9, TSLA. No act was passed. PAR #11482505.

1. In 1796, the Tennessee Constitution granted the right to vote to all freemen—including those of color—who were twenty-one, possessed a freehold, and had lived in the county for six months prior to an election. In 1835, the new constitution dropped the freehold requirement but granted the franchise only to free white males over twenty-one who were citizens of the United States and had been residents of the county for six months. Francis Newton Thorpe, comp. and ed., *The Federal and State Constitutions Colonial Charters, and Other Organic Laws of the States, Territories, and Colonies,* 6 vols. (Washington, D.C.: Government Printing Office, 1909), 5:3418 (1796), 3433–34 (1835).

66. Gaspar Sinclair, Jefferson County, to Mississippi Assembly, 1825

To the Honable the Senate and House of the Representatives of the State of Mississippi in General Assembly, Convened.—

The petition of Gaspar Sinclair

Humbly Sheweth

That he is ~~now~~ a very old man, being eighty four years old, and is now disposed to close his affairs in this world, and by a proper provision, prepare for a better—To do this conscientiously, your petitioner is disposed to discharge all ~~his~~ debts due by him, and more especially his debts of gratitude—However praiseworthy may be this disposition in the ordinary intercourse of men, yet, your petitioner is estoped in this ardent feeling of his heart by the prudent policy of the State,—which forbids the emancipation of slaves without the special licence of the General Assembly—Your general principle of policy says, that slaves may be emancipated for great and signal services, for long and peculiar fidelity—On this ground I pray you to pass an Act of Emancipation in favor of negro man, named James, and his wife named Franky—James aged about fifty-five years and Franky about fifty years—without any child or expectation thereof—

Your petitioner has been possessed of James about seventeen years and Franky, about twenty-five years, and since the death of his wife, about the year 1808, they have been to him the Kindest and best friends in his sickly and solatary course through this life—Without a relation ~~about here~~ in the Country, they have been Kind, patient, affectionate, to him under every change of circumstance—being dependent alone on them for the management of his plantation and care of his property, they have been industrious, faithful & honest and thereby furnished ~~all~~ those cumforts which all desire in this world—but your Petitioner would more especially call the attention of your Honble Bodies, to the care and attention of those valuable friends in my hours of affliction by disease—Tho by nature your petitioner has been blessed with a tolerable good constitution, yet he has been greatly distressed and his life sometimes dispaired of from a cut which he rec'd many years ago across the foot—inflamation often attaches to this wound and your petitioner has been deprived of the power of walking out of his house, and mortification threatened for several months, accompanied with agony which no language can properly convey to you. In this situation without any white friend about your petitioner, these faithful slaves have alternately laid by him every night for three months at a time, and by constant watchfulness and care given to your petitioner all the relief in their power, ~~and~~ which could only have been obtained from them—Your Petitioner will provide amply for their comfort and support, by giving them the use of land for life, and as much personal property as will be equal to all their wishes, ~~in this life~~—and then this property I propose to leave ~~by~~

to a poor infant orphan, now in the care of your petitioner and these black friends, by the name of Ann Maria Eliza Stephens-

With this view of the powerful motives which operate on the Heart and Conscience of your Petitioner, he most Humbly Entreats Your Honble Bodies, to award him this his only and last Request, which he expects ever to ask of his Government—

And your Petitioner as in duty bound will ever pray—

[signed] Gaspar Sinclair
Jefferson County—
Decr. 30 1825

SOURCE: Petition of Gaspar Sinclair to the Senate and House of Representatives of Mississippi, 30 December 1825, Records of the Legislature, Petitions and Memorials, 1825, RG 47, MDAH. Rejected. PAR #11082502.

67. Basil Chastang, Mobile County, to Alabama Legislature, ca. 1826

the Members of the Senate and House Representatives of the State of Alabama General assembly convened.

The Petition of the undersigned Basil Chastang of the County of Mobile, humbly represents that he is the rightful owner of certain slaves to wit Nancy and her four children Gertrude, Francois, Catherine and Fostin, all of whom have been faithful and useful to your petitioner and his family and he is desirous of liberating them from slavery. He therefore prays that your Honorable body will pass an act authorising your petitioner to manumit the said slaves above named and Your petitioner as in duty bound will ever pray &c.

[signed] Basil Chastang

SOURCE: Petition of Basil Chastang to the Members of the Senate and House of Representatives of the State of Alabama, ca. 1826, Records of the Alabama Secretary of State, Legislative Bills and Resolutions, ADAH. Granted.[1] PAR #10182602.

1. "An Act to Emancipate Coloured Woman Slave Named Nancy and Her Four Children . . . ," signed by Governor John Murphy, 11 January 1827, in Records of the Alabama Secretary of State, Administrative Division, Enrolled Acts, 1826–27, 131, ADAH. The son of Dr. John Chastang, a prominent Mobile surgeon, Basil Chastang became one of the wealthiest free blacks in Alabama.

68. Wilmington Union Colonization Society to Delaware Assembly, ca. 1827

To the honourable the Senate and House of Representatives of the State of Delaware.

The Memorial of the Wilmington Union Colonization Society respectfully solicits your attention to the condition of the free negroes and free mulattoes in this country. Your memorialists are greatly mistaken, if this condition ~~do~~ does not present to our Statesmen a subject deserving their most anxious care and requiring all their wisdom.

The free people of colour now constitute a considerable part of our population; and they are fast increasing. Their natural increase is as rapid, as that of white persons; and every year, many are added to their number by the enfranchisement of slaves.

These people are in one of the most important, if not the most important, classes of our population—the labouring class; and it is not necessary to remark, that they do in various ways affect this class. The effect produced by the diminution of respectability, not to say degradation, of the labouring class, by which many, who would be the most useful members of the community, are driven from their proper sphere, to oppress society with their burden instead of profiting it by their labour, has consequences not easily calculated.

There is a more important view of this subject. We have liberated the free people of colour from physical restraint. So far as conduct is concerned,—the right to pursue the dictates of their own judgements or inclinations,—they have all the freedom secured by our constitution and laws. But we do not allow to them the means of moral restraint, without which freedom will not be discreetly used. Our laws do not and cannot permit them to enjoy the most important civil priveleges. They cannot elect nor be elected to any office; they cannot serve on a jury, so that trial by jury, a most important feature of which is trial by one's peers, is not allowed to them; they can not be heard as witnesses in a court of justice in opposition to the interest or in contradiction of the testimony of a white person.

Our manners are and must be as unfavorable to them as our laws. We will not permit them to associate with us. We will not tolerate any notion of equality with them. We will not act in reference to them nor will we suffer them to act in relation to us, except upon ~~up~~ the unquestioned principle, that they are in a state of ~~degration~~ degradation, to which we will not descend, and from which they must not expect to rise.

The consequence is, that those powerful motives, which form the palladium of morals and the safe-guard even of laws, and which enable men to be free without abusing freedom, the love of reputation, the desire of respectability, the dread of reproach, the value of character, are either unknown to them or have little influence.

In these observations your Memorialists intend no accusation against our laws or our manners. Our separation from these people is the effect of moral causes, the foundation of which we could not safely remove; amalgamation would demoralize society; the consequence of breaking up the present distinctions would be not to raise the free coloured people, but to sink all to a state of degradation yet unknown.

Your Memorialists believe, that every one will assent to the correctness of their conclusion, that the increase of these people among us, as they must increase if they remain among us, is an alarming consideration If we will reflect upon the progress of this increase, we shall see, that their numbers in a few years must be troublesome, independent of the deleterious influence, which has been noticed, upon the labouring class, and independent of the danger threatened by this growing evil. This danger is of two kinds. As to one;—will not crimes increase as rapidly, as their numbers?—As to the other,—brought up, as these people are, in the sight of our priveleges, will they consent to be excluded from them?—Numbers will give power,—and at all events, will afford facility for secret mischief, if not encouragement to open violence. Are not these people by their very condition our enemies? Do we, or can we, bind them to us or to our laws by any ties of common feeling or reciprocal obligation, by the influence of gratitude or respect? Must ~~we~~ they not feel themselves to be, as we treat them, aliens to our common weal? When therefore your Memorialists ask the question,—Will prudence permit such a heterogeneous population to take root in our soil and grow up into power among us?—does not the reflecting mind anticipate every argument, which they could urge for the removal of these people? We ought not to conceal this evil from ourselves. Let us consider, that this condition is still in infancy; that the real character of this population is not yet disclosed. The negro, when emancipated from slavery, retains many of the habits of thinking, which had formed themselves in bondage. Among these, there are always fear and deference, sometimes affectionate regard for white people. We have not yet reached the time, when these habits have not a general and powerful influence. They are however wearing off by degrees; time is planting other feelings in their place; and he is a careless observer, who does not see, that the character of this population is undergoing, in the particular, to which allusion is here made, a constant change.

In illustration of some of ~~our~~ these remarks, your Memorialists could cite the laws of several States expelling free negroes from their limits. They will mention only the Act of our own General Assembly of 1811 prohibiting free negroes from coming from other States into this State.

The difficulty heretofore has respected the removal of the free people of colour. The question has been, how or where can they be removed? The answer to this question will, for its reception, depend upon the opinion, which is entertained of the necessity of the measure. If we are indifferent about a measure, a slight inconvenience attending its execution may seem to be an insurmountable obstacle. That this population can be removed from our soil, and that this removal can be effected with ease by the power of this nation, your Memorialists consider to be perfectly certain. This certainty, they believe, will be apparent to every one, who will examine the subject.

The American Colonization Society has obtained on the coast of Africa a place to receive these people. It is proved by experience, that the climate suits their constitution. The soil is fertile, beyond what we have any knowledge of, and the country is pleasant and most advantageously situated. There is ample room for all the coloured people in the United States, and their posterity, for generations,—place for the growth of a mighty nation. Nature herself points to Africa, whence the progenitors of these people were brought, and where is still their kind, as the ~~place~~ country, to which they should be restored.

The American Colonization Society was organized in December 1816. In December 1821 they succeeded in obtaining a suitable district of country for their purpose. It was to be expected, that an undertaking, the chief operations of which were upon another continent, would be attended by some disasters. The history of the settlement of many of these States ~~wou~~ fully illustrates this remark. It was also to be expected, that the change from the climate of this country to that of Africa would have no inconsiderable effect upon the health even of people of colour. At first, it was not known how to guard against the effects of this change, and there were no conveniencies upon the spot to aid any endeavours for this object. The society has had to contend with difficulties and has surmounted them. It is now known, when is the best season for arrival upon the coast of Africa; and what measures should be pursued for preserving the health of the emigrants. A colony has been planted; and it flourishes. It is proved by experiment, that these people can be removed to that country and comfortably and advantageously settled. The expenses of removal and the time consumed by the voyage are also ascertained by experiment. The removal of the first emigrants cost, for each, fifty dollars. This expense has been gradually diminished and the expense of the last removals did not exceed on an average ten dollars for each emigrant. The present perfect state of navigation renders the voyage of little account. A vessel departing from this country in the ~~February~~ first part of February will reach this colony during March.

Can there be a doubt, when we see, that this voyage can be performed in less than two months and at the expense of ten dollars for each emigrant, that this nation can remove, and with facility, this population?

The question has been suggested, Will these people consent to go? Your Memorialists might answer this question by ~~t~~ stating the fact, that this Society has always found more desirous to go, than they had means to remove. They however say confidently, that if so much of the resources of the National Government were applied to this object as to make facilities for this removal general and common, there can be no doubt, that this whole population would flow in a current in that direction. It would be understood, that in Africa, the land of their fathers, are fertile fields and pleasant skies, and that a nation is forming there, in which they can establish themselves in comfort and independence, in the undisturbed enjoyment of the rights of man.

The view, which your Memorialists have taken, concerns our own safety, the measures, which enlightened policy requires us to pursue? May they not bring before you another view? May they not ask, Is there no obligation upon us to restore these people to their country?

We have emancipated them from slavery; but we have given to them, we can give to them, none of the advantages of freedom; none of those great advantages, of which if we were deprived, we should deem ourselves slaves. Can we permit them to remain in this state of humiliation? Do not the highest considerations require, that if we can not admit them to the participation of the rights of freemen on our own soil, we ought to place them, where they will not be driven from society and set without the influence of every noble principle, by the very circumstances of their condition?

The Wilmington Union Colonization Society deeply impressed with the importance of this subject have deemed it their duty to bring it before the honourable the Senate and House of Representatives. The course which the National Government will pursue in relation to it must depend upon public opinion; and this opinion will be greatly influenced by deliberations and resolves of the State Legislatures. It is among your highest duties to guard against occasions of evil; to take care reasonably to eradicate whatever may threaten calamity to ourselves or to posterity. Your Memorialists believe, that no subject deserves more careful attention, than that, which they have now submitted to you. They are satisfied, that you will not le[t] it pass without examination, and that you will consider of the best means to promote the measure, which your Memorialists have briefly explained and which they believe to be of vital concern to the happiness and prosperity of this country.

By Order of the Society

[signed] Robert Porter Chairman

SOURCE: Petition of the Wilmington Union Colonization Society to the Senate and House of Representatives of Delaware, ca. 1827, General Assembly, Legislative Papers, DSA. Resolution passed.[1] PAR #10382701.

1. The Delaware General Assembly passed a resolution supporting "one of the grandest schemes of philanthropy that can be presented to the American people." It did so not only as a "requisite for our prosperity" but also as an essential element "to our safety." Congress, it said, should assist in removing free persons of color who wished to emigrate to Africa. *Laws of the State of Delaware, Passed at a Session of the General Assembly, Commenced and Held at Dover, on Tuesday the Second Day of January, in the Year of Our Lord, One Thousand Eight Hundred and Twenty Seven* (Dover: J. Robertson, 1827), 158.

69. Littleton P. Henderson, Accomack County, to Virginia Assembly, 1827

To the honourable the General Assembly of Virginia

The petition of Littleton P. Henderson most respectfully showeth.—That some time in the year 182   the overseers of the Poor of the County of Accomack by virtue of a provision of the Act of Assembly concerning slaves free negroes and mulattoes proceeded to sell at public auction many of the free negros residing in the said county, the proceeds arising from which sale have been paid into the public Treasury to the Credit of the Literary Fund[1]—Amongst the number of free negros thus sold by the said overseers of the Poor, there was a certain Jim Outten who at the time of the sale was in the city of Baltimore, & who had never been in custody of the said overseers of the poor. Your petitioner conceiving the sale to be conducted according to law & ~~not~~ knowing the character & worth of the said Jim Outten was induced to bid for him and actually bought him at the price of $50, all which will fully appear by the receipt of the overseers of the poor given to your orator by them for the purchase money which is here with exhibited—Your petitioner further showeth that not long after purchasing the said Jim Outten and as soon as your petitioner attempted to exercise the rights of ownership over the said Jim Outten he commenced his action *in forma pauperis* in the County Court of Accomack against your petitioner and at the last August term of the said Court he recovered a judgment against your petitioner and was restored to his former rights and privileges all which will fully appear by a complete copy of the record in the said suit herewith filed & prayed to be taken as evidence touching the premises—Your petitioner conceiving that he has a just and equitable demand against the president & directors of the Literary Fund humbly prays that your honourable body will authoriz & require the president & directors of the Literary fund to refund to your petitioner the purchase money paid by him for the said Jim Outten & legal interest thereon (as he never derived any benefit from the services of the said negro) together with the cost of suit incurred by your petitioner in defending the same & your petitioner will ever pray &c.

[signed] Littleton P. Henderson

SOURCE: Littleton P. Henderson to the Virginia General Assembly, 11 December 1827, Legislative Petitions, Accomack County, VSA. A bill was drawn. PAR #11682708.

1. Used to finance education, the Literary Fund was supported by escheats, confiscations, and forfeitures. The proceeds obtained from selling emancipated slaves who remained in the state went into this fund. *Fifth Annual Report of the Library Board of the Virginia State Library* (Richmond: Davis Bottom, 1908), 13.

70. Mechanics of Charleston to South Carolina Assembly, ca. 1828

To the Honorable the President and Members of the
Senate of S. Carolina

The Petition of Sundry Mechanics of the City of Charleston
Respectfully sheweth;

That your Petitioners suffering under the distress incident to the situation of those who have to live by their labor, from the decay of Trade, and want of Employment, ventured to lay their Humble Complaints before the Legislature at the last Session. That the Memorial which they then had the honor of submitting was signed by a very large number of the Wealthiest and most Respectable Inhabitants of this City, who were deeply impressed with the necessity of counteracting by a Wise and Provident Legislature, the Causes that had already produced so much evil, and were likely to produce so much more; and that they were encouraged to hope that your Honorable Body, moved by the many weighty considerations which present themselves to every one who seriously reflects upon the subject, would be induced to interfere by some effective measure on their behalf.

[Your] Petitioners, however, were disappointed in their hopes; not, as they have been informed from [the disposition] of your Honorable Body to afford them the relief for which they prayed, and of [which they are] much in need, but because, owing to the great press of Business, and the shortness of the Session, [their] petition never came fully before the Legislature.

Your Petitioners, therefore, beg leave again to call the attention of your Honorable Body to the subject of their complaints, which they will now proceed to state.

Your Petitioners believe it to be a fact which admits of no doubt, that the conditions of White Mechanics in the City of Charleston, is, of late years, become so unprosperous, as to hold out to those who would be willing to become Tradesmen, and to gain their livelihood by honest and laborious Industry in their avocation, a prospect full of gloom, and almost of Despair. For obvious reasons, the competition of Negro and Colored Workmen, whether Bond or Free, supposing anything like an equality of skill, is too powerful [to overcome] by persons situated like your Petitioners. They can live on a great deal less than white men, with such notions of what constitutes the Necessaries of Life, as universally prevail among [white] men in this Country possibly can; even with the strictest economy. Slaves, particularly, are exempted [from] some of those expenses that fall heaviest upon the Poor; such, for example, as Doctors' Bills, and the other expenses of Sickness; and with these they are exempted, from all the harassing cares and fearful anticipations that accompany the Poor man's reflections upon the future. Add to this, that the greatest cause of extreme poverty, the tendency which it has to depress the spirits, to break the energies, and ultimately to debase the character of its victim, is scarcely known to them;—Hence, in Seasons of Difficulty and Distress, while the white Mechanic, frustrated in all his efforts to better his condition, unable to get work, or to collect the wages of his labor, surrounded with a family, perhaps, for which he finds himself every day less liable to provide, sinks into despair, and falls a victim to vicious and idle habits:—The Slave finds his situation in no wise affected by the Times, except by the possibility which he contemplates without emotion, that he may exchange a Master whom he has helped to ruin, for one better able to indulge him in the privileges he has been accustomed to enjoy. Another circumstance well worthy of notice, is, that many of the most opulent Inhabitants of Charleston, when they have any work to be done, do not send it themselves, but leave it to their Domestics to employ what Workmen they please; it universally happens that those Domestics prefer men of their own Color and condition; and, as to a greatness of business thus continually passing through their hands, the Black Mechanics enjoy as complete a monopoly, as if it were secured to them by Law.—

When, in addition to these causes, your Honorable Body take into consideration others, that it is unnecessary to mention, as well as the hardships and difficulties inseparable from the condition of those who have to depend upon their daily labor for their daily bread, you cannot be surprised to learn that the number of White Mechanics in this City is every day diminishing more and more; some of them betaking themselves to other and less useful employments; others, emigrating, with the little capital they may have got together, to distant places; while others, again, less fortunately situated, too surely fall victims to adversity, and become at once, a burthen to themselves and to Society. On the other hand, it is a fact which must strike the most superficial observer, that almost all the Trades, but especially those of Carpenters, Bricklayers, Plaisterers, Wheelwrights, House=painters, Shoe=makers, &c are beginning to be engrossed by Black & Colored workmen; that these are multiplying in a prodigious ratio; and, that Charleston, already swarming with a population of Free Blacks, and of Slaves, more Licentious than if they were Free, must, in a very short time, be in the condition of a West India Town, which it will be impossible to defend without a Regular Military Force.

Your petitioners assure your Honorable Body, that the comparative decrease of the white Population of this City, mainly owing to the causes that have been pointed out, is even now, visible and alarming and must be every day, progressively greater; and they submit it to the Wisdom of the Legislature, whether their case is not recommended to its most serious consideration, by every motive which can influence them, either as Men, or as Politicians.

Your Petitioners pray for such relief in the premises, as to your Honorable Body it may seem most expedient to grant them; but, especially, in the following particulars:—

1st. By an Act passed at the Session of 1822, it is made unlawful to hire to any Slave, his own time; and in case any Slaves be permitted by their Owner or Owners to hire out his own time, he is made liable to Seisure and forfeiture, according to the form prescribed by the Act of 1820. The object of this Statute, was evidently twofold; 1st, to secure to the Owner, all the wages of his slave's labor, and 2d to secure to him (what was even more important to himself, and far more so to the public) a complete control over his conduct and pursuits. This salutary Law, however, fell dead-born—it has never been in any manner carried into execution—It is easily evaded by a Certificate from the Owner, that the Slave is in his employment; and such is the indolence of Mankind, that there are but few owners who do not prefer turning loose their Slaves upon the Community, with such a Certificate, to hunt for Work, although they profit less by it, than put themselves to the trouble of making the contract, and thus receiving the full price of the Work. Your Petitioners respectfully suggest, that this Act of 1822, ought to be so amended and explained, as to make it completely effective of its purposes.

2d. With a view rigorously to enforce the execution of that Law, as well as of any other, that in its wisdom, your Honorable Body may see fit to make, touching the premises, your petitioners are desirous of forming themselves into an Association by the style of "the Charleston Mechanics' Association." They therefore, pray that they may be [permitted to form such an Association] and your Petitioners, as in duty bound, will ever pray, and so forth.—

[signed] Wm. McKewn Prest
Aaron Barton V.P.
Henry J. Egan, Trea
Henry C [Gifken?]
James [Moins?]
Willa Johnson
John Bonner 22 Ellery St.
Richard Leake 212 Meeting St
William MacMillan
[101 additional signatures]

SOURCE: Memorial of the Mechanics of Charleston to the South Carolina General Assembly, ca. 1828, Records of the General Assembly, 1811-#48, SCDAH. No act was passed.[1] PAR #11382813.

1. The 1822 law made it "altogether unlawful for any person or persons to hire any male slave or slaves, his or their time." A generation later, in 1849, following complaints about self-hired women, the assembly stipulated that female slaves should also be denied this privilege. *Acts and Resolutions of the General Assembly of the State of South-Carolina, Passed in December, 1822* (Columbia: Daniel Faust, 1823), 13; *The Statutes at Large of South Carolina* (Columbia: A. S. Johnston, 1840), 462; *The Statutes at Large of South Carolina* (Columbia: T. S. Piggot, 1858), 578.

71. Charleston City Council to South Carolina Senate, ca. 1828

To the Honble
The President Members
of the Senate
The Memorial of the City Council of Charleston respectfully Sheweth

That the Grand Jury of Charleston District have presented the number of Schools publicly kept for the instruction of persons of Colour in reading and writing as injurious to the Community. Your Memorialists concur fully with them in this opinion—To be able to read and write is certainly not necessary to the performance of those duties which are usually required of our Slaves, and on the Contrary is incompatible with the public Safety. The facility with which the knowledge of the Art of writing will enable persons of this class to carry on illicit traffic, to communicate privately among themselves and to evade those regulations that are intended to prevent confederations among them, renders it important that the Law prohibiting them being taught should be rigidly enforced.[1] This Law prohibits Slaves being taught to write. The facilities however that are afforded them by the means of Schools professedly kept for the instruction of Free persons of Colour, will soon render this knowledge very common in our community. It is impossible to distinguish between the free and the slave of our coloured population and therefore it is extremely difficult to detect violations of the Law—We know of no remedy so effectual and at the same time so little liable to objection as the absolute prohibition of all s[c]hools for the instruction of coloured persons. Tho the instruction of Slaves in reading is not liable to all the objections which exist against their being taught to write, yet ~~it~~ while it does not contribute to increase their Comfort and happiness it may seriously affect the peace and good Order of our Society. It has been the policy of some evil minded persons to publish inflammatory writings and to circulate them among these people. The perusal of such publications cannot fail to be injurious. It is also difficult to prevent those who can read from attaining also the art of writing. These circumstances render it important that the prohibition against the instruction of Persons of Colour in reading and writing should be general.

There is another subject realating to our Coloured population which Your memorialists would bring to Your attention. It has been ascertained that Slaves and free persons of colour have been employed by their owners and others, as salesmen in Stores and Shops, and generally as clerks to traders of different descriptions. This is an increasing evil and it is impossible to ~~tell~~ determine where it will stop. It not only deprives a white population from employments which have hitherto afforded a support to many, but introduces the coloured population and especially slaves, into situations which are inconsistent with their condition. Your memorialists respectfully suggest that as the system of slavery is so interwoven with the constitution of our society that even if our interests permitted it would be impossible to eradicate it, it becomes highly important that the regulations necessary for maintaining this State of things in peace and security should be permanently established and regularly maintained. To effect this it is necessary to fix as far as possible the grade of employments in which such persons may be employed and to exclude them by Legislative enactment from all others. At first view it may be regarded as unnecessary interference with [t]he rights of owners, but when we consider how deeply the welfare of the State is involved in this subject, that impression must yield to views of more serious import. As domestics, cultivators of the soil, labourers, and labouring mechanics, they have always been employed. These by common consent are admitted to be their appropriate avocations, but beyond these to any engagements which require the exercise of greater intelligence and improvement they should not be allowed to aspire. Without some regulations on this subject we preserve the seeds of disquiet in the very constitution of our Society. We would not attempt to point out the particular enactments that may be necessary, but pray that such may be adopted as you may deem most expedient. . . . [six pages concerning internal improvements]

[signed] Jos. Johnson
Intendant

SOURCE: Petition of the Charleston City Council to the President and Members of the Senate, ca. 1828, Records of the General Assembly, #207, SCDAH. Granted.[2] PAR #11382809.

1. In 1740, following the Stono Rebellion, the South Carolina General Assembly prohibited slaves from learning to write.

2. In 1834, the assembly passed a law prohibiting anyone to teach a slave to read or write. The penalties for whites included a fine not exceeding one hundred dollars and imprisonment for not more than six months; for free blacks, the penalty included a public whipping not exceeding fifty lashes and a fine not exceeding fifty dollars. Any free black or slave who kept a school or other place of instruction would receive the same punishment as that prescribed for free persons of color who taught slaves to read or write. *Acts and Resolutions of the General Assembly, of the State of South Carolina, Passed in December, 1834* (Columbia: E. F. Branthwaite, 1834), 13.

72. John Jonah Murrell et al., Christ Church Parish, to South Carolina House, 1829

To the Honourable the Speaker and Members of the House of Representatives of South Carolina—

The Memorial of the Freeholders and Other Inhabitants of the Parish of Christ Church respectfully Sheweth—

That Your Memorialists, Planters of South Carolina, from the vicinity of their property to Charleston, from their parish being surrounded by navigable water leading directly to, and occasioning much intercourse with that City, and from the great Northern road passing through their parish in its whole length are peculiarly exposed to the great evil of absconding slaves and their ruinous depredations—

Your Memorialists are aware that these causes have long combined to produce this evil, but they have within these latter Years only, found it operate to an extent producing great irregularity and disorder among their slaves, and now leading directly to a state of insubordination and danger affecting the lives of individuals and the security of property—

This state of things is operating, Your Memorialists believe, in every part of the lower and middle divisions of the State, as they are informed by the inhabitants of other parishes, and it cries aloud for the interference of your Honourable House—They think it unnecessary to say any thing of the increasing efforts made by enthusiasts out of Carolina, to poison the minds of our domestic people, these must be met in a different way, and cannot hurt us if the Southern states are true to themselves; but they would distinctly state their conviction, that great mischief has been already done, and is daily increasing by the misguided zeal and unguarded movements, acts and conversation of persons within our own State, owning little or none of the property they so earnestly and so unceasingly crave to meddle with, yet living and supported by the agriculture of the country—

Prior to the passing of the Law of 1821 entitled an Act to increase the punishment inflicted on persons convicted of murdering any slave,[1] and *for other purposes therein mentioned,** it is asserted by your Memorialists without fear of contradiction the Slaves of this part of South Carolina were in every respect more obedient and better servants, and infinitely more trust-worthy and faithful than they have been subsequently. Since the passing of that Law, changes in the prices of our crops and consequently in the fortunes of many of our fellow Citizens have taken place, and these changes have carried to Charleston for sale, large bodies of negroes. The unrestrained intercourse of these with free blacks and low and worthless white people, during their sojourn there, has infused into the minds of the negroes ideas of insubordination and of emancipation, which they carry with them when sold into every part of the State—

Your Memorialists have referred to the Law of 1821, as a period from which the evils of running away have increased upon them and upon the low country, and they do not hesitate to say, that this law has produced a most baneful influence on the conduct of the negroes—The persons who projected that Law stated, no doubt, that they were actuated by motives of great humanity, but Your Memorialists with much deference to Your Honorable Body undertake to assert, that they

---

* No other purposes are mentioned in this act!

were not practical Southern Planters, otherwise they would have foreseen that the Law would be useless, and even hurtful to those whom it professes to protect; these persons were not Southern Legislators, for if they had been, they would have known that *changing the nature of the penalties in the case of negroes*—that inflicting the punishment of death on a white man for killing a slave, *who is a property, instead of exacting a fine for the loss of that property,* was placing the white inhabitants on a footing which would not be admitted by Juries of our Countrymen, and hence that the penalty would never be inflicted in any case however enormous; for the very effect of the law as your Memorialists will presently shew, is to produce upon the part of the negro, such acts of violence, as call immediate vengeance down upon him—Your Memorialists therefore deny unequivocally the policy, much less the necessity, of such a law as that of 1821, unless to satisfy the morbid feelings of those who wish to interfere with our slaves; and they further assert that the negroes of South Carolina were better protected by the Laws and penalties which were founded by our forefathers, on the dictates of common sense and the nature of the property, than by the law of 1821; for the Old laws were practical, reasonable and therefore carried into execution, while the new law which inflicts death without benefit of clergy on a white for Killing a slave, apparently admits of no mitigation or exception even if the slave should have ravished his daughter, attempted to Kill himself, or burnt his dwelling, and is therefore only productive of injury to the slave, to his owner and to the country.

Your Memorialists will now proceed to shew in their own case, the real and practical effect of the Law of 1821 and Your Honorable Body will not be surprised at the consequences, when the concise and artful manner in which the law has been drawn up is considered, its peculiar fitness to impress upon the minds of Slaves, (to whom it is too often read,) that they are now on a different footing as regards their owners and the whites, from what they formerly were; a footing approaching nearer to a State of emancipation from their authority, and of course to a State of unrestrained liberty and licentiousness—

And first—This Law prevents Planters and Overseers from turning out to put down even large gangs of runaways, unless under very aggravating circumstances; because they will not subject themselves to be tried for their lives by City Juries having notions and prejudices as to the property, and of course as to the principle of the law itself, different from what every planter and owner of country property must have; nor will they expose themselves to endure the expense, vexation, and loss of time, to which they may be and in some instances have been made liable under this law, although in the end honorably acquitted—

Secondly—The negroes finding a backwardness on the part of their owners and the neighbors to turn out, are encouraged to run off without cause or with a view to commit depredations. Finding these are not closely pursued, others are encouraged to follow the same course, and those at home become disorderly and insubordinate—It is well known to Your Honorable body, *that a State of security in crime like this described,* must lead to greater and yet greater atrocities, hence the depredations upon our property, crops and cattle, have been enormous.—

Thirdly—Such negroes as have in consequence of this combination of fatal circumstances remained out for Years, at length cease to respect the whites, become reckless of consequences, and choosing their opportunities during the sickly season of the Year or when individuals are alone and supposed to be defenceless, attack them with a view to destroy them—

Fourthly the end of this chain of consequences proceeding from a most injudicious and fatal law, the act of 1821, is death to the misguided Slave and destruction to the property of your Memorialists, as will appear from the following facts supported upon the evidence of affidavits,

In 1822 a negro belonging to the Estate of Spring, but formerly the property of a Parishioner deceased, absconded and came into the parish as a runaway. In 1824 a fellow belonging to Mrs Legare joined him as a runaway was shot and killed in his company—In 1825 a family five in number purchased at the sale of A. Vanderhorst, absconded and joined the same ringleader—They continued out until October last, when the Children surrendered (one having been born in the woods) the Father and Mother having been both shot and killed—In 1827 three Negroes belonging to a Parishioners Estate returned in like manner after the sale of his effects, as runaways. One of them in January last snapped a gun heavily loaded with Slugs at one of Your Memorialists, who met him in the woods and who immediately shot the negro. Another of these three negroes in October last attacked another of Your Memorialists with a knife fifteen inches long, stabbed him in the hand and would have cut his throat, but for assistance rendered in time to save him. In 1828, runaway slaves were collected from various parts of the Parish, one was Killed upon the spot, and another severely wounded for the second time and taken, in January last Eighteen Slaves the property of one of your Memorialists went off under their driver and of these one fellow has been shot and killed, while the house of the owner has been pillaged by his own slaves, ten of whom are still out in a neighbouring parish—

The death of these negroes has been brought on them by the aggravating circumstances attending their depredations, which were no longer to be tolerated or borne with—One negro taken some months ago, declared on his trial, that he had in three weeks destroyed Forty head of Cattle, and many of Your Memorialists are altogether prevented from keeping Stock of any Kind, from these causes, after having had large gangs of cattle, sheep and hogs entirely destroyed—

Your Memorialists could swell this statement with many circumstances at once ruinous to them as well as most vexatious in their nature, for many of their slaves although not killed by gunshot, have been transported or have died in the woods and of diseases occasioned by running away. But they will not wear out the patience of Your Honorable Body, they would now rather, briefly, but with the utmost earnestness appeal for redress from so grievous a state of anarchy, occasioned by a spirit of infatuation which is abroad in our country touching our negroes; they would in truth and sincerity, and in the name of humanity to their slaves, call for a repeal of a Law (the act of 1821) which lays the foundation of such waste of blood and property, and for a reestablishment of the Old State laws formerly in force—. They would ask as a means of undeceiving their misguided people, as a means of enabling Your Memorialists and all planters throughout the State, to bring their own and all other negroes into that state of subjection and perfect control, without which they speedily bring destruction on themselves and ruin on their owners—They would ask of this Honble Body, to pass an Act, declaring every Slave who shall hereafter abscond or runaway, or who may now be absent, as outlaws and deprived of the benefit of the Laws and out of the protection of the State, after the lapse of thirty days from his work without his Owners permission—And Your Memorialists as in duty bound will ever pray—

[signed]	John Jonah Murrell	Joseph Maybank
	Henry English	J Hibber
	Elisha Whilden	D [Jervey?]
	George W D Scott	A. V. Toomer
	Frederick Steding	Paul Weston
		[13 additional signatures]

SOURCE: Petition of John Jonah Murrell et al. to the Speaker and Members of the South Carolina House of Representatives, 1829, Records of the General Assembly, #90, SCDAH. Referred to the Judiciary Committee. No act was passed. PAR #11382913.

1. The law of 1821 imposed the death penalty for murdering a slave. In 1834, an appeals court judge wrote, "This change I think made a most important alteration in the law of his [a slave's] personal protection." It "elevated slaves from chattels personal to human beings." Quoted in George Rogers, "Slavery in South Carolina," in *Dictionary of Afro-American Slavery,* ed. Randall M. Miller and John David Smith (New York: Greenwood, 1988), 704.

73. Elias Naudain, Kent County, to Delaware Assembly, 1829

To the honourable the Senate and house of Representatives of the State of Delaware in General Assembly met

The Petition of the subscriber humbly represents that on the 22nd day of February 1826 there was bound to him by John Wright one of the Justices of the peace for Kent County, a Negro boy named Joshua Rodney to serve for the term of four years one month and eight days or untill he should arrive at lawfull age, that the said Joshua ran away from me and left my employment on or about the night of the nineteenth or twentieth of February last, that on the night of the nineteenth my blacksmith shop was burned down between the hours of 11 and 12 oClock at night, that the said Joshua went to Philadelphia, and remained ~~and remained~~ there until the night of the 23d August, when he returned to my neighbourhood and remained concealed until the night of the first of September on which night my stable was burnt down and six head of Horses burnt in it, the fire took place about the same time of the former, between the hours of 11 and 12 at night that the said Joshua was discovered by two persons during the fire concealed within about thirty or forty paces of the fire, that the said Joshua was lodged in the public Jail of Kent County on the second of September last and still remains there at the expense of your petitioner, on examination he stated that he did not put the fire to the stable, but that himself and another Negro boy of Your petitioner a slave called James Lee was together and that James fired the building. when James was arrested, he stated that they were together but that Joshua put the fire to the building. That upon application to the Supreme Court they granted me a permit to Sell the said James Lee out of this state, That upon a representation of the case to the attorney general at the Court of quarter sessions held in December last he declined prosecuting the said Joshua, as there could be no positive proof of the fact, and his character could not be brought in question, the said Joshua was first bound to Ceasor Knight who had his dwelling house burned down and all his property in it burnt, he then sold him to Outen Laws who had his dwelling house fired twice. He ran away from Mr Laws and came to your petitioner, and not knowing his character purchased his time of Mr Laws—Your petitioner therefore prays that you will take his case into consideration, and grant him a permit to Sell the Said Joshua out of this State for the balance of the time that he may have to serve him

And Your petitioner will ever pray &c
[signed] Elias Naudain
February 5t—1829

SOURCE: Petition of Elias Naudain to the Senate and House of Representatives of Delaware, 5 February 1829, General Assembly, Legislative Papers, DSA. No act was passed. PAR #10382904.

74. Martha Smith Green, Williamson County, to Tennessee Assembly, 1829

To the honourable the general assembly of the State of tennessee, your Petitioner Martha Smith Green, humbly Sheweth to your honours that She was married to Thomas, C, Green on the 10th day of January 1828 and in three weeks after your Petitioner was Married Clearly Discovered a disposition of heart, and temper of mind in her husband that She feared would destroy all her Prospects of happiness and Render her life miserable, your Petitioner did Constantly use every Exertion of warm affection towards her husband that heart was Capable of, hopeing he would Reciprocate her Love, and Reform His manners towards her, But your Petitioner had the mortifycation to See, that all and every attempt

She made of the tenderest nature Proov,d abortive, and that when your Petitioner was in Publick Company With her husband, he would at Such times make use of Such opportunities to display an uncommon Childish fondness towards her And as Soon as we ware Retired from company he would then Commence the most abusive language and threats of Punishment To the Constant terror and dread of your Petitioner, and when your Petitioner would Remonstrate Against Such acts of abuse He the Said Green, to Retaliate, would accuse your Petitioner of Want of affection to him, and did accuse your Petitioner Repeatedly of being too intimate with a young Gentleman, a near Relation of Said Greens, at other times he did accuse your Petitioner of being Intemate and guilty with his Negro man (Jim) to the great mortifycation of your Petitioners feelings, and your Petitioner farther Sheweth to your honours that on the Second Sabbath in July of the above date, as well as She now Recollects, on the Said day a Young Negro woman Came to the house where your Petitioner and her husband live,d and in a few minutes Said Green Commenced Playing with and handling Said Negro Girl in an indecent manner. your Petitioner did Reprove him for Such Conduct, and ordered the Negro away, and Said Green imediately went in Pursuit of the Negro girl, as your Petitioner Plainly Saw, and was absent from the house as your Petitioner believes Near one hour and a half, and when he Return,d to the house, Saw that your Petitioners feelings was much hurt with his Conduct And Said Green did acknowledge that he was Carnally With the Said Negro Girl, and Said if your Petitioner would forgive Him he never would do the like again, your Petitioner told him if he Would Keep to his Promise then made, She would try to forgive him. He again in a Short time commenced his former abusive language and Continued to do So, untill about the Second week in August At which time the Said Green, Put all his threats and abuse Into Practice by Severely beating your Petitioner in Such a Manner that She Carried the markes of his Violence, on her body For twenty weeks; in the night following the day, in which your Petitioner was thus maltreated by her husband, She made an attempt to escape to her fathers, for the Purpose of Claiming his Protection, but was Pursued by Said Green, with Negroes and Dogs, and was overtaken at Some distance from the house, and Was taken back by Said Greens Negro man with some degree of Violence, by the express order of Said Green, to the Great fear and Terror of your Petitioner; the day after your Petitioner attempted to Escape to her fathers, She was taken Very ill, of a feevor, and does Religiously beleive, that the ill treatment of her husband was the Cause of Her Long Protracted and dangerous illness, Some Short time after your Petitioner was take Sick, her half Brother Col. Kearney came to See her, and through his influence, the Said Green, consented that your Petitioner might be Carried to her fathers, for the Purpose of being Convenient to the Physician, where your Petitioner lay Dangerously ill Eighteen weeks, her life was dispared off [*sic*] by her Physician and all her Kind friends who Visited her duering Her Long illness, your Petitioner farther Sheweth to your honours that while She lay Sick at her fathers the Said Green did frequently Treat her ill, and abused her Mother and eldest Sister; at one time While her fevor was Very high and your Petitioner was suffering Much Pain, the Said Green Slapt her on the Cheek with his Hand in an abusive maner, at another time when there was company at my fathers house, the said Green, came into the Room where I Lay Sick and began to abuse me in the Presence of my mother And Sister, and threatened me with the Cowhide when he got me Home again, at this time my father drove Said Green off and forbid Him again visiting his house dureing my illness, your Petitioner Dureing her illness, did believe she would die, and determined in Her own mind not to devulge the maltreatment of her husband which took Place at his house, to No Person; but as Soon as your Petitioner Discovered there was a Probability of her again being Restored To health, She did beleive it was her duty to inform her Parents of the ill treatment of her husband, while liveing with him at His house and did So, as She had determined never again to Live with Said Green as his wife, haveing lost all Confidence In him;—Therefore your Petitioner Prays your honours in General assembly to Pass an act for her benefit, Secureing the Right of all the Property She may hereafter acquire by honest Industry or donation of friends and your Petitioner will Ever Pray &c. &c.

[signed] Martha S. Green

State of Tennessee }
Williamson County } This day Personally appeared the above Petitioner Martha Smith Green, before me Joshua Farrington An acting Justice of the Peace for the County aforesaid And made oath that the facts stated in her Petition Are true and that this application is not made by—Collusion between her and the Said Thomas, C, Green

But in truth and Sincerity
Sign,d and Sworn to before
Me this 19th day of September 1829

[signed] J. Farrington Martha S. Green
Justice of the peace

To whom it }
may concern } We the subscribers were invited by Mrs Martha Greene [*sic*] lately Miss Martha Denson daughter of William Denson of Williamson County to visit her at the house of her father, in the summer of 1828 when rising out of a spell of illness of 18 weeks duration, that she might have an opportunity of asking our opinion, about her duty in a certain case which had lain with great weight upon her mind during her long and tedious illness. We the undersigned—waited upon her according to her request. She informed us that Thomas Greene her husband, to whom she had been married not more than a year, had given her such extreme ill treatment previ-

ous to her illness, & from which ill treatment she thinks her long & severe illness proceeded, that she did not feel willing to live with him any longer, and the particular question on which she wished our opinion when we should hear her grievances related; was the following—Whether or not she as a professor of the Christian religion, could consistently with a good conscience & in the fear of God, refuse to live any longer with Mr Greene as his wife. The abuse and ill treatment she said she had received from her husband previous to her illness was such as the following. Viz. That he had been unfaithful to his marriage vows by associating too familiarly with a certain black woman of her acquaintance in the neighbourhood; that what she saw with her own eyes, was that which convinced her of his crim. con. with this black woman; that on a certain sunday shortly before she was taken sick she saw her husband follow said woman from her own house till they disappeared that about an hour after they disappeared her husband returned; that she charged him on his return [with having] intimate connection with this woman that he acknowledged this was the fact, that he shed tears on this occasion and insisted if she would forgive him this time he never would treat her so any more. She also informed us that on a certain evening when they had a family dispute, she left the house & with a small negro girl whom her father had given her she attempted to escape to her fathers; that her husband pursued her, and whipped her all the way back to the stele with beech switches and whipped her very hard. That once when she attempted to escape from him in the night, & had been gone some time before he awoke, he set his tracking dogs on her which wer[e] very fierce though they did not siege her, as she & her little girl squatted in a loop of the fence, and made out to keep them off. That her husband and one of his negro men came up, and he ordered her to get on the negro's back, whom he ordered to carry her back to the house. With this order she refused to comply, apprehending much danger from it, as she was in a family way at the time. He then forcibly set her on the negro's back, who when he carried her back to the house set her down very hard. From which resulted the most serious consequences; and as she thinks her eighteen weeks sickness. When this unfortunate young woman mentioned her husband whipping her; Mr Denson her father desired that we should see her back, which was accordingly made bear by her sister in the most decent & modest manner the nature of the case would admit. On that part of her back where stripes are generally inflicted we saw sundry large welts, of a bluish or livid colour, which appeared to us to be raised by an instrument of correction. And we knew of no other way in which such appearances could be made on the human frame & therefore had no doubt then; nor have we any yet they were made by whipping; the existence of these bale looking welts was not a matter of hear say with us we saw them plainly with our own eyes & examined them minutely.

Notwithstanding all this statement; & what we ourselves saw we gave no opinion at that time to the question [th]is young lady asked us. We viewed it quite a delicate thing to give an opinion on such a subject, an opinion that might operate to the everlasting separation of husband & wife. We thought justice & the sacred dictates of our duty imperiously required us to see the husband & wife face to face before we should hazard an opinion on so serious a subject. We accordingly appointed another day to meet & notified Mr Greene to attend. ~~Mr Green~~ He attended & we heard both their stories face to face. Greene contradicted almost every word Mrs Greene stated, in the most positive manner. Here the matter was fairly at issue the one positively affirming & the other as positively denying. No Witnesses were introduced on either side.

The undersigned were disposed to give unlimited credence to Mrs Green's statements, for sundry reasons such as the following. 1 They saw plainly the marks of the stripes on her back. 2. In refusing to live with her husband she leaves a fine full home, a beautiful & fertile plantation & one amongst the finest houses in the County, to go back to reside with an aged father on rent land. We have no idea, that any young woman in her senses would do this without the most imperious reasons. These reasons, the undersigned have no doubt, this unfortunate young woman must have had. Otherwise they cannot account for her conduct, on any principles of human action with which they are acquainted. 3. Throughout the whole of this conversation, this grossly injured young female appeared to converse with a ~~the~~ Countenance sincere, earnest and consistent. This did not appear to be the case with Mr Greene in the opinion of the undersigned & the undersigned did and still do think that Mrs Greene was ~~still~~ extremely backward to publish her husband's faults & ill-treatment of herself any farther than necessary for her own safety & justification. Nay so far was any thing like this from being the case, That they do believe, had she died by her long illness, as was for a long time expected by herself, her family, her neighbors, & her Physicians; [we] never would have known his base treatment of her. For it was not untill after she found she was likely to recover that her parents & the family were made to know [about how she was treated] And when she told her father she could not be [made] to live with Mr Greene any more, the old Gentleman was manifestly struck with the utmost surprise which showed he knew but little about it [until] his daughter was in the way of recovery. The undersigned [witnesses] not doubting in the least, but the whole deposition of Mrs Greene is strictly true, do most conscientiously give it as their opinion that she is justifiable [in her] refusing to live any longer with her husband.

[signed] Robt Henderson V D M [*sic*]
R. McGavock

The undersigned was not present at the second meeting when Mr. Green was named to be present, but am decidedly of the same opinion with the above named gentlemen as by them expressed—

[signed] Garner McConnico
18.th Sep. 1829

SOURCE: Petition of Martha Smith Green to the Tennessee General Assembly, 19 September 1829, Legislative Petitions, #138-1829, reel 11, TSLA; Deposition of Robert Henderson and R. McGavock, September 1829, Legislative Petitions, #106-1829, reel 11, TSLA; Deposition of Garner McConnico, 18 September 1829, #106-1829, reel 11, TSLA. Granted.[1] PAR #11482911.

1. Martha Smith Green was granted the privileges of a single woman, which meant she could buy and sell property, make contracts, and conduct a business or trade in her own right. Gale W. Bamman and Debbie W. Spero, eds., *Tennessee Divorces, 1797–1858; Taken from 750 Legislative Petitions and Acts* (Nashville: Gale Bamman, 1985), 39.

75. Joshua Thuman, Hardeman County, to Tennessee Assembly, 1829

To The Honble the General Assembly of the State of Tennessee now in Session,

The Petition of Joshua Thuman a Citizen of Hardeman County Would humbly represent to your Honorable bodies that being a colored man although born a free man and engaged in business by which many persons have open accounts with him, yet so it is some delicacy is felt by Magistrates in Suffering him to prove the Said accounts when rendered necessary by his own Oath He therefore prays your honorable bodies to pass an act for his relief in the premise making it lawful for Judges Magistrates &c to allow him the privilege as referred to aforesaid Your Petitioner submits a Certificate here with annexed by which it will appear that his character among ~~the~~ his neighbors is fair and without reproach and your Petitioner in duty bound will ever pray &c—

[signed] Joshua thuman

The Subscribers are well acquainted [w]ith Joshua Thuman the Petitioner above. they Know him to be a Citizen of the County and Town, and can safely say that for moral character and respectability of deportment he is to be Esteemed by all.

Sep 26, 1829

[signed]	E R Belcher	Rufus P. Naly
	Jno. H. Bills	Dry Brown
	Wm. W. Atwood	S. C. Alsobrook
	John Rogers	Geo Lingerfelt
	V. D. Barry	T. W. Pinckard
		[27 additional signatures]

SOURCE: Petition of Joshua Thuman to the Tennessee General Assembly, 26 September 1829, Legislative Petitions, #107-1829, reel 11, TSLA; Certificate, E. R. Belcher et al., 26 September 1829, ibid. No act was passed.[1] PAR #11482904.

1. Despite his failure to "prove his accounts," Joshua Thuman (also spelled Thurman) saved enough to buy his slave sister Harriet. *Private Acts Passed at the First Session of the Twentieth General Assembly of the State of Tennessee. 1833* (Nashville: Allen A. Hall and F. S. Heiskell, 1833), 129.

76. Joseph Mickle, Kershaw District, to South Carolina House, 1829

To the Honourable The hous[e] of Representatives of the State of South Carolina

The Petition of Joseph Mickle of Kershaw District respectfully sheweth; That on the 8th of September 1828, the services for five years, of a free man of colour, named James Walker, was offered to the highest bidder, by the sheriff of Kershaw District. The sum claimed in behalf of the state for said Walkers arearage taxes, was two hundred dollars, and fifteen dollars 37 ½ cents for costs.

Your Petitioner bid that amount, for which he gave his note, payable to the state of South Carolina. Your Petitioner finding his bargain a *hard one,* petitioned your Honourable body to grant him an indulgence in the payment of said note untill the first of January 1830, which was granted.

About the first of last April, the said James Walker made his escape into North Carolina, where he was born, raised, and well known.—In consequence of a reward offered in the news papers by your petitioner, Walker was apprehended, and lodged in the Gaol of Fayettevill. As soon as your petitioner got notice of this apprehention, he dispatched Mr. James B. Berry (who knew Walker, and saw him sold) with the necessary documents to establish the Justness of his claim to the services of said Walker, for five years from the 8th September 1828. On Mr Berry's arrival, he demanded Walker of the Gaoler, who positively refused to deliver him up, alledging at the same time, that Walker was a free man, and would soon be declared so by a proper authority.

By a reference to the accompanying papers marked A & B containing Mr. Berry's account of the transaction, and Mr. Tasmers opinion, your Honourable body will discover the manner in which your petitioner has been deprived of the services of the said James Walker.

Your Petitioner living a distance from Camden, had no knowledg of the Character of James Walker, or he certainly would not have purchased a man, that was a continual pest to society, and augmenting his expences from the day he bought him.

Your Petitioner therefore prays, that your Honourable body will exonerate him from paying the two hundred dollars for the Taxes of the said James Walker (the costs are paid) and order that the sheriff deliver up the note to your Petitioner.

[signed] Jos. Mickle
28th Octr 1829

SOURCE: Petition of Joseph Mickle to the South Carolina House of Representatives, 28 October 1829, Records of the General Assembly, #104, SCDAH. Granted.[1] PAR #11382917.

1. In December 1828, the House granted Mickle an extension on his note. In December 1829, the House Ways and Means Committee recommended that Mickle be "discharged from the payment of his note" entirely and that the sheriff of Kershaw District be credited with two hundred dollars. "Walker is a fellow of dangerous principles and habits," the committee said, "whose removal from the state is to be regarded as an advantage to the public." The Senate concurred, and the resolution became the official response of the assembly. *Acts and Resolutions of the General Assembly of the State of South Carolina, Passed in December, 1828* (Columbia: D. and J. M. Faust, 1829), 28, 29; *Acts and Resolutions of the General Assembly of the State of South Carolina, Passed in December, 1829* (Columbia: D. and J. M. Faust, 1830), 83.

77. Inhabitants of Sampson, Bladen, New Hanover, and Duplin Counties to North Carolina Assembly, ca. 1830

To the Honourable the General Assembly of the State of North Carolina now in Session.

The petition of Sundry Inhabitants of the Counties of Sampson Bladen New Hanover and Duplin humbly Sheweth, that our Slaves are become Almost Uncontroulable they go and come when and where they please and if an Attempt is made to correct them they fly to the Woods and there Continue for months and years commiting grievous depredations on Our Cattle hogs and Sheep and many Other things. And as patrols are of no use on Account of the danger they Subject themselves to and their property. Not long since three patrols two of which for Executing their duty had their dwelling and Out houses burnt down, the Other his fodder stacks all burnt.

Your petitioners pray that an Act of the General Assembly may be passed during the present Session of your honourable body Compelling Each Captain in the Afore named Counties to divide their companies into four Equal divisions which shall be Numbered 1.2.3.& 4. and One Man Shall be Chosen out of Each Company as a Captain or commander of that Company the Rest to be Submissive to his Orders ~~xorders~~ under pen[al]ty of fifty Cent and the Captain or Commander on Neglect or Refusal to Comply with the duties named in Said law Shall pay the Sum of ten dollars, and the first Company Shall be compeled so soon as appointed to search their Respective districts for Runaway Slaves in all the Suspected places houses or thicks where they may Suppose any Runaway or Runaways are concealed with the priviledge of Shooting and destroying all Runaway Slaves who may Refuse to Submit to Said Authority, And Said Company Shall Continue to make Such Search at all times when Necessary for the

Space of three months and shall during the time perform all the duties Required by law for patrols to perform, and at the Expiration of three months the Company No.2 Shall take place and perform in like manner as the first and so Continue untill the whole have served And for Compensation to said Company, the Rewards Already Offered by Owners of Slaves for Apprehending Runaways and on all Others those that have bin Runaway any time Under Six month fifteen dollars and from Six months to One year twenty five dollars and for more than One year fifty dollars which Shall be paid by the Owner of Said Runaway Slave to the Use of Said Company before they give him Up, and all property they may find in the possession of Runaways where the Owner of Said property Cannot be found.

Whereas Many Negro Slaves are Allowed by their Owners to Raise and keep dogs and follow them at large that do great Injury to Our Stocks and if we kill there dogs they will then kill Our dog, Our horse, or Our Cow.

For Remedy Whereof Your petitioners humbly Request that an Act be passed Compelling all persons Owning Slaves at the time of giveing in their list of taxable property to give in on Oath all the dogs their Negroes are Allowed to Raise keep or follow them on the first day of April preceding the time of giveing in their list or Any time Since and pay a tax of five dollars on Each dog so given in. And your petitioners as in duty bound Shall Ever pray,

[signed] P. Cromartie — George A Dyer
Hanson W, Herring — Silas Herring
R W Cromartie — Richard Registe[r]
John Cromartie — G. Downing
A. Cromartie — D, Melvin Senr
[68 additional signatures]

Your petitioners further request your Honerable Body if the method above proposed does not meet your approbation, that you will take our case into consideration & pass such a law, or grant us such relief as you in your wisdom shall think best.

SOURCE: Petition of Inhabitants of Sampson, Bladen, New Hanover, and Duplin Counties to the North Carolina General Assembly, ca. 1830, Records of the General Assembly, Session Records, Miscellaneous Petitions, November 1830–January 1831, NCDAH. Granted.[1] PAR #11283004.

ON FOLLOWING PAGES: A petition from residents in four North Carolina counties in the 1830s expressing their concern about slave unrest. The petition was unusual only in that it came from the inhabitants of several different counties. In theme, tone, argument, and expression of fear, it was similar to many of the documents written to legislatures about the same time. (Courtesy of the Department of Cultural Resources, Division of Archives and History, Raleigh, North Carolina)

To the Honourabl the General Assembly of the State of North Carolina now in Session.

The petition of Sundry Inhabitants of the Counties of Sampson Bladen New Hanover and Duplin humbly Sheweth, that our Slaves are become Almost Uncontroulable they go and come when and where they pleas and if an Attempt is Made to correct them they fly to the Woods and there Continue for Months and years Commiting greevous depredations on Our Cattle hogs and Sheep and Many Other things. And as patrols are of No Use on Account of the danger they Subject themselves to and their property. Not long since three patrols two of which for Executing their duty had their dwelling and Out houses burnt down, the Other his fodder Stacks all burnt.

Your petitioners pray that an Act of the General Assembly may be passed during the present Session of your honourable body Compelling Each Captain in the afore named Counties to divide their companies into four Equal divisions which shall be Numbered 1.2.3.&4. and One Man Shall be Chosen out of Each Company as a Captain or commander of that Company the Rest to be Submissive to his Orders ~~[illegible]~~ under pennelty of fifty Cent and the Captain or Commander on Neglect or Refusial to Comply with the duties Named in Said law Shall pay the Sum of ten dollers, and the first Company shall be compelled so soon as Appointed to search their Respective districts for Runaway Slaves in all the Suspected places houses or thicks where they may suppose any Runaway or Runaways are concealed with the precilidge of Shooting and destroying all Runaway Slaves who may Refuse to Submit to Said Authority, And Said Company Shall Continue to make such Search at all times when Necessary for the Space of three months and shall during the time perform all the duties Required by law for patrols to perform, and at the Expiration of three Months the Company No. 2 Shall take place and perform in like Manner as the first and so Continue untill the whole have served And for Compensation to Said Company the Rewards Already Offered by Owners of Slaves for Apprehending Runaways and on all Others those that have bin Run away any time Under Six month fifteen dollers and from Six months to One year twenty five dollers and for more than One year fifty dollers which Shall be paid by the

Owner of Said Runaway Slave to the use of Said Company before they give him Up and all property they may find in the possession of Runaways where the Owner of Said property Cannot be found.

Whereas Many Negro Slaves are Allowed by their Owners to Raise and keep dogs and follow them at large that do great Injury to Our Stocks and if we kill there dogs they will then kill Our dog, Our horse, or Our Cow.

For Remedy Whereof Your petitioners humbly Request that an Act be pass'd Compelling all persons Owning Slaves at the time of giving in their list of taxable property to give in on Oath all the dogs their Negroes are Allowed to Raise keep or follow them on the first day of April preceding the time of giving in their list or any time Since and pay a tax of five dollars on Each dog so given in. And your petitioners as in duty bound Shall Ever pray.

P. Cromartie
Hanson Wm. Herring
R. & W. Cromartie
John Cromartie
A. Cromartie
J. Cromartie
E. Herring
Rogers Lee
D. H. Spearman
William Spearman
Geo. W. Armway
John Wright senr
Alew Dickerson
Sterling Canady
James Carr
Amos Herring
George Dyer
Silas Herring
Richard Rogers
Wiley Herring
Phillip Herrington
Wiley Hall
Love Co.
Robin Bickstaff
Eli Leacaman
John Cashwill
Owen Jones
S. Cain
W. Young
M. Monroe
James O. Anders
G. Downing
D. Melvin senr.
D. J. Patterson
John Monroe
Daniel Melvin sr
David Cain
John Love McDaniel
Wm. Smith sr
Ivan Horn
G. Melvin
J. Smith
Richard Magee
Robert Fermidge
J. Melvin jr
Walters
Edith Lee

Geo. W. Huffman
Jno. Treadwell
Owen Fennell
Wm. K. Devane
Richard Parish
Wilson Maldraws
James Herring
Nathan Herring
Stephen Herring Jr
Enoch Anders
Raiford Carroll
James Newton
Geo. Fennell
Lewis Highsmith
Isaac Newton

Reuben Rogers
James Mashburn
Charles Page
John Hennesey
Amariah Bland
Alx Hawes
David Wells
James McCalebb
James Rogers
Wm. J. Cogdell
James Meredith
Joseph Stringfield
Amos Johnson
James Cook

William McVirrah
J. D. Beatty

Your petitioners further request your Honorable Body if the method above proposed does not meet your appro=bation, that you will take our case into consideration & pass such a law, or grant us such relief as you in your wisdom shall think best.

1. The North Carolina General Assembly instituted a one hundred dollar penalty for anyone who enticed, or harbored and maintained, a runaway slave, and it created new procedures to form and maintain slave patrols. The county courts could levy a tax of ten cents per "each taxable slave" to help defray expenses, appoint patrol committees of three persons in each captain's district, and command patrollers "to visit the negro houses in their respective districts as often as may be necessary, to inflict a punishment not exceeding fifteen lashes on all slaves they may find off their owner's plantation without a proper permit or pass." *Acts Passed at the General Assembly of the State of North Carolina, at the Session of 1830–31* (Raleigh: Lawrence and Lemay, 1831), 12, 17–18.

78. Samuel Miller to the Mississippi Legislature, ca. 1830s

To the honorable members of the Legislature of the State of Mississippi convened at the Seat of government, at Jackson, in said state

Your petitioner Samuel Miller would respectfully represent to your honorable body, that in consideration of the honesty and fidelity of a negro woman, slave named Martha Tyler aged about 30 years, belonging to your petitioner: he has determined to emancipate said negress, should such a step meet the approbation of your honble body. Said negress your petitioner has owned and possessed for many years passed; and who since she has been in his servitude, has by her upright ~~&~~ and honorable conduct, rendered herself a favourate of your petitioner: so much so that he has resolved, by all the means within his power to aid her final emancipation. Your petitioner is aware, that the inclination of the public is somewhat opposed to the grant of such privelige; in consequence of the frequency of such applications: but when considerations, overbalancing those of public interest, require the exercise of such privelige; your petitioner is assured, that there will be found an inclination in your honble body, to further the philanthropic views of the master; who desires in this manner to recompence the faithfulness and integrity of his Servant. Your petitioner reflects, that he is now advancing in years and knows not at what hour the hand of death, may prevent his paying this last act of benevolence and kindness to a servant endeared to him by years of faithful servitude—Your petitioner has therefore resolved *in time* to attempt the consumation of a ~~the~~ purpose, which might be defeated by longer delay.

With these considerations presented your petitioner hopes that your honble body, will coincide with his views and meet his expectations, by the passage of legislative provision permitting her emancipation upon such terms as to your honble body may seem meet; and as in duty bound your petitioner will Ever pray &c

[signed] Samuel Miller

In aid of the object of this petition We reccommend the views of the petitioner to the consideration of the Legislature—
[signed] C. Rawlings

SOURCE: Petition of Samuel Miller to the Mississippi General Assembly, ca. 1830s, Records of the Legislature, Petitions and Memorials, 1817–39, RG 47, MDAH. No act was passed. PAR #11000012.

79. Jeremiah Gill, Jefferson County, to the Mississippi Assembly, 1830

To the Senate and House of Representatives of the State of Mississippi in General Assembly convened.

The humble petition of Jeremiah Gill, respectfully represents to your Honorable Body, that he is a free man of colour, and by the industry and economy of many years, he has been able to accumulate a sum of money sufficient to purchase, from Mr. Caleb Reed of the County of Jefferson, his, your petitioner's wife Amy, and his daughter Betsey.—That he is now advanced in years, and being apprehensive, that in the event of his said wife and daughter's surviving him, they may, through the tyranick grasp and relentless cupidity of some unfeeling wretch, be deprived of that portion of liberty, which the sweat of your petitioner's humble brow has purchased for them.—Your petitioner further begs leave humbly to represent to your Honorable Body, that in the decline of life, ~~he is~~ he is very solicitous, so far as the humility of his situation may enable him, to provide against any event that may deprive his said wife and daughter of their liberty, and to prevent the yoke of bondage from being fastened upon their defenseless necks after his death, he now humbly implores the aid of the protecting shield of your legislative body.

Through the kind indulgence of those Gentlemen of his County, whose benevolence and sense of justice has induced them to bestow upon your humble petitioner, the benefit of their names, hereunto subscribed, he begs leave to represent to your Honorable Body, that the character of your petitioner is that of a peaceable, orderly, sober industrious honest and submissive man of colour, & that the characters of his wife and daughter are equally good and irreproachable. In the event of their surviving your petitioner he, before his death, and they afterwards, will be able to give satisfactory guarrantees against the contingency of their becoming expensive to the State or to any County or Corporation therein in which they may reside, as well as of their orderly, peaceable and submissive deportment and character.—

Wherefore your petitioner humbly prays that your Honorable Body would manumit and forever absolve from the bonds of slavery, his aforesaid wife and daughter, and enable them to assume the Sir-name of Gill and be called and Known by the names of Amy Gill and Betsy Gill, and that their manumission may be subject to any condition or conditions which your Honorable Body may deem reasonable, humane and liberal.—And your humble petitioner will ever pray, &c.

his
Jeremiah X Gill
mark

We whos names are hereunto subscribed, being acquainted with the petitioner, Jeremiah Gill, a free man of colour, do concur with him in the representations of the foregoing petition, and recommend the prayers thereof to be granted by the legislature of our State

[signed]
John J. Robertson
A. K. Macleod
John Airs
R. Dunbar
A. B. Sims
James Kelly
Dnl McKey
J. E. Stampley
A. G. [Dornpoole?]
Hiram Baldwin
[6 additional signatures]

SOURCE: Petition of Jeremiah Gill to the Mississippi Senate and House of Representatives, 1830, Records of the Legislature, Petitions and Memorials, 1830, RG 47, MDAH. No act was passed.[1] PAR #11083005.

1. A bill was drafted concerning Gill's wife and daughter, but it never became law. See "A Bill to Be Entitled 'An Act to Emancipate Certain Slaves Therein Mentioned,'" 23 November 1830, Records of the Legislature, with above petition.

80. Austin Grisham, Williamson County, to Tennessee Assembly, ca. 1831

To the Honble,

The Senate & House of Representatives of the State of Tennessee, Now in Session—

Your Petitioner Austin Grisham would most respectfully represent, that several years ago Mr. Henry A. Burge departed this life, leaving a widow & two infant Children, Thomas & Mary—He died without having made a will, and left Considerable property—that sometime after his death, his widow was appointed guardian for his two infant Children, and took upon herself the discharge of the duties pertaining to the appointment, which will, if Considered necessary, be proven by the order of the ~~Davidson~~ Williamson County Court, making the appointment—Your petitioner states that on the 23rd day of July 1829, and after the sd. appointment was made, he intermarried with the sd. Widow of the sd. Mr. Henry A. Burge; that at the time of sd. marriage she had the Controul of several slaves belonging to her wards, that among them is a boy, named Nathan, Now, between eleven and twelve years old—Your Petitioner States that for three or four years back, this boy, Nathan, has been in the Constant habit of running away; that he has employed all the means he Could, himself, devise, to prevent it; that he has obtained the aid of other experienced Persons to the same object, but has failed in every expedient—the habit is increasing—And your Petitioner doth verily believe that nothing short of actual Confinement will, or Can restrain him from an indulgence in this vice—He says that he is a boy of more than ordinary Capacity, And he doth believe if the habit Complained of, should increase with his years (and he doth believe it will) he will be lost to the heirs, perhaps, entirely, by absconding, & finding a residence in some place or county where they Cannot find him, or, if found, from which they Cannot take him—

Your petitioner states that by law he has no right to sell him, tho' he is Confident it would be to the advantage of the heirs that he should be sold—He further states that his wife, the guardian of the heirs, is extremely anxious that he should be sold; that her security is also desireous that it should be done

Therefore, your petitioner respectfully solicits your Honorable Body that you would pass a law directing him the sd. negro boy Nathan to be sold, or authorising your petitioner to sell him, upon such terms as shall deem proper to you, and with such modification as will secure to the said heirs the money arising from the sale, and the interest thereon.

And your Petitioner as in duty bound will ever Pray.

[signed] Austin Grisham . . . [docket information]

Some twelve or fifteen months ago, I was in want of a boy, and upon some inquiry was informed that I could hire one of Mr. Austin Grisham—And upon application to him he agreed to hire me a black boy named Nathan, ten or eleven years old.

I took possession of him, and was very much pleased with him.—He was ~~ob~~ obedient, active, & intelligent far beyond most boys of his age whom I had ever seen

—In about two weeks, (my belief is) after I had taken possession of him, in my absence, he ran away. And upon inquiry as to the Cause, I was satisfied he had none—In a day or two, I saw Mr. Grisham and informed him of the boy's departure and he then told me, it was his habit, but he had hoped he would not do so, while I had him, as the boy had Promised him he would not—After three or four days' inquiry I got him; And, being much pleased with him as a servant, and anxious to Keep him for a time, I resolved to pursue Such Course as would break the habit, if possible, and therefore, I only *talked* to him of the impropriety of his conduct, when I [told] him in such language as I am Confident he Perfectly understood—From his manner & his language he seemed to regret what he had done, & promised faithfully that he would not repeat the act—On the very next day, however, without any earthly cause, he absconded again, And after three or four days' inquiry & search I found him—I then joined Punishment to advice, and he again promised, faithfully, that he would do so no more—In six or seven days he repeated the offence, and eluded my search for about a week—when I got him, I had an iron Collar made for him & put a large padlock on it, and in this Condition set him about his business—On the same night ~~on~~ which this was done, he eloped again and I resolved to have nothing more to do with him & so notified Mr.Grisham—I believe he could not be reclaimed & believe it, still.

[signed] James I. Dozier
Nov 21, 1831.

I am the security of Mrs Eliza Grisham, late Burge, the Widow of Mr. H. A Burge, deceased, and Guardian for her two infant Children, Thomas & Mary Burge—I Know the Negro boy Nathan, whom Austin Grisham, the present husband of the sd. Eliza, is anxious to sell, and have no objection to his doing so, indeed, I am of opinion that it should be done, as he is the most habitual runaway, I ever Knew of his age—He is a boy of, greatly more than Common Capacity, And I think it more than probable, that if his Cunning & disposition to runaway shall increase with his years, that he may have the adroitness, before the sd. infant children, Thomas & Mary Burge shall have arrived at the age of twenty one to escape entirely. Given Under my hand this day of November 1831

[signed] Jas. Condon

SOURCE: Petition of Austin Grisham (also spelled Gresham) to the General Assembly, ca. 1831, Legislative Petitions, #18-1831, reel 18, TSLA; Deposition of James I. Dozier, 21 November 1831, ibid.; Deposition of James Condon, November 1831, ibid. Granted.[1] PAR #11483110.

1. As his wife's guardian and Thomas and Mary Burge's stepfather, Austin Grisham was permitted to sell "a certain negro boy slave named Nathan" for the best price he could obtain. *Private Acts Passed at the Stated Session of the Nineteenth General Assembly of the State of Tennessee. 1831* (Nashville: Allen A. Hall and Frederick S. Heiskell, 1832), 224–25.

81. James Spare et al., New Castle County, to Delaware Assembly, 1831

To the Honorable Senate and House of Representatives of the State of Delaware in General Assembly met.

The Memorial of the undersigned inhabitants of New Castle county, respectfully represents: That the public tranquillity of New Castle county, in common with other parts of the State, has been much disturbed by rumours of intended insurrectionary movements among the black portion of our population. To such a height did the alarm arise, that it was deemed prudent in many places, to take precautionary measures, not entirely in accordance with the laws of the State, yet believed it to be loudly demanded, in order to quiet the excitement, which existed far and wide on this delicate and dangerous subject.

Your Memorialists are not aware that any conspiracy had really been formed, or any time fixed upon, for a general insurrection; yet they are fully satisfied, that for some time past, attempts have been made to prepare the minds of that portion of our population, for such an event. This they believe, has been done at meetings, held under the pretence of religious worship; and they also have reason to think, that many, if not *all,* the black preachers, who come into *this* State, from *other* States, are regular and constant preachers of sedition, to our slaves and free blacks at their night meetings, where no whites are present. This opinion is not hazarded lightly, but is founded upon the voluntary disclosures of some of the black people, who have been present at such meetings.

While your Memorialists are fully sensible of the great importance of religious worship, in all well regulated communities, and would not abridge the religious privileges of any portion of our population, or take aught from the opportunities of religious instruction, which might be offered to our blacks; they must respectfully solicit the interposition of the Legislature, to prohibit all *nocturnal* assemblies, of our coloured population, under any pretence whatever; and further, that the ingress of free blacks into this State, upon the plea of preaching, be also made unlawful. Your memorialists would respectfully call your attention, to the fact, that while the blacks received their religious instruction, from white preachers of the gospel, and had their class meetings, prayer meetings and camp meetings, conducted by white instructors, the public mind was tranquil, and can it be doubted, that they were as carefully instructed in *religious* duties *then,* as they are *now,* by their ignorant and fanatic black preachers?

Your Memorialists also believe, that the public safety and peace require, that it should be declared unlawful, for slaves, or free blacks, to own or possess fire arms and other military weapons. At the present time our blacks are well armed, almost every man possessing an efficient gun. Whether in the present excited state of public feeling, this should be permitted, is submitted to the wisdom of the Legislature.

In calling the attention of the Legislature to this important subject, your memorialists disclaim the least wish, to abridge any privileges, which they think, can be granted, or continued to that unfortunate class of people, consistently with the safety and quiet of the State. But they *cannot* shut their eyes to the fact, that a deep and growing discontent, pervades the blacks, not only in this State, but throughout the Union, which they fear, is assuming a most dangerous aspect; and they believe the time has fully arrived, when it has become the part of prudence, to take such precautionary measures, as may appear best calculated to avert the threatened danger.

November 25, 1831.

[signed]	James Spare	Wm Wilson
	Zachariah Jones	John Dugless
	Abm. S. Crawford	John C manlove
	Charles Jones	John M. Woods
	Collins Tatman	Levi Henderson
		[15 additional signatures]

SOURCE: Petition of James Spare et al. to the Senate and House of Representatives of Delaware, 25 November 1831, General Assembly, Legislative Papers, DSA. Granted.[1] PAR #10383201.

1. In 1832, lawmakers prohibited free people of color from possessing a "gun, pistol, sword or any warlike instrument" unless they first obtained a written certificate signed by five or more "respectable and judicious citizens of the neighborhood." Section 2 of the law forbade free blacks from gathering in groups of more than twelve after ten o'clock at night unless supervised by three "respectable white men." The penalty for assembling illegally was a fine of ten dollars. *Laws of the State of Delaware [Passed at a Session of the General Assembly in 1832]* (Dover: n.p., [1833]), 208–9.

82. A. P. Upshur et al., Northampton County, to Virginia Legislature, 1831

To the Legislature of Virginia, The petition of the undersigned, citizens of County of Northampton, respectfully represents:

By the last census of the U. States it appears that there are in this county 3573 whites, 3734 slaves, and 1334 free persons of colour. By a comparison with the census of preceding years, it also appears that the proportion of free persons of colour to our white inhabitants is annually increasing. A fact of this sort under any circumstances, would be a source of well founded uneasiness. The free persons of colour in Virginia, form an anomalous population, standing in a relation to our society, which naturally exposes them to distrust & suspicion. Inferior to the whites in intelligence & information; degraded by the stain which attaches to their colour; excluded from many civil privileges which the humblest white man enjoys, and denied all participation in the government, it would be wholly absurd to expect from them any attachment to our laws & institutions nor any sympathy with our people. On the other hand, the enjoyment of personal freedom is in itself a sufficient mark of distinction between them & our slaves, and elevates them, at least in their own opinion, to a higher condition in life. Standing thus in a middle position between the two extremes of our society, and despairing of ever attaining an equality with the higher grade, it is natural that they should connect themselves in feeling & interest, with the slaves among whom many of their domestic ties are formed, and to whom they are bound by the sympathies scarcely less strong, which spring from their common complexion. Independent, therefore of any particular facts calculated to excite our alarms, the worst evils might justly be apprehended from such an increase of their numbers as would give them confidence in their physical power, while it would enlarge their means of information, facilitate their intercommunications, and thus add to their capabilities of mischief. Unhappily, however, this is no longer a subject of mere speculation. The scenes which have recently passed around us contain a melancholly & impressive lesson upon this subject, to which the most careless and supine among us cannot be inattentive—The caution which these scenes suggest, is of peculiar importance to us.

From the number of our free negroes, and from the idle & vicious habits of most of them, we have stronger reason than exi[s]ts in most of our counties, to suspect dangerous intrigues with our slaves;[1] nor can we be insensible to the great aid which our slaves would derive from that source, in any actual attempts against us. Our peninsular situation also, cutts off from us that prompt assistance from other parts of the State, on which every County exposed to the harrow of a servile insurrection, would naturally rely. While, therefore, we have full confidence in our power of self defense under all circumstances, and while we entertain no fear that any attempt of that kind would be ultimately successful, even against our own unassisted efforts, we might justly apprehend greater difficulty in suppressing it, and more disasters from its progress, than would be looked for in most other places. Deeply impressed with these considerations we have met together in our respective neighbourhoods, in order to consult on the most expedient mode of getting rid of our free negroes, whom we regard as a most prolific source of evil to our community. In these meetings we have adopted the following resolutions:

1st. Resolved, That it is absolutely necessary, not only to the correct government of our slaves, but also to the peace & security of our society, that all free persons of colour should be promptly removed from this county.

2nd. That, as a measure of this sort will necessarily produce much private inconvenience and suffering, we will endeavour so to effect our object as to render the calamity as little oppressive as possible.

3rd. That we will not willingly entail upon any other white community an evil which we feel to be intolerable to ourselves.

4th. That the free negroes of our county ought, if practicable, to be sent to Liberia in Africa.

5th. That to effect their removal, John Eyre, John Addison, John T. Wilson, John C. Parramore, Abel P. Upshur, John Goffigon, Jesse Simpkins, Daniel Fitchett, John Ker, George Yerby, James Goffigon, William G. Smith, Levern E. Parker, Little Upshur, Edmund W. P. Downing, Nathaniel J. Winder, Nathaniel Burris, and William S. Floyd, be a committee to borrow a sum of money not exceeding fifteen thousand dollars for the payment of which a tax shall annually be imposed upon each citizen of this county equal to the tax he may pay to the State; so that such tax be at least equal to his revenue tax of the present year, until the principal and interest shall be paid.

6th. That the committee appointed by the 5th resolution be authorised to open a correspondence with the Agent of the Colonization Society, to ascertain what aid can be immediately, or in a short time afforded by that Society, for the removal of the free negroes from this county to Liberia, in Africa.

7th. That so soon as the sum authorised to be borrowed by the 5th resolution, or such part thereof, as the Committee shall think necessary to borrow shall be obtained . . . [the Committee shall] make known the same to the free negroes, & to make arrangements for ~~thir~~ [their] removal to Liberia of such of them as are willing to go there.

8th. That our representatives in the Legislature be instructed to use their best exertions to procure the passage of a law giving effect to the preceding resolutions; and if no such law can be procured, that they devote themselves zealously to any & every other plan of legislation which may be calculated to rid us promptly, effectually, & entirely of our free coloured population.

9th. That our representatives be instructed to vote for every measure, whether of a general or local character, which may have for its object the removal of the free people of coloure~~d population~~ from the state at large or any part thereof.

10th. That after the arrangements from their removal have been made, we pledge ourselves not to employ, or have any dealings with any free negros in the county.

11th. That we pledge ourselves not to rent to any free negro any house or land, and that we will forthwith give notice to those with whom we have contracted to quit on the 1st day of June next.

12th. That we earnestly recommend to the owners of vessels in this county, immediately, or as soon as practicable, to discontinue the use & employment of slaves and free negroes on board their vessels; as we do firmly believe the practice dangerous to the peace & safety of our society.

13th. That a Petition to the General Assembly in conformity with the preceding resolutions, and more particularly the 5th, be forthwith prepared and presented to the Citizens for their signature.

14th. That the proceedings of this meeting be communicated to the Citizens of Accomack County, in such manner as the Chairman of this meeting thinks best, with a request of concurrence on the part of the Citizens of that County, with the views & objects of the Citizens of this County. It will be perceived from these resolutions, that we are willing to rely for the accomplishment of our Object, upon our own resources alone, without asking any assistance from the treasury of the State. Should it however, fall in with the course of public policy, to extend such assistance to particular communities circumstanced as ours is, we shall acknowledge it on our part with proper gratitude. Yet we do not solicit any such support. The evil of which we complain is found to be no longer endurable, without the most serious dangers to the peace &

security of our county, & we are willing to rid ourselves of it at every sacrifice & every hazard.

The corrupting influences of that part of our population have long been felt as a serious impediment in the way of our prosperity; & the time has now arrived, when we can no longer doubt that they are equally hostile to our personally [*sic*] safety. We therefore earnestly yet respectfully pray that such a law may pass as will enable us promptly to carry into effect such of the ~~foregoing~~ preceding resolutions as are properly the subjects of legislation. And as we are not without apprehension, from the number & character of those on whom such a law will operate, that it will not be executed without some opposition, we trust that it will be ~~granted~~ armed with all adequate sanctions, from whatever source such opposition may arise, & your petitioners will ever pray

[signed]	A P Upshur	Robert J Nottingham
	Geo. L. Yerby	Thos I Nottingham
	Jas. Goffigon	J W Leatherberry
	William Dunton	Victor A Mast
	Jno. T. Wilson	S B Nottingham
		[186 additional signatures]

SOURCE: Petition of A. P. Upshur et al. to the Virginia Legislature, 6 December 1831, Legislative Petitions, Northampton County, VSA. Granted.[2] PAR #11683101.

1. In 1830, free blacks represented 15 percent of Northampton County's total population and 26 percent of its black population. Slaves and free blacks combined made up 59 percent of the county's total. In Virginia, free blacks represented 4 percent of the total population and 9 percent of the black population. Slaves and free blacks combined made up 43 percent of the state's population. *Fifth Census; or, Enumeration of the Inhabitants of the United States, 1830* (Washington, D.C.: Duff Green, 1832), 84–85; Ira Berlin, *Slaves without Masters: The Free Negro in the Antebellum South* (New York: Pantheon Books, 1974), 136–37, 396–99.

2. *Acts Passed at a General Assembly of the Commonwealth of Virginia, Begun and Held at the Capitol, in the City of Richmond, on Monday, the Fifth Day of December, in the Year of Our Lord, One Thousand Eight Hundred and Thirty-One . . .* (Richmond: Thomas Ritchie, 1831), 23. Though pertaining to only one county, the act was deemed "sufficiently important" to be included among the public acts.

83. Inhabitants of New Bern to North Carolina Assembly, 1831

To the Honorable the Senate and House of Commons of North Carolina, in General Assembly.

The Memorial & Petition of the undersigned citizens of the Town of Newbern,

Respectfully sheweth unto your honorable body, That many of the free negroes residing in the Town of Newbern, claim the right of voting for a Representative of said Town in the House of Commons, and that fifty or more actually exercise that right. Your petitioners further shew, that those who advocate this claim to one of the highest & most important privileges of Freemen, allege, that it is conferred upon this class of inhabitants by the ~~eighth~~ ninth section of the Constitution of this State, which declares,

Sec-9. "That all persons possessed of a freehold in any town in this state having a right of representation, and also all freemen who have been inhabitants of any such town twelve months next before and at the day of election, and shall have paid public taxes, shall be entitled to vote for a member to represent such town in the House of Commons Provided always, that this section shall not entitle any inhabitants of such town to vote for members of the House of Commons for the county in which he may reside; nor any freeholder in such county, who resides without or beyond the limits of such town, to vote for a member for s~~uch~~aid town.["]

Your Petitioners respectfully shew unto your Honorable Body, that they are sincerely of opinion, that the term *Freemen* is inapplicable to this class. It is a term well known to the Common Law, which at the time of the adoption of the Constitution, was, (with exceptions irrelevant to the subject matter) the law of the land. A Freema[n] Your Memorialists beleive, is by that standard, also a lawful man, "*Homo liber et legalis*" one who is not restrained from making contracts of any kind, except such as are forbidden to all citizens generally; one who can sit on juries, and can participate in the administration of the law—one against whose life & character the testimony of a slave is not admitted. Your Memorialists need not remind your Honorable Body that, our law does not recognise this class of persons as possessing these rights and immunities, or as having the capacity to acquire them; they are forbidden to contract marriage except with thier own class—they have not the capacity to become qualified to sit on juries, as the peers or equals of the Freemen of the State: they are not called upon to aid in the execution of the civil or criminal process of the law: they may be subjected even to the punishment of death on the testimony of a slave. Can these disabilities belong to the Freeman? Is it not a paradox in American polity to say, that a man shall exercise what has always been deemed the ~~brightest~~ highest & noblest trust and power which can be confided to the citizen of a free country, and yet himself be socially degraded by the *general* law of the land.

But your Memorialists would invite the attention of your Honorable Body to a very brief view of our civil history, as connected with this class of persons, from which they think an ines[tima]ble argument may be drawn against thier claim. It is notorious as matter of history, that the African race were originally introduced into this State as *Slaves;* they remain such, except only so far as thier disabilities and incapabilities have been removed by the statute law of the land. It would hardly be contended, that the master alone could confer upon the slave so important a right and power as the right of suffrage: Its consequences would be at once most momentous to the State, and exceedingly liable to abuse. It would, moreover, be at least as great an act of power as the naturalization of an alien, which by the common law, could only be done by the sovereign legislative authority. We find by the preamble of the act of 1777, chap 109, that previous to that statute, the intervention of the courts was not necessary to emancipate a slave; the Legislature of that day denounced the freeing of slaves, as then practised, as "evil & pernicious," and one which ought to be guarded against "by every well-wisher & friend of his Country." The Constitution was adopted in December, 1776, and declares in its preamble, that it is formed by the Representatives of the "Freemen" of North Carolina. What Freemen? The slaves, who had then been freed by thier master alone, and whose freedom is denounced as the consequence of an evil & pernicious practice? Surely not. It will be recollected that the Legislature of 1777 was composed of many of the Patriots who formed the Constitution in 1776, and who of course were well acquainted with the meaning and spirit of that instrument. Your Memorialists have understood, and they beleive, that for many years immediately following the adoption of the Constitution, no claim to suffrage was asserted on thier behalf, and that it has been declared by some of the venerable men who were contemporary with the formation of the Constitution, that they did not vote in the election of the delegates who framed it.

If this declaration be true, your Memorialists humbly conceive that it is decisive against thier claim; for, when the Congress of 1776 announce themselves in the preamble to the Constitution, as the "Representatives of the Freemen, &c", the question occurs, "what Freemen?" and if thier constituents were the *free white* men *alone,* as your Memorialists sincerely beleive, then a ready explanation is afforded of the sense in which they use the same term in the ninth section, when they prescribe the qualifications for the voters for the House of Commons. Your Memorialists have thus far considered the question in a merely legal view; but there are other considerations of infinite moment, and intimately connected with the happiness & honor of our country, which give to this question an awful importance. A very large portion of our population are slaves, and recent occurrences must deeply impress on your Honorable Body the vital necessity of keeping them in a state of discipline and subordination. Your Memorialists beleive they hazard nothing, in saying that permitting free negroes to vote at elections, contributes to excite & cherish a spirit of discontent and disorder among the slaves.—During the heat of party contest, they are counted & caressed by both parties, and treated apparently with respect & attention. When the slave sees him whom he regards as his associate and equal, and who, is perhaps in fact his brother, thus respectfully treated by men of high character,—when he sees that his favour is eagerly sought, and even his prejudices flattered, we respectfully ask your Honorable Body, if the barrier of *opinion* which alone keeps him in subjection, is not effectually under-mined? With these practices is combined, almost necessarily, that of treating them for their votes. The slaves intermix with them, and indeed, are often auxiliary to the practises upon thier free brethren. Drunken free negroes and slaves intermixed, parade our streets at night, and enjoy a riotous license of the most disgusting & fearful character. Will not practises such as these, in the language of the late eminent Judge, when speaking of conduct far less dangerous, "naturally excite in the slave, discontent with their condition, encourage idleness & disobedience, and lead possibly in the course of human events, to the most calamitous of all contests, *a bellum servile;* a servile war."

Your Memorialists humbly pray your Honorable Body by Declartory act, a Resolution, to ascertain and determine the true construction of the Constitution upon the subject matter of this their Memorial.

New Bern December 6th 1831

[signed] Jos L Fowler, Thomas Watson, Danl Jackson Jr, Moses W. Jarvis, Moses Jarvis, Wm C Hunter, Henry Dewey, Jno Street, Thos Sparrow, Alexander Meadow [154 additional signatures]

SOURCE: Petition of Inhabitants of New Bern to the General Assembly, 15 December 1831, Records of the General Assembly, Session Records, NCDAH. Referred to the Judiciary Committee. No act was passed.[1] PAR #11283108.

1. Free blacks were stripped of the vote in North Carolina following the ratification of the 1835 state constitution. John Hope Franklin, *The Free Negro in North Carolina, 1790–1860* (1943; reprint, Chapel Hill, University of North Carolina Press, 1995), 116–20.

84. Inhabitants of Craven County to North Carolina Assembly, 1831

To the Honourable the General Assembly of the State of North Carolina;

The undersigned inhabitants of the County of Craven, beg leave to represent to your Honorable body a grievance, to which they are subject, and which must continue to oppress them, unless it is remedied by the intervention of your honourable body.—

Your Petitioners reside upon Neuse River and the adjacent Creeks above the town of New Bern, and are much injured and interrupted both in their avocations, and in the management of their farms and negroes, by the large gangs of slaves, who come up from the Town of Newbern and the neighbourhood thereof, in boats, with passes from their owners or those having the control of them, to sell, buy, traffick, and fish in the neighbourhood of Your Petitioners, to their great annoyance and manifest injury.—

Your Petitioners further shew unto your honourable body, that the passes given to the said slaves are for a month's or more duration, and under their sanction, they trade with, and Corrupt the Slaves of your Petitioners, induce them to runaway, and when runaway employ them, in dragging skimming nets for the purpose of Catching fish, and pilfering the farms of your Petitioners.—Your Petitioners would call the attention of your Honourable body, to the grievance of permitting Slaves to fish either during the night or day, without the presence of a white person, and to the many facilities and advantages which those enjoy who live on the water, have the command of a boat, and who thus elude the vigilance of the Patrol, and escape from performing the labour due to their owners.—To the end therefore that your Honourable body would take into consideration the law with regard to the subject of granting passes to Slaves, ~~and of pem~~ thus indirectly permitting the owners of Slaves to nullify, the acts of Assembly with regard to Slaves hiring their own time, and likewise the Subject of trading with Slaves,[1] and also the indiscriminate permission given to them to fish at large upon the waters of this State, your Petitioners have deemed it Expedient to lay before you this Exposition of their grievances, with the humble hope, that they may be remedied by the interposition of your honourable body.—

[signed]	William Gatlin	Silas Gaskins
	Allen Ernest	Ephraim Arthur
	Charles Kelley	Arthur Gaskins
	Levin Gaskins	Guilford Gaskins
	Daniel Gaskins	Reding Wiley
		[46 additional signatures]

SOURCE: Petition of Inhabitants of Craven County to the North Carolina General Assembly, 19 December 1831, Records of the General Assembly, Session Records, NCDAH. Granted.[2] PAR #11283107.

1. In 1794, the North Carolina General Assembly passed a law prohibiting slaves from hiring out their own time. In addition, slaves were not permitted to go about as free persons, even with the consent of their owner. According to laws passed in 1787 and 1788, slaves were forbidden to barter and trade "any Commodities whatsoever." John Spencer Bassett, *Slavery in the State of North Carolina,* Johns Hopkins University Studies in Historical and Political Science, vol. 17 (Baltimore: Johns Hopkins Press, 1899), 335–36 (self-hire); John D. Cushing, comp., *The First Laws of the State of North Carolina,* 2 vols. (Wilmington, Del.: Michael Glazier, 1984), 2:609, 633–34 (bartering and trading).

2. In 1831, North Carolina passed a law prohibiting anyone from working "any seine, set net, skimming net, fish trap or slide" on the Neuse River below New Bern or on the Neuse and Trent rivers above New Bern from sunset on Saturday to sunset on Monday during the four months from mid-January to mid-April. Slaves violating the act would receive thirty-nine lashes "on his or her bare back." *Acts Passed by the General Assembly of the State of North Carolina, at the Session of 1831–32* (Raleigh: Lawrence and Lemay, 1832), 129–30.

85. Citizens of Charles City and New Kent Counties to Virginia Assembly, 1831

To the Honourable Legislature of Virginia

The undersigned, inhabitants of the County of Charles City and New Kent beg leave to represent to your honourable body, that it is the almost universal custom with the owners of mills in this county, and indeed in the whole of the lower part of the state to employ, coloured persons, *slaves,* to attend to their Mills and to do the duties of miller—That the grievances under which they labour in consequence of this custom, are burdensome and ought to be redressed Few or none of those thus employed are honest, and we are all of us constantly subjected, to ~~much~~ great inconvenience & much vexation, in geting returned to us from the mills what we are by law entitled to receive And the numerous cheateries and deceptions, to which we are subject are of that nature that it is very difficult to detect them, and even when detected, it is pretty much at the discretion of the mill owner whether the offender, shall be punished, or the grievance redressed,—In the neighborhood of almost every mill there are located squads of free negroes, who it is believed are sustained almost entirely, by the millers, with the unlawful gains, taken from their customers And these slave millers are a sort of link of communication between our slaves and the free persons of colour, by which we believe much injury is done to our best interests—how these evils are to be remedied, we are all willing to submit entirely to your wisdom, but take leave to suggest that if a law were passed, requiring every owner of a mill to keep employed as his miller a white man, & for the purpose of insuring their employment only of such as were honest, make it necessary that he should obtain from the court of the County a certificate of good character much if not all of the grievance under which we labour might be redressed—all which is respectfully submitted.

[signed]	Wm F Walker	Henry Bowy
	Jno Minge	Robt. C. Walker
	John W. Bradley	John L. Egmon
	Jno B Christian	Edmund Christian
	Littleberry H Bradley	R. W Christian
		[53 additional signatures]

SOURCE: Petition of Citizens of Charles City and New Kent Counties to the Virginia General Assembly, 27 December 1831, Legislative Petitions, VSA. Rejected. PAR #11683108.

86. Residents of Maury, Bedford, Giles, Hickman, Williamson, and Lincoln Counties to Tennessee Assembly, ca. 1832

To the Honl. The Legislature of the state of Tennessee—

The subscribers having understood and learnt that an act was passed at the last Session of your Honl. body, Entitled "An act to amend the Laws of this State in relation to the government of slaves and for the persons of color," one Section of which makes it an indictable offence for "any owner or other person having charge of any slave or slaves,["] to "permit him or them to go about the Country under pretext of ~~pratici~~ practicing medicine or healing the Sick."[1] Without pretending to question ~~of~~ the [wisdom] of this law, as one [of a] general ~~nature~~ character ~~and that in its general aplication,~~ or denying that in its general operation it may not be productive of much good, yet we would most respectfully ask of your Honl. body to [modify] its general operation so far as to permit, a negro man, named Jack, the property of Mr. William H. Macon of Maury County, t[o] practice ~~sing~~ as ~~heretofore~~ he has been heretofore doing. We ask this from a full knowledge of the Character, of this boy; though he may be a *slave,* yet in the opinion of the undersigned, his character for honesty and ~~fair~~ correct deportment, is fair [an]d not often excelled by many who profess to possess more than he does—In his profession, we speak from our knowledge of his practice we are free & happy to say that he has practised with great & unparalled success, for many years, none having any cause to complain of either a want of fidelity or success among his patients. We are residents the Several Counties of Maury, Bedford, Giles, Hickman, & Williamson, and Lincoln, and ask the passage of this Law, granting permission to this ~~boy~~ to practice, with a firm belief that the public good will be advanced by its pas[sage] from our knowledge of the character of this boy, and his practice for Several years—

Subscribers from the County of Maury

[signed]

A L. Pickard
Johnston Craig
Reubin Reynolds
Milledge S Durham
Ezekiel Hogges
Wm B Brown
Jansen [Colkril?]
Edward Grimes
James Grimes
henry Grimes
[121 additional signatures]

[Doctor Jack has] bin healing diseases more or less for the last Six or Seven years and has done much good and not any harm [to anyone] that ever has bin laid to his charge

[signed] John Boon

Subscribers from Bedford County

James Y. Green 1
Hugh McClelan 2
James McClelan 3
C. C. Cathey Dr 4
J N Rainey Jr
Edward Walker
Wm J Sanders
[torn page]
John M Dawson
Thomas Atkerson
Milton Powell

I do Certify that I have bin acquainted with the general character of Dr Jack for the past Three years and know him to be an honest faithfull slave, I am also acquainted with his skill in the art of healing disease and know it to be very good and not easy to be exceded he has . . . [torn page]

This is to certify that I had a case of sickness in my family caled by the phisitions the D[ropsy?] & baffled the[ir] skill which I do believe Dr Jack has made a firm cure wheather or not his medicine cured or no I cant tell but this I do c[e]rtify that sencible releaf was felt on taking the first dose & continued to mend & is at this time in good health—

[signed] . . . [illegible]

I believe that nature has wisely (& graciously) formed roots, & herbs, to meet every complaint incident to the human species, & that [if] men would study to grow acquainted with them & their uses, & would drench less with drugs, the world would be people'd a great deal sooner, & mankind would enjoy a great deal more health & strength.

An old observer . . . [certificates omitted]

Terms For engaging with Doctor Jack

Those who wish to Imploy Jack, must send me their notes, payable on the 25th of decr—next

William H. Macon

(Certificate)

State of Tennessee }
Giles county }

I do (hereby) certify that my wife (Amelia) was taken unwell about the first of Augst 1829—she complain'd of great misery in the back & loins, together with a numbedness in her thighs, ~~about~~ which threw her to bed about the 19th of the same month.

I Immediately applied to a physician, who (formerly) waited on my family—from whom she took medicine for about six weeks without receiving any benefit—I then applied to another, who (I thought) to be the best physician in the county, who attended on her about one month without the least (apparent)

benefit, but she still grew worse & it was the opinion of the most of my neighbors that she must sink under her complaint (if not speedily remov'd)

In this case she was when about the first of decr following I imploy'd Doctor Jack (a colored man) belonging to William Macon of Maury county, Tenn—ten miles west of Columbia, who undertook her, he commenced with roots, & (to my great astonishment) in a few days she began to amend, & in a few weeks was up & attending to her ordinary business of life—& I believe she is as well (at this time) & enjoys as good health as she has done for several years—

Given under my hand, July 6th *1830*

[signed] Wade Barret

SOURCE: Petition of Residents of Maury, Bedford, Giles, Hickman, Williamson, and Lincoln Counties to the Tennessee General Assembly, ca. 1832, Legislative Petitions, #11-1832-1a-4, reel 12, TSLA; Testimonials concerning Doctor Jack, 1829–31, #294-1831-1-7, reel 12, TSLA. Some of the pages are torn, and some of the signatures are illegible or too faint to decipher. The extant signature pages contain the signatures of 121 residents. Rejected.[2] PAR #11483208.

1. The law stipulated that the owner would be subject to indictment in the county court and a fine to be determined by the court. The slave would receive up to twenty-five lashes. *Public Acts Passed at the Stated Session of the Nineteenth General Assembly of the State of Tennessee. 1831* (Nashville: Allen A. Hall and F. S. Heiskell, 1832), 122–23.

2. For other petitions in Dr. Jack's behalf, see Petition of Citizens of Tennessee to the Legislature, August 1843, Legislative Petitions, #189-1843-1-2, reel 17, TSLA; Petition of the Ladies of Tennessee to the Legislature, August 1843, Legislative Petitions, #189-1843-3-4, reel 17, TSLA; *Journal of the House of Representatives of the State of Tennessee at the Twenty-Fifth General Assembly, Held at Nashville, on Monday the 25 Day of October, 1843* (Knoxville: E. G. Eastman and L. Gifford, 1844), 180; and *Journal of the Senate of the State of Tennessee at the Twenty-Fifth General Assembly, Held at Nashville* (Knoxville: E. G. Eastman and L. Gifford, 1844), 190. For a biographical sketch of Dr. Jack, who died in Nashville in 1860, see Loren Schweninger, "Doctor Jack: A Slave Physician on the Tennessee Frontier," *Tennessee Historical Quarterly* 57 (Spring/Summer 1998): 36–41.

87. Stephen Lytle, Nashville, to Tennessee Assembly, ca. 1832

To the Honble, The Senate & House of Representatives of the State of Tennessee, now in Session—

Your Petitioner, Stephen Lytle, a man of Color would most respectfully show, that several years ago, his master, William Lytle Esq of Nashville, ~~and who is one of your Honorable body,~~ after having owned him for many years, agreed with him, yr. petitioner, that if he would pay to him (Mr. Lytle) the sum of four hundred dollars, that he should be free—Your Petitioner states that when the proposition was made by his master, he embraced it with a determination that if honesty, industry & frugality would enable him to procure the four hundred dollars, he would be free.

He states that his labors were successful & he paid to his master, the money, which by agreement, was to be the price of his freedom, and for the truth of this statement he refers your Honble Body to the letter of his master to Mr. James I. Dozier of the date of the 17th of April 1832, & also to the letter of Mr. Dozier of the same date, to his master, both of which letters are prayed to be read as part of this petition—they are marked A.

Your Petitioner States that by his own labor he has purchased his wife, Charity, of Mr. John Spence, and has actually paid him the money for her, which will more fully appear by referring to the Original Bill of Sale executed by Mr. Spence to him, dated 29th July 1825, which Bill of sale is asked to be read as a part of this petition—it is marked B.

Your Petitioner States that since he purchased his said Wife, Charity, as is herein before stated, she has born one child, a girl, whom he has named Mary Shepherd Lytle, now about four years old.

He states further that on the 14th day of May 1829, at a time when he verily believed he was a free man he purchased of a Mr. Amos Sawyer of the Town of Nashville, a lot of ground, in the said Town, that he has paid for it, and Mr. Sawyer has Conveyed the same to him by deed bearing date the 19th day of April 1832, which will more fully appear by referring to the deed, which is respectfully asked to be read as part of this petition—it is marked C.

Your Petitioner states that on the 1st day of May 1832 he purchased of Mr. Amos Sawyer another piece of ground in the Town of Nashville, which will more fully appear by referring to the bond of Mr. Sawyer for the Conveyance of title, which is asked to be read as a part of this petition—it is marked D.

Your Petitioner states that he is an unlettered man, unable to read or understand the laws of his Country—but he declares to yr. Honble body, that he did most confidently believe he was a free man, and as such had right to contract   that he had by his own labor earned the money to pay for himself, for his wife and for the first lot he purchased of Mr. Sawyer.

It is unnecessary for yr. petitioner to state to this Honble body, every member of which has always enjoyed liberty, that best of human blessings, what his feelings of regret, surprise, and mortification were when he was first informed, on the 17th of April 1832, that he was not by law a free man, and that his wife & his child were, by law, the slaves of your petitioner's master.

Your Petitioner has lived in Nashville from the time of his early youth, *there* he has toiled with his hands day after day & year after year, *there* he has acquired a reputation which he will show to your Honble body is of respectable estimate:— And *there* are all his associations and feelings—his preferences are *there*—his attachments are *there*—he could not live and enjoy life *any where* else

He is informed that the Second Section of the act of 1831, Session acts, page 121.2. prohibits his emancipation & that of his wife & child, "except on the express Condition, that" he & they shall immediately remove from the State of Tennessee, and unless his master & the master of his wife & child shall before their "emancipation enter into bond with good & sufficient security,["] in a sum equal to their respective values, Condition that they nor either of them and each of them "shall forthwith remove from" the State of Tennessee.[1]

If your Petitioner Could Consent to leave the spot where he has lived, for nearly fifty years, he believes, that by promising that he would never return, he could give the security, as to himself, required by the statute; but he has no hope that for his wife and his child he could get such security, and he believes they are, and will be wholly unable to do it. He is then reduced to this sad condition: To remain here a slave for life, or, to leave the State, his wife, his child, his property, and all upon earth, which he regards with affection—He would state to your Honble body that he has no fear of being made a slave of himself, or that his wife or child ~~would~~ will be reduced to that situation, during the life of his master—he knows better—he can Confide & he knows it, in his integrity—But if he, who is an elderly gentleman, should be *called away*—your Honorable body knows what would be the state of this Petitioner, without his explanations. And you know too, what would be the condition of his wife & child. Before he would leave the State and separate himself from his wife & child, dear as liberty is to him, and galling as are the chains of bondage, he would remain a slave.

Your Petitioner presents to this Honorable body the testimony of men of high character, proving the reputation of both his wife & himself, and respectfully, but earnestly solicits you, that you would by an act for his benefit, & the benefit of his wife & child ~~dec~~ declare someway, by which they can be free, *and continue to remain in the State of Tennessee,* and whereby his purchases of land or lots; may be made valid. And as his master has permitted him to assume *his name,* he prays that yr. Honble body may confirm it—He asks that you would for him & in his behalf, & that of his wife & child make such provision as from the facts herein set forth, you shall believe ought to be made. And as in duty bound, he will every pray &c

his
Stephen X Lytle
mark . . . [page omitted]

We have Known a man of Color named, or Called, Stephen Lytle for many years, and we can state that he is, and always has been, so far as we Know or believe, an industrious, punctual, truthful honest man—It is due to him, to say, that he is a man of good character. We do not know his wife Charity, to[o] well, but state that We have never heard her honesty questioned

[signed] Wm Carroll — Jas. Grizzard
Felix Robertson — Saml Seay
Duncan Robertson — Saml V.D. Strout

John Robertson Stephen Cantrell
And[rew] Hynes [24 additional signatures]

In addition to the above I have to State, that I know his wife, Charity for twenty two years, and that she is as trust worthy as any Woman of Color
[signed] Alpha Kingsley
M Young

I have been well acquainted With Stephen from his infancy to this time, and has [labored] gd. [for] me for the Term of twenty five years, with his wife Charity about twelve years & they are entitled the above character
June 28th. 1832
[signed] Will Lytle

SOURCE: Petition Stephen Lytle to the Tennessee General Assembly, ca. 1832, Legislative Petitions, #140-1833-1-3, reel 13, TSLA; Certificate, Will Lytle et al., 28 June 1832, ibid. Granted.[2] PAR #11483320.

1. See *A Compilation of the Statutes of Tennessee, of a General and Permanent Nature, from the Commencement of the Government to the Present Time* (Nashville: James Smith, 1836), 279; John Codman Hurd, *The Law of Freedom and Bondage in the United States,* 2 vols. (Boston: Little, Brown, 1858–62; reprint, New York: Negro Universities Press, 1968), 2:92.

2. In 1833, the Tennessee General Assembly emancipated Stephen Lytle, his wife, Charity, and his daughter, Mary Shepherd, but it permitted them to remain in Tennessee only if Lytle paid "sufficient security to the county court of Davidson, for their good behaviour, and also that they will not become a public charge." *Private Acts Passed at the First Session of the Twentieth General Assembly of the State of Tennessee. 1833* (Nashville: Allen A. Hall and F. S. Heiskell, 1833), 142.

88. Samuel H. Osborne to Mississippi Assembly, ca. 1833

To the Honorable the Senate and House of Representatives of the State of Mississippi

Your petitioner Saml. H. Osborne begs leave to represent to your honorable body that he has recently purchased as a Slave, an infant child called Margaret whom he verily believes to be the issue of white parents who by fraud or some disgraceful device have caused said child to be brought to the State and sold as a slave—And as it is the wish of your petitioner to Educate said Child and raise her as one of his own Children he prays your honorable body to emancipate said child by the name of Indiana Osborne and restore her to what he honestly believes to be her natural rights.
[signed] Saml. H. Osborne

SOURCE: Petition of Samuel H. Osborne to the Mississippi General Assembly, ca. 1833, Records of the Legislature, Petitions and Memorials, 1817–39, RG 47, MDAH. Granted.[1] PAR #11000010.

1. To prove his case, Osborne held the child up before the legislature. It was "the sense and opinion" of the legislators that Indiana Osborne was the offspring of free white parents. She was therefore "emancipated and set free from slavery" and "invested with all the rights, privileges, and immunities" of white females in the state. *Laws of the State of Mississippi, Passed at the Seventeenth Session of the General Assembly, Held in the Town of Jackson* (Jackson: George R. Fall, 1834), 169–70.

89. David Harding, Davidson County, to Tennessee Assembly, 1833

To the General Assembly of the State of Tennessee now in Session

The Petition of David Morris Harding a citizen of the county of Davidson & State aforsaid

Represents to your Honorable body that he is at this time in possession of a certain negro man named Major who was formerly the property of the late William Harding the Brother of your Petitioner—that his said Brother in his lifetime had designed and intended to emancipate said slave Major in consequence of his long and faithful services—but that his intentions were frustrated by the death of his said Brother who died suddenly and without having made a Will—After his death, in making distribution of his property said slave was distributed to the Wife of my said Brother, and she being willing that said slave might be enabled to obtain his freedom as his former master had intended ~~told,~~ agreed that as he had been valued to her at the sum of Four Hundred Dollars your Petitioner, might take him at that price, with a view to secure to him his freedom—Your Petitioner states to your honorable body that the said slave has paid to him the said sum of Four Hundred Dollars, and he is now desirous that he may be emancipated, and he represents that said Slave Major, is about Thirty five years old, that he has been a most valuable and faithful slave, that he is strictly honest, sober, and industrious, and in fact a man of uncommonly good character for a man of his color, and your petitioner entertains no doubt that if emancipated he will make, an orderly and respectable Citizen, wherefore he prays your Honorable Body to pass an act emancipating said slave Major and as in duty bound he will ever pray &c

[signed] David M. Harding
September 27th 1833

SOURCE: Petition of David M. Harding to the Tennessee General Assembly, 27 September 1833, Legislative Petitions, #144-1833-1-2, reel 13, TSLA. Granted.[1] PAR #11483308.

1. The assembly authorized the Davidson County Court to free Major "Provided, that

the provisions of the act of 1801, chapter 27, requiring security to indemnify the county and State, be in all things complied with." *Private Acts Passed at the First Session of the Twentieth General Assembly of the State of Tennessee. 1833* (Nashville: Allen A. Hall and F. S. Heiskell, 1833), 94.

90. Philip Lindsley et al. to Tennessee Assembly, 1833

To the General Assembly of the State of
Tennessee

We undersigned, members of the Tennessee State Colonization Society and other citizens of Tennessee, would respectfully invite your honourable body to a consideration and adoption of the means which shall be best calculated to effect the removal of our free coloured population in a manner consistent with the rights and interests of every portion and description of persons within the limits of this commonwealth.

Your memorialists deem it superfluous to enlarge on the disabilities and degradation necessarily entailed on the manumitted African, so long as he remains in the country where his colour will be regarded as the index of an inferior and servile caste:—and they deem it equally superfluous to specify the evils which a population, occupying so doubtful, anomalous and humiliating a position in the midst of us, may inflict upon all other classes of the community. They do not presume to offer information or to construct an elaborate argument upon these delicate and momentous topics. They doubt not that the entire subject, in all its bearings, is as obvious to yourselves as to them; and that you estimate the interests involved with as deep a solicitude, with as honest a patriotism, and with as generous a philanthropy as the most enlightened and benevolent of your constituents could desire.

Believing, as they do, that much may be done to mitigate, if not utterly and immediately to eradicate the evils acknowledged to exist, and which are rapidly and fearfully augmenting—and believing that the auspicious moment for decided energetic action has arrived: Your memorialists exercise the common right of freemen in requesting the seasonable interposition of legislative wisdom and counsels to save the commonwealth from the dangers and calamities threatened, and from all the difficulties and embarrassments which the population referred to may hereafter create.

The American Society, for Colonizing in Africa, the Free People of Colour of the United States, with their own consent—founded, sustained, directed & controlled by a large number of the purest, wisest, and most respected statesmen, jurists and patriots of the South and the North—has been labouring in the noble cause, during the last twelve or fifteen years, with an efficiency and success unparalleled in the annals of colonial enterprise. Notwithstanding the extremely limited pecuniary resources of the National Society, (resulting almost entirely from private charity and individual benefactions ~~until very recently,~~) a flourishing colony of *American Negroes* has been planted on the western coast of Africa. With the history, statistics, present condition, and cheering prospects of this incipient *African Republic,* you are perfectly acquainted: and their brief memorial could add nothing on this score worthy of your notice.

The Tennessee State Colonization Society has in view the same great object with the parent institution,—while it restricts its immediate operations to our own state. The free negro of Tennessee will be conveyed to the home of his fathers in the first instance and in preference to all others. To this single object do your memorialists solicit your present attention. And should you accord with them in sentiment, you will doubtless adopt such measures and make such appropriations as will accelerate the important work now in progress, and which is but feebly sustained by a few individuals, & with means totally inadequate to the grand achievement contemplated.

Your memorialists confidently submit the cause of humanity and of their country to your unbiased judgment and mature deliberation. And, as in duty bound, they will ever pray, &c.&c.

Nashville, October 25 1833.

[signed] Philip Lindsley — President of the Tennessee State Colonization Society.

John Shelley
Jno P. Erwin Tr: Ten State Co. Soc
Geo. Brown
R. H. McEwen
James Hamilton
Nathl Cross
H. L. Douglass
F. M. Jones
William S Mayfield
[158 additional signatures]

SOURCE: Petition of Philip Lindsley et al. to the Tennessee General Assembly, 25 October 1833, Legislative Petitions, #203-1833-1-4, reel 13, TSLA. Granted.[1] PAR #11483306.

1. The assembly provided ten dollars for each free black removed by the Tennessee Colonization Society from middle Tennessee to Africa. The total expenditure could not exceed five hundred dollars in any given year. *Public Acts Passed at the First Session of the Twentieth General Assembly of the State of Tennessee. 1833* (Nashville: Allen A. Hall and F. S. Heiskell, 1833), 75.

91. Ned Hyman and Elizabeth Hagans, Martin County, to North Carolina Assembly, 1833

To The Honorable The General Assembly—
of North Carolina—

The petition of Ned Hyman (a slave) humbly complaining sheweth unto The Honorable The General Assembly ~~aforesaid,~~ that your petitioner now residing in the Town Williamston in the County of Martin ~~& state aforesd~~ and by occupation a farmer—was born some fifty four or five years ago ~~the property &~~ slave of one Jno. Hyman of Bertie County, that ~~sd~~ Jno. Hyman died when your petitioner was about the age of fourteen, that your petitioner then became the ~~slave and~~ property of his then young Master Samuel Hyman—during three years (the minority) of his ~~sd~~ young master ~~Saml.~~ he was hired out to the highest bidder,—that after ~~sd~~ three years of hired service he was taken home by his ~~sd~~ Master Saml., in whose possession and under whose control ~~and management~~ your petitioner lived and served from that time up to the death of his ~~sd~~ Master Saml—which happened some time in the year 1828—Since that time your petitioner ~~with little exception~~ has been under the control of the Executor of his ~~sd~~ decd. Master. Your petitioner would further state, that during this long period and through every change of Master or service your petitioner has been a faithful and an honest servant to the interest of him or her whom it was his duty to serve—and of this he hopes he can give the most satisfactory testimonials. Your petitioner would further state that some time about his Twenty-seventh year he intermarried with one Elizabeth Hagans a free woman of Colour with whom he has lived in friendship and harmony with little or no exception ever since; (and altho your petitioner has been informed that the sd union or marriage did not constitute your petitioner & sd Elizabeth "husband & wife" in the Legal acceptation of that phrase—yet your humble petitioner would ask the indulgence of your Honorable body and hope that it will not be considered at all presuming, to use these words, through out the remainder of this petition and the other writings accompanying it, when ever there may be necessity for them or either of them, instead of words—of like import—) Your petitioner would further state, that through the indulgence and advantages which his kind & benevolent master extended to him, aided by his own industry prudence and frugality and seconded by the virtues and exertions on the part of your petitioners wife—Elizabeth, (~~not less profitable,~~) your petitioner has had the good fortune to accumulate an estate worth from from five to six thousand dollars; consis~~s~~ting of lands chiefly live stock negroes and money, the right & title to all which except the money is vested in your petitioners wife Elizabeth—Your petitioner would further state that it was the wish of his decd Master Saml. Hyman expressed to his family often times during his last illness that your petitioner after his death should do service as a slave to no person—but that as far as was consistent with the Laws of the State he wished him to be free—alleging as the reasons, that your petitioner had been a trusty faithful and obedient servant to him through a long period of years; that your petitioner was getting old; and that for the future he wished him to serve himself or language to that amount.—Your petitioner would further state that in furtherance of this kind and benevolent wish of your petitioners decd Master for your petitioners future freedom and happiness, his Executor Jno. S. Bryan has (at your petitioners request) sold your petitioner to your petitioners sd wife Elizabeth.—that your petitioner by his sd. wife Elizabeth has three children Penny, Sarah and Ned—the Two daughters are of full age, the son nearly so—that your petitioner has been informed that by, either the death of his sd wife Elizabeth or a change in her feelings or disposition towards your petitioner, your petitioner might not only lose his whole estate but even that portion of freedom and happiness which, by the kindness of his wife he is now permitted to enjoy. But your petitioner in justice to his kind and affectionate wife Elizabeth would further state, that she is not disposed at all to abridge in the least degree the liberty or happiness of your petitioner but wishes and desires (if consistent with the will of the Honorable The Genl. Assembly ~~aforsd~~) that the same may be inlarged & increased—that she is therefore perfectly willing and anxiously desires to give up her sd title to your petitioner to the Honorable Genl. Assembly ~~aforesaid~~ that they may confer the same (by an act of manumission) to gether with such other liberties and privileges & immunities as other free persons of Colour now by law enjoys,—upon your petitioner—that to this end & for this purpose ~~to sd~~ Elizabeth the wife of your petitioner will unite with your petitioner in praying The Honorable Genl. Assembly ~~aforsad~~—that they would take his case into consideration and ~~to~~ pass such an act in favor of your petitioners manumission ~~they~~ as they in their wisdom may deem meet and proper—that in Confirmation of the sd Elizabeths sincerity in this prayer and request she will most willingly Sign this petition with your petitioner—Your petitioner considers that further enlarging might be trespassing too much upon the time of The Honorable the Genl. Assembly aforesaid—But in conclusion however your petitioner would further state that from the facts already stated it must be apparent in what an unpleasant and grievous situation your petitioner is placed—He has by laboring ~~of~~ in the nights and at such other spare times as his master would give him and by his prudence and frugality acquired an estate which (say nothing of the uncertainties of life) he has not the assurance of enjoying even for a day—that he in a single hour might be placed in a worse condition than the day he began this life—that your petitioner has by his faithfulness and extraordinary attention to his masters business and interest secured his esteem and favor and obtained his sincere wishes that your petitioner should be freed—& the nearest your petitioner has been able to approach an end so desirable to his decd Master, is, to have had the title to your petitioner vested in your petitioners ~~sd~~ wife ~~Elizabeth~~—that it must be evident to the Honorable The Genl. Assemble from these facts in what a precarious condition, stand the property, ~~the liberty~~ and [e]ven the happiness itself of your petitioner—Your petitioner together with his wife Elizabeth therefore pray the Genl. Assembly aforsd in tender consideration of his unhappy and grievous condition to pass such an act for his benefit and relief, as in their wisdom may seem meet & in their justice may seem right & proper & your humble petitioners as in duty bound will ever pray &c—signed—

Test Wm. B. Bennett

E. S. Smithwick

his
Ned X Hyman
mark

her
Elizabeth X Hagans
mark

SOURCE: Petition of Ned Hyman and Elizabeth Hagans to the North Carolina General Assembly, 23 November 1833, Records of the General Assembly, Session Records, NCDAH. Referred to the Committee on Propositions and Grievances. No act was passed. PAR #11283305.

92. John Waddell to North Carolina Assembly, 1834

To the Honorable the General Assembly of North Carolina.

The Memorial of the undersigned a native citizen of North Carolina respectfully represents to your Honorable body that during the last Fall, he visited the state of Louisiana & purchased land on Red River in that state & returned with the view of removing negroes from North Carolina to the land so purchased: That he shipped twenty two slaves on board the Brig Enconium, bound from Charleston, South Carolina to the City of New Orleans & became a passenger with his brother & divers others in said Brig:—He represents that said Brig was an American Vessel, commanded by an American & engaged in the lawful trade between the cities of Charleston & New Orleans—Within fifty six hours after her departure from Charleston & at midnight she struck & was wrecked on the Coral reefs of Abaco:—The passengers with great difficulty & after having been confined for many hours to the wreck & having lost everything, escaped impending destruction by the kind assistance of the Inhabitants of the Island.—Here after some delay they were enabled to procure a small vessel which conveyed the passengers & crew, sixty nine in number to the Town of Nassau in the island of New Providence.—Upon their arrival in the harbour of Nassau, your Memorialist with his companions in misfortune, confidently anticipated the reception which all civilised nations extend to the unfortunate.

Crowded together in a craft too small to allow even the ordinary comforts of such a situation and literally without food, they asked permission to land that they might obtain the means of subsistence:—this was denied them:—& to their inexpressible astonishment they were informed that they should hold *no* intercourse with the shore, not even for the purpose of procuring food.

In vain did your Memorialist & his companions demand the reason of such treatment:—insult was added to injury & they were told that if they presumed to hold the forbidden intercourse with the shore, their vessel should be immediately fired upon by a British sloop of War then lying in the harbour.

After some hours of this humiliating treatment though there seemed no pretense for it, your memorialist & those with him were subjected to the further indignity of having the vessel in which they were, ordered up under the guns of the sloop of War & within pistol shot of her, where they remained for some hours in the attitude of prisoners:—By the manly interposition of one of the passengers, who was a British subject & had friends on the island, the passengers after great delay & many petty insults were permitted to land at 8 oclock at night.—

Early on the following day, the negroes belonging to your Memorialist & the other passengers, forty five in number, were taken on shore by the order of the Lieutenant Governor of the island & carried before the Officer of the Customs, where they were asked if they desired their freedom & upon an affirmative answer, they were *immediately liberated* & directed to repair to the quarters of a Black Regiment in the Town of Nassau, where they would be accommodated, until they could obtain suitable situations.—Some days after this event & when there ~~xxxxx~~ were vessels about to sail to New Orleans, your Memorialist through the American Consul, addressed a note to the Governor asking if there were any obstacle to his proceeding on his voyage with his property & to this note couched in language as respectful as your Memorialist was capable of making it, the Governor replied that if your Memorialist presumed to interfere with the manumitted slaves, it would become his duty to *hang him & all accessories.*—

Thus has your Memorialist been not only unfortunate in having been shipwrecked & delayed in his proposed settlement in Louisiana, but has been plundered of his property while going from one part of the United States to another.—

It is not for your Memorialist to comment on this transaction—he cannot trust himself to do so lest he be betrayed into expressions unsuited to a Memorial.—Nevertheless were it pardonable, he would add, that a tame submission by our Government to such an outrage, is impossible & Your Memorialist appeals to his native State to make common cause with her sisters of the South on this most delicate but vital subject:—If it be Known that the British Islands, so near our coast & upon which so many vessels are liable to be thrown by stress of weather, need only be reached to establish the freedom of our Slaves & that the power of Great Britain, guarrantees their safety, it will be holding out a *premium to insurrection* & the condition of the South be rendered even more anxious than it has heretofore been.-

[signed] John Waddell

SOURCE: Petition of John Waddell to the North Carolina General Assembly, 8 December 1834, Records of the General Assembly, Session Records, NCDAH. Resolution passed.[1] PAR #11283408.

1. The North Carolina General Assembly passed a resolution condemning the action of the British. The assembly defended the right of property in "persons" as well as "things." *Acts Passed by the General Assembly of the State of North Carolina, at the Session of 1834–35* (Raleigh: Philo White, 1835), 94–95.

93. Sally Dabney, Richmond, to Virginia Assembly, 1834

To the Honorable the General Assembly of the State of Virginia.

The Memorial of Sally Dabney respectfully represents, that she was a slave till about the year 1818, when she was purchased by her husband Cambridge Dabney a free man of color of the City of Richmond, and continued his property until the period of his death in the year 1826; that her said husband always intended to leave your memorialist free at his death, but held her in slavery during his life to prevent the separation which would have been the necessary consequence of her emancipation, since your Memorialist would have been required by the laws of the Commonwealth to remove to another clime.

Your Memorialist further states that at the death of her said husband he bequeathed all his property of every description excepting some few articles of furniture to her, which he believed was sufficient to constitute her a free woman without the formality of a deed of emancipation. That such was his intention is sufficiently manifest from the whole body of his said will, the provisions of which would have been totally nugatory if made in relation to a slave who cannot own property. In addition to the evidence afforded by the will itself, the fact is clearly established by the affidavits of several respectable witnesses subscribing said will, who testify that they believe such to have been his intention and wish. These affidavits your Memorialist refers to with confidence in support of her statement.

In consequence, however, of the failure on the part of her said husband to express that which he obviously and clearly intended, your Memorialist finds herself in the novel attitude of a slave without an owner, or a free person without any evidence of her right to freedom; and she is thereby daily rendered liable to imprisonment for unlawfully going at large without permission from her owner, or to be sent out of the state for remaining contrary to law within its limits. If your memorialist belongs to any one, she has become the property of the Commonwealth, because her husband has no heirs living who are free persons capable of inheriting her as a slave; but she thinks it might easily be established that she is entitled to her freedom; but if in this she may be disappointed, she cannot believe the Commonwealth would deprive her of rights which she obviously acquired by the known intention of her husband, nor can she believe that the great State of Virginia would cause her to be again sold as a slave, and receive the proceeds of her sale into the public coffers.

Your memorialist states and refers to the accompanying affidavits to sustain her statement, that she has resided in the City of Richmond from her infancy, and has ever borne a good and irreproachable character; That she is now at least forty five years of age, and though she is again married and has been now for five or six years, she has not become the mother of any children nor is it reasonable in the common course of nature to expect that she will have children in future.

Your Memorialist thinks her case is a peculiarly hard one, and out of the ordinary course of events; and she humbly prays your honorable body to take it into consideration, and pass a law recognizing her freedom and granting her permission to remain in the state with her present husband & friends, or make such other provisions to suit her case as your honorable body may think right & proper, and as in duty bound she will every pray &c

Sally Dabney
X
her mark . . . [docket information]

State of Virginia }
City of Richmond } S.S.

Personally appeared, this 15th day of Decr A.D. 1834, before me a justice of the Peace in and for said City, Bartholomew Graves, a resident of the City of Richmond and made oath, that he is well acquainted with Sally Dabney a free woman of Color of said City, and has known her for more than thirty years past; that she has always borne a good character, and is about forty five years of age, has no children, and there is no probability that she will ever have any; That she was a slave up to about the year 1818, when she was purchased by her husband Cambridge Dabney a free man of Color, who died about six or seven years ago, ever since which period his relict Sally Dabney has been considered and recognized as a free woman. Given under my hand this 15th Day of Dec 1834

[signed] Wm Allison JP

State of Virginia }
City of Richmond } to wit:

This 16th day of December A.D. 1834, personally appeared before me a justice of the peace in & for said City, Isaac White, a resident of said City and made oath that he is well acquainted with Sally Dabney, a free woman of Color of said City, who maintains a good reputation and fair character; That he was one of the subscribing witnesses to the will of her late husband, Cambridge Dabney a free man of Color, since deceased; in which will dated 7th Novr. 1826 the said Cambridge bequeathed to his said wife Sally Dabney all his property with the exception of an inconsiderable legacy to his Niece Doria; That he the said Isaac White understood at the time of witnessing the said will, that it was the intention of the testator to leave his said wife Sally free; and that she has ever since had the reputation of being a free woman, and as he believes is justly entitled to be so considered and recognised.

Given under my hand the day & year first above written.

[signed] Wm. Allison JP

SOURCE: Petition of Sally Dabney to the General Assembly, 20 December 1834, Legislative Petitions, Richmond City, VSA; Affidavit, Bartholomew Graves, 15 December 1834, ibid.; Affidavit, Isaac White, 16 December 1834, ibid. Granted.[1] PAR #11683414.

1. Noting that Dabney's husband "recognized her right to freedom by making several bequests to her," the Virginia General Assembly relinquished the commonwealth's "right, title, and interest" in her and permitted her to remain in Virginia "as a free person, until some person claiming as next of kin, or as a creditor of the estate of Cambridge Dabney, shall assert and maintain a right to her as a slave." *Acts of the General Assembly of Virginia, Passed at the Session of 1834–35, Commencing 1 December, 1834, and Ending 12 March, 1835* (Richmond: Samuel Shepherd, 1835), 242.

94. David Hemphill et al. to South Carolina Legislature, 1835

To the Honorable, the Legislature of South Carolina

The prayer of your petitioners, the undersigned, shows, that many citizens of this commonwealth are seriously aggrieved by that law passed in the Legislature of So. Ca. the seventeenth of December 1834 entitled an act to amend the laws in relation to slaves & free persons of colour—That is to say—we are aggrieved with so much of the first section of said act, as forbids us to teach our slaves to read—With the other parts of said act we have no controversy.[1] Your petitioners b[e]lieve that not only ourselves but thousands of worthy citizens of this State are aggrieved by this law; and really desire it repeal[ed]. Your memorialists would respectfully suggest that the law in question will have a tendency injurious to the well-being of this community. And your memorialists believe that it will be a *dead letter* generally except when roused by malicious persons in order to punish better men than themselves. In many places this law could not be enforced. A jury could not be made [to] see how the teaching of slaves to read the scriptures, or any book strictly religious, (which is all we desire) could jeopardize any interest human or divine. Your memorialists would further state their conviction, that very many good citizens, in the best sense of the word, have left, and are now purchasing to leave, and will continue to leave, the State, because of the law in question. Your memorialists therefore are perfectly certain that said law tends to depopulate the State.—This law is also believed by many (and some of your memorialists are of this opinion) to invade the rights of conscience, and so doing to be unconstitutional; and it is not all unusual to hear prudent men say "we are prepared to disrespect such a law." It is painful to a good citizen to be compelled from a sense of duty to violate the laws of the land—Your Memorialists also think that the Hon. Legislature, that passed this law did not duly weigh its *efficiency.* Your memorialists cannot imagine any motive, which could have influenced a learned Legislature to enact such a law; except simply the law of self-defence; and your memorialists, think that this law cannot answer the purposes of defence. Because the ability to read exists on ~~nearly~~ probably every plantation in the State; and it is utterly impossible for even the *masters* to prevent this:—as is apparent from the cases in which servants learn to write by stealth, although all masters are very watchful to prevent this. The probability that *abolition fanaticism* will ever rise higher than it has done is not very great, yet we have found ourselves perfectly competent to defend ourselves without any such aid as that law in question contemplates.—And cannot we always do so? Besides is it no[t] very questionable whether intelligence is more productive of dangerous insurrection than *ignorance*? And would not demagoueism [demagogism] among intelligent slaves be as comparatively harmless as among intelligent freemen? And, your memorialists soberly believe, that the state has less to fear from even general intelligence (for which we are not pleading) among slaves, than that ignorance contemplated by the law in question—which when carried out would make ourselves the fit dupes of every Nat Turner who might chance to pass along. And if Imperial Rome could manage even a classic *slavery,* and a large part of their slaves, also the best trained soldiers in the world, the Romans excepted, does chivalrous South *Carolina* quail before gangs of cowardly Africans with a Bible in their hands? Let it not be said!!

But Your Memorialists would grow tedious were they to present every argument which willingly offers itself in support of our petition for repeal of said law. Nor do we make any apology for thus plainly appealing before your Hon. body as memorialists—It is the right of freemen. We wish our rights only. We are perfectly aware that the law for whose repeal we now petition is daily *violated and* ever ~~xxxlic and~~ will be; and your petitioners believe that it would be both politic and prudent to repeal said law.

[signed]	David Hemphill	S, Alexander
	Jas Lowry	A P Nicholson
	John McKnight (York)	Hillory Montgomery
	Geo McKnight	W D Henry
	Philip Williams	[113 additional signatures]

SOURCE: Petition of David Hemphill et al. to the South Carolina Legislature, 1835, Records of the General Assembly, #1812, SCDAH. No act was passed. PAR #11383503.

1. The other provisions prohibited anyone from employing a colored person as a "clerk or salesman in any shop, store, or house used for trading," instituted new penalties for selling "spirits to slaves," and forbade anyone from gambling with slaves. *Acts and Resolutions*

of the General Assembly, of the State of South Carolina, Passed in December, 1834 (Columbia: E. F. Branthwaite, 1834), 13–15; John Codman Hurd, *The Law of Freedom and Bondage in the United States,* 2 vols. (Boston: Little, Brown, 1858–62; reprint, New York: Negro Universities Press, 1968), 2:98.

95. Basil Brawner, Prince William County, to Virginia Assembly, 1835

To the General Assembly of Virginia

Your petitioner Basil Brawner respectfully represents to your Honorable body that heretofore a mulato called and known as William Hyden was apprehended in the County of Prince William and committed to the Jail of the said County as a runaway, that the said Hyden was confined in the Jail of the County, aforesaid, and advertised as the Law in such cases direct, and was by order of the County Court advertised for Sale & no person having claimed him, and he not having proved his Fredom, he was offered at public Auction for Sale by your petitioner as Deputy for Michael Cleary, then high Sheriff of Prince Wm County, on the first day of January 1834. When one Robert Lipscomb being a bidder, and making the highest bid became the purchaser of said Hyden, as the agent of a trader, or dealer in slaves, and he Lipscomb informed your petitioner, that his principal would pay the purchase money in a fiw [*sic*] days, the said Hyden was returned to Jail to await the arrival of the said trader, who in a short time came and being requested refused to pay the amount which he had authorised the said Lipscomb to bid. Your petitioner afterwards sent the said Hyden to the Town of Fredericksburg and to the City of Richmond by one Col. James Fewell of Prince William, (who had a number of slaves to be offered for sale,) to be sold if the amount of the said Robert Lipscombs bid could be obtained for him, the said Hyden was offered for sale to sundry persons in Fredericksburg by Fewell & Myself, he was also offered in Richmond by Fewell; all of Whom refused to purchase him at any price, on account of his colour all alledgin that he was too white, the said Fewell returned him to your petitioner in the Town of Brentsville, where he offered him for sale on a court day, several traders were present, all of whom refused to make any offer for him, alledging that his colour was too light and that he could by reason thereof too easily escape from slavery and pass himself for a free man, and whilst your petitioner was endeavouring to sell the said Hyden he made his escape, and although your petition[er] has mad[e] every exertion in his power to regain possession of him he has not been able so that your petioner was compelled to report to the county court aforesaid his proceeding under their order, ~~of~~ and to pay all the expense that arose from aprehension, confinement, advertising &c, without having received any part of the sum of money which was bid for him the said Hyden. Nor has your petitioner any prospect or hope of being reembursed the expense so paid by him, that Robert Lipscomb to whose bid the said Hyden was cried out, if legally bound to your petitioner for the sum bid by him $452 is wholy unable to pay any part of it, as is well know by several of your Honorable body, and if your petitioner had or could obtain a Judgment and Execution against him they would be without avail. That the former Sheriff of this county, Michael Cleary now stands charged on the books of the Auditor of Public accounts with a large sum of Money which your petitioner will be compelled to pay unless your Honorable body will release him from it, although he has not received nor has he any hope of receiving one cent of the same. Your petitioner beg leave to represent to your honorable body that it was the impression of all who saw and conversed with said Hyden that he was born free, that the said Hyden allway asserted that he was born free in the State of New York, was the son of a white woman and was educated in that state, which was evident from his pronunciation, at the age of 14 he went to the State of Ohio where he continued about three years, when the increase of that population with Whom he associated became so numerous as to induce the constituted authorities of that State to enact severe Laws in relation to the police of the State, which compelled all persons of his colour, which was not able to comply with the requisitions of the Laws, to seek an asylum else where, and that he in endeavouring to return to New York his nativity, and not being acquainted with Virginia Laws attempted to pass through said state without evidence of his freedom, and for want of such evidence, he was apprehended and committed to Jail, and dealt with as a runaway slave, that your petition from conversation had with him and conversation had by other persons in his presence whilst he the said Hyden was confined in Jail, has a strong belief, and so have others whose certificates he present with this his petition that the said was free born, his knowledge of the Geography of New York his acquaintance with the cities, Towns, rivers & the trade of the state, is calculated to convince any person that he was born, raised, & educated & migrated, as he the said Hyden himself represented to your petitioner & others. Your petitioner ~~will as the reason of his being~~ therefore prays your Honorable body to pass an act releasing him and the said Michael Cleary from the payment into the Treasury The sum of money charged as aforesaid upon the books of the Auditor of Public accounts, in consideration that he has not received any part of the same and for the reasons above set forth can never expect to receive any part thereof. And your petitioner as in duty bound will ever pray &c.

[signed] Basil Brawner

January 22nd 1835

Prince Wm County towit,

I James Fewell, do hereby certify that I saw Wm Hyden the man refered to in this petition several times whilst he was in prince William Jail, and made sundry inquiries of him in relation ~~of~~ to the scituation of some of the Towns, rivers, and the kind of vessels that, traversed certain rives in the state of New York all of which he answered correctly that in addition to his dialect and education induces me to believe that he was born & raised in the north and I have no doubt but that he was free born. I took him to Fredericksburg and Richmond by request of B. Brawner where I offered him at public auction & but could not get a bid for him. I also endeavored to sell him at private bargain it was also without avail all said that it was evident that he was free born and was so bright that he might easily escape from slavery. I could not sell him at any price and returned him to said Brawner in Brentsville when the boy ran off and I have not heard from him since, given under my hand this 22nd Jany 1835

[signed] Jas Fewell

Prince William County towit,
I certify that I saw Wm Hyden the man referred to in this petition whilst he was confined in the Jail of Prince William, and always considdered his case ~~desperate~~ one of oppression, he was a bright Mulatto, and as I believe born free, this belief is founded upon his representations, which carried with the reason I have no doubt but that he was free born

22nd Jany 1835
[signed] M B Sinclair

SOURCE: Petition of Basil Brawner to the General Assembly of Virginia, 20 February 1835, Legislative Petitions, Prince William County, VSA; Certificates, James Fewell and M. B. Sinclair, 22 January 1835, ibid. Rejected. PAR #11683519. (Original is not included in microfilm edition.)

96. John Moffett, Rockbridge County, to Virginia Assembly, 1835

To the General Assembly of Virginia

The petition of John Moffett now of the county of Rockbridge, humbly represents. That, he has very recently been informed, that an act has passed your honorable body granting permission to Scipio & Peggy his wife persons of colour to remain in this commonwealth—

Your petitioner formerly lived in the county of Augusta and about eight or nine years ago suffered great loss by the burning of his barn and subsequently by the death of horses and cattle. The barn was set on fire by a young negro girl about fifteen years old (the property of your Petitioner) who was tried before the county court of Augusta, and on her trial, the said Peggy wife of Scipio was a witness, when many persons became convinced that, the said Peggy had instigated the girl Lucinda to commit the incendiary act; but your petitioner at that time had no such impressions—Subsequently after Lucinda had been sent out of the country, your petitioner lost horses and cattle as was believed by poison and he as well as many of his neighbours became satisfied that the said Peggy who was well known to be intelligent, artful and vindictive, had contrived or executed the plans that caused the loss of his property—

Your Petitioner having suffered much in property and deeply in feeling after much reflection, Sold his land and most of his personal property, (the land at a reduced price) ~~and~~ abandoned the neighbourhood of his birth and relations, and for some years has been without a settled home, during which time had lost sight of the said Peggy—Since the commencement of the present winter your Petitioner has in order to settle himself permanently, purchased a valuable farm in the county of Rockbridge and a few days since when about to take possession of it, to his great surprise learned that the said Scipio and Peggy his wife were living on an adjoining farm and had obtained permission to remain in the commonwealth—

Your Petitioner cannot feel secure in the possession of his property while the said Peggy is permitted to remain in the country and if time were allowed, he feels satisfied that he could produce evidence to your honorable body that his apprehensions are not without foundation—

Your petitioner would therefore pray either that the law permitting said Scipio & Peggy his wife to remain in the commonwealth may be repealed or that the whole matter may be submitted to the county court of Rockbridge for its decision—and your petitioner will ever pray

[signed] John Moffett

SOURCE: Petition of John Moffett to the Virginia General Assembly, 21 February 1835, Legislative Petitions, Rockbridge County, VSA. Referred to the Committee for Courts of Justice. No act was passed. PAR #11683509.

97. John Hawkins, Caroline County, Maryland, to Delaware Assembly, 1837

To the Honourable General Assembly of Delaware.

The petition of John Hawkins a man of color, and resident of Caroline County and State of Maryland, humbly represents, That a certain John Cooper now deceased formerly a resident of Kent County, and State of Delaware, by his Deed purporting to be a Deed of manumition bearing date the 29th day of December 1809, which is hereby produced, declared the manumition of certain of his negroe Slaves, That he discharged the said negroes according to the provisions of the said deed, That amoung them was a Woman named Lydia, with whom your petitioner intermarried, and raised a family of children, That afterwards in the year 1826 The said John Cooper residing in Kent County, and state of Delaware, And your petitioner and his wife Lydia, and their Children, Charity, Sally, & John, in Caroline County and State of Maryland: A certain Richard D. Cooper, a son of the said John Cooper, and a certain John Willoughby, who had intermarried one of his daughters, induced the said John Cooper, to believe that in consequence of the said negroes being at large in Maryland, by the Laws of that State he was liable to heavy penalties, and that he would be exonerated therefrom, by executing a deed for said negroes, The said John Cooper under that impression, executed to them the said Richard D. Cooper and the said John Willoughby—And to Samuel B. Cooper, Ezekiel S. Cooper, and Maria Dawson his other children, a deed for ~~the~~ certain of the negroes contained in the manumition, and their decendants, which was recorded in the records of Caroline County, and State of Maryland—

Your petitioner farther States, that it never was the intention of John Cooper by this deed, to affect the freedom rights of the said Negroes mentioned in the said deed of manumition, or their descendants, but that he was seduced to make the deed, by the representation of Richard D. Cooper, & John Willoughby, That although the names of Samuel B. Cooper, Ezekiel S. Cooper & Maria Dawson—appear as bargain[ers] in the deed, they had no knowledge of the transaction, and have never pretended to claim any right under it, That the insertion of their names was one of the artifices, by which John Cooper was deceived That although one thousand Dollars is mentioned as the consideration in the deed, no money or other consideration was ever paid,

Your petitioner farther states, that some short time after the execution of the last above mentioned deed, John Willoughby & Richard D. Cooper seized on a number of the above mentioned negroes, and put them in confinement with an intention of selling them to southern traders, which coming to the knowledge of John Cooper he and his son Samuel repaired to the place and found them in the custody of Richard D. Cooper, and the said John Cooper, ordered him ~~pre~~ [per]emptorily to release, and discharge them, which he did the people returned to their homes, and were never again in any manner molested during the life of the said John Cooper—

Your petitioner further states that some time in the month of April last, John Willoughby in the night, at the head of a gang of armed men, seized on his three children, Charity, Sally & John, and a number of the other negroes and their Children included in the manumition of John Cooper, and violently and forciable caried them from Caroline County, to the Jail of Queen Anns County, with a view to sell them to foreign traders, or to carry them to the South himself, where your petitioner understands he has gone, That three several petitions for freedom, each including a family, were filed in Queen Anns County Court, Their Counsil found the deed of manumition defective in consequence of not being executed, and acknowledged according to the Laws of Delaware, One of the cases was tried and a Verdict was obtained for the petitioners, upon the ground that

John Cooper had permitted them to be moved from Delaware to Maryland against law. And John Willoughby well knowing the same facts to exist in another of the cases, Confessed a Judgment—The case of your petitioners Children is still pending in Queen Anns County Court, and he is instructed by Council that their legal claims depend upon other grounds—

A cause so dear to him, your petitioner is unwilling to risque upon an uncertain event; to adjudge his children to Slavery would be a case of peculiar hardship—John Cooper never incured any expense for them, they have been raised from their infancy by the means of your petitioner the fruits of his labor, he has riased them with tenderness and care, and he has indeavoured to instruct in the duties of their lowly station, and they have but lately attained the age of maturity—

Your petitioner is now in vale of years, beyond the age of Sixty. he had looked to his children as the support of his declining life. If bereft of them his remaining days must be spent in Sorrow, imbittered by the reflection that they are passing their lives in Climes where Slavery dos not wear the mitigated carracter, which belongs to Delaware & Maryland—

These considerations having induced your petitioner humbly to pray the Honourable Legislature of Delaware to give effect to the humane intentions of John Cooper, and to that end an act may be passed declaring the manumition executed by him to be good and available as if the same had been originally been done according to the Laws of Delaware

[signed] John Hawkins
By Wm Carmichael

SOURCE: Petition of John Hawkins to the General Assembly of Delaware, 17 February 1837, General Assembly, Legislative Papers, DSA. Granted.[1] PAR #10383702.

1. The act granting Hawkins's request was entitled only "An Act to Confirm a Deed of Manumission, Therein Mentioned. Private Act. Passed at Dover, February 18, 1837." *Laws of the State of Delaware, Passed at a Session of the General Assembly, Commenced and Held at Dover, on Tuesday the Third Day of January, in the Year of Our Lord, One Thousand Eight Hundred and Thirty-Seven* (Dover: Samuel Kimmey, 1837), 158. For the contents of the act, see General Assembly, Legislative Papers, Enrolled Bills, 1837, 292, DSA.

98. Greenberry and Caroline Logan, Brazoria, to Texas Legislature, 1837

Republic of Texas,

To the Honorable the Senate and house of Representatives of Texas in Congress assembled

The humble petition of Greenberry Logan a free man of color, respectfully represents, That he was born a slave in the state of Kentucky and was emancipated by his father David Logan; that having acquired the trade of a blacksmith he was induced to emigrate to this country ~~where~~ and arrived here in the year 1831 where he has lived ever since. That in the fall of the year 1835 he joined Captain Fannin's Company and was at the battle of Conception That he was afterwards a private in Captain York's Company and was one of those who volunteered to march into the Town of San Antonio under Colo. Milam, when it was taken by the Texan's; and that he was badly wounded in the right arm by a ball's passing through it, on, the 5th of December 1835, in the storming of said Town, and was afterwards honorably discharged, for the truth of all which he will refer to Colo. Hill a member of your body who was present at the taking of said town, and to Capt. Wm T. Austin and others who were present at the taking of said town. That he is now thirty eight years of age, infirm in body, and has almost entirely lost the use of his right arm by occasion of the wound received as before mentioned. That your petitioner had hoped that after the zeal and patriotism evinced by him, in fighting for the liberty of his adopted Country, and his willingness to shed his blood in a cause so glorious, he might be allowed the privilege of spending the remainder of his days in quiet and peace, but your [petitioner] has been informed that the Constitution contains a clause which prohi[bi]ts all free persons of color from coming to or remaining in the Country, unless by the consent of Congress. Your petitioner therefore humbly prays that Congress will pass a law permitting your petitioner to remain in the Country.

And your petitioner as well for himself as for his wife Caroline, and the said Caroline for herself, also respectfully represent to Congress, That the said Caroline is a free woman of color and has been married to said Greenberry Logan for about three years, that she has no children, and is anxious to remain in the Country That your petitioners have been living in the Town of Brazoria for the last three years and are now engaged in keeping a boarding house; and they pray that the said Caroline may also be permitted to remain in the Country

And as in duty bound they will ever pray &c
~~Ju~~ March 13th 1837
[signed] Greenberry Logan Caroline Logan

We the subscribers citizens of Texas being well acquainted with Greenberry Logan do certify that he is a man of good character, well behaved, and of good demeanor—That the matters set forth in the petition the subscribers believe to be true: and they recommend that a law be passed authorizing the said Greenberry Logan and wife to remain in the Country.

[signed] Geo. B. McKinsly
R. J. Townes
David Mills of Somervill [testifies separately] I
Jn. Selden have known Mr. Logan for
R Mills upwards of Ten years and

Edmund Andrew
Pat. C. Jackson
F. W Douglass
Theordore Bennet
Jas Collinsworth
[13 additional signatures]

have always Known him to
be an honest upright man
& has uniformly conducted
himself as a good citizen

SOURCE: Petition of Greenberry and Caroline Logan to the Texas Senate and House of Representatives, 13 March 1837, Records of the Legislature, Memorials and Petitions, RG 100, TSL-AD. No act was passed. PAR #11583702.

99. Samuel Seay, Davidson County, to Tennessee Assembly, 1837

To the Honourable the Senate and House of Representatives of Tennessee

The Petition of Samuel Seay a Citizen of the County of Davidson would respectfully represent to your Honourable Body that he is the owner of a negro man by the name of Peter commonly called Peter Loury [*sic*] about 27 years of age whom he is desirous the Legislature should emancipate or authorize the County Court of Davidson County so to do. As an inducement to the Legislature to grant this request Your Petitioner would state that said negro was raised in the County of Davidson, & that from his youth upwards he has been distinguished for his fidelity and industry, that he has always demeaned himself submissively and humbly towards white persons and ~~has always~~ seemed inclined to obey the Laws of the Community in which he lived that by his attention to business he has not only accumulated money enough to pay for himself but has also purchased a hack and horses with which he can earn a sufficient support ~~for~~ to prevent his ever becoming a charge to the Community in which he lives. But as a further security to prevent his becoming chargeable to the County, Your Petitioner proffers to give ample security against such an evil whenever your Honourable Body shall direct him so to do. he hopes the premises considered that the Prayer of this Petition will be granted

October 1837
[signed] Saml Seay

We the Undersigned Citizens of Davidson County believe from our knowledge of Peter Lourys Character that it would not be inconsistent with the interest of our Citizens for the Legislature to emancipate him

[signed]
Saml Seay
J. T. Hill
Ephraim H. Foster
R. H. McEwen
Jno M Bass
Thomas Fletcher
Stephen Cantrell
Henry Ewing

Alpha Kingsley H L Douglass
[30 additional signatures]

SOURCE: Petition of Samuel Seay to the Tennessee Senate and House of Representatives, 2 November 1837, Legislative Petitions, #156-1837, reel 15, TSLA. No act was passed.[1] PAR #11483702.

1. Two years later, in 1839, Samuel Seay again requested that Lowery (as he spelled his name) be allowed to remain in Nashville. The petition was rejected, and the assembly passed a law making self-hire and property ownership among slaves—"permitting slaves to act as if they were free persons of color"—indictable offenses. The fine was only five dollars, however, and Lowery continued to operate his hack-driving business. Petition of Samuel Seay to the Tennessee General Assembly, 4 November 1839, Legislative Petitions, #138-1839-1-2, reel 15, TSLA; *Acts Passed at the First Session of the Twenty-Third General Assembly of the State of Tennessee. 1839–40* (Nashville: J. Geo. Harris, 1840), 82–83; Records of the Davidson County Court, Minute Book, 1850–53, 6 March 1851, 135–37, Davidson County Courthouse, Nashville, Tennessee.

100. Rebekah, Sullivan County, to Tennessee Assembly, 1837

To the honorable the General Assembly of the State of Tennessee in Session at Nashville Sept 1837 the petition of the undersigned a free woman of Color in Sullivan County humbly sheweth—that your petitioner formerly belonged to Joseph Wallace who by his last Will and Testament bearing the date the 5th of July 1829 directed her to be emancipated after his decease—that said Joseph Wallace died in Feby 1835—and his said last Will and Testament was duly proven in open court agreeable to law—that your petitioner is ready at any time to give the necessary security for the indemnity of the County &c—but fears the operation of the late law, by which emancipated slaves are compelled to leave the state in a given time—Your petitioner humbly represents that she is a native of this state—that she is now far advanced in life—that all her children with the exception of one were sold into other states shortly after her master's decease—that she now lives in the neighborhood of that remaining child and of her aged husband with whom she earnestly desires to pass the remnant of her days—she therefore humbly prays your honorable body to pass a law permitting her, on sufficiently indemnifying the county, to remain in the State during her life—and your petitioner as in duty bound shall pray &c

[signed] Rebekah

We the underwritten Citizens of Sullivan County respectfully represent to the honorable the General Assembly of the state of Tennessee in Session at Nashville, that they have long resided in the vicinity of Joseph Wallace now deceased and have been acquainted with the above petitioner Rebekah both before and since her emancipation—that they believe her to be a woman of peaceful disposition and industrious habits and have no doubt she will be a useful member of society—they therefore respectfully request your honorable body to grant the prayer of her petition

[signed]	John Miller	Joseph Hobough
	James Crockett	Phillip Hobough
	Edward Cox	Samuel Cox
	John Cox	Daniel B. Bradley
	Jacob Cox	Abraham Cross
	[Dietirich?] Hobough	Jesse Cross
	George Pile Jun	

SOURCE: Petition of Rebekah to the Tennessee General Assembly, 10 November 1837, Legislative Petitions, #113-1837, reel 14, TSLA. Tabled. PAR #11483703.

101. William W. Dunn, Barnwell District, to South Carolina Assembly, 1837

South Carolina }
Barnwell District }

To the Honorable the Senate and House of Representatives of the said State—

The petition of William W. Dunn of the District of Barnwell—

Respectfully Sheweth—

That your petitioner is the owner of a little Boy, by the name of William, about twelve years of age—

That the mother, of the said Boy, is of a very light yellow complexion, and his father a white man.

That although the said Boy is the child of a coloured woman, he is nevertheless so very white and of so good a complexion, as not to create even a suspicion on the mind of the most critical observer, who was not acquainted with the fact, of his being in any degree related, by consanguinity, to a person of colour.—

That the said Boy has, in his raising, been kept, thus far, separate and apart, from the Society of coloured people, And has, consequently, not imbibed any of the principles or habits peculiar to them.—

That it is contrary to the wishes, as well as, it is, inconsistent, with the feelings of your petitioner, to retain in slavery, a person, who approximates, so closely in identity of colour, habits and appearance to that of the White man—

In accordance therefore with these considerations as well as, many others, good and valid, Your petitioner respectfully solicits your Honorable body to pass an Act, granting your petitioner leave, and authorizing him to emancipate the said little Boy William, with permission for him to remain in the State.—

And your petitioner will pray &c.—
the 1st Decr. 1837.
[signed] William W. Dunn

SOURCE: Petition of William W. Dunn to the South Carolina Senate and House of Representatives, 1 December 1837, Records of the General Assembly, #14, SCDAH. Referred to the Judiciary Committee. No act was passed. PAR #11383702.

102. James Paterson, Richland District, to South Carolina Assembly, 1838

To the Honorable Senate & House of Representatives

The Humble Petition of James Paterson Sheweth. That he is a free man of Colour, & that by a Long life of Care and industry he has been inabled to buy his wife Sarah, & his two Children George & Mary who are Slaves by the Law of the land & the property of your Petitioner—

Your Petitioner farther sheweth That he is very desireous of setting said slaves free, but that by the law of the Land he is unable to do so—Wherefore your Petitioner most humbly intreats your Honorable body to manumit the said slaves Sarah Paterson George Paterson & Mary Paterson—so that the honest industry, the unwearied Pains and untireing efforts of a Father & Husband may not be lossed to him intirely; and your Petitioner will ever Pray—

his
James J P Paterson
mark

South Carolina }
Richland District }

We the undersigned are well acquainted with James Paterson the within Petitioner—He is an honest Careful industrious man who by a life of constant industry has been inabled to buy his wife & children—and we do—for the purpose of incouraging Similer Conduct in others of his grade & for the purpose of doing to him but an act of Justice—most cordially recommend that the prayor of the Petitioner by [*sic*] Granted—

[signed] Wm. M Kennedy
Jesse Arthur
Thos. Wells
P.M.Buttes [testifies separately] I know nothing of his having purchased a family I believe him an industrious well behaved boy—respectful & always knowing his place

Adam Edgar
Jos A Black
James Boatwright
Benj Rawls
F. H. Elmore
B. F. Taylor
[6 additional signatures]

SOURCE: Petition of James Paterson to the South Carolina Senate and House of Representatives, 1838, Records of the General Assembly, #2923, SCDAH; Certificate, William M. Kennedy et al., ca. 1838, ibid. Rejected.[1] PAR #11383805.

1. "It would be inexpedient except as a reward for great and distinguished merit," a committee report read, "to depart from the principles and policy of the law which forbids the emancipation of slaves." A decade earlier, Paterson, a carpenter by trade, had petitioned the general assembly with a similar result. Following his death, however, Sarah, George, and Mary, though legally slaves, lived as free people of color. Petition of James Paterson to the South Carolina Senate, 27 November 1828, Records of the General Assembly, #73, SCDAH; Marina Wikramanayake, *A World in Shadow: The Free Black in Antebellum South Carolina* (Columbia: University of South Carolina Press, 1973), 38; United States Manuscript Population Census, 1850, Richland County, Columbia, S.C., 10.

103. Free Persons of Color of Fredericksburg to Virginia Assembly, 1838

To the Honorable Legislature of the State of Virginia.

The undersigned humbly beg leave to represent unto your Honorable body that they are free people of color residing within the jurisdiction of the Corporation of Fredericksburg and natives of the State of Virginia—some of them descendants of soldiers of the revolution—others having been ~~been~~ personally engaged in aiding the efforts of their country in the late War with England—That many of them are possessed of property, real as well as personal, & have therefore an abiding interest in preserving the peace and good order of the community—They beg leave further to represent that so general has become the diffusion of knowledge, that those persons who are so unfortunate as not to be in some slight degree educated, are cut off from the ordinary means of self=advancement & find the greatest difficulty in gaining an honest livelihood[1] In consequence of this condition of things and of the prohibitory statutes of Virginia on this subject, the Undersigned have been heretofore compelled to send their children abroad for instruction. The expense attendant upon this course, though heavy to persons of small means, is the least important part of the evils growing out of it. The residence of their children in the North not merely deprives them of the fostering care of their parents, but unavoidably exposes them to the risk of having their minds poisoned by doctrines alike inimical to the good order of society & distructive of their own interests.[2]

Moved by these considerations, your petitioners humbly beg that an Act may be passed, authorizing a school in the Corporation of Fredericksburg, for the instruction of the free people of color resident therein—subject never the less to such conditions & restrictions as to your honorable body may seem necessary & proper—And your petitioners will ever pray &c &c

The above petition having been duly Considered a Majority of the company select Mr. James Willkins to be the bearer of the same to the representative of Spotsylvania County

[signed]	Adolph Richards	Washington Simmons
	Edward Dbaptist	Lawson phillips
	James Wilkins	William Thornton
	William Dbaptist	Shelton Phillips
	Thrashley Simmons	Thornton Fox
		[6 additional signatures]

[Edward and William DeBaptist and Thrashley Simmons signed the petition twice, once at bottom of the petition and once on an attached signature page; only the signature page is included here.]

SOURCE: Memorial of Free Persons of Color of Fredericksburg to the Virginia General Assembly, 16 March 1838, Legislative Petitions, Spotsylvania County, VSA. Rejected. PAR #11683834.

1. In 1831, the Virginia General Assembly prohibited "all meetings of free Negroes or mulattoes at any school-house, church, meeting-house or other place for teaching them reading or writing, either in the day or night, under whatsoever pretext." Free blacks who broke the law were subject to corporal punishment of up to twenty lashes, administered at the discretion of the justice of the peace. Whites who broke the law faced a fine of up to fifty dollars and a jail term of up to two months. *Supplement to the Revised Code of the Laws of Virginia: Being a Collection of All the Acts of the General Assembly of a Public and Permanent Nature, Passed since the Year 1819* (Richmond: Samuel Shepherd, 1833), 245.

2. The petition was in response to a law prohibiting free blacks from sending their children out of the state for an education. Children in violation could, upon returning, be "bound out" until age twenty-one and then forced out of the state. Benjamin DeBaptist and his three sons worked as contractors; they owned horses, carriages, real estate, and slaves. Later, the DeBaptists and others migrated to the North. June Purcell Guild, comp., *Black Laws of Virginia: A Summary of the Legislative Acts of Virginia concerning Negroes from the Earliest Times to the Present* (Richmond: Whittet and Shepperson, 1936; reprint, New York: Negro Universities Press, 1969), 112; Luther Porter Jackson, *Free Negro Labor and Property Holding in Virginia, 1830–1860* (Washington, D.C.: American Historical Association, 1942), 140, 154, 157, 218; W. B. Hartgrove, "The Story of Maria Louise Moore and Fannie M. Richards," *Journal of Negro History* 1 (January 1916): 26.

104. William Goyens, Nacogdoches County, to Texas Legislature, 1838

To the Hon: the Senate and House of Representatives of the Republick of Texas in Congress Assembled

The Petition of William Goyens of the County of Nacogdoches and Republick[1] aforesaid would most respectfully show and represent unto your Honorable Body, that he is unfortunately a man of colour—And consequently his rights and interests have not in his humble opinion, been so reserved and protected by the general Laws of the Republick in relation to the interests herein after mentioned, as the rights of others whose colour is different from his.—That he emigrated to this Republick in the year 1820. That from peculiar circumstances which it is now too tedious to mention, not withstanding he was born free, he has all most been compelled, twice to purchase that freedom by his hard & honest labour—That from the date of his emigration he has ever been identified with the feelings and interest of the Anglo American population And has born his humble part in their struggles—

That he has had the honour to obtain some what the confidence of his superiors and has to the best of his feeble ability for the last five years, been more or less engaged in publick services connected with the Indians and for the last two yea[r]s he has had the honour to have been appointed a regular Indian Agent—for the Cherokee Tribe—And trusts that he has discharged that agency with satisfaction to those who have employed him and benefit to his cuntry—That during the war he has the satisfaction to know that he contributed to its support, by furnishing horses provisions and money—Small as may have been these services they were at least equal to his ability—That he has a family of children & a wife whom he has endeavoured to support with respectability and having also some servants, he certainly fills the requisitions of the law in being the head of a family—And as he thinks consequently under the Colonization Law entitled to Land—He has however made no application therfor since he has reason to fear from the peculiar provisions of the late land law his application would be rejected—He has never at any previous period, obtained Land as a Colonist or other wise except by fair purchase for a valuable consideration—

Under all the circumstances he ventures therfore to make this his first application before your Honorable Body that a League & Labor of Land may be granted him as a Head Right[2] and that a Law may be passed to that effect in his favour—And in duty he would ever pray &c.

[signed] William Goyens

SOURCE: Petition of William Goyens to the Senate and House of Representatives, 5 May 1838, Records of the Legislature, Petitions and Memorials, RG 100, TSL-AD. Rejected. PAR #11583803.

1. After Sam Houston defeated the Mexican general Antonio Lopez de Santa Anna at San Jacinto on 21 April 1836, Texas operated as an independent nation for nine years. It was recognized by the United States in 1837 and by various European countries between 1839 and 1841.

2. The constitution of 1836 guaranteed every head of family "already in the Republic" a "League and Labor of Land," a Texas unit of more than four thousand acres. *New Handbook of Texas,* 6 vols. (Austin: Texas State Historical Association, 1996), 3:1180–81; J. Villasana Haggard, *Handbook for Translators of Spanish Historical Documents* (Austin: University of Texas Press, 1941), 78.

105. William Lewis, Tuskaloosa, to Alabama Legislature, 1839

To the Honorable the Senate and House of Representatives of the State of Alabama in General Assembly convened.

The undersigned respectfully represents unto your Honorable body that he is a free man of color aged about thirty two years That he was born in the city of Charleston State of South Carolina and there continued to reside untill February Eighteen hundred and thirty six, when he came to the city of Tuskaloosa under a contract with Maj. Wm. B. Allen, (a citizen of the latter place) to serve him two years for a stipulated sum. The circumstances which induced that contract were these—Your petitioner was raised to the Carpenter's and House-joiner's business, and married a coloured woman then a slave of Mrs. Lucretia Horry of Charleston. Mrs. Horry dying in the fall of the year 1835, his the petitioner's wife became the property of Maj. Allen, in right of his wife who removed her to Tuskaloosa at the time first aforesaid

Your petitioner states that he has been married to his wife ten years, and was forced to follow her from Charleston or submit to a separation which his feelings would not brook as long as he was permitted to follow her.

Your petitioner states that he has always endeavoured to demean himself humbly and respectfully towards all persons, having been taught that the only way to pass through life smoothly was to attend to his own business.

He begs leave to refer to the following testimonials of Character &c. that your Honorable body may be advised of his standing &c.

In view of all which the undersigned most humbly entreats your Honorable body that he may be permitted to remain within the State of Alabama a free man, on giving such security for his good behavior &c. as may be thought proper,

And your petitioner will ever pray &c.

[signed] William Lewis

I hereby certify that I believe the foregoing to be correct and that the petitioner has, as far as my knowledge extends, behaved himself humbly and prudently, as much so as any colored free person in the country.—I therefore sign his petition, and believe those who know him will do the same.

[signed] William B. Allen

I became acquainted with William Lewis a coloured man about two years ago—having employed him to work for me as a house-Carpenter. I think him remarkable for his humility, prudence and industry—in fact I know of no Coloured man, whether a Slave or free, more so.

[signed] Henry W. Collier

SOURCE: Petition of William Lewis to the Senate and House of Representatives of Alabama, 1839, Records of the Alabama Secretary of State, Legislative Bills and Resolutions, ADAH; Certificate, William B. Allen, ca. 1839, ibid.; Certificate, Henry W. Collier, ca. 1839, ibid. No act was passed. PAR #10183901.

106. Citizens of Charleston Neck to South Carolina Assembly, ca. 1840

To the Honorable the Senate and House of Representatives of the State of South-Carolina

The Memorial of the Subscribers, Citizens of Charleston Neck, Respectfully Sheweth, That

That portion of the Parish St. Philip which is most thickly settled, and immediately proximate to the city of Charleston, is at present destitute of an efficient system of Police or local government adapted to its peculiar condition. The vicinity of Charleston, where an independent and well organized government prevails, exposes our inhabitants to evils much greater than those which are incident to other communities. The privileges which are enjoyed by the residents of Charleston Neck, and their exemption from the burden of taxation which the citizens of Charleston are obliged to bear, have rendered a residence amongst us peculiarly desirable to all persons whose conduct might expose them to the operation of the police regulations of the city. The consequence has been, that disorderly houses, unruly negroes, and wicked and depraved persons of every class, have resorted to the Neck, and endanger the security and comfort of its inhabitants. As might have been anticipated under these circumstances, the number of shops where spirituous liquors are retailed, has been multiplied, without any corresponding want on the part of the community. Encouragement has been given to unprincipled men by the success of others in the practice of vice; and within a few years it has been demonstrated, that there are persons now living in the heart of our society, who disregard our most salutary laws—who live in the habitual practice of corrupting our slaves—tempting them to theft and robbery, and promoting a general state of insubordination and depravity.

Examples may be cited of avowed disregard and audacious resistance to the law, and of attempts to intimidate our fellow citizens by threats of assassination from its vindication. Crimes of the most flagrant character have been committed amongst us, and the evil combination which prevails against the peace and prosperity of our community amongst those who enrich themselves by plundering us, has reached so deplorable an extent, that a sense of danger to every individual has wrought conviction of the necessity of some well regulated Police for our protection, and the establishment of law and order.

Your Petitioners have been informed, that it is not unusual for shop keepers to sell spirituous liquors in various places on the Neck, without any license whatever; that dissolute negroes are allowed to loiter in crowds about these shops—that on the Sabbath especially, when duty to God and man requires that peace and quiet should pervade our streets, they have been infested by worthless and turbulent negroes, who are intoxicated at these dens of wickedness; and when all the earnings of their labor and the fruits of their villainies, have been transferred to their seducers, are turned into the streets and roads, to disturb by their profanity, insolence and bestiality, the virtuous portion of our population, and disgrace the moral character of our community.

Intemperance, with its long train of vice and misery, must at all times render our slaves discontented and insubordinate; and licentiousness extinguish the wholesome moral force of fear, which should be stronger than the sword of justice. These results are not now only in apprehension, but have already manifested themselves.

Your Petitioners, after mature deliberation upon this serious and threatening aspect of our condition, deem it their imperative duty to apply to your Honorable Body for the passage of the following bill for the Regulation of Commissioners of Cross Roads for Charleston Neck.

The Laws regulating the Commissioners of Cross Roads for Charleston Neck, as they at present stand, are so scattered throughout the different Acts of Assembly, as to render it difficult for the Commissioners themselves to ascertain rightly what are their legitimate powers; and those powers have been granted to suit times and circumstances so entirely different from the present, as to render it manifest to every one, that some change is necessary. Your Memorialists would therefore submit to your Honorable Body, the subjoined Bill, in which it will appear that they ask for the Commissioners of Cross Roads, but few powers not already secured to them. The chief aim of the Bill is, to bring into a condensed form, the duties and powers which at present belong to the Commissioners of Cross Roads, an object which must be alike desirable to the Commissioners who are to execute the laws, and the citizens upon whom those laws are to operate. The new powers praye[d] for and embodied in the Bill, are those relating to the assessment of an annual tax upon all lots of land inhabited by a majority of slaves, or free persons of color; a capitation tax upon all free persons of color, and also a tax upon all persons of color, whether slaves or free, who keep a store or shop any where within the local limits of Charleston Neck. Also, the amendment of our Patrol Laws, so as to give the appointment of Leaders of said Patrol to the Commissioners of Cross Roads, instead of the Captain of the Beat of Charleston Neck, and to attach to said Commissioners the power to try defaulters, and to collect the fines imposed on the same.

As regards the assessment of a tax upon persons of color residing on the Neck, the late City laws seem to render such a measure absolutely essential. The imposition of taxes by the city on colored people has been so severe, that they have been driven almost entirely to the Neck. Wherever congregated, they have depreciated the value of all property around them, and have in many instances rendered themselves a complete nuisance to the neighborhood. Your Memorialist can see no good reason why they should thus receive what the city has thrown off as an offensive and useless part of their population. They therefore pray your Honorable Body to meet this prohibitory law of the city, by the enactment of the clause subjoined in the Bill, which they believe will have a countervailing tendency.

The appointment of Patrol leaders by the Board of Commissioners, the trial of defaulters for non-performance of Patrol duty, by said Board, and the appointment of its own Collector of Fines, appear to your Memorialists a manifest improvement upon the present system. There are at present upon Charleston Neck, at least 600 persons liable to perform Patrol duty; and as the whole of this number are under the control of one Captain, it must be apparent, how impossible it is for him, to give so large a Patrol proper arrangement and classification. In most places in the State, embracing so dense and numerous a population, the powers to regulate the Patrol are given to the municipal authorities. Your Memorialists are therefore of opinion, that this power should be assigned the Commissioners of Cross Roads, who should be for Charleston Neck the proper guardians of public tranquility and good order.

The other objects suggested in the subjoined Bill, your Memorialists believe, will appear of such importance to your Honorable Body, that they are content barely to suggest them, confident that your wisdom and correct judgment will induce you to pass the bill as prayed for.

And your Memorialists will ever pray, &c.

[no signatures]

SOURCE: Petition of Citizens of Charleston Neck to the South Carolina Senate and House of Representatives, ca. 1840, Records of the General Assembly, #2125, SCDAH. Granted.[1] PAR #11384012.

1. Several acts passed the legislature for "the better regulation" of slaves and free blacks in Charleston Neck. In 1842, lawmakers gave magistrates and freeholders authority to inflict up to twenty lashes and impose a ten-day jail sentence on slaves who misbehaved, and they in-

stituted a two dollar capitation tax for free blacks who lived in the Neck. In 1845, they granted commissioners of Cross Roads on Charleston Neck permission to build a guard house and to incarcerate "all such slaves and free persons of color as may be found violating the laws." Those violating the patrol law would receive corporal punishment unless the owner of the slave or the guardian of the free black paid a fine of not more than one dollar. *Acts of the General Assembly of the State of South Carolina, Passed in December, 1842* (Columbia: A. H. Pemberton, 1843), 238–40; *Acts of the General Assembly of the State of South-Carolina, Passed in December, 1845* (Columbia: A. G. Summer, 1846), 344.

107. Jehu Jones Jr., Philadelphia, Pennsylvania, to South Carolina Senate, 1840

To The President & Members of the Senate—of the State of South Car
Gentlemen Senators

The Subscriber a Native of Charleston in South Carolina, where he did reside for upwards of forty five years, without reproach, by trade a Tailor, & who served the State faithfully Ten years in the 17th Regiment under The Command of the late Colonels John Ward, Keating Lewis Simons & Robert Y. Hayne, without the Slightest censure, haveing been prevailed upon by Gentlemen of great respectability, to leave my peaceful & Happy Home, to Emigrate to Africa, with promises of great Remuneration in money & valuable Lands, made by the Friends of the American Colonization Society to Engage my Services for Liberia—But after I accepted the proposal & left Charleston for the Express purpose, to Enter into The promised arrangement, in New York—and the City of Washington, with Revd R R Gurley & others I found that the whole matter of promise was merely a delusion, and although the Subscriber was Seriously impressed in Charleston, with the Conviction, that all was fair & upright in the proposal made to him, and was advised by one of the most Eminent and pure Councillors in Charleston at that time 1832, to accept the proposal, viz Six hundred dollars per annum for my Services to assist in giving instruction in a School, a Town lot in Liberia, & a farm of valuable lands in the Country, also Two hundred dollars per annum as Assistant Editor of the Liberia Herald, Besides a Town Lot for my wife & each of my children; I Scarsely need to add, for your information, That I was disapointed in the whole matter & concern, on my application to those who held up The promise, of Large Sallery & honorable Employment for my services—those very gentlemen who profess to Engage to Councill, & to urge me forward in a Business, they inform me was praiseworthy—Soon as they found me afar from Home, without any prospects to Return to Charleston Abandoned me to my fate, among Strangers Jealous of new commers, without friends, without funds & without Employment. I should have returned home immediately in d[i]sgust with the Erroneous Philantrophy held up to me, But knowing The Laws of my Native State, which I Ever did Respect forbid me, return, I at once made up my mind to search for a Home & locate myself in Some desirable Situation where I could ma[i]ntain my wife & family—after Eight years diligent Search, I have failed to accomplish my design—I Cannot find a place that I can Reconcile myself to Live in—My wife also is unhappy—Like myself She cannot adopt the manners & Habbits of the North—under Such Circumstances and with an ardent desire to visit the grave of my Father, the Spot where I was Born, grew up & lived respectably for Nearly half a centry—where I am intimately Known The Recollection of many acts of Kindness that I have receved of the hands of South Carolinians generally, at Home & in the North will make me feel Happy, once more to mingle with & Embrace the Friends & associate of my youth—Therefore I respectfully beg the Legislature of my Native State to permit my Return to South Carolina—

[signed] Jehu Jones—184
Locust Street—Philadelphia

October 1840

Philadelphia—28th October—1840—

I certify that I have known Jehu Jones, formerly of Charleston South Carolina, during my residence in Philadelphia, that from his general character & my own knowledge of him, I feel myself authorized, confidently, to state that he is entitled to the character of a sober, industrious, & moral man, that his conduct has been such as to obtain for him the good opinion of the community in which he now lives, & to warrant the conclusion that he would merit the same good opinion in South Carolina, should he be permitted to return there.

[signed] Wm. Drayton—

SOURCE: Petition of Jehu Jones Jr. to the South Carolina Senate, October 1840, Records of the General Assembly, #47, SCDAH; Certificate, William Drayton, 28 October 1840, ibid. Rejected. PAR #11384007.

108. Citizens of Brazoria County to Texas Legislature, 1840

To The Honourable The Senate and House of Representatives in Congress assembled

We the undersigned residents of the County of Brazoria respectfully represent,—that a free coloured man named James Richardson, a native of Philadelphia, Sixty years of age, and by occupation a vender of oysters and refreshments, who has resided in the County since 1832, being desirous of remaining in the Country of his adoption, We hereby attest—that the aforesaid James Richardson from his industry, sobriety, and correct deportment has been in good repute since his emigration to Texas;—that he has been in the service of the Republic, having belonged to the garrison of Velasco[1] commanded by Capt Thomas Bell in 1836,—that from the circumstance of his being in the habit of entertaining travellers between Velasco & San Luis, at his house, which is the only one on the road & midway between those towns, he is useful to the public in a situation suitable to his class and at a locality where a white person equally serviceable could not be expected to reside;—that from his age and character and the fact of his having no descendants, as well as from the isolated situation of his dwelling, he is not liable to cause or promote any of the evils for whose protection the Laws prohibiting the residence of Free persons of Colour in this Republic were designed[2] and moreover, that for the reasons above stated we conceive that his case is entitled to the consideration of Your Honorable Body and worthy of being excepted from the operation of the Laws aforesaid.

Therefore We Respectfully pray—that an Act be passed to exempt the aforesaid James Richardson from the disability of permanently residing in this Republic to which the Laws referred to would subject him, to this end that he may be permitted to remain in his present and long accustomed abode and to continue in the useful advocations he has heretofore pursued, whereby both he and Your Petitioners will receive favour.

Brazoria County 19th of October 1840

[signed]	H N Walcott	Reuben M Potter
	Ambrose Crane	S. C Lyon
	D R Walker	Tho. L Green
	[ink smear]	A Underwood
	Henry Brewster	[ink smear]
		[13 additional signatures]

SOURCE: Petition of Citizens of Brazoria County to the Texas Senate and House of Representatives, 19 October 1840, Records of the Legislature, Memorials and Petitions, RG 100, TSL-AD. No act was passed. PAR #11584001.

1. Located near the mouth of the Brazos River, the fort at Velasco was the site of the first battle between the Mexicans and Texans prior to the revolution (1832). It was also the site where the Mexican president Antonio Lopez de Santa Anna signed the peace treaty on 14 May 1836, giving birth to the Republic of Texas. Lewis W. Newton and Herbert P. Gambrell, *Texas Yesterday and Today* (Dallas: Turner, 1949), 115, 150–51.

2. In 1840, the Texas General Assembly passed a law requiring free blacks who entered Texas to post a thousand dollar bond or be sold to the highest bidder for one year. The successful bidder would exercise "all the rights of ownership." H. P. N. Gammel, comp., *The Laws of Texas, 1822–1897,* 5 vols. (Austin: Gammel Book, 1898), 2:151–52. An earlier proposal to ban free Negroes entirely passed the General Council of the provisional government in 1836 but was not signed by the governor. Ibid., 1:1024–25.

109. Fanny McFarland, Houston, to Texas Legislature, 1840

To the Honorable the Senate and House of Representatives of the Republic of Texas in Congress assembled

The petition of Fanny McFarland humbly represents. That in the year 1827 being thirteen years ago she was brought to this country by William McFarland Esq who in consideration of her long and faithfull services to himself and his family gave unto her freedom in the year 1835. That at the time of the Mexican invasion[1] your petitioner was a resident of the town of San Felipe De Austin from which place she was driven by said invasion loosing all that she possesed in the world, Your petitioner further represents that in the year 1837 she took up her abode in this City and by her industry prudence and economy she has been enabled to gather together a little property, she would further represent that she ~~would~~ has four children held as slaves in this Republic so that all her hopes and prospects in this life lie here. And Your petitioner would beg leave to urge upon your Honors the hardships of being obliged in her *old age* to leave her children to sacrifice her hard earned property, to be obliged to part from fr[ie]nds of years standing to be obliged to leave [her] only home and be turned loose upon the wide world, And Your petitioner begs that when Your Honors take all these things into Consideration Your Honors will in your wisdom grant her Your gracious permission to spend the few remaining days of her life as a resident and Citizen of this republic. And your petitioner will ever pray &c

[no signature]

We the undersigned Citizens of Houston and Republic of Texas would respectfully second the petition of Fanny McFarland a free woman of Colour to remain as a Citizen of this Republic. And hereby reccomend her as a good and usefull Citizen, ~~and as a fit~~

Houston October 30 1840

[signed]	Ro. Wilson	1
	J. T Callihan	2
	Jas H. Clark	3
	W. M. Burch	4
	Wm. A. Elliott	5
	W K Wilson	6
	C M McGee J.P. H.C.	7
	W E Miller	8
	John W Markle	9
	J. H. Jackson	10
	[70 additional signatures]	

SOURCE: Petition of Fanny McFarland to the Texas Senate and House of Representatives, 30 October 1840, Records of the Legislature, Memorials and Petitions, RG 100, TSL-AD; Certificate, Robert Wilson et al., 30 October 1840, ibid. No act was passed. PAR #11584006.

1. The Texas revolution began 2 March 1835, when Texans defeated Mexican troops at Gonzales. Later, Texans besieged San Antonio, culminating in its surrender on 10 December 1835 and the withdrawal of Mexican forces from Texas. Early in 1836, a Mexican army under Santa Anna invaded Texas, winning a battle at the Alamo on 6 March 1836 but losing at San Jacinto on 21 April 1836.

110. Peggy Rankin, Montgomery County, to Texas Legislature, 1841

To the Honorable the Senate and House of Representatives of the Republic of Texas in Congress Assembled

Your memorialist Peggy Rankin of Montgomery County respectfully represents to your honorable body that she is the Owner of a Certain Mulatto Woman named Siney and her three Children Emily, Mahulda and Milton. The Mother of the said Siney was given to your memorialist by her father when a Child and was by her raised. The said Mulatto Woman Siney was born the property of your Memorialist has been tenderly raised and has been taught such labor as are generally performed by free White females she has ever been a faithful and obedient Servant and has been remarkably kind and attentive to your Memorialist in her infirm old age who is now in her 86th year. Knowing that according to the Course of Nature she Cannot long Survive, and being anxious to reward her kindness and obediance she is desirous to have her emancipated. As an additional cause your memorialist is Well aware that her late husband Robert Rankin in his life time intended that the said Mulatto Woman should remain in Servitude only during the life time of your Memorialist.

Your Memorialist further represents that all her Children and heirs are of full age and Consenting to the emancipation of the said Mulatto woman Siney

Your memorialist further represents that neither memorialist nor the estate of her deceased husband are indebted so that emancipation of the Woman Siney Cannot prejudice Creditors and the heirs of your Memorialist are ready and Willing to enter into such ~~as~~ obligation as may be required of them to prevent the said Mulatto Woman Siney and her Children from becoming a public Charge. Your memorialist therefore prays your honorable body to emancipate the said Mulatto Woman Siney And your memorialist as in duty bound will ever pray &c

Montgomery County
October the 25th 1841
[signed] Peggy Rankin

We the undersigned Children, and heirs of the estate of Robert Rankin and Peggy Rankin (of full age) do hereby give our Consent to the emancipation of the Mulatto Woman Siney mentioned in the foregoing memorial of Peggy Rankin and unite with her in praying your honorable body to grant her petition

[signed] W M Rankin
F T Rankin
John Rankin
James Rankin
[two illegible signatures]

SOURCE: Petition of Peggy Rankin to the Congress of the Republic of Texas, 25 October 1841, Records of the Legislature, Memorials and Petitions, RG 100, TSL-AD; Certificate, W. M. Rankin et al., ibid. No act was passed. PAR #11584102.

111. W. H. Merriwether et al., Albemarle County, to Virginia Assembly, 1842

To the General Assembly of Virginia.

Your petitioners beg leave to call your attention to a law of our State which we think calls loudly for amendment. The subject is not more particularly interesting to us, than the other citizens of the commonwealth, and we are aware that general laws should not be altered upon slight consideration, and that the question may be asked "why petitioners should call the attention of members to a subject which is equally interesting to themselves and has heretofore escaped their notice.["]

This oversight, we attribute, partly to the great interest felt in general politics, which seem to absorb every other question; but more particularly to the fact, that those immediately interested are unrepresented in your honorable body.

It is in behalf of the fair daughters of Virginia, that we appeal to your gallantry; and we may say to your justice, to redeem them from that law which oppresses with its iron grasp those upon whom misfortune has already laid her heavy hand. In the name of the forlorn and the desolate widow we approach you and ask that she may not be ground into the dust. In the name of our beloved and adored Virginia, we entreat that her proud escutcheon may be no longer blotted with the foul stain of oppressing those whose class is the very emblem of wretchedness, beyond any other civilized and christian country on the face of the earth. In the name of the *bereft* who is already deprived of every source of earthly joy and happiness, we entreat that you will not bereave her of that little portion of comfort which has been awarded to her in other lands, by the proud lords of creation.

It is well known to every member of your honorable body that the civil law, the prototype of the municipal regulations which prevail over the continent of Europe, places the wife almost on an equality with the husband; in so much that the common law which we received from our Anglo Saxon ancestors has been thought very illiberal in its provisions for widows. But even this gives the widow one third of the real estate (at any time during coverture[1] possessed by her husband) for her life. And one third of all other property in fee simple.[2]

There is a species of property in our State, which in the early periods of Legislation was sometimes considered as real and then as personal property, but in the changes of the law, our rugged forefathers seem to have forgotten what was due to their better halves, giving to them only the rights which they hold in real estate, without guarding those rights as they are in landed estate.[3] That is by a sort of legerdemain, they declared that slaves should be real or personal estate alternately, just as it might best subserve the interest of the males, disregarding entirely the rights of the softer sex. When a man marries, all his wife's slaves become his immediately; but when he dies those very slaves do not revert to the widow as land would; but she only gets a life estate of what he may not have sold in his life time; or may not be necessary to pay his debts after his death.

Slaves are in their nature personal estate, and the law declares them such in every case except that of Dower.[4] And if we will examine this subject more closely we will find that this is the very last kind of property of which we should wish to have a life estate. In money and every other kind of personal estate the use may be considered as at least equal to the interest; But this is by no means the case with slaves for taking them in families as they are generally allotted in dower, and the expense is nearly equal to the profit, sometimes even greater; and our court of appeals has decided that even when the slaves are an actual charge and the widow wishes to give them up, she cannot do so without the consent of the reversioners.[5] Can there be a greater mockery than this? You pretend to give the widow something for her support, and instead thereof compel her to bear a charge for the benefit probably of persons not at all related to herself, and very remotely to her deceased husband.—"She has asked for a fish, you give her a serpent; she asked for bread and you give her a stone."

The small value of slaves held for life is evidenced by the fact that most widows die insolvent or nearly so. Like other agricultarists they rely upon the growing crop to pay their expenses and if that should fail the year of their deaths nothing is left for their creditors. And in those sections of the state where wheat is the staple, the failures have been such for a succession of years, that the farmer has realized no profit but the increase of his slaves.

But were we to close our eyes and shut our hearts against the claims of those whom the Almighty has made dependant on our protection, and fold our arms in utter selfishness, there are yet other considerations which should induce us to give the widow a fee simple estate in the slaves allotted to her for dower.

The prosperity of the State would be promoted by placing widows in a situation less embarrassed, which would enable them to attend to the improvement of the soil. And frequently the public interest as well as their private good would be promoted by allowing them to sell slaves which may be unprofitably employed, or may be so unruly or dishonest as to be a pest to them and the whole neighborhood. But the law to secure the rights of reversioners, prohibits under every circumstance the removal of the slaves from the State.

It has been wisely ordained by our Creator, that the father should have authority over his children, to restrain them from evil, and encourage them in good courses, and the law has enforced this authority by giving him the power of withholding his property from a disobedient child. Many children have the misfortune to lose their fathers in infancy, while their mothers if spared are their proper guardians, and their authority would be much increased if they had the full control their dower slaves.

The great use of property is to provide against the misfortunes which are incident to our natures. In the full vigor of health and the day of prosperity, we may fearlessly rely upon our own exertions to provide those things which are necessary for our support. But when the frame is weakened by sickness, and the spirits broken by adversity, or when the desolate widow is deprived by an inscrutable dispensation of providence, or the more cruel neglect of an unworthy husband, of his aid in the support of the babes of her bosom; then is felt that heart sickening dependance which deprived of all aid so often "brings the gray hairs in sorrow to the grave." Then the true value of fortune is felt by the giver, as well as the receiver.

How numerous are the cases where some member of a family falls into this situation, or rather how rare are the instances that prosperity smiles upon every child of the household: May God avert such a misfortune from each and all of the children whom you have left at your smiling homes: but should it prove otherwise and your own heads should "lie cold before that dreadful day;" "if your departed spirits are permitted to revisit this world" of woe, they will certainly rejoice that by granting the amendment now asked, you have put it in the power of your broken hearted widow to give a pittance, to an unfortunate or even imprudent child, to save her or him from utter penury, and their offspring from being turned entirely adrift upon the world's cold charity.

'Tis for reasons like this that the English Judges have decided that the law abhors a perpetuity, and by their decisions have broken down entails as effectually as our laws. In fact we can see plainly in our law as it now stands, the same spirit which supported the entails and family settlements in England.

One of the peculiar aggravations of the law, as it stands at present, is that if a man becomes embarrassed, he is obliged to surrender his reversionary interest in his mother's dower, to be sold for a mere song when that very interest, if under the control of his mother might furnish a support for his family, without taking any thing from the rest of her children.

Although we hope that in the greatest number of instances, filial piety is amply sufficient to ensure every attention to an aged mother, yet there are many cases where the attention of children would be much increased by knowing that a mother had something to dispose of.

Even in an economical point of view it is very desirable that the slaves should be held in fee simple instead of being divided into two estates. Such a division materially lessens the value of the property, and there can be no doubt that the fee simple in all the negroes held as dower in this State would be worth millions more than the life estate, and reversion held separately, and would bring it in the market.

In fact what we ask you to give the widow or rather take from the children, that is, a reversion, in one third of the slaves, is worth very little to the children at the time the dower is laid off; being generally estimated at half of the fee simple, say one sixth of the interest of the slaves, whilst all other property is left undisturbed.

The cause of humanity too as well as the interest of the husband, would be promoted by giving the wife and widow an interest in rearing the young negroes.

We beg you will excuse us for dwelling on a subject which you no doubt understand better than we do, and which will present to you other views overlooked by us. But we cannot for a moment believe that giving it the calm consideration of statesmen, forgetting that you are giving up something to your own wives (if such cold selfishness could restrain you for a moment), but laying aside self, and looking entirely to remote posterity—reflecting that you have sisters and daughters as well as wives, whose hearts will be warmed by the consciousness that you have been the blessed instrument of reinstating their rights so long withheld; you cannot refuse to grant our petition.

[signed]	W H Merriwether	Wm M Keblinger
	Alonzo Gooch	H Massie
	Chas Lucas	Andrew Sample
	J. Z. Banet	James Alexander
	Richd Mathews	Andrew McKee
		[6 additional signatures]

Charlottesville Feb 3/42
Dear Sir

Inclosed is a petition which has only been handed round a few minutes [under] candle light and it is not now dark.

I send it with the small number of names rather than wait because it is all important that it should be [put] before the legislature as soon as possible.

I hope you will present it Saturday;

I shall get more signatures and send [you] another petition next week

Your family are all well

Very Respectfully yrs

[signed] W H Merriwether

SOURCE: Petition of W. H. Merriwether et al. to the Virginia General Assembly, 5 February 1842, Legislative Petitions, Albemarle County, VSA; W. H. Merriwether to Alexander Rives, 3 February 1842, ibid. No act was passed. PAR #11684205.

1. *Coverture,* in law, is the status of a married woman.

2. *Fee simple* is the ownership of land with unrestricted rights of disposition.

3. Between 1705 and 1792, slaves in Virginia were defined for some purposes as real estate rather than as chattel property. The same was true in Kentucky between 1798 to 1852 and Arkansas between 1840 to 1843. Slaves in Louisiana were designated as "immovables" in some cases and "real estate" in others. The historian Thomas D. Morris observes, "For one reason or another rules of real property law were applied to slaves in some instances in over one-third of the jurisdictions that made up the slave South." Slaves considered as real property could not legally be sold on speculation to distant locations. This, of course, was not adhered to in practice. Thomas D. Morris, *Southern Slavery and the Law, 1619–1860* (Chapel Hill: University of North Carolina Press, 1996), 64.

4. A *dower,* in law, is the portion of a man's estate—usually one-third of the real estate—that his widow inherits for life.

5. A *reversioner,* in law, is a person who has a right to receive an estate.

112. P. N. Nicholas et al., Henrico County, to Virginia Assembly, 1842

To the General Assembly of Virginia

The undersigned respectfully represent that at a Public meeting of the Citizens of Richmond and County of Henrico held at the Capitol on the 9th day of Decr. 1833 for the purpose of adopting measures to prevent the absconding and abduction of their slaves beyond the limits of the state A society was formed subject to the following rules and regulations, adopted by said meeting

"1st. Resolved that it is expedient that the owners and employers of slaves in the County of Henrico and city of Richmond, do form a Society for the prevention of the absconding or abduction of their slaves and for the detection and recovery of such as shall have absconded or been abducted beyond the limits of the State. In a word, for the protection of their slave property

2nd. That such persons as shall subscribe and contribute towards the raising of a fund for the objects of the Society and shall annually hereafter contribute towards the maintaining and continuing the same shall constitute the members thereof

3rd. That there shall be a Board of Directors consisting of Sixteen members, five of whom may act and of whom eight from the city and eight from the County shall be chosen by the general meeting forthwith, to continue in office till the third Monday in December 1834 and till a new election shall take place. That they shall choose from among themselves a President Vice President and Secretary and that they shall appoint a Treasurer. That there shall be an annual general meeting held by the society on the third Monday in December in each and every year for the election of Directors

4th. That the fund and all means and modes for giving effect to the first Resolution shall be ordered and governed by the Board of Directors who shall have power to adopt such Rules and Regulations for their own government as to them shall seem fit and proper

5th. That in giving effect to the first resolution it shall be a primary object to recover the slaves of members of this society gone or carried beyond the limits of the state, to discover the means and mode by which they effectuate their escape without detection and to provide suitable countervailing remedies, the expense of which shall be defrayed out of the funds of the Society

6th. That all other persons to be employed for the purpose of giving effect to the first resolution shall be appointed by the Board of Directors and that the said Board shall also fill any vacancies in their own [Board].

7th. That the Board of Directors shall on behalf of the Society adopt such measures to give effect to the first resolution as to them may seem fit, and to that end shall have power to make application to the Authorities of the state, county and city, and to employ persons and to reward them out of the funds of the Society pursuant to their regulations"—In pursuance of the above resolutions a Board of Directors was appointed, who, in accordance with the powers conferred on them appointed a President, Vice President Secretary and Treasurer. And in pursuance of a resolution also adopted by said meeting, committees were appointed to solicit and collect subscriptions from the citizens. That the said committees collected a considerable sum of money and paid the same to the Treasurer (the late James Rawlings decd) appointed by the board of Directors. That by authority of the board of Directors a part of the fund thus subscribed was disbursed to promote the objects of the Society. The residue amounting as far as can be ascertained to nearly one half the amount collected remained in the hands of the Treasurer at the time of his death which occurred in the year

That at a meeting of the Directors held on the 7th day of August 1839 a Treasurer was appointed to supply the vacancy, with instructions to ascertain the amount due by the late Treasurer, in performance of which duty he reports that the Executor of the deceased Treasurer acknowledges a balance due the Society from his Testator, but declines to pay the same to the Treasurer, on the ground, that no one is authorised to give him a legal receipt for the same—In consideration whereof and the more effectually to secure the object of this Society in guarding its members and owners from the loss of their slave property, and aid in preserving the peace and quiet of the community, we respectfully ask your honourable body to grant us an act of Incorporation, with power also to give to the Executor of the deceased Treasurer, a legal receipt for the amount of money due the Society—and to collect, receive and disburse, all or any sums of money which may be voluntarily contributed or otherwise subscribed in aid of the Society

[signed]	P. N. Nicholas	Sam. S. Myers
	James Bosher	J.H. Eustace
	John Goddin	Isaac Davenport
	Ro. A. Mayo	Thomas Nelson
	J A. Goddin	WillByr Chamberlayne
		[12 additional signatures]

SOURCE: Petition of P. N. Nicholas et al. to the Virginia General Assembly, 8 March 1842, Legislative Petitions, Richmond City, VSA. Referred to the Committee of Courts of Justice. No act was passed. PAR #11684212.

113. Commissioners of Raleigh to North Carolina Assembly, 1842

To the General Assembly of the State of North Carolina

The Memorial of the undersigned Commissioners of the City of Raleigh respectfully represents unto your Honorable Body, that in the humble opinion of your Memorialist many defects exist in the Statute laws of the State relating to Slaves and free person of colour, and they therefore beg leave respectfully to call your attention to the policy, if not the absolute necessity in some cases of so amending these laws as to supply such defects.—It is well known that for years past a band of unscrupulous fanatics, living under the same Government and protected by the same laws with ourselves, have been using every exertion to produce discontent and ultimately to engender rebellion amongst the Slaves of the South:—Appeals have been made to the worst of passions—Every epithet which detraction and madness could furnish has been unsparingly applied to the Slaveholder:—Emissaries clothed in the garb of benevolence have been sent amongst us either to carry on the work of insurrection or to seek out weapons for detraction. Pamphlets, handbills, newspapers disgusting and revolting pictures have been circulated throughout the Northern States intended to poison the public mind, and well calculated to increase that fanatical spirit which threatens the peace and happiness of the Country.—What might have been the result of the efforts of men thus unfuriated [*sic*], had not timely steps been taken to counteract them, no patriot or christian can contemplate without horror.

The Slave holding States have been forced, in self defence to increase the rigour of their internal police in relation to Slaves and free Negroes. The Legislature of this State has passed a variety of laws for this purpose and made every provision as they thought for their faithful and prompt execution.—Amongst which laws are those passed in the years 1830 and 1831, forbidding slaves to teach each other, and prohibiting their being taught by white persons, to read or write, figures excepted,—forbidding Slaves to go at large as freemen, or to preach or exhort in public—requiring emancipated Slaves to leave the State within ninety days after their emancipation—forbidding the migration of free Negroes into this State,—and prohibiting their intermarriage with Slaves—These and a variety of other laws were enacted not only to protect the value of slaves as property, but to preserve that due subordination Amongst them, and the free Negroes which was likely to be disturbed by occurrences in other sections of the Country and by the machinations of the reckless spirit of Abolitionism, which was springing up at the North.—The policy of these laws under the exigencies which occasioned them, cannot be doubted.—They have nevertheless almost entirely failed to meet the object of the Legislature on account of the loose way in which they have been heretofore executed.—

We would beg leave to call attention most particularly to the law which forbids slaves and free persons of Color, under any pretence whatsoever to preach or exhort in public or to act as preachers or teachers in any prayer meeting or association for worship where slaves of different families are assembled. The spirit of this law is daily violated in many sections of the State particularly in the Towns and villages where it is less difficult for them to congregate in large numbers. It is evident the Legislature meant by this enactment to prevent the assembling of different families of negroes to carry on religious worship under *their own direction* or by teachers or exhorters *of their own colour.* They have learned from the fatal experience of others that in such assemblies, so managed, insubordination and rebellion might be preached under the garb of religion.—It certainly was neither their intention nor desire to deprive this species of population of the advantages of religious instruction.—They well knew that every opportunity had been and would continue to be afforded them to attend religious worship in Churches and at other places where white persons would officiate and where due order would be preserved.—They could not have intended therefore to allow the law to be evaded and its objects defeated by one or two white persons attending such meetings, thereby given them the *appearance* of being under the control and direction of whites.—Nor could it have been the intention of the Legislature to permit negroes to assemble at night from various families and engage in religious exercises by *praying* and *singing.*

Such a construction is a mere quibble and destroys all the efficacy of the law. Yet it is resorted to sometimes by respectable men, and may hereafter be resorted to by bad men, to defeat the objects of the Legislature and to keep up a practice which can in no way benefit the slave, but which on the other hand must inevitably result in the most injurious consequences both to him and his master.—Your Memorialists therefore beg that the said law may be rendered more efficient either by extending its provisions—increasing the severity of the punishment, or making such alterations or amendments thereof as will render it more explicit, and thereby disarm those who encourage its violation by the miserable quibble to which they resort for their justification.

There is but one other law to which we shall particularly call your attention:—We have reference to that which prohibits the migration of free Negroes into this State and the return of such persons after having been absent for more than ninety days.[1] The provisions of this laws [*sic*] are rendered perfectly nugatory by the ease with which its punishments may be evaded.—The negro forfeits $500, for which Judgment is to be entered up under proper process, and if the penalty is not paid within the time allowed by the sentence of the Court, he is to be hired out. Experience shews that no one will give more than a nominal price for a negro hired under such circumstances owing to the many facilities he has to escape and go beyond the reach of the master—The offender is thereby enabled to provide some friend, with the means to hire him, who permits him to go at large either to renew his violation of the law in other parts of the State or to go beyond its limits ridiculing the cobweb character of those laws from whose meshes he so easily escaped. Many instances of this kind have occurred since the passage of the law.—We beg leave to call your attention to what most persons consider another defect in this enactment. The free negro migrating into the State is to have twenty days notice given him before legal process can issue to subject him to the penalties of the law. Thus there is time allowed him to infuse into the minds of the slave population principles adverse to their happiness and tending to disaffection or rebellion.

And can it possibly for one moment be alledged that every effort should not be made to keep from amongst us those free negroes who have resided in northern Cities where the doctrines of abolitionism are openly as well as secretly advocated and advanced?—Instances might be cited where free Negroes who had visited northern Cities were enabled to return into the State and retain their residence here for years—So defective are the provisions of the law that when notified at one place the offender has only to rest contented until the twenty days have nearly expired and then move to some other place, which device he repeats as often as there may be occasion for so doing.

This species of population is annually becoming more and more troublesome. In some sections of the State they are nuisances of the worst kind.

We speak of them as a class. Occasionally you find instances of the greatest industry and honesty—But they are mostly especially those who have taken up their residences in the suburbs of the towns indolent and worthless, living not by labour but by depredations upon their neighbors—by trading with slaves and by midnight robberies.

Perhaps no part of the Country is more infested by this population than that in which your Memorialists reside.—They have had ample opportunity to know what is their character and how injurious their example and contact are to the slaves. Many amongst them can read,—And occasionally may be found one who is able to write well.—That any information which may be thus acquired is used to the injurious influence of the Slave is not within the knowledge of your Memorialists, but surely it behoves wise Legislatures to provide against the evil consequences of such a state of things.—We are far from desiring that any policy should be adopted in reference to these people which would be considered harsh or unjust.—The peace of the community—their own safety, and the happiness of the slaves, however require that something should be done.

So far, many of those enactments which were intended for wise purposes have failed to remedy the evils complained of owing either to their own inefficacy or the manner which they have been enforced.—The facilities for rapid communication between the different parts of the country, by means of Rail Roads, the ease with which information may be secretly obtained from the most distant quarter, and used for evil purposes, render it necessary that some alteration should be made in the internal police of those States in which the institution of slavery exists.—No good man should desire to create any unnecessary alarm in reference to the efforts which have been made in some sections of the Northern States to produce dissatisfaction amongst our slaves. Their own good however, and the interest and safety of the community demand that energetic means should be adopted to remedy those evils which exist, and which must sooner or later produce their bitter fruits.—Your Memorialists entreat that your Honorable Body will take this matter under consideration and act in relation thereto as your wisdom may advise to be best for all concerned. They do not wish to be considered as dictating. They regard the defects of the laws which they have brought to your notice as public grievances, and certainly worthy of your consideration. What is best to be done is not for them to say, nor would they presume to point out what is the true policy to those whose province it is to provide for the public safety by the passage of wise laws, for which duty they are taken to be fully qualified.—Should your Honorable Body consider it wise not to pass any general law on this subject they beg that such provisions may be made as will protect the community in which they live from the many evils they have attempted to show must originate from permitting the laws to remain as they now are—

And your Memorialists as in duty bound will ever pray &c &c.

Raleigh Nov 8th AD 1842

[signed] T. Loring, Intendant

SOURCE: Petition of the Commissioners of Raleigh to the North Carolina General Assembly, 8 November 1842, Records of the General Assembly, Session Records, NCDAH. No act was passed. PAR #11284206.

1. This law was also passed during the 1830–31 session. John Hope Franklin, *The Free Negro in North Carolina, 1790–1860* (1943; reprint, Chapel Hill: University of North Carolina Press, 1995), 69.

114. S. T. Robinson et al. to South Carolina Assembly, ca. 1843

To the Senate & House of Representatives of the State of South Carolina

Your Petitioners Citizens of the said State shew That the persevering efforts, in some parts of our Union, to intermeddle injuriously with our slave population, furnish increased motives for vigilance on our part not only in repelling interference from abroad, but in a stricter government at home That the judicious government of our slaves at home, is liable to mischievous disturbance from the importation of vicious or criminal slaves from other States That as laws have been passed by the States, Southwest of us,[1] prohibiting the importation of Slaves into those States merely for Sale and not the property of residents or emigrants passing through them, This State and the City of Charleston in particular, have become the common place of meeting between the Slave dealer from places north of us, and the purchaser South West of us—That the motive of the Slave dealer is not only to approach as near as he can to his buyer, but to remove the slave as far from his old range, & from notorious bad character as possible That while on Sale here many vicious slaves are palmed upon careless or confiding Citizens among us, and their mixture with our own, has had a sensible influence upon the docility and usefulness of our slaves. That your Petitioners are not to be confounded with those inimical to Southern interests who oppose the removal of Slaves from State to State under any circumstances We propose to confine the admission of Slaves into this State, to those brought here by their owners residents in this State, and those the property of emigrants passing into or through this State, and we propose to prohibit under proper sanctions, the introduction of slaves into this State *merely for Sale* and lastly we propose that additional Sanctions should be added to that part of the Act of 1740 which prohibits the slave from sleeping or living out of his master's premises or of those of some white person appointed by the master And your Petitioners pray the passage of such Laws as may attain these objects

[signed] S. T. Robinson — Alfred Huger
Saml D. Stoney — Chs. Edmondston
Wm H. Peronneau — Daniel Ravenel
C Gadsden Hume — John Robinson
James Ravenel — A Tobias
[87 additional signatures]

SOURCE: Petition of S. T. Robinson et al. to the South Carolina Senate and House of Representatives, ca. 1843, Records of the General Assembly, #2824, SCDAH. Referred to the Judiciary Committee. PAR #11384301.

1. In 1827, the Alabama assembly passed "[a]n act to prohibit the importation of slaves into this state for sale or hire." In 1832, a revised law permitted certain groups—guardians, heirs, legatees, distributees, and husbands—to enter the state with slaves. *Acts Passed at the Eighth Annual Session of the General Assembly of the State of Alabama, Begun and Held in the Town of Tuscaloosa, on the Third Monday in November, One Thousand Eight Hundred and Twenty-Six* (Tuscaloosa: Grantland and Robinson, 1827), 44–45; *Acts Passed at the Thirteenth Annual Session of the General Assembly of the State of Alabama, Begun and Held in the Town of Tuscaloosa, on the Third Monday in November, One Thousand Eight Hundred and Thirty-One* (Tuscaloosa: Wiley, McGuire and Henry, 1832), 12–18. In 1837, Mississippi passed "[a]n act to prohibit the introduction of slaves into this State as merchandise, or for sale." The act was

repealed in 1846. John Codman Hurd, *The Law of Freedom and Bondage in the United States,* 2 vols. (Boston: Little, Brown, 1858–62; reprint, New York: Negro Universities Press, 1968), 2:148.

115. Citizens of Halifax County to North Carolina Assembly, 1844

To the General Assembly of the State of North Carolina,

We the undersigned, citizens of Halifax County—in the Exercise of a right guaranteed to us in the Constitution would respectfully Call the attention of your honorable body to a subject which we think should claim your serious consideration, that is: the a[l]teration or amendment of the present law concerning ~~runaway~~ negroes—imposing some heavy penalty upon any runaway negro that is caught with a gun,—or is known to have one—We have suffered greatly in the County from the lameness of the present law, in this particular, It has become a common occurrence now for runaway negroes to provide themselves with guns in this County, & to use them in providing themselves provisions, & by threats to intimidate and frighten the timid thereby rendering their apprehension Extremely difficult—almost impossible, We know of two, at this time, in the vicinity of Weldon that have guns & have used them as above stated—One farmer have lost by them seventy five hogs, they alleging as the reason they stold from him in particular—that he ~~thatx~~ hunted for them; they sent him word, that if he would not hunt for them again—they would not Kill any more of his hogs—but if he did, they should kill him; Another respectful Citizen of this County was shot by them, returning home in the night—the above statement is not Exaggerated but a plain statement of facts—and we do think they call loudly upon your honorable body for some salutary enactment to put a stop to such monstrous outrages of the well being and order of society—We would respectfully suggest to your honorable body the passage of a law upon the subject, based on the following principles, to wit—the negro to be hung, & the state pay the owner for him, & that no one to be held accountable for shooting him while, in the woods,[1] Your honorable body, may perhaps think that the above principles of a law would be too strong, We dare say they are—but we feel so sincerely the importance of putting an immediate stop, to such dangerous examples, we do think that strong remedies ought ~~out~~ to be used, We leave the matter with your honorable body, hoping and believing, that your will not turn a deaf ear to the grievances of a portion of fellow citizens, & that you will enact Such a law as will have the effect desired by your petitioners

[signed]	Wm. M. Moody Jr.	G W Ivey
	N.M. Long	L M Long
	Rice B Pierce	B W Bass

Lawrence C Pierce
W H Day
B.J. Spruill
John Ivey
[7 additional signatures]

The Select committee to whom was referred a memorial ~~from~~ of from sundry Citizens of Halifax County have duly considered the same and report that the memorialists state in their petition that several run away slaves had committed serious wrongs & injuries by the use of guns, on the said citizens, ~~by~~ in the wanton destruction of their hogs & cattle, and that in one instance a respectable and useful inhabitant had been fired upon by them and seriously wounded, because of his efforts to cause them to be arrested, And ~~And~~ that the most insolent threats had been made of general destruction of the cattle & hogs of the petitioners if any further attempts were made to bring them to justice. The Committee entertain no doubt but the memorialists have been grossly outraged and injured by the said run away slaves and if the present laws do not afford adequate remedy for the evils complained of, it would unquestionably be the duty of the present General Assembly to provide new guards for the public safety & security. For doubtless it is the duty of the Legislature to provide a remedy for every evil which afflicts society, coming within the competency of the Legislative power. The remedy suggested by the memorialists is that authority should be given by law to kill ~~any Slave to sh~~ run away Slaves while lying out, ~~lurking~~ in the woods swamps & other secret places doing serious injury to the public and that the State should pay for such slaves when so killed. Your committee have no hesitation in declaring it to be their opinion that such a law would be unnecessarily cruel & sanguinary; would lead to great abuses and would render slave property insecure and consequently diminish its value. But it is important to inquire whether the law as it exists at present, is not sufficient to suppress the evil of which complaint is made, and therefore render further legislative on the subject unnecessary.

In the twenty second section of the one hundred & eleventh chapter of the revised States [statutes] it is provided, that when run away Slaves lie out in obscure places killing cattle & hogs and committing other injuries to the inhabitants of this State it shall be lawful for any two Justices of the Peace to issue proclamation against such slave or slaves, requiring him or them for[th]with to surrender him[self] or themselves; and it is made the duty of the Sheriff, when required by the said Justices, to take with him such power as he may deem necessary for effectually apprehending such run away slave or slaves and if after such proclamation such slave or slaves do not immediately surrender him[self] or themselves, then it is declared to be lawful for any person or persons to kill & destroy such slave or slaves, without accusation or impeachment of any crime for the same. By the same law, slaves whether run away or otherwise, are prohibited from using a gun in the woods, and is liable to be whipped if found so offending.

These provisions ~~your~~ the Committee believe ample to suppress the mischief complained of, if duly enforced, and desire to be discharged from the further consideration of the subject.

Jan. 8, 1845

[signed] A. Joyner
Chairman

SOURCE: Petition of Sundry Citizens of Halifax County to the North Carolina General Assembly, 14 December 1844, Records of the General Assembly, Session Records, NCDAH; Report of Select Committee, 8 January 1845, ibid. Rejected.[2] PAR #11284403.

1. In 1741, North Carolina lawmakers had passed a comprehensive act governing servants and slaves. In a section concerning runaways "lurking in Swamps, Woods, and other obscure Places, killing Cattle and Hogs," the law permitted any two justices of the peace to declare them outlaws who could be shot on sight "without Accusation or Impeachment of any Crime for the same." In 1796, an act provided compensation to owners whose slaves were killed as outlaws in Bladen, Halifax, Granville, Cumberland, Perquimans, Beaufort, and Pitt counties; the next year a similar act was passed in Warren, Onslow, and Chatham counties. John D. Cushing, comp., *The First Laws of the State of North Carolina,* 2 vols. (Wilmington, Del.: Michael Glazier, 1984), 1:93; *Laws of North-Carolina. At a General Assembly, Begun and Held at Raleigh, on the Twentieth Day of November, in the Year of Our Lord One Thousand Seven Hundred and Ninety-Seven, in the Twenty-Second Year of the Independence of the Said State: Being the First Session of the Said Assembly* (n.p., 1798), 4. For the repeal of some of these laws, see *Laws of North-Carolina. At a General Assembly, Begun and Held at the City of Raleigh, on Monday the Nineteenth Day of November, in the Year of Our Lord One Thousand Eight Hundred and Ten, and in the Thirty-Fifth Year of the Independence of This State* (n.p., 1811), 40.

2. The assembly did pass a law instituting a fine of one hundred dollars for anyone convicted of selling, bartering, or delivering to a slave "any gun cotton, fire arms, swords, dirks or other side arms, unless these articles be for the owner or employer, and by the written order of the owner or employer." *Laws of the State of North Carolina, Passed by the General Assembly, at the Session of 1846–47* (Raleigh: Thomas J. Lemay, 1847), 107.

116. Jacob et al., Halifax County, to North Carolina Assembly, 1844

To the honourable the Legislature of the State of North Carolina the petition of Jacob, Mary, Patsey[,] Meriwether and Matilda free persons of Colour, humbly represents that Philip E. Vass formerly of the County of Halifax in the State of Virginia by his last will and testament in writing duly executed according to the Laws of the Commonwealth of Virginia and duly admitted to probat in the County Court of the said County of Halifax, emancipated your petitioners Jacob and Mary and such of the slaves of his father's Estate then undivided as should be alloted to him in the division, and appropriated the sum of two thousand dollars for the purpose of purchasing lands in the state of North Carolina upon which to settle his said slaves in the manner particularly directed in his said will. Your petitioners Patsey, Meriwether and Matilda were assigned or alloted to the said Philip E. Vass in the division of the slaves of Philip Vass the Elder the father of the said Philip E. Vass; And by a decree of the Circuit Superior Court of Law & Chancery for the County of Halifax in a suit brought by your petitioners against Isaac Medley the executor of the said Philip E. Vass decd. they were declared to be free persons under and by virtue of the will aforesaid. For full and more perfect information on the subject they refer to a copy of the will of the said Philip E. Vass decd. a copy of the Record of a suit in the County Court of Halifax in the State of Virginia for the division of the Estate of Philip Vass the Elder decd. both of which are regularly certified by the Clerk of the said Court; and also a copy of the Record of the suit brought by your petitioners against the Executor of the said Philip E. Vass decd. in like manner certified by the Clerk of the Circuit Superior Court of Law & Chancery for the said County of Halifax—Your petitioners respectfully represent to your Honourable body that by the Laws of the Commonwealth of Virginia they will not be permitted to reside within its limits; and they have been informed that the Laws of North Carolina also forbid the immigration of free persons of Colour into that State. They have been advised that they cannot have the benefit of the provision made for them in the will of their late master unless they are permitted to remove to the State of North Carolina; and in confirmation of that opinion they beg leave to state that James Young the agent or trustee appointed to execute that part of the will of the said Philip E. Vass decd. which relates to the emancipation removal and settlement of his slaves, brought his suit in the Circuit Superior Court of Law & Chancery for the County of Halifax (Virga.) against the Executor of the said decedent, to recover the sum of two thousand dollars appropriated by the will to that object; and the Court declared it's [*sic*] opinion to be that the money could not be recovered unless the trust could be executed in the manner prescribed by the will that is by the removal of your petitioners to the State of North Carolina; and it suspended it's final action upon the case to enable them to profer their petition to your Honourable body. They are very poor and entirely destitute of the means to remove to any of the United States or to any other Country in which the laws would suffer them to reside and unless they can have the benefit of the provision made for them in the will aforesaid they are at all times liable by the laws of Virginia to be sold as slaves. They therefore cast themselves on the indulgence of your Honourable body and humbly entreat that the benevolent intentions of their former master towards them may be suffered to be carried into execution by removing the restrictions which now prevent their availing themselves of all the benefits of the provision made for them in his will. And your petitioners as in duty bound will ever pray &C.

[no signatures]

SOURCE: Petition of Jacob et al. to the North Carolina General Assembly, 20 December 1844, Records of the General Assembly, Session Records, NCDAH; Report of the Committee of Propositions and Grievances, 26 December 1844, with Senate Committee Reports, November 1844–January 1845, box 4, NCDAH. Rejected.[1] PAR #11284401.

1. Philip E. Vass published his last will and testament on 8 August 1831, providing for the freedom of Jacob and Mary and "allotted slaves" Sam, Meriwether, Patsey (or Patty), and Matilda. Vass died the next year, but the executor of his estate failed to comply with Vass's desire to send the slaves to North Carolina because free people of color were denied entry into that state. The executor held the group as slaves for eight years. Finally, Jacob, Mary, and the others brought a suit *in forma pauperis* in the Circuit Superior Court of Halifax County, Virginia, for their freedom. They were successful. North Carolina, however, denied them entry. Patty Daniel asked to remain in Virginia with her husband, but that request was also denied. The former Vass slaves moved to Ohio. On the eve of the Civil War, Meriwether returned to Halifax County, Virginia. A nephew and niece of Philip Vass claimed that he had "forfeited his claims to freedom" by returning to the South. Being in "indigent circumstances and lawful heirs of Philip Vass," they asked that he become their slave. Copy of Records of the County Court, Halifax County, Virginia, George B. Ewing and wife vs. Isaac Medley Sr. et al., November 1832, in Petition of Jacob et al. to the North Carolina Legislature, 20 December 1844, Records of the General Assembly, Session Records, Senate Committee Reports, November 1844–January 1845, box 4, NCDAH; Petition of Patty Daniel to the Virginia General Assembly, 14 December 1842, Legislative Petitions, Halifax County, VSA; Petition of Philip Vass and Emily B. Haden to the Virginia Senate and House of Delegates, 1860, Legislative Petitions, Halifax County, VSA. For relevant statutes, see petition 129 below.

117. Elisha Blackmon to South Carolina Assembly, 1845

To the Honorable the Senate & House of Representatives of the State of South Carolina.

The humble petition of Elisha Blackmon sheweth into your Honble Body that Samuel McCorkle late of Lancaster District died about the Year 1839 leaving an estate of negroes to be disposed of according to his last will & testament in the following manner to wit—"After the foregoing directions to my Executors (which concern the payment of his debt by hiring the negroes) I do further direct that my Executors Apply to the Legislature of the State of South Carolina and use their best endeavours with the same to procure the Emancipation of them all that is my Negrost that is named Lydia and her children Named John Bob Lund Isaac Simpson & Harriet and Should they fail to procure the Emancipation of them in this state then and in such Case I direct my Executors to transport all of them to the Nearest nonholding slave state in the United States or to the Free Colony in Africa if they Choose to Go there to live; I will that my Executors shall hire them out for such length of time as will Raise a sum of money sufficient to pay of all Reasonable Expenses for to accomplish the same my Design and for to Compensate them for their trouble & Expense in the executing of this my Will and testament"—

After the above, directions are given concerning the care the children should take of Lydia the mother the distribution of the household furniture & what articles to be sold for payment of debt: After which comes the following to wit— "I have Relations and Kindred, but it is not my Will that they or any of them should Enjoy any part of the Property I may die possessed of and lastly I do humbly Constitute & do appoint Thos. Small Senr Elisha Blackmon Abrm Auten Executors of this my last Will and testament"—

Your Petitioner further sheweth that he qualified as Executor under the will & took upon himself the execution thereof but has been considerably harassed & prevented from executing the desires & intentions of his testator by bills filed against him in the Court of Equity & such instituted in the Law Court by persons representing themselves to be the next of kin of said McCorkle—That Amos Blackmon and Raleigh Hammond have filed a bill against your Petitioner as Executor in the name of one Milly Gordon who is represented as the next of kin & who as it is said sold her interest to the said Blackmon & Hammond for the sum of one Dollar

Your Petitioner further sheweth that the said bill in the name of Milly Gordon attempted to set aside the will on the ground that it was contrary to the laws of the State & it was then advised by the Chancellor that your Petitioner should at the next session petition your Honble Body agreeably to the directions of s'd will to emancipate s'd negroes & that s'd McCorkle left no next of kin, but those very remote, not nearer perhaps than second cousins—and that if said Blackmon & Hammond recover; the next of kin will not be benefitted but by the trifling sum of the one dollar aforesaid—

And your Petitioner further sheweth that the said negroes viz. Bob John. Lun. Isaac, Simpson & Harriet are notoriously the offspring of the body of the said McCorkle (dec'd)—Your Petitioner has often heard him say so & furthermore that it was one of the strongest wishes of his old age to effect their emancipation— The said negroes are of good character not given to vice but well behaved & obedient. They are all young stout and of industrious habits fully able to make a support. (their mother Lydia having died ~~ae~~ about the time of testator's death)—The said negroes are extremely anxious to have that freedom designed for them by their Father & to which they are justly entitled as your Petitioner believes by the Laws of South Carolina

And your Petitioner now prays your Honble Body as the Executor of Samuel McCorkle (dec'd)—in as much as he was so directed by the Will & the s'd negroes being the offspring of the body of said McCorkle, they desiring their emancipation being of good character & industrious habits & the next of kin being very remote & not likely to be benefitted in any event—having bartered away their interest—to emancipate the said negroes to wit Bob John Lun Isaac

Simpson & Harriet in order that the purposes & directions of the last Will & testament of Samuel McCorkle (dec'd) may be carried out & accomplished by— Your Petitioner as his Executor. And your Petitioner will ever pray &c—

Nov 24 1845

[signed] Elisha Blackmon

SOURCE: Petition of Elisha Blackmon to the South Carolina Senate and House of Representatives, 24 November 1845, Records of the General Assembly, #32, SCDAH. Referred to the Committee on Colored Population. No act was passed. PAR #11384502.

118. James H. Hanson, John W. Hanson, and U. Rasin to Missouri Assembly, 1846

To the Honl. the Senate and House of delegates of the State of Missouri—

The undersigned petitioners respectfully represent to your honl. body that the Statutes of the state in relation to slaves, prohibits their removal from other states to be introduced into the said state of Missouri, Excepting such as are slaves for life—The undersigned have become possessed of Certain Slaves in the state of Maryland under the will of their grand father, having only a term of years to serve, namely—

Negro Man Isaac James	28 Years old	7 Years to serve
Isaac Scott	23 Years old.	12 Years to serve
Mary Ann Bryan	18 Years old.	17 Years to serve
Sarah Jane Bryan	17 Years old.	18 Years to serve
Ben. Jones	18 Years old.	17 Years to serve
Retty Scott	19 years old	16 Years to serve

The said slaves were all willed to be free at the age of 35 years, Since the period of Making the said bequest, the undersigned have removed to the state of Missouri and have all permanently become Citizens, by a residence of about Eight Years, also the Mother of the undersigned by whom most of the said slaves was raised and for whom they all manifest a warm attachment desiring to remove from their present homes to reside in the said State of Missouri with and about the family in which they were raised—

The undersigned further state that in their present situation altho they are very likely slaves the whole income arising from their labour does not more than pay the expenses of supporting them, and the women with their Children are a burthen upon the hire of the Men. they are placed and under the supervision of an agent in such homes as he is enabled to procure, without the comforts and attention that they would naturally receive from those who would feel an interest in and for them. If the said slaves could be removed to the [area] where the undersigned reside they would become a source of profit, and would enjoy

~~themselves~~ all the Comforts that [a sincere] regard for their health could produce. They are now subject to the control of persons who cannot feel any other interest for them than the profit of their labor, and those that are incumbered with children are left to seek such homes as they can obtain suffering in some cases for actual necessaries for their support—

Now the undersigned petitioners respectfully ask Your honl. body to permit by special act the introduction of the said slaves into the State of Missouri, to be set free as they shall respectively arrive at the age of 35, the evidence of which will appear by the will of the late Benjamin Harrison of the County of Kent in the said State of Maryland which said will by copy could be transfered to the records of the County to which the said negroes shall be removed—

And Your petitioners will ever pray

[signed] James H. Hanson
John W. Hanson
U Rasin
intermarried with Martha H. Hanson

SOURCE: Petition of James H. Hanson, John W. Hanson, and U. Rasin to the Missouri General Assembly, 1846, Records of the House of Representatives, 14th General Assembly, 1st Session, 1846–47, RG 550, MoSA. Granted.[1] PAR #11184603.

1. See *Laws of the State of Missouri, Passed at the First Session of the Fourteenth General Assembly, Begun and Held at the City of Jefferson, on Monday, the Sixteenth Day of November, Eighteen Hundred and Forty-Six* . . . (Jefferson: James Lusk, 1847), 301.

119. Ambrose Lewis, St. Louis, to Missouri Assembly, 1846

To the Hon. the General Assembly of the State of Missouri

The undersigned Petitioner, begs leave most respectfully to State, that he was born a free man of Color in the town of Petersburg, State of Virginia, together with his wife—that he has five children living with him, three daughters and two sons, all born in said State of Virginia—that he has with him three grand children, two born in Virginia and one in the State of Missouri—The names of his children are Peggy Butcher (a widow) Caroline Lewis, Mary Lewis, Ambrose Lewis and Edward Lewis, his grand children are Henry Lewis, John Lewis, and Phillis Butcher—none of them of full age, except Peggy Butcher—

Your Petitioner states that he came to the State of Missouri in the year 1841—and has resided here ever since & is well Known to many of the most respectable Citizens of the City of St Louis & State of Missouri as a well behaved, orderly and reputable man—but so it is, the laws are now such that he & his family cannot procure the necessary license to remain here, (not having been here since Jan. 1840) and he is now ordered after thirty days to depart the limits of the State—

Without troubling your bodies with a long petition, he asks you, if deemed expedient to pass an act authorizing him and his family named to remain in this State, on his Complying with the laws in other respects—He refers your body to the undersigned recommendations for his Character and standing, and prays you to act in the premises as your Laws of justice dictates.

St Louis, 24th December 1846—
[signed] Ambrose Lewis

SOURCE: Petition of Ambrose Lewis to the Missouri General Assembly, 1846, Records of the House of Representatives, 14th General Assembly, 1st Session, 1846–47, RG 550, MoSA. Granted.[1] PAR #11184605.

1. See *Laws of the State of Missouri, Passed at the First Session of the Fourteenth General Assembly, Begun and Held at the City of Jefferson, on Monday, the Sixteenth Day of November, Eighteen Hundred and Forty-Six* . . . (Jefferson: James Lusk, 1847), 282.

120. Jonathan Lipps et al., Carter County, to Tennessee Assembly, 1847

State of Tennessee }
Carter County }

October 30th 1847 To the Honerable General Assembly of Tennessee now in Session

where as the Law now in force is not sofisiant Respecting slaves and cullard free persons living and cohabbiting togeather with free white persons—we therefore the underneath subscribers do most earnist and humbly pertishon and pray that the honerable Legislat[ure] of tennessee would take the mater into consideration and make a more efectual law on the subject we think a law to this afect would be much better that the five hundred dollars that is now on a whit pers on living and cohabbiting togeather with culard persons should be turnd over onto the person whoe ownd the slave if he sufered his slave to live with or cohabbit with any white person or if any free cullard person should so live or cohabbit togeather that the person on whose land they should live should be subject too the five hundred dollars fine also—and that the informer of such case should have one half of the fine and the state of tennessee the other half for as the Law now is it is only an expence to the state as such persons is hardly ever worth any thing for we have well tryd it we have informed against them and taken them up to cort and they take the benifit of the insolvant law and take the oath and go rite to living togeather again and leave the state to pay the cost of the suit and the grate evil not remided [remedied] any at all which evil we think is a scandle and disgr[a]ce to human natuer and raising up the worst sociaty on earth in our cuntry for as it now is in a few years more we will not know what blood our children are incurring for we think that such malgamation of blood is hatefull in the sight of god and good men we tharefore your humble pertishenrs do ever pray your honarable body to take the matter in too your most serious concideration and pass the above prayd for law or some other law on the subject that you may in your wisdom think best so it is soficiant to stop the grate evil pray neglect us not

[signed] Jonathan Lipps
Edward Lane
David Bishop
Tennessee Bishop
Alfred C Williams
Stephen Lewis
Peter B. Elliott
Samuel Anderson
Daniel Lipps
Michael [Grindstaff?]
[91 additional signatures]

SOURCE: Petition of Jonathan Lipps et al. to the Tennessee General Assembly, 31 October 1847, Legislative Petitions, #33-1847, reel 17, TSLA. Rejected. PAR #11484703.

121. Oscar Taliaferro, Richmond, to Virginia Assembly, 1847

To the General Assembly of Virginia the Petition of Oscar Taliaferro a man of color most respectfully sheweth—

That your Petitioner was until about the year 1842 the slave of Mr James Blakey of the city of Richmond, & during the time of such servitude earned, by such means as were allowed him by the indulgence of his master, for his own use, sums of money amounting to $400. These sums he lent as he accumulated them, to his said master to keep for him, & to account with him for; & in the year 1842 the circumstances of his said master became so embarrassed, that your Petitioner was in danger, not only of losing as he did the money lent him, but of being himself sold to the south, & separated from his wife a slave in Richmond. In this fearful extremity he was permitted by his master to make his situation known with a view of avoiding evils greater than the loss of his money—by obtaining a master in the city. He found one in Mr George Taylor of Richmond, who purchased your Petitioner, & who having heard the above statement confirmed by Mr Blakey subsequent to the sale, urged your Petitioner to exert himself to accomplish the object to which his previous accumulations had been made, & kindly promised to manumit him as soon as he should reimburse him the sum then paid Mr Blakey—

Your Petitioner succeeded in his efforts to return by installments of from one to fifty dollars & by occasional services, the purchase money, except the amount which his present master contributed & Mr Taylor has been willing & anxious at any moment for nearly two years to execute the promised deed of manumission upon the alternative (as he originally conditioned) that, he your Petitioner—should obtain from your honorable body permission to remain in the commonwealth—or should remove permanently to some other state. But the wife of your

Petitioner is a slave; the property of Mr Myers of this city, & a deed of manumission, by driving him from the Commonwealth, would separate him from her forever. Your Petitioner when accumulating the fund he lost by the pecuniary embarrassments of his former master was animated with the hope of being able to procure the freedom of his wife as well as his own. It was that which stimulated him to work while others rested, & to deny himself indulgences which others enjoyed, & again after (some two years since) satisfying the claims of his present owner, he had every prospect of accomplishing this object—only secondary as resulting from it to the great object to which his efforts previously had been directed for years, when he was prostrated the last summer at the Hot Springs of Va: by severe indisposition, during which,—attendance,—board & the Drs bills swallowed up a considerable part of his accumulations for that object—& now—increased years & enfeebled health prevent him from cherishing any such hope. He cannot, without your kind interposition enjoy the freedom he has so long struggled for, & the society of the being he cannot abandon. He therefore prays your Honorable Body to permit him though he should receive his manumission to remain in the State.

Test
George Taylor

his
Oscar X Taliaferro
mark

I have a personal knowledge of the truth of all the facts stated in the above Petition as occurring at the time I purchased Oscar & subsequent thereto—& I believe that sums in the aggregate *at least equal* to the amount stated, were placed from time to time in his former owners hands. Mr Blakey having since I purchased Oscar confirmed his statement previously made me to that extent. I should be gratified to see his Petition granted by the General Assembly.

[signed] George Taylor
Novr 26th 1847—

SOURCE: Petition of Oscar Taliaferro to the Virginia General Assembly, 15 December 1847, Legislative Petitions, Richmond City, VSA; Statement, George Taylor, 26 November 1847, ibid. No act was passed. PAR #11684703.

122. Harvey Dean et al., Bedford County, to Tennessee Legislature, 1847

To the Honbl Members of The Tennessee Legislature, now Sitting at Nashville—

The undersigned members of the ~~Tennessee~~ Grand Jury, for the County of Bedford & State of Tennessee, would respectfully petition your Honorable body, to pass some law for the more effectually preventing negroes from selling, meats, chickens, fruits &c, upon public days, at public places—. Your petitioners have seen & felt the evil effects of the System now prevailing upon that subject. The only way most of the things thus sold are obtained is by stealing—And your petitioners amongst others suffer from their petty thefts—

Your petitioners feel great diffidence in suggesting to your Honorable body any plan; but having thought ~~a great deal~~ much upon the subject they would respectfully suggest that you pass a law authorizing any person, when they see negroes thus trading, to have them taken up before a magistrate & publicly whipt, unless the negro can produce a written permit from his or her master or mistress, authorizing them thus to trade—

Your petitioners believe that such an act would be highly beneficial, and is called for by the community—[1]

Hoping that your Honl Body will think favourably of their petition—and as in duty bound your petitioners will ever pray—&c—

[signed]	Harvey Dean	Benjamin F. Clayton
	David Green	T. I. Culley
	Hilliard Dixon	[illegible]
	Wm C. Chandler	Daniel Lacy
	W. R. McFarlin	D. C. Sriver
	William Phillips	Jesse Harris
		Newcom Thompson sr

SOURCE: Petition of Harvey Dean et al. to the Tennessee Legislature, 20 December 1847, Legislative Petitions, #123-1847, reel 18, TSLA. Referred to the Committee on the Judiciary. Rejected. PAR #11484701.

1. An 1813 law prohibited slaves from selling articles "not of their own manufacture, without permit." Later, a law prohibited slaves from selling "any article whatever" without permission. The general revised code enacted more than a decade after this petition was submitted prohibited slaves from buying or selling "any goods, commodities, or other things" and free blacks from peddling or bartering "market stuffs or other articles." The punishment included five to thirty-nine lashes. John Codman Hurd, *The Law of Freedom and Bondage in the United States,* 2 vols. (Boston: Little, Brown, 1858–62; reprint, New York: Negro Universities Press, 1968), 2:91; *The Statute Laws of the State of Tennessee, of a Public and General Nature* (Knoxville: F. S. Heiskell, 1831), 315; *A Compilation of the Statutes of Tennessee, of a General and Permanent Nature, from the Commencement of the Government to the Present Time* (Nashville: James Smith, 1836), 676; *The Code of Tennessee, Enacted by the General Assembly of 1857–8* (Nashville: E. G. Eastman, 1858), 516, 525.

123. Nicholas N. Nixon, New Hanover County, to North Carolina Assembly, 1848

To the Honorable, the General Assembly of the State of North Carolina—

The Petition of Nicholas N Nixon of the County of New Hanover, respectfully represents to your Honorable body, that he is the owner of a certain slave by the name of Sam, and that he is desirous to emancipate and set free said slave—Your Petitioner shows that said slave Sam is now between the ages of fifty five and sixty, as your Petitioner has been informed and believes—Your Petitioner further represents to your Honorable body, that said slave Sam was formerly the property of the late Robert Nixon who died in the year 1809, and from that time up to the year 1832 said slave was the property of the late Christian Nixon widow of said Robert Nixon, and that during the whole time that said slave belonged to said Christian Nixon, he was entrusted by her with the management of her property, superintending her farm, overseeing her other slaves, carrying her produce to market, making sales of the same and making all her necessary purchases; and in all these different offices of trust and confidence he was always found to be faithful, irreproachable, assiduously devoting himself to the performance of the extraordinary duties and services required of him—

Your Petitioner further represents to your Honorable body, that he has been informed and verily believes, that about the year 1822, the kitchen of the said Christian Nixon, situated near her dwelling house was consumed by fire, and that said dwelling house was saved from destruction principally by the extraordinary efforts of said slave Sam, who at the risque and peril of his life succeeded in protecting it from burning.

Your Petitioner further shows to your Honorable body, that he is one of the Executors of the last Will of said Christian Nixon who died in the year 1832, that she was the relation and intimate acquaintance of your Petitioner, and your Petitioner well knows the great desire of said Christian Nixon that said slave Sam should be emancipated as some remuneration for his meritorious services while in her possession, and that with the view and for the sole purpose of carrying her wishes into effect, she conveyed said Sam to the late Christopher Dudley, by whom he was conveyed to your Petitioner without any valuable consideration being given for him, and solely with the intent on the part of said Christopher Dudly [*sic*] that your Petitioner would procure the emancipation of said slave—Your Petitioner therefore prays your Honorable body that said slave Sam may be emancipated and set free, and that hereafter he may exercise all the rights and privileges which are enjoyed by other free persons of colour in this State—And Your Petitioner as in duty bound shall ever &c

[signed] Nichs N. Nixon
~~Jas T. Miller~~

To the Honorable the General Assembly of the State of North Carolina—

The undersigned citizens of the County of New Hanover, respectfully represent, and do hereby certify to your Honorable Body, that they are at this time, and have been for many years past, acquainted with the slave named Sam, known generally as Sam Nixon, being the same referred to in the Petition on the previous pages of this sheet, that his moral and steady deportment, his industrious habits, his devotion to the interests of his late mistress, his courteous humility in the presence of white men, and his irreproachable character generally, entitle him to the favourable consideration of your Honorable Body—

[signed]	Jas T. Miller	Owen Fennell
	W. C. Bettencourt	David K. Futch
	N. F. Nixon	J D Jones
	John Dawson	J Walker
	Geo Davis	L H Marstellon
	C. C. Bettencourt	Wm A Wright
	Jos. M. Foy	

SOURCE: Petition of Nicholas N. Nixon to the North Carolina General Assembly, 1 December 1848, Records of the General Assembly, Session Records, House Committee Reports, November 1848–January 1849, NCDAH; Testimonial of the citizens of New Hanover County to the North Carolina General Assembly, ca. November 1848, ibid. The Committee on Propositions and Grievances recommended that the "prayer of the same be not granted." Report of Committee on Propositions and Grievances, 10 January 1849, ibid. No act was passed. PAR #11284804.

124. Nathaniel Brinkley et al. to Delaware Assembly, ca. 1849

To The Sennate and The house of Repprepresentative of the State of Delaware

The Petition of the undersigned Inhabitants of the State of Delaware Respectfully Asks That you will take Measures for affecting Sutch chanege in The Laws of this State as to Exempt free people of collar inperticular From being compeled to Exhibit a pass or a certificate To astablish our freedom when we have occasion to pass or Travel from This State to any other as for instance From this State to the City of Phila or pennsylvania By Steemboat or Stage. we have been Exceedingley anoyd And poot to veary Considiable inconvenience and Eaven compeled To Leave the boat and thare by entirely defeated From accomplishing our just and lawful business Because we have not a pass or a certificate from some White pearson now mater whe [who] it is so he be white. This we believe to be a grate greviance and unjust in all its bearings we pay our taxes Regularly Every year For Support of goverment Then why may we not be Permited to pass or travel from This State to any other In persuit of our just and Lawful business or any peart of The Community we are free men jet we are gilty of a [crime] A thing That was not in our power to controle yeat it was The will of him who made us To be his accountable Creation We are Sivil we designe no intent to hurt or Injure any of The Human family but wish well To all yet we are liable To be arrested when Travling on our lawful buisness to be Put in prison pervided we do not Exhibit a certificate or Pass signid by a white man which appears to be Sufficent thogh his Charector be mutch blacker Then our Skins This odious Law perticularly we desire may be expunged From The Statew bookes[1] Togather with Several oather Inactments Equilly oppressive to us as freeman for we have None [known] two or three pearsons of some of our acquaintance to Be put in prisson in new castle and some in dover And we have had ot [to] raise money To hire Some white pearson To go up to new castle and Sartify to thear freedom If not they must Stay Six weaks in prison Accordain to The Laws of The State of Delaware And receave no compenation for Lost time This we think To [be] a grate greavances for we have To pay our tax as a other men and yeat we are not Pearmited To have That rite That our constution holds out to all of its free mail Sitisons

And as being free tax paing Sitison of this commonwealth we will Respectfully mension one or two oather laws which we Think unnecessary and we ~~wish~~ think unjust That we cannot own or have a gunn in our persession Without a permet from a Justice of The peace allso We may not assemble to gather for Religious wriship in our own churiches and re main Thare beyound the Hours of ten oclock at night with out having the presanc of three white men amoungst us we have no objection of the companys of white men in our meetings at church If [coming] of thear own will and peasable visits among us Jeat [yet] desire thear pressiance may not be obbligatary on Such an occsion but we may be left at Liberty To Precure our quite peaceable Religious worship with out The aid or presince of white men or any how as aother Religious Societes are permitid to Do

our worth in murderkill hundred is Thirty Thousand five Hundred and Thirty five Dollars and from That we pay one hundred and fifty two Dollars and Sixty Seven Cents in Murderkill hundred and Alowing the Same in other hundreds our worth would be 132.tho 200.dol 50 cts And our tax would be Throw [through] out this county then Nine hundred 10 Dollars 2 cts This we pay Eveary year why Then are we debeared from Travling Throw or out of this State in persuit of our own bisness with out being Liable to be put in prisson or de nied The rite To go by steem bote with out a pass

This we be leav to be a grate greavance and unjust in all its baring Therefore we pray you well take into Consideration and Expung theas Laws from your books so as to give us aright to Travel as men and not as bruts So the undsine pertissioners Do Ever pray

[signed] Nathaniel Brinkley | Venson Summars
Prince Caldwell | William Brinkley
Calab Berry | Nathan Gibbs

Palm Caldwell	Palm George
Thomas Caldwell	Jack Bayard
	[20 additional signatures]

SOURCE: Petition of Nathaniel Brinkley et al. to the Senate and House of Representatives of Delaware, ca. 1849, General Assembly, Legislative Papers, DSA. No act was passed. PAR #10384901.

1. In 1849, free blacks from outside the state were permitted to visit friends and family in the state for a maximum of sixty days. Previously, the visiting period had been six months. Authorities checked travelers closely. Two years later, in 1851, nonresident free blacks were prohibited from entering the state entirely. *Laws of the State of Delaware, Passed at a Session of the General Assembly, Commenced and Held at Dover, on Tuesday the Fifth Day of January, in the Year of Our Lord, One Thousand Eight Hundred and Forty-Nine* (Dover: S. Kimmey, 1849), 319; *Laws of the State of Delaware, Passed at a Session of the General Assembly, Commenced and Held at Dover, on Tuesday the Seventh Day of January, in the Year of our Lord, One Thousand Eight Hundred and Fifty-One* (Wilmington: Johnson, Chandler and Harker, 1851), 591–92.

125. J. W. F. Jackson et al. to Delaware Assembly, 1849

To the Honorable the Senate and House of Representatives of the State of Delaware in general assembly met,

We the undersigned Citizens of the State of Delaware, beg leave to represent That there is a Certain mulatto man by the name of Samuel D. Burris, well known to a large portion of the community who[se] Conduct is highly reprehensible indeed, being a notorious character, who is going about the country We beleve persuading and enticing Slaves Servants and apprentices to run away and leave their Homes, to the great disadvantage of the Community.

Last year this said Burris was accused, apprehended, tried and found Guilty agreeable to Law, after which he was sold ~~sold~~ as a servant, and bot by some man, who suffers him to go about amongst us and continue the same unjustifiable employment,

We therefore request Your Honors to pass some Law to reach his Case and effectully stop such conduct and you [*sic*] petitioners will as in duty bound ever pray &c

[signed]	J.W.F. Jackson	Thomas Martindale
	Wm Slaughter	Joel Clements
	John [undecipherable]	W. K. Lockwood
	John P. Coombe	Thomas Purnell
	James Lord	Thomas B. Lewis
		[19 additional signatures]

SOURCE: Petition of J. W. F. Jackson et al. to the Senate and House of Representatives of Delaware, 16 February 1849, General Assembly, Legislative Papers, DSA. Granted.[1] PAR #10384903.

1. On 8 February 1849, an act gave free blacks who enticed slaves away from their owners twenty-four hours to leave the state. If the guilty person returned, he or she would receive a public whipping of sixty lashes. A second law, passed on the same day, granted discretionary power to sheriffs to hire out "idle and vagabond free negroes." *Laws of the State of Delaware, Passed at a Session of the General Assembly, Commenced and Held at Dover, on Tuesday the Fifth Day of January, in the Year of Our Lord, One Thousand Eight Hundred and Forty-Nine* (Dover: S. Kimmey, 1849), 412–16.

126. Residents of Rutherford County to Tennessee Assembly, 1849

To the Representatives of the people of Tennessee in Legislature assembled,

Your memorialists, the undersigned, respectfully submit to your attention, the existing laws, legalising upon certain conditions, the sale of spirituous and vinous liquors.—They have observed their effects upon the moral and social condition of the country; and feel constrained to express the conviction, that the act of the general Assembly, authorising the Keeping of tippling houses, militates against the best interest of the people. The evils consequent upon the act of 1846,[1] are apparent, in the relaxation of industry, the loss of property, the outbreaks of violence, the instigation to crime, the neglect of education, the abatement of public spirit and enterprise, the increase of taxes, the ruin of domestic happiness, the debasement of morals, the desecration of religion, the corruption of elections, and the increase of want and misery amongst that class of our population who are addicted to intemperance If your Honorable Body desires proof of these assertions, we refer your daily observations to the purlieus of the tippling house, to the streets of our cities and villages, to the neglected fields of labor, to the records of our courts; and Saddest of all, to the hearth Stone, where the despairing wife weeps, over her destitute and miserable children—Feeling their truth, we cannot remain callous, Knowing that these evils exist; that they are increasing and will accumulate until the Legislature shall interpose; we appeal to you to the organs of the public mind; the conservators of public morals, and promoters of the general prosperity; to act, to restrain and to Save—Public Sentiment is fast, arousing itself, against the sensual policy of arming the selfish with poison to slay their fellow men for pay—It is awakening from the lethargy produced by the clamors of the tippler and his inebriate victims—It is rapidly producing a current of opinion against the existing law, So strong, that even demagogues will leap into it.

We venture the assertion that a majority of the people of Tennessee when fairly tested when the question shall be stripped of the extraneous influence of party passion and strife, will declare their opposition to a law by virtue of which the public morals, the public peace and health are sold for revenue, in the form of a tax upon tipplers—It would be a slander upon them to alledge, that they were in favor of a moral and physical pestilence that is daily and nightly attempting by the most seductive blandishments, to infuse its taint into the bosom of every family.

Aside from pecuniary considerations; the existence of tippling houses, is pregnant with one other great end, standing out even now in strong relief, but ~~xxx~~ more fearfully ominous for the future—There is a class, a race of population amongst, but not of us: a class, that Providence has permitted the Caucasian to hold in subjection, a subjection now rendered necessary by our relative positions, for the ending of which the most sagacious political economist can see no time—Whether true or false the theory has been adopted and is now acted upon, that the ignorance of that class is necessary to its degradation; and its degradation to our security—And this class, having no intellectual and but little more culture to restrain and direct them; from whose want of sympathy and untutored passions, we have the most to fear, are gradually, but surely becoming inebriates—In vain are incidental restrictions, when the great evil is tolerated—In vain are the oaths of reckless men the violation of which no witness can Know.

That slaves, ~~do~~ procure and drink; that the excess in use of ardent spirits is becoming the pervading passion of their class, we know; but we cannot see and cannot Know, how, or when, or where, the poison is dealt out to them, or the oath of the seller violated—We trouble at the consequences, to which this may lead—The white man, has cultivated intellect, and strong endearments to subdue, or restrain him in his madness; yet when his passions are inflamed by drink, his desperate hand breaks the dearest ties, and spills the most cherished blood=But what is to restrain besotted Slavery from filling the land with blood and conflagration? The details might be imagined, but they are too horrible for reflection.

Public opinion may do much to restrain and limit; but it requires law to eradicate the evil—We beseech you therefore to repeal all laws legalising the sale of ardent spirits in tippling houses, or elsewhere; We p[r]ay you to erase from the Statute book, a law that [covers] us with Shame, by the ineffectual attempt to preserve the morals of the Slave, whilst it tempts the master to debasement—Do this, and your memorialists will vouch for the support of the people, and for the approbation of all the good and virtuous—

[signed]	Jno. Jones	J. J. Abernathy
	James F. Fletcher	Thomas G. Sweeney
	Charles Ready	B. W. Avent
	Jn: Leiper	Erasmus D. Hancock
	R. G. Ellis	W G McKnight
		[98 additional signatures]

SOURCE: Petition of the Residents of Rutherford County to the Tennessee General Assembly, 19 December 1849, Legislative Petitions, #7-1849, reel 18, TSLA. Rejected. PAR #11484904.

1. The 1846 law permitted whites to sell "spirituous or vinous liquors" to slaves with an

owner's permission. *Statute Laws of the State of Tennessee, of a General Character; Passed since the Compilation of the Statutes by Caruthers and Nicholson, in 1836* (Nashville: J. G. Shepard, 1846), 289–93.

127. Citizens of Warren County to Mississippi Assembly, ca. 1850s

To the Honourable Senate & House of Representatives of the State of Mississippi in assembly convened

Your Petitioners, Citizens of the County of Warren, would respectfully represent, that one William Newman and Candis Newman his wife people of colour were formerly slaves of a family by the name of Newman who resided in the County of Warren, most of whom have departed this life. These being faithful and favorite family servants, It was the wish and intention of this family to procure in some way their freedom—The heads of the family dying without effecting this objective which they so much desired, William and Candis came to the representatives of the family who sold and conveyed them to their present owner with a distinct understanding that they were to be emancipated so soon as it could conveniently and legally [be] done. This understanding, Mr. Hazard their present owner is honorably endeavoring to carry out and is not only willing but is anxious that they should obtain their freedom.

Through the kindness and indulgence of their present master, they have lived for many years under his protection in a manner free, yet without enjoying any of the rights pertaining to a State of freedom. During all this time they have been humble and respectful in their deportment towards every one, honest, temperate and industrious and faithful in the performance of every trust—so much so as to secure the confidence and esteem of all who know them. Their intercourse and dealing have been entirely with white people and have carefully avoided commingling with or having transactions with slaves—

Your petitioner would further represent that during the prevalence of the terrible scurge that prostrated the City of Vicksburg for three years in succession William Newman as the whole community can bear witness rendered the most important services to both City and Country. Services never to be forgotten and worthy of being generously rewarded. When this dire disease spread terror and alarm everywhere; when the stoutest heart quailed before it—when all communication between town and Country ceased, when the Citizens of Vicksburg were suffering for the necessaries of life he fearlessly "braved every danger" and where his services were needed by day or by night they were generally tendered—at all times and in every part of the City might be seen William Newman with his little wagon faithfully and carefully distributing supplies to the suffering and afflicted which had been kindly furnished by the planters and in return bringing back—making purchases and executing orders for the people in the country—all these various transactions confided to him he executed with an honesty and accuracy that would have done honour to the most upright and exact business man. In fact, while these epidemicks prevailed, his house was not only a depot for the Country [provisions] but a receiving, forwarding and distributing office of goods letters & papers—

Your Petitioners in view of their good & exemplary conduct through life, their industry and integrity more especially for the services magnanimously rendered in times of danger and distress, feel it a privilege—and that it is justly due these persons to petition the legislature in their behalf and sincerely hope that by a suitable legislative act their freedom may be granted them. Your petitioners believe they are deserving of it and entitled to it, nor do they believe that their freedom would be attended with any injurious consequences to the State or to any individuals. Your Petitioners would therefore humbly pray &c

[signed] Washn. E. Green — Thos. J. Finney
David Gibson — F[ranklin] White
Ben Johnson — O. H. Perry
Hal. W. Green — F J Hume
W. F. Gaines — F C, Wadsworth
[199 additional signatures]

Mr Speaker

The select committee to whom was referred the petition of sundry Citizens of Vicksburg & Warren County, in behalf of one William Newman and his wife (persons of color) have had the same under consideration and instructed me to report that in their opinion the prayer of said petitioners should not be granted—

[signed] J C Newman Chr—

SOURCE: Petition of Citizens of Warren County to the Mississippi Senate and House of Representatives, ca. 1850s, Records of the Legislature, RG 47, MDAH. No act was passed. PAR #11000022.

128. John Dixon and Sarah Dixon, Alexandria, to Virginia Assembly, 1850

To the General Assembly of Virginia

Your petitioners John Edward Dixon, a slave belonging to Miss Sally Griffith of the Town of Alexandria, and Sarah Dixon his wif[e], humbly represent to your Honourable Body,

That William H. Fitzhugh Esq of Ravensworth in the county of Fairfax, departed this life on the day of May 1830, and by his last will and testament among other things bequeathed to his wife Anna Maria his slaves to hold and enjoy until the year 1850, at which time the said slaves were to become free; that your petitioner Sarah Dixon is one of the said slaves so emancipated by the will of the said William H Fitzhugh; that your petitioners were married some years since with the approbation and consent of their respective owners and before the retrocession of Alexa[ndria], where the law would have allowed her to remain in the event of her emancipation and have ever since lived upon terms of peace and happiness.

Your petitioners further represent that by the existing law of Virginia "if any emancipated slave shall remain within this state more than twelve months after his or her right to such freedom shall have occurred, he or she shall forfeit all such right and may be apprehended and sold by the overseers of the poor of any county in which he or she may be found, for the benefit of the literary fund," and that your petitioner Sarah in consequence of her emancipation by the will of the said Fitzhugh, is compelled to depart this commonwealth, or to be apprehended and sold by the overseers of the poor.

In an alternative so dreadful and harassing to the feelings of your petitioners, they humbly pray and beseech your honours, for a few moments to contemplate their distressing condition.

Being drawn together by those inscrutable impulses of the human heart that impel one to sympathise in the condition and feelings of another and so living together bound by these ties of feeling and sympathy, they have brought into the world offspring

And now it is that this terrible alternative is placed before them—that your said petitioner Sarah is either to be shipped to the inhospitable climes of strangers at home or abroad, or to be apprehended, sold and sent far away to the Southern Market. If your petitioner Sarah is compelled to suppress all those natural feelings of affection and love for her husband and the companions of her infancy; and to leave the place ~~home~~ of her birth and of her earliest and dearest associations; to carry with her a small and helpless offspring, (for your petitioner John being a slave is incapable of supporting them), and among strangers unknown and uncared for to seek a livelyhood and subsistence for them and herself, your petitioners humbly represent that misery, wretchedness and starvation must be their fate.

Your petitioners further represent, that they have always borne a good character; that your petitioner Sarah has ever been a good, peaceable, and orderly slave; that she has always conducted herself to the satisfaction of her owners and of the citizens generally, and in support of which statement they respectfully refer to the annexed certificates marked exhibit A. B. C. ~~&D~~ prayed to be made a part of this petition; and further that they will always hereafter continue to behave in the same orderly and peaceable manner.

In consideration of all which your petitioners humbly beg and pray, that your honours will grant your said petitioner Sarah permission to remain within this commonwealth free and without being liable to be apprehended and sold, upon such terms and conditions as to your honours may seem necessary and proper to preserve the dignity and purity of the law; and to afford your petitioners such other and further relief as you may deem meet and equitable

Your petitioners will ever pray &c

[signed] John Edward Dixon

Sarah Dixon.—

Alexandria County, towit,

Personally appeared before me the subscriber a justice of the peace in & for the County aforesaid B. G. Newton and made oath that all the matters and things in the annexed petition of John Edward Dixon and Sarah his wife are true to the best of his Knowledge & belief—Given under my hand and seal this 11th day March 185

Geo Wise {seal}

Ravensworth Fairfax County Va.

Feby 15th 1850

Understanding that the bearer of this Sally Dixon wishes to become a resident and get employment in Alexandria, I take pleasure in recommending her as an honest and industrious Woman. She is a good Cook and a first rate washer and Ironer and I have no doubt that any business She may undertake She will give entire Satisfaction

I have Known Sally for many years and have always Considered her a very nice woman and particularly amiable in her disposition and I sincerely hope she may do well—

[signed] George Burke

Drans[e]ville Mar 7th 1850

Sarah Dixon the wife of John Dixon (a Slave the property of Miss Griffith of Alexandria) lived in my family a few years since. It gives me much pleasur— to say that I considered her then as I now believe her to be ~~now~~ a very respectable Girl—Honest, faithful, and respectful to *all.*

She was then the property of Mrs A M Fitzhugh of Ravensworth in the County of Fairfax Va my family parted with her with regret in consequence of ill health—

[signed] Jas D. Kerr

The bearer, Sally, was formerly one of my Servants, and [worked] about my house—She is quite a good Cook, and would no doubt be a useful servant in almost any family—

I have always found her quiet and orderly, Civil and respectful in her demeanour, and in her general deportment amiable and well disposed—

[signed] A M Fitzhugh
March 1850

SOURCE: Petition of John and Sarah Dixon to the Virginia General Assembly, 13 March 1850, Legislative Petitions, Alexandria City, VSA; Certificate, George Burke, 15 February 1850, ibid.; Certificate, James D. Kerr, 7 March 1850, ibid.; Certificate, A. M. Fitzhugh, March 1850, ibid. Referred to the Committee for Courts of Justice. No act was passed. PAR #11685012.

129. G. Mason, John A. Washington, and Dennis Johnston, Fairfax County, to Virginia Assembly, 1851

To The Genl Assembly of Virginia.—

Your Memorialists, Justices of the Peace for the County of Fairfax, beg respectfully to call your attention to the Law concerning "Suits for Freedom," which is to be found under the CVI. C. of the Code of Virginia.[1]—

By this, it will be perceived, that it is made the duty of Justices of the Peace in this Commonwealth on the "Complaint" of any one conceiving himself to be unjustly detained as a Slave, to issue their precept in writing giving him in charge to an Officer of the Law, to be produced before the Circuit Court of the County or Corporation (as the Complainant may elect) at the next Term thereof, & in the mean time to keep him at the expense of the person Claiming to be the owner.—

Whatever may be the true interpretation of this word "Complaint," your Memorialists state the fact, that it has been claimed that a mere allegation, without the requirement of an Oath, by the Counsel of the Complainant, was sufficient ground on which such precept should be granted, & that both in this, & in an adjoining County precepts have been granted by Justices of the Peace on such mere allegation of Counsel, unsupported by any evidence whatsoever, & the owner divested of his property.—It is therefore to be presumed, that this construction of the Law, may be generally acted on; & thence the necessity of endeavouring to point out the evils & injuries the Community may be subjected to by the Statute as it at present stands.—For any Judicial authority to issue a warrant to deprive a man of his property, on every mere allegation on Oath (& there certainly ought not to be even an inchoate proceeding without one*) of such a fact by an ignorant or interested party, is to countenance any false or frivolous pretext, & must lead to the most vexatious & imperious Consequences in our State of Society.—

It is well known to your Honble Body, that in the present age of illumination & philanthropy, there is a very numerous Class of people in the United States, who hold the doctrine that there can be no property in persons; & most unfortunately our border Counties in this State, are now inundated with emigrants from the North, many of whom doubtless hold this doctrine, & therefore in consonance with their tenets, could most conscientiously swear that every Slave in Virginia, was "*unlawfully detained* as such."—But, if a precept is to be granted, to deprive a man of his Slave, even *without* the formallity of an Oath, can it be doubted that any of them would hesitate to make the "Complaint"?—If then, such a proceeding as has been claimed, can be had, as it has been had, on a mere allegation of a third party, unsupported by evidence, for one Slave, it can with equal propriety be had for any number, and against every man; consequently they might be deprived of their labour for an indefinite time; for where or how could they—under such circumstances—obtain security for double their value (the only means by which they can regain possession of their Slaves) when the Slaves would most probably abscond so soon as returned into the possession of their alledged owners?—Or if they remain in "charge" of an Officer of the Law, as prescribed by the Statute, in the event of such Security not being given, as he is not required by the terms of the Statute to commit them to Jail, but, only to "keep them at the expense of the person claiming to be the owner," what security is there, that they would not abscond, as the whole proceeding may have been a mere device to get them out of the masters possession to afford them that opportunity?—And if they did, how could their owner be indemnified for their loss?—The Law makes no provision whatever for that.—Yet should they not abscond, a man by such a divestment of his Labour, would have all his opperations broken up for an unlimited time; & if about to emigrate he & his Family would be stopped certainly for months, perhaps years, to his utter ruin: for it is not uncommon that suits of this sort, under one pretext or another for hunting up Testimony, are kept in the Courts for that length of time**.—

In the former Law, which this repealed, this same word "Complaint" was used, but there, the party complained of, *even before taking his Slave out of his possession,* was required to be *summoned to "answer the Complaint,"* that a fair opportunity might be afforded him by offering Testimony—if he possessed it—rebutting that of the Complainant, & it was only in case of his failing to appear to answer such Complaint, or give the Security demanded—which, by the by, was only *one half* of that required by the present Law—that the Justice was authorised to order the party Complaining into the Custody of an Officer for safe keeping.—That under the present Law, on a new Complaint, without any summons for the owner to appear & be heard in defence of his rights, a wholy ex parte proceeding—a proceeding ever savouring of Tyranny, & entirely at variance with the Spirit of all our institutions—is entertained, in ~~th~~ absence of the slightest shaddow of proof of even presumptive Freedom, & a man is divested of his property without any Security whatever for its restoration, or remuneration for the injury he may sustain from its loss.—

Every Negro or mulatto is prima facie a Slave in Virginia.—This is the rule of Law.—Freedom, in those colors is only the exception.—But, it may be said, that the Law in its Spirit of humanity, should lean to Freedom.—Be it so.—But the Law should not lean so far to Freedom, as to work the perversion of Justice & derogation of Right.—The Claims to Justice, are as Strong on the side of the alledged owner, as that of the Complainant for Freedom.—It should be fully & fairly meted out to both, & the Rights of one as scrupulously protected as those of the other.—Thence the necessity of a careful & Speedy examination into the facts of the Case, upon due summons given, before a man be finally deprived of the use of his property; tho' it might be wise that the Complainant should be taken into the Custody of the Law, so soon as complaint was made on Oath, to prevent the possibillity of his being unfairly dealt with, or carried beyond its protection.—But, it would seem to be contrary to every principle of Justice, that so summary & peremptory a procedure as is directed by the present Law should be allowed, & that upon wholy exparte Testimony—much less, on no Testimony at all—without allowing the party complained of even a hearing; a privilege granted under every other Law of our Land, before a man is divested of his property, except in the single case of Attachment, where ample Bond & Security, is always first required of the Claimant.—And what Surety or redress does this Law allow to the master for all these deprivations of Right, should the Complainant not sustain his Claim to Freedom?—None whatever, but the mere Contingent liability of a person found aiding & maintaining him in his Claim.—

'Tis true, this Law declares that if the person claiming to be the owner, or some one for him, shall enter into Bond "*approved by the Officer having the Complainant in charge*" (—& here, mark the wide & culpable discretion given by this Law to the honest Constable, for the Complainant may be given into the charge of such, & he may take security or not at his pleasure) equal to *double* the value of the Complainant conditioned to have him forthcoming before the Court at its next Term, the Officer Shall deliver to him the Complainant.—This requirement, if faithfully & discreetly discharged, would be difficult (under the peculiar risks of the Case, as adverted to above) to be complied with even by a resident—unless a man of wealth—it would be next to impossible, by a Stranger.—If not complied with, the slave *must* remain in charge of the Officer "*at the expence of the person claiming to be his Owner.*"—Thus, actually prejudging the Case, without any evidence whatever; depriving a man of his property (for every Negro or mulatto, in this State, is presumed to be that man's Slave, in whose possession he is found, until the contrary is shown) & then subjecting him to a heavy expence, *because of the very wrong that had been done him!*—At a subsequent stage of the proceedings, to wit, at the next Term of the Court—which if the petition should be filed, & it is most likely to be as at the option of the Complainant, in the Superior Court, might be months off; he may in the discretion of the Court be hired out, but there is no provision for his being hired out sooner; & consequently the whole interval between his being taken into Charge, & the Session of the Court is inevitably lost to the alledged owner, while he is as certainly taxed with the expence of keeping him, be *his titled ever so good,* if he cannot give Bond & Security.—Yet, even after he is hired out, the hire (which can only be paid to the master by order of the Court, after the termination of the Suit in his favour) would probably be a very inadequate compensation for his time, as that hire would not be one half of what could be obtained for him in the South, where he is generally about to be carried, when such an action as this is instituted.—To say nothing of the heavy expences certainly to be incurred—the time & trouble the alledged owner must necessarily give to the case, & the much greater loss he may be subjected to by detention here, if emigrating, or in the Sale of his Slave, as there is no species of property more fluctuating in its value.—

It may be said, that there is no doubt an action for damages under the present Law would lie, in the event of Freedom not being established.—This, is probably true in the abstract; but *against whom* it would lie, with any chance of recovery, it is difficult to conceive.—It could not lie against the Slave, if he is decided to be such.—If against his next Friend (who generally makes the Complaint, as the party is almost always in duress) it would be his Father or Mother, or some near Relative, all of whom would also be Slaves, or at best worthless Free Negroes, from whom no damages could be recovered.—So in fact, the whole hope of redress, would be narrowed down to an action on the case under the Statute against the person found aiding & maintaining him in his petition for Freedom.—To say nothing of the difficulty of establishing this charge—for these things are generally done in secret—he would almost always be found—if found at all—some person of very little means; for men of property rarely, if ever engage in such matters in this state.—Thus, it is evident, that while the owners losses must be certain & heavy, in any event, the chances of recovering damages at all, would be next to none.—

But besides the loss of his Slaves labour, his own detention & charges while superintending the Suit—the chances of depreciation in value, & the certain expense of his maintenance in every Case, there is no provision whatever made by this Law, for the owner's even recovering Costs should Judgment be rendered in his favour!—This, is certainly an anomaly in our jurisprudence, & is surely contrary to every principle of Justice & Right.—

In a late case, where some of our Fellow Citizens of the County of Clarke in pursuit of their fugitive Slaves, were indicted in Harrisburg Pennsylvania, for an alledged assault, tho' on Trial they were acquitted, Yet the Court undertook to saddle them with the Costs of the prosecution!—This, was undoubtedly a great Judicial wrong; one that has aroused the indignation of not only every Slave owner, but of every honest man who has heard of it.—Yet, it was but a Judicial wrong, which might be repaired upon appeal; but here is a Law of Virginia, which if it does not declare that the Costs are to be paid by the defendant, even when Judgment is given in his favour, leaves him at least to bear—even in that event, without hope of recovery—not only his own Costs, but all the expence of the maintenance of his Slave, who had been most probably prompted by some interested

Knave to Subject him to a costly & troublesome Lawsuit, while his only hope of redress, is an action against some foreign Fanatic, beyond the Jurisdiction of our Courts, or some intermedling & pennyless Pettifogger, who in ninety nine cases out of the hundred, would not be able to pay the first farthing of Damages!—

Surely to be a Slave holder, ought not yet a while in Virginia to be considered so infamous a Condition, that he is to be—whether rightfully or wrongfully assailed—first, without a shaddow of testimony, or even a hearing, divested of his property for an unlimited time; & then, that property kept at his sole expence; & then, subjected to all the costs & charges of a judicial procedure, without a hope of redress.

If it is still to be the magnanimous policy of Virginia, that every Negro or Mulatto within her limits, should have the opportunity of asserting his Freedom, then it is but Justice *that the State* should, in the first instance, bear the expences of such a proceedure.—Of this Policy, we do not pretend even to express an opinion, much less presume to condemn; but, we do think her generosity should be exhibited in some other way, tha[n] at the sole expense of the unfortunate Master!—It is enough, that he should be subjected to these charges (as in all other actions) if Judgment is rendered against him.—

It may be said, that no wrong has ~~been~~ yet awhile been experienced under this Law.—That may be true, for it has been only a few months in existence; but that is no reason why it should not be substituted by one more explicit & just in its provisions.—That alone, is a wise & good Law, which is so framed, that no wrong *Can* be perpetuated in its execution.—The past, even if we had had the experience of a lapse of years, as to its innocuousness, is no sufficient pledge for the future, when now the Spirit of Fanaticism is so widely abroad, exerting its most baleful influence in every way on this institution of Slavery.—

Under these Considerations, we pray your Honble: Body to enact such a Law, as while it shall effectually provide for maintaining the rights of the Complainants for Freedom, those of the Master, may be equally Secured; & above all, that there may be a speedy preliminary examination of each Case before a Justice or Justices, where the Complaint shall be made, so that Masters may be saved from the consequences of false & frivolous pretensions, & the heavy expences incident thereto.—

With this view, we have had carefully prepared a Bill, that accompanies this Memorial, which we believe will be found on examination to fully meet the exigencies of the Case, & most respectfully pray that it be enacted into a Law.—

[signed] G. Mason of Hollin Hall
John A. Washington
Dennis Johnston

*"The right of the People to be secure in their persons, houses, papers & effects, against unreasonable searches & seizures, shall not be violated; & *no warrant shall issue*, but upon probable cause, *supported by Oath or Affirmation*,

& particularly discribing the place to be searched, & the person or things to be seized."— 4.A. Amendment Constitution of U.S.—

**Of this, one of your Memorialists can speak of his own knowledge, having been several years Since (& how much worse would it be now!) Sued by four of his Slaves for their Freedom, at the instigation of a Yankee Lawyer; where the case was kept in the Courts for *Five years,* & tho' ultimately decided in his favour, the Costs, Lawyers fees & other expences, joined to what he had to pay for their apprehension, for they attempted to run off to the North, as soon as the case was decided agst: them, amounted to more than their value.—

SOURCE: Petition of G. Mason, John A. Washington, and Dennis Johnston to the Virginia General Assembly, 14 January 1851, Legislative Petitions, Fairfax County, VSA. Rejected. PAR #11685109.

1. A 1795 law gave persons illegally detained as slaves the right to bring suit and be assigned counsel. A 1798 law prohibited persons belonging to emancipation societies from serving on juries in such cases and stipulated that all such suits had to be tried immediately. The most comprehensive code on this subject, entitled "Act of January 17, 1818–January 1, 1820," allowed any persons believing themselves illegally detained as slaves to file a complaint against the person who assumed ownership. Magistrates were required to issue a warrant summoning the presumed owner to answer the complaint. Defendants were commanded to give bonds with security "equal at least to the full value of such complainant" and to appear before the next session of the superior, county, or corporation court. Plaintiffs without funds could sue *in forma pauperis.* The same strictness "as to *form,*" one judicial decision explained, "is not required in actions for freedom as in other cases." When such an action was brought by a person for himself or herself as well as children, the declaration of trespass and assault, formal in other cases, could in these instances be informal. *Acts Passed at a General Assembly of the Commonwealth of Virginia, Begun and Held at the Capitol, in the City of Richmond, on Tuesday, the Tenth Day of November, One Thousand Seven Hundred and Ninety-Five* (Richmond: Augustine Davis, 1796), 16–17; John Codman Hurd, *The Law of Freedom and Bondage in the United States,* 2 vols. (Boston: Little, Brown, 1858–62; reprint, New York: Negro Universities Press, 1968), 2:6; *Acts Passed at a General Assembly of the Commonwealth of Virginia: Begun and Held at the Capitol, in the City of Richmond, on Monday, the Fourth Day of December, One Thousand Seven Hundred and Ninety-Seven* (Richmond: Augustine Davis, 1798), 5; *Digest of the Laws of Virginia, Which Are of a Permanent Character and General Operation; Illustrated by Judicial Decisions* (Richmond: Smith and Palmer, 1841), 869–71.

130. Eleanor Vaughan et al., Halifax County, to Virginia Assembly, 1851

To The Honourable the Senate, and House of Delegates for the Commonwealth of Virginia Sitting in General Assembly.

Your Petitioners Elleanor Vaughan, Frances Vaughan, Susan Vaughan, William Vaughan, America Vaughan, Sarah Vaughan, Margaret Vaughan, and

Dicey Vaughan, respectfully represent and Shew unto your Honourable bodies, That Craddock Vaughan lately a resident of the County of Halifax, and State of Virginia, made a last will, and testament in writing, which has been duly admitted to probate in the Clerk's office of the County Court of Halifax, by which he emancipates your petitioners, and intends to give them the full, and free enjoyment of all the rights, and immunities of Free persons of Colour—That the said Testator in his life time nourished, and raised them as his own children, and paid them every regard which a paternal Care for their interests seemed to require—That though they were by laws of the land necessarily regarded as Slaves, (their mother being a slave), and are now taken by the laws to be noted as Free negroes—they are in fact, and in truth much more than three fourths white so far as blood is Concerned, and in Colour almost entirely so—That the said Ellanor [*sic*] is their mother, and Dicey was a favorite of her master—the rest being his children—

Your petitioners further represent that the said Craddock Vaughan though in his lifetime a man of Intemperate habits, had by industry and unusual economy accumulated an Estate, of not less than seven or eight Thousand dollars—all of which he bequeathed to his Executors to be held and Controlled for the joint, and exclusive benefit of your petitioners (except Dicey whose support and maintainance for life is charged upon his Estate)—that said Estate Consists of Seven Slaves all of whom are valuable, and whose value will Continue to increase—Since all are young, and several of them are children. of acres of land very productive, and finely located on Dan River, of a large stock, and such perishable property as is usually attached to such a farm. that he left at his death sufficient means on hand to pay off, and satisfy every debt which he owed, and they believe the acting Executor has already liquidated the same. that after his death in October last, George W. Purkins Esqr one of his Executors, and who is the one acting, and managing the Estate, employed immediately a white man to live upon, and manage the Farm, and to Control every thing, and keep order in and about the premises, and that so far they have heard no complaint among their neighbors of any disorderly conduct on their part. Your petitioners are perfectly aware of what they will be excused for terming, a popular prejudice, which exists to a very great extent in Virginia against that Class of persons, among whom their lot is now most unfortunately cast—but

They fondly indulge the hope that however just in most instances the indulgence of such emotions may be, and however apt in those instances to reach even the honourable legislators of Virginia—that such feelings have not become so radically fixed in the minds of enlightened Statesmen as to preclude a fair, and impartial discrimination where Circumstances will justify it—they think they come before you with no ordinary case, and with no usual claims upon your attention—they are themselves in their own estimation~~aton~~ beyond the sphere of the Free negro Class generally so degraded, and yet they are, they hope, sensible of the humbleness of their position—they have been respectably raised, know how to conduct themselves—and have always conducted themselves well—and mean to continue to do so, for they know perfectly well how much their welfare depends upon their own good conduct—they have Estate sufficient left them by proper management, to place them beyond the temptations commonly held out to that class of persons, they have been taught always to look to their own labour for a support, and they are neither too proud, too indolent or so foolish as to neglect to labour—but they are attached by all the ties of humanity to the place of their birth. they have friends and relatives near them from whom it would be heartrending to part. They pray your Honourable bodies therefore, in the discharge of your high and responsible duties to reflect upon their situation, and pass such a Bill as will allow them under proper restrictions to remain within the limits of the State of Virginia Such a Bill might be framed as they humbly conceive, which would secure to them the enjoyment of their liberty here, and yet fully provide against any contingency which may arise rendering it either disagreeable to their neighbors, or impolitic to the public for them to remain—And Your petitioners pray that this their petition may be heard and granted, will as in duty bound every pray &c. &c. &c.

Eleanor Vaughan,
Frances Vaughan,
Susan Vaughan
William Vaughan,
America Vaughan,
Sarah Vaughan,
Margaret Vaughan,
Dicey Vaughan.
By their Attorney

SOURCE: Petition of Eleanor Vaughan et al. to the Virginia Senate and House of Delegates, 15 January 1851, Legislative Petitions, Halifax County, VSA. Referred to the Committee for Courts of Justice. No act was passed. PAR #11685103.

131. Horatio McClenaghan, Marion District, to South Carolina Senate, 1851

To the Honorable the Senate and house of Representatives of the State of South Carolina and in General Assembly convened.

The Petition of the undersigned Horatio McClenaghan of Marion District Respectfully sheweth, that he is, or was, the owner, at the time of their deaths, of two negro fellow slaves by the respective names of Daniel & Sutton, who were convicted by a court of magistrates and freeholders for Grand Larceny. (Breaking the store of one Alison H. Brown.) and the verdict of the jury was as follows.

"That Daniel & Sutton, receive to day (May 21 1851) one hundred lashes on the bare back; and to be well inflicted; and that after receiving their punishment be conveyed to the common Jail of this District, therein to be confined for the space of four months from the date hereof; and moreover to receive during their Confinement on the first Monday in said four months, the further punishment of fifty lashes each."

Your Petitioner Respectfully presents, that the said slaves were valuable, that they remained in Jail from the day above stated, until the 5th day of Septr when Daniel Died, and on the 11th day of Septr 1851 the other fellow also *died.* That the sickness of which they died, was, (as the certificate of the attending Physician shews) produced by the imprisonment and punishment inflicted; That they lived long enough to receive the punishment of the whipping 300 lashes each, but died before the expiration of the Term of the imprisonment; and that when the last whipping was inflicted; they were at that time so reduced with fever; that in being brought out for punishment, they were unable to stand & were insensible to the punishment inflicted—They lived but a short time after the last whipping.

Now, your petitioner Humbly conceives that it is peculiarly hard, that he should be subjected to the entire loss of his slaves, and cannot reconcile it to his mind, to believe, that the State of South Carolina, will, for a violation of the law by his slaves, subject him to the full and entire loss, when it is manifest, *that their deaths, were Consequent, upon the Execution of the sentence pronounced by the said Court.*

Your petitioner, in asking Compensation from your Honorable body, is aware, that by the laws of the state, payment to the owner is only allowable, in capital cases, punishable with death; Yet in this *peculiar case,* he conceives, that it comes within the *spirit of the law,* if it is not to the letter. Because in carrying out the Execution of the sentence of the court, Death did ensue, which is the same to your petitioner, as if they had been put to death for a capital offence.

Your Petitioner therefore prays your Honorable body, to grant such compensation, as, under the circumstances, you may consider that Justice will approve.

And Your Petitioner as in duty Bound prays.

[signed] Horatio McClenaghan

SOURCE: Petition of Horatio McClenaghan to the South Carolina Senate, October 1851, Records of the General Assembly, #2844, SCDAH. Rejected. PAR #11385105.

132. T. W. Sweet et al. to Alabama Legislature, 1851

To the Hon. the Legislature of the State of Alabama:

Your petitioners believe the comfort, the health, as also the wealth of the people would be augmented by the multiplication of sheep in our State. Under existing circumstances they are almost forced to confine themselves to one kind of meat—they are at least limited in their enjoyment of one agreeable & healthy kind. A large portion of the State is eminently adapted to the rearing of this economical stock: the very places where cotton wool cannot be grown, are the very places where sheeps wool can. Shall such places, covering a large area, rich with the appropriate food, remain a waste? The sheep is said, by the agricultural writers, to be one of the best fertilizing machines on a plantation.

Without trespassing with views which might be extended, we state that the efforts of many in this matter are discouraged, often thwarted by the unreasonable number of dogs in the country—not only among the whites, but among the slaves. And although there is a Statute making it penal in masters to permit slaves to have dogs, it has remained a dead letter for years, & the same influences causing this will continue to operate—practically it is no protection.

There is one way in which we think this evil can be diminished if not removed. Two dogs on a plantation we deem entirely sufficient for all valuable purposes. Taking each above that number would tend greatly to abate a nuisance affecting seriously the wealth of the agricultural population, & the comfort, if not the health of all the people.

Wherefore we earnestly ask of your honorable bodies a trial of this or some efficacious remedy.

[signed]	T. W. Sweet	E. Pickens
	John C. Mcnair	Saml H. Gilmer
	J. M Morgan	T. P. Ferguson
	D A Boyd	S. Donoghey
	Abner Jones	J W Prichard
		[44 additional signatures]

SOURCE: Petition of T. W. Sweet et al. to the Alabama Legislature, 15 December 1851, Records of the Alabama Secretary of State, Legislative Bills and Resolutions, ADAH. This petition was sent to delegates representing Mobile and Tallapoosa counties. No act was passed. PAR #10185102.

133. Citizens of Wilkinson County to Mississippi Assembly, ca. 1852

A Memorial, addressed to the Legislature of Mississippi.

To the Honorable Senate and House of Representatives, of the State of M[i]ssissippi, in general assembly convened:

The subscribers, citizens of the county of Wilkinson and State of Mississippi, would respectfully represent to your Honorable Bodies, that, Whereas, there is generally to be found about our towns and villages a certain class of lawless and unprincipled persons, whose chief occupation is an illegal traffic with negroes, bartering whiskey for pigs, poultry, meal, corn &c., &c., thus corrupting the morals and injuring the health of the negroes, to the great detriment of their owners, and the imminent danger of the community;[1]—and, whereas, the present system of Patrols, which has been in vogue from time immemorial, has not only been found entirely inefficient, but worse than useless by operating as a license to the base and vicious, to visit negro-quarters for dissolute and immoral purposes. We, therefore, pray your Honorable Bodies to enact a law, authorising the Board of Police to appoint a proper and suitable, and competent person for each town, village, or Captain's Beat where such officer may, by them, be deemed necessary, to serve as Patrol for the term of two years from the date of the regular session of said Police Court; that, each person so appointed be commissioned by the Governor, and, before entering upon the duties of his office, be required to take an oath, in addition to the usual oath of office, to faithfully discharge, by day and by night, to the best of his abilities, the duties of the office of Patrol according to law, &c; and be also required to enter into bond, with sufficient security, in the penalty of from $500, to $1500, as the Police Court may direct, payable to the Governor, with the condition that he will well and truly discharge the duties of the office of Patrol; and that each patrol, thus appointed, upon the faithful performance of the duties of his office, shall be entitled, at the discretion of the Board of Police, to salary of from $400 to $800, according to the importance of his respective station, besides the perquisites to which he would be entitled under the present laws.

That should said patrol be convicted of any malconduct, or misdemeanor in office, whatsoever, his commission shall be revoked, and the person so removed, shall thereafter be rendered incapable of holding the office of either Patrol, Constable, or Justice of the Peace.

That each Patrol shall have the power to appoint an assistant or deputy, who shall take the oath of office as above prescribed; a[n]d thereupon such assistant or deputy shall have power and authority to perform all the acts and duties enjoined upon the principal.

That the duties of said Patrol, in addition to those required of patrols under the present system, shall be faithfully to aid and assist in preserving the peace, and in executing the criminal laws of the State; to give information, without delay, to some Justice of the Peace or other proper officer, of all riots, routs, and unlawful assemblies; and of every violation of the penal laws, which may come to his knowledge in any manner whatsoever; to apprehend any slave found off the premises of his or her owner, without a pass, or some letter or token, whereby it may appear that he or she is proceeding by authority from his or her owner, or some person having power to direct; also, any slave found offering or carrying any article for sale, without proper authority so to do, and carry him or her before some Justice of the Peace, to be, by his order, punished according to law; to seize any article, whatsoever, offered or carried for sale by any slave without written permission, from some person having power to grant it, specifying each article thus permitted to be sold; and to seize any gun, powder, shot, or other weapon unlawfully in the hands of any slave, and deliver all articles thus seized to some Justice of the Peace, to be by him disposed of according to law; to give information against and to prosecute any free negro, or mulatto, who shall keep or carry any arms in contravention of law, &c., &c. In short, said Patrol might be, advantageously, invested with all the powers of a Constable and supervisor of public roads.

Your petitioners would respectfully call the attention of your Honorable Bodies, to the fact, that it is a common practice with some shop-keepers, particularly during the Christmas Holidays, to have, in and about their shops, crowds of negroes, drinking, fiddling, dancing, singing, cursing, swearing, whooping and yelling, to the great annoyance and scandal of all respectable and order loving persons. And that negroes, having charge of teams, frequently drive them very fast and not unfrequently absent themselves from them, or fall asleep upon their waggons, and thus leave their teams to go along the public roads of their own accord, without any person to guide them, to the imminent risk of the lives of persons who may be passing them, especially in vehicles. We, therefore, pray your Honorable Bodies to enact a law making it penal for any merchant, store, or shop-keeper, to encourage or allow any noisy or clamorous assembly of negroes, about his or her store or shop.

Also, for any person to drive a team at a greater speed than a brisk walk of the animals usually employed in teams; or to allow his team to go along a public road without some person to guide and manage it. And, for any slave to be drunk, or engaged in any riotous, clamorous or disorderly conduct in any public place, store, shop, street or public road. And for such further action on the premises as to your Honorable Bodies seem meet and agreeable; and your petitioners, as in duty bound, will ever pray, &c.

[signed]	William L. Cage	A P Rodney
	P. E. H Lovelace	W B Mitchell
	W. O. Rodney	L. L. Babers
	N R Scudder	R. A. Ford
	John N Hunter	Johnsa Dorsey
		[53 additional signatures]

SOURCE: Petition of Citizens of Wilkinson County to the Mississippi Senate and House of Representatives, ca. 1852, Records of the Legislature, Petitions and Memorials, 1850–59, RG 47, MDAH. Granted.[2] PAR #11085201.

1. An 1822 law forbade liquor retailers from selling to "servants" without an owner's permission. In 1823, a law prohibited anyone from buying, selling, or receiving "any commodity whatsoever" from a slave without permission from the "master, employer, or overseer." The penalty included paying the master a sum equal to four times the value of the commodity, plus a fine of twenty dollars. Later, the fines were increased. The laws remained in force over the years. *Laws of the State of Mississippi* (n.p., [1822]), 472; *Laws of the State of Mississippi* (n.p., [1823]), 63; *Laws of the State of Mississippi, Passed at the Sixteenth Session of the General As-*

sembly, Held in the Town of Jackson (Jackson: Peter Isler, 1833), 129; *Laws of the State of Mississippi, Passed at the Regular Session of the Mississippi Legislature, Held in the City of Jackson January, February, and March 1850* (Jackson: Fall and Marshall, 1850), 100–102; Rena Humphreys and Mamie Owen, comps., *Index of the Mississippi Session Acts, 1817–1865* (Jackson: Tucker Printing House, 1937), 204–5, 285–89.

2. See *Laws of the State of Mississippi, Passed at a Regular Session of the Mississippi Legislature, Held in the City of Jackson, January, February, and March, 1852* (Jackson: Palmer and Pickett, 1852), 484–86.

134. Moses America et al., Kent County, to Delaware Assembly, ca. 1853

To the Honorable, the Senate and House of Representatives of the State of Delaware in General Assembly met:

The petition of the subscribers, free colored citizens of Kent County, humbly represents:

That the two Acts passed by the General Assembly of the State of Delaware, March 5, 1851, one entitled "An act in relation to free negroes and slaves," and the other entitled "An act to amend the Act entitled [']An act concerning apprentices and servants,[']" are grievously oppressive, and we call on the Legislature in which we have no voice, [(]except that of our Heavenly Father,) to relieve us from the burthens imposed by said Acts, which are heavy and hard to be borne in this enlightened age and land, where the hand of oppression is stayed from all except our unfortunate race. We endeavor to perform the duties of good, orderly citizens, and it bears hard on us not to be allowed the privilege of seeking to do better elsewhere without losing our residence and being subjected to arrest, fine, imprisonment and sale, provided we return temporarily to visit our families and friends. We, like our white brethren, are seeking the consolations and peace of the christian religion, and not to be permitted to assemble together, as we have been accustomed, to ask counsel of God for the salvation of our souls hereafter, and for making us more upright in this life, works against both our spiritual and temporal interest; and to have our little ones taken from us upon slight pretexts by those desiring their services without adequate reward, is very hard, and causing all those to emigrate who can conveniently leave the homes of their families and childhood.[1] We approach you with great diffidence, but with confidence, and in all sincerity, that you will, under God, do something for our relief, to encourage us to become more intelligent, better citizens, and to seek more generally that best of wisdom to be found in the sanctuary, all being believers in a common religion which teaches, that as *ye would that others should do to you, do ye even so to them.* We hope and pray that your honorable bodies, as your wisdom may deem it meet, to repeal the aforesaid acts, and otherwise ameliorate our condition, and we hope by our good conduct hereafter that we shall show that your acts were dictated not only by humanity, but the best interests of the State; and as in duty bound will ever pray, &c.

[signed]	Moses America	Purnel Carlisle
	Francis Brown	Charles Smith
	Richard Jacobs	William Adkins
	John Draper	George Brown
	Alexander Bell	James Robinson
		[17 additional signatures]

SOURCE: Petition of Moses America et al. to the Senate and House of Representatives of Delaware, ca. 1853, General Assembly, Legislative Papers, DSA. No act was passed. PAR #10385301.

1. For residency status, see petition 124, note 1, above. The law also prohibited free blacks and mulattoes from attending political gatherings and religious camp meetings. Fines of twenty and ten dollars, respectively, were to be assessed against wrongdoers. *Laws of the State of Delaware, Passed at a Session of the General Assembly, Commenced and Held at Dover, on Tuesday the Seventh Day of January, in the Year of Our Lord, One Thousand Eight Hundred and Fifty-One* (Wilmington: Johnson, Chandler and Harker, 1851), 591–92, 599–601.

135. Joseph F. McDonald et al., Harrison County, to Texas Legislature, 1853

To the Honorable the Senate & House of Representatives of the State of Texas

The undersigned J F McDonald respectfully represents that he is the owner of a negro man known by the name of Henry Moore who is about forty years of age and of black complexion—that said Henry has faithfully and obediently served him and all others to whom he has belonged and who have had him under their charge and that his faithfulness industry integrity and general good deportment have enable him in addition to the service rendered his master to accumulate a sufficient sum of money to purchase his freedom and he now desires by paying me the said McDonald his ~~master~~ master his value in money to obtain his freedom and I the said McDonald upon these terms am willing and desirious to emancipate and set him free from servitude and grant him personal freedom and liberty so far as he in accordance with the law may be permitted to enjoy the same—

And we the undersigned Citizens of Harrison County and State of Texas respectfully represent and say that we have long known the said negro man Henry, that he is a man of fixed honesty integrity industry and general good deportment and conduct and that he is respectful and humble in the presence of the white population regardless of their rank or condition in life and that he would remain and continue so to be if emancipated from servitude and permitted to remain in the state of Texas—and that we believe that if the said Henry were emancipated and permitted to remain within the limits of the state of Texas that his deportment and conduct would tend to the promotion of public order and decorum among all upon whom he might have or exert any influence—and that he would studiously avoid creating discontent and dissatisfaction among slaves with their condition and we believe that he would promptly discourage and discountenance the attempt in others so to do and that he would endeavor to suppress such a feeling if he found it existing—and we believe that as a negro he would be a friend of order and decorum and that his ~~residen~~ residence in the state after emancipation would not prejudice or have a tendency to prejudice the well being and interest of society or of individuals—and we believe that he would rely upon honest labor integrity and industry for a support and that by these means he would support and maintain himself and acquire enough in this way to sustain him in infirm old age so that he will not become or be a public charge and finally we are willing for him to be emancipated and remain in the state of Texas and reside among us if after emancipation he may desire so to do

Wherefore we pray your Honorable body to pass an act authorizing the said McDonald to emancipate the said Henry in the state of Texas and authorizing the said Henry upon and after his emancipation to be and remain permanently in the state of Texas emancipated and set free from involuntary servitude

[signed]	Joseph F. McDonald	T T Gregg
	C- A- Frazer	Saml P Taylor
	S R Peny	Edward Clark
	E C Beuzley	T. A. Harris
	H Key	N W, Eames
		[12 additional signatures]

SOURCE: Petition of Joseph F. McDonald et al. to the Texas Senate and House of Representatives, 8 December 1853, Records of the Legislature, Memorials and Petitions, RG 100, TSL-AD. No act was passed. PAR #11585306.

136. W. G. Veal et al., Hopkins County, to Texas Legislature, 1854

To the Honorable Senate & House of Representatives of the State of Texas:

Your Petitioners, citizens of the County of Hopkins, and state of Texas, would respectfully represent unto your Honorable Body, that there is now living in said County of Hopkins a "Collered Boy," Called and Known by the name of "Europe", about the age of Seventeen years. It is commonly reputed that he was born of a free *white* woman. We Know the said Boy well—personally—and we can say of our own knowledge that he is peaceable—good tempered—and orderly. He desires to remain in the State. He was brought here some years since by a widow woman, now deceased; and it is the wish of "Europe" now to remain in the State.

Your Petitioners respectfully ask your Honorable Body to pass an act to grant permission to said Boy "Europe" to remain in the State of Texas; and as in duty Bound &c.

[signed]	W. G. Veal	J C [Burson?]
	John H. Cullum	K E Matthews
	H, C. Russell	E. D. McKenney
	G, H, Crowder	Carrol Crisp
	A, O. French	J. S. Stout
	A. M. Birdwell	

SOURCE: Petition of W. G. Veal et al. to the Senate and House of Representatives of Texas, 12 January 1854, Records of the Legislature, Memorials and Petitions, RG 100, TSL-AD. Rejected.[1] PAR #11585401.

1. The Committee on State Affairs ruled that the petitioners' request did "not come within the meaning of the law which prohibits free persons of Collour remaining within the limits of the State." The committee report is included with the above petition.

137. J. Malachi Ford, Walterboro, to South Carolina House, 1854

To the Hon, the Speaker & members of the house of Representatives of So, Ca,

The Petition of J. Malachi Ford of Walterboro in Colleton District, respectfully sheweth unto your Hon. Body, that sometime in the month of July 1853, two felons, named Thomas Motley & Wm. Blacklege, from Richland District, whilst on a visit to Colleton District, Committed many outrages, with their ferocious dogs, upon Slaves, in that portion of the district, comparatively uninhabited by white persons, and amongst others, murdered a Slave at Parker's ferry, after inflicting the most outrageous and inhuman barbarities, hitherto without a parallel in a Civilized Country, and for which they were convicted by a Jury of the Country & Suffered the extreme penalty of the Law, on the Gallows.—That shortly after the commission of these barbarities, the said Felons absconded from the Parish, and attempted to make for Charleston District, and probably thence out of the State:—That a Warrant was issued for their arrest, but no Constable or Deputy Sheriff could be induced to go in pursuit of them:—That under these circumstances your Petitioner was called upon to act as Special Constable, which he eventually consented to do, especially for the vindication of public justice:—That he pursued the said felons for upwards of fifty (50) miles, through a very Sickly country, day and night, (from which he contracted fever) & eventually succeeded in arresting them at one Thos. Limehouse's, almost on the very lines of Charleston District, Carried them to the town of Walterboro, & delivered them to the Sheriff of Colleton District, in whose custody they remained until their trial, & conviction at Fall Term 1853, and subsequent execution.—That through the instrumentality of your Petitioner, the said felons were induced to point out the place where the body of the murdered Slave was secreted, & subsequently found, & without which important evidence said felons may never have been convicted, & brought to Justice; & thus one of the most barbarous murders in the history of civilized nations would have passed unpunished,

That for these valuable services, rendered to the State, for the vindication of her laws, for protection of our Slave property, & that, too at the risk of Petitioner's life, from the malaria of a sickly country, & from desperate armed felons, your Petitioner has never yet received compensation, not even the petty costs of a Constable:—That your Hon. Body cannot but see, that such petty costs, would be wholly inadequate to compensate your Petitioner, & that the small sum of two hundred($200) Dollars, which he now respectfully Submits, he is, at least entitled to, your Petitioner prays may be ordered to be paid to him.

And your Petitioner will ever pray &c—

November 24th 1854—

[signed] J. Malachi Ford

SOURCE: Petition of J. Malachi Ford to the South Carolina House of Representatives, 24 November 1854, Records of the General Assembly, #47, SCDAH. No act was passed. PAR #11385401.

138. Agricultural Society of St. Paul's Parish to South Carolina Assembly, 1854

To

The Honb Senate & Representatives of the State of South Carolina

We the following Committee, J Raven Mathewes Senr, J B Grimball, F Fraser Mathewes, Wm. Brisbane & Geo Morris, having been unanimously appointed at a regular and full meeting in May last of the Agricultur Society of St Pauls Parish to memorialize your Honbl Bodies, at the present Session upon the subject of the inefficiency of the Law against hireing Slaves without the assent or Knowledge of the Owners and also, the crime of harbouring Runaways,

Reported, at a very recent meeting (6 inst) That we had been prevented from carrying out its instructions, in consequence of several members of the Committee, being absent from the State during the long and severe Epidemic of last Summer, upon which the Society urged upon the Committee the necessity of immediately presenting their views to the present Session of the Legislature on so important and harrassing a subject to the State, The Slave Holding, and Agricultural Interest in General

We therefore, respectfully submit the following from among many similar Complaints as illustrative of the nullity of the Law as it now stands The following decisions have recently taken place in the Commercial City of Charleston, which are antagonistic to the Agricultural Interests of the State and if so continued, will impair all confidence in a Title to this property so valuable, at least for Taxable purposes. Mr Wm Westcoat, a member of the Society and a large Planter and Owner of Slaves, reported to the Society, that last spring, one of his negroes, ranaway from his plantation, was gone two months, took him out a vessel in Charleston action entered and no redress, in the fall, a carpenter fellow ranaway, was taken out of a Vessel in Charleston loading for Europe, action entered and no redress Judge Cooper presiding, said in order to convict it was necessary for Mr Westcoat to prove that the person hiring was aware that his slaves were runaways, on both occasions his runaways were hired by Colored Men, The Honbl J B Campbell a member of the Legislature was the Attorney employed in both these actions, to whom we respectfully beg to leave to refer, Another Member, Mr J Fraser Mathewes, also a Planter & Owner of Slaves, reports to the Society, that about two years ago, he with two Police Officers in Charleston captured, a negro woman & her two children, who had absconde[d] three years before, whilst in the yard & employment of a Free Mulatto woman he prosecuted and Judge Elliott, who presided charged the Jury, that unless they were satisfied that the woman knew, she was employing a runaway they could not convict her under the Law and accordingly she was acquitted, tho it was proved that Mr Mathewes negro was employed without a Ticket or Badge

Mr J B Grimball, reports to the Society, that it is the practice of masters of Vessels, who frequent the Pon Pon River, for the purpose of obtaining gravel for Charleston Market, to hire out slaves without our knowledge and against our wishes, at night to load their vessels, thus imposing on them a laborious task at the time, which ought to be devoted to rest, and also encouraging habits of Intemperance and disorganization

Your Petitioners are aware, that cases involving difficulties of a like nature, have been brough[t] before the Courts of the State, without redress to the owners In consideration of the above Your Petitioners pray Your Honbl Bodies to afford them, that protection which their Interests require and the policy of the State demands

St Pauls Parish
7h December 1854
[no signatures]

SOURCE: Petition of the Agricultural Society of St. Paul's Parish to the South Carolina Senate and House of Representatives, 7 December 1854, Records of the General Assembly, #83, SCDAH. No act was passed. PAR #11385404.

139. Hervey Currie et al. to Tennessee Legislature, 1855

To the Legislature of Tennessee

Your petitioners Citizens of the State of Tennessee would respectfully present for the consideration of your honorable body the propriety of passing more stringent laws for the punishment of negroes guilty of burning Cotton Gins and other out houses the Commission of such crimes is on the increase to an alarming extent there having been three Gins burned in this vicinity doubtless by negroes quite recently only a few miles distant from each other Your petitioners are of opinion that there is too much at stake in the burning of Cotton Gins to be passed over with so light punishment it is frequently the case that in the burning of Cotton Gins the owner is damaged to the amount of from one to five Thousand dollars as was the case of one of your petitioners (H. Currie) whose Gin was recently set on fire and burned by a negro in the neighborhood the evidence of his guilt being of such a character as not to leave a doubt on the mind of any one acquainted with the circumstance and yet all the punishment which could be inf[l]icted according to the Statutes of Tennessee is Thirty nine lashes In view of the danger to which we are exposed your petitioners would most earnestly pray your honorable body take into Consideration the importance of passing a law punishing offenders of this class ~~by hanging~~ with the same punishment that is inflicted for the burning of dwellings and other out Houses and in duty bound your petitioners would ever pray

[signed]	Hervey Currie	L. Taliaferro
	Thos R. Tuggle	James A. Rogers
	M B Drake	Philip Yancey
	A. W. Allison	Jno Irving
	J. H. Cobb	Robt. W. Hargrove
		[114 additional signatures]

SOURCE: Petition of Hervey Currie et al. to the Tennessee Legislature, 11 December 1855, Legislative Petitions, #24-1855, reel 20, TSLA. Granted.[1] PAR #11485501.

1. Any slave found guilty of "willfully and maliciously" setting fire to any barn, stable, crib, outhouse, ginhouse, manufacturing establishment, bridge, or "steamboat or lighter" would suffer death by hanging unless the jury recommended a milder punishment. *Public Acts of the State of Tennessee, Passed at the First Session of the Thirty-Second General Assembly, for the Years 1857–8* (Nashville: G. C. Torbett, 1858), 18–19.

140. Citizens and Mechanics of Smithville to North Carolina Assembly, 1856

To The General Assembly of the State of North Carolina, at the Session of 1856

Your memorialists, citizens of Smithville in the County of Brunswick, some of us Mechanics, considering the great injury done us by Colored persons in taking contracts at a lower rate than we can afford, thereby depriving us of the means of supporting our families, pray your Honorable bodies to pass an act to prevent free colored persons from becoming contractors for any mechanical work such as building houses vessels &c. And especially to pass more stringent laws against slaves hiring their own time The evil has become a serious one, and we most earnestly believe that sound policy no less than our own interest requires that white mechanics should be protected against the competition of colored persons whether free or slave

[signed]	W R Dosher	G.W. Reaves
	S W. Lehew	Wm. R. Davis
	C. B. Daniel	Jos, T. Thompson
	Lafayette Dosher	A, M, Guthrie
	Asa Dosher	Geo W Stout
		[48 additional signatures]

SOURCE: Petition of Citizens and Mechanics of Smithville to the North Carolina General Assembly, 1856, Records of the General Assembly, Session Records, NCDAH. No act was passed. PAR #11285609.

141. Samuel McCulloch Jr., Jackson County, to Congress of Texas, 1857

To the Honourable Congress of Texas

The Petition of Samuel McCulloch Jr. of Jackson County, respectfully represents, that he emigrated from the United States to Texas, in the family of his Father, Samuel McCulloch the elder, also of Jackson County, in the spring of the year 1835—being then a single man—That when the Revolution commenced he entered the military service of Texas, as a private in the Matagorda Volunteer Company, commanded by Captain James Collinsworth, and under his command he participated in the storming of the Fort at Goliad, on the 9th of Octo. 1835. In that action he recieved a severe wound in the right shoulder, which laid him up, a helpless invalid, for nearly a year, and has made ~~left~~ him a cripple for life.—He was the only one of the Texan Troops wounded in that action, and the first whose blood was shed in the War of Independence.

Your petitioner, while Texas was a part of the Republic of Mexico, was, by the Constitution and Laws, a citizen of the state, and as such entitled to lands as a settler;—but he never made application for any lands, nor ~~does he hold~~ has he ever received any from ~~in~~ the Country. And now, having by marriage become the head of a family, he is desirous of settling in life, and of performing the duties of a citizen;—but he unhappily finds that by the Laws of the Country, for the Independence of which he has fought and bled, and still suffers, he is deprived of the privileges of citizenship by reason of an unfortunate admixture of African blood, which he is said, without any fault of his, to inherit from a remote maternal ancestor;—nor can he, without the beneficent action of Congress, recieve the lands to which he was entitled under the Mexican Government.—Your petitioner refers for the truth of the foregoing statement to the accompanying copy of his military discharge and the evidence of John P. Barden Esq—and the Honl. Mr. Patton and the Honl. Mr. Southerland, of the House of Representatives To those Gentlemen and all others who may know him, he would also respectfully refer for testimonials of his general good demeanour.

Your Petitioner prays your Honourable body to take his case into consideration; and that he may be allowed to recieve from the Government the quantum of land that is allowed to other persons who were citizens of the Country before the declaration of Independence;—and, as he wishes to make Texas the home of himself & his posterity, he further prays your Honl. body that he and his children may be allowed to enjoy the privileges of Citizenship in this Republic.

And your petitioner, as in duty bound will ever pray &c.

[signed] Saml. McCulloch, Jr.

Matagorda Sept—14th 1857

I do hereby certify, that I knew Samuel McCulloch in the year 1835 at the time he joined Capt—Geo—M Collinsworth's company as a volunteer on the 6th or 7th of October of that year on the Lavacca River & that he was engaged in the attack made by said Company on the Fort at Goliad on the night of the 9th of said month, to the best of my recolection, & in the said attack was wounded by the enemy by a gun-shot in the right shoulder which wound permanently disabled him rendering his right arm useless—I have known him & seen him occasionally since 1835 up to the present time & beleive that his wound received at Goliad rendered him forever unfit for active duties—I further certify that he was the first man who entered the Fort—

[signed] John Duncan

The State of Texas } Before me Henry D. Starr
County of Jackson } Clerk of the County Court
in & for said County, duly bonded & Commissioned personally came and appeared, Benjamin J. White, a citizen of said County & State, to me well known

and a credible Witness, who being duly & solemnly sworn deposed & said—Towit:

"I Benjamin J. White being solemnly sworn depose & say, that I am well acquainted with Samuel McCulloch—And that I knew him when he joined the Company of George M Collingsworth [*sic*] in the Service of the Republic of Texas on the 6th or 7th day of October A.D. 1835 as a volunteer, and I know; that he was engaged in the attack made by said Company on the Fort at Goliad, on the 9th of October at about 12 oclock at night and to my Knowledge, he was wounded in said attack by the enemy, by a gun shot in the right shoulder, which disabled him and rendered his right arm useless, and I was by his side when he was wounded—and that he is the person he represents himself to be. I also know, for I have known him personally ever since

[signed] Benj. J. White"

And the said affidavit was signed & sworn to by the witness before me
Witness my hand & the seal of the County Court
this Sept 16th AD 1857
[signed] Henry D. Starr Clerk CCCJ

SOURCE: Petition of Samuel McCulloch Jr. to the Congress of Texas, 23 November 1857, Records of the Legislature, Memorials and Petitions, RG 100, TSL-AD; Certificate, John Duncan, 14 September 1857, ibid.; Deposition, Benjamin J. White, 16 September 1857, ibid. No act was passed.[1] PAR #11585702.

1. The Committee on Judiciary recommended postponement "on the ground of inexpediency & unconstitutionality." Earlier, in 1840, Samuel McColloch Jr.; his sisters Jane, Harriet, and Mahaly; and one other family member obtained an exemption from the law requiring immigrant free blacks to be sold as slaves. *Laws of the Republic of Texas, Passed at the Session of the Fourth Congress* (Houston: Telegraph Power, 1840), 151–53; *Laws of the Republic of Texas, Passed at the Session of the Fifth Congress* (Houston: Telegraph Power, 1841), 4, 5.

142. Citizens of Hardeman County to Tennessee Assembly, 1857

To The Senate & House of Representatives, of the State of Tennessee, }

We the undersigned Citizens of Hardeman County Do Most humbly & respectfully petition Your Honorable Body, to take into consideration, the importance of passing a law, to prevent, Negroes preaching; in this our State, as we believe, its practice, alike, baneful, to the negro, and dangerous to the public weal & safety, Injurious to the great mass of negroes who attend such worship, because the minister in a great majority of cases, is entirely, unlettered and hence cannot understand and properly expound, the great & essential truths of the

Bible, But much oftener promulgates dogmas, militant to the true religion of Christ, producing effects fatal in its opperations upon the minds & moral natures, of his, deluded followers; And not only is this so, but we believe, that in many instances the religious societies of our country allow such preaching, to supersede appointments that might otherwise be made by regular members of the liscenced clergy, who are qualified to preach and explain to the negro the Blessed Revelations of Holy writ that in a wise & merciful dispensation of Providence has been given to man,

Thus at once interposing a barrier, to the proper moral culture of our collored population, and at the same time entailing upon society an evil of considerable magnitude, by assembling in great numbers under pretext of Divine worship, crowds of disorderly blacks, that much oftner ends in the p[r]opagation of mischief, than the diffusion of useful knowledge and moralizing influences, In fact Your ~~||||||~~ petitioners believe that the frequent insurrectionary outbreaks that disturb the repose, tranquility and sometimes even safety of communities, are much oftner, the fruits, of these gatherings, and the pernicious doctrines, there disseminated, than the effects, of any, or all other causes, whether immediate or remote, And hence we humbly & respectfully pray that your Honorable Body pass a law that will effectually protect us from the evils, and dangers that must continue to follow the practice of a system, unauthorized as we think by the plainest principles of moral and Social Law

[signed]	C. H. Anderson	T H Hancock
	W. W. McCarly	H Bullington
	Asa Cox	M O Pearce
	Holman Southall	G W Wells
	J. C. H. Fowler	J C Welty
		[24 additional signatures]

SOURCE: Petition of Citizens of Hardeman County to the Tennessee Senate and House of Representatives, 3 December 1857, Legislative Records, #94-1857, reel 20, TSLA. No act was passed. PAR #11485702.

143. Citizens of Coffee County to Alabama Assembly, 1857

The State of Alabama

Coffee County

To the Honorable the senate and House of Representatives for the State of Ala in General assembly Convened we the Undersigned Citizens of Coffee Co. pray your honorable Boddy that you pass and [*sic*] act for the benefit of Narcissa Daniel a free colored Girl of about seventeen years of age.

Said Narcissa Resides with the family of Mr Allen Daniel a highly Respectable & Citizen of our County Mr Dani[e]l is late of ~~Sumter~~ Marion *Co Ga* from whence he removed to this State and this County bringing Said Girl with him

Said Narcissa was raised from infancy by *Mrs* Daniel wife of said Alen Daniel she (Narcissa) having been a [favorite] child (and it is asserted from a reliable sorce [*sic*] that she is the offspring of a white woman of high family)

Narcissa assigns as some of the reasons for applying to and praying your honorable boddy for the passage of such an act, that she knows Mrs. Daniel as her best friend and that she would preffer a state of bondage to that of a sepperation and we your petitioners pray that boddy will pass and [*sic*] act Giving her the right to reside in your state

Respectfully

[bottom of page torn and damaged]

[signed on second page] Isaac H. Watson, Huey Gilles, Powell Smith, Joseph Williams, Burrel Rudd, Samuel Colbert, James Howell, David Wilson, John Prince, James Curey

[44 additional signatures]

SOURCE: Petition of Citizens of Coffee County to the Alabama Senate and House of Representatives, 7 December 1857, Records of the Alabama Secretary of State, Legislative Bills and Resolutions, ADAH. No act was passed. PAR #10185701.

144. Lucy Andrews to South Carolina Senate and House, 1858

To the Honorable, the Senate, and House of Representatives, of the Legislature, of the State of South Carolina—

The humble Petition of Lucy Andrews, a free Person of color, would respectfuly represent unto your Honorable Body, that she is now sixteen years of age, (and the Mother of an Infant Child) being a Descendant, of a White Woman, and her Father a Slave; That she is dissatisfied with her present condition being compelled to go about from place to place, to seek employment for her support, and not permitted to stay at any place more than a week, or two, at a time, no one caring about employing her—That she expects to raise a family, and will not be able to support them—That she sees, and knows, to her own sorrow, and regret, that Slaves are far more happy, and enjoy themselves far better, than she does, in her present isolated condition of freedom; and are well treated, and cared for by their Masters, whilst she is going about, from place to place, hunting employment for her support. That she cannot enjoy herself, situated as She now is, and ~~therefore~~ prefers Slavery, to freedom, in her present condition. Your Petitioner therefore prays that your Honorable

Body, would enact a law authorizing and permitting her to go voluntarily, into Slavery, and select her own Master, and your Petitioner will, as in duty bound, ever pray &c—

her
Lucy X Andrews
mark

SOURCE: Petition of Lucy Andrews to the Senate and House of Representatives of South Carolina, 1858, Records of the General Assembly, #2811, SCDAH. Referred to the Committee on Colored Population. No act was passed.[1] PAR #11385806.

1. On two subsequent occasions, Lucy Andrews petitioned the South Carolina General Assembly to become a slave, but she was denied. In 1861, she noted that her infant child had died. In 1863, she said that her husband, Robbin, and her two children, Emily and Robbin, were owned by Henry Duncan, a kind and benevolent master. She wished to live on his plantation with her husband and children. Petition of Lucy Andrews to the Senate and House of Representatives of South Carolina, 20 November 1861 and 25 November 1863, Records of the General Assembly, #97 and #11, SCDAH. See also Certificate, J. R. Hunter et al., ca. 1861, ibid., #97; Report [of the] Committee on Colored Population, ca. 1861, ibid., #97; and Statement, R. S. Beckham, 25 November 1863, ibid., #11.

145. Citizens of Chester District to South Carolina Legislature, ca. 1859

Chester District So. Ca
To the Legislature of S. C.

Your Petitioners would respectfully suggest to your Honorable Body the propriety and necessity of taking into consideration the deplorable condition of the free Negroes of the State, and of taking some action in their behalf. We consider them the most degraded people that live in a civilized community. We of the South understand the Negro character. We know that naturally they are indolent, lazy, improvident, destitute of forethought, and totally incapable of self government. With such proclivities they are incapable of supporting themselves, and should have some one to arouse their dormant faculties and direct their labors, But apart from themselves they have decidedly a demoralizing influence upon our slave population. Their indolence and imprudence are deleterious to the young and unexperienced slaves, and their shanties are the ready receptacles of stolen property and a place of rende[v]ous for badly disposed slaves, where they meet to drink, gamble, & plot mischief.

We regard their condition socially and politically as most deplorable and consider them proper subjects for Legislative action. We would therefore humbly pray that you would enact some law for their relief, by placing them in a happy state of bondage, the place where God designed the African to be. ~~If your~~

~~Honorable Body be not disposed to grant this boon to these unfortunate people; then we pray you to appropriate a fund and~~ have ~~them removed to Liberia~~ and thus relieve the state of their contaminating influence.

	Names	Names
[signed]	R A Pagan	Jos. T. Walker
	L. D. Smith	J. A. Ready
	E. T. Atkinson	Jas Turner
	[illegible]	Henry Pratt
	D B [ink smear]	J H Carter
		[77 additional signatures]

SOURCE: Petition of Citizens of Chester District to the South Carolina Legislature, ca. 1859, Records of the General Assembly, #1843, SCDAH. Rejected. PAR #11385908.

146. Citizens of McClennan County to Texas Legislature, ca. 1859

To the Hon Legislature of the State of Texas.

The petition of the undersigned citizins, residents and property owners of the County of McClennan respectfully represent, That the maintenance of the institution of negro slavery, with due subordination of slaves to masters as heretofore existing is all important to the interests and well being of the State. That one of the great operating causes in corrupting the minds of the poeple by infusing sentiments hostile to the institution of Slavery is the free and unlic[e]nsed circulation of incendiary documents and antiSlavery newspapers through the post-offices of the State. Another cause of discomfort, loss and injury to masters, and all honest and law-abiding citizens, is the intercourse with slaves of persons w[h]ether vagrants or temporary sojourners, who in many cases are voluntary or hired emissaries of northern associations; or individuals laboring to destroy slavery in the Southern States, instigating desertion or conspiracy and insurrection. That althoug[h] legal evidence can be obtained that these infamous and dangerous offenders are diligently pursuing their object by the means mentioned, yet they are intirely safe from prosecution and conviction, and may securely pursue their iniquitous course. Therfore we pray your Honorable body, that such new measures of prevention and punishment may be enacted as will reach the evils enumerated. Aiming only to present in general terms the evils existing And to pray for relief in general, we do not presume to prescribe Special or precise remedies; but submit to the wisdom and discretion of the Legislature the devising and adoption of such enactments as will afford sufficient remedy for the great and growing evils and danger under consideration.

[signed]	Richd Coke	F C Downs
	Thos. Harrison	J. D Wallace

B. D. Chenowith	Thos Walker
L. F. Puckett	J. H. Mullens
J. M. Smith	J W Maddin
	[131 additional signatures]

SOURCE: Petition of Citizens of McClennan County to the Texas Legislature, ca. 1859, Records of the Legislature, Memorials and Petitions, RG 100, TSL-AD. No act was passed. PAR #11585905.

147. Johan Perret, Kemper County, to Mississippi Legislature, ca. 1859

To the Honorable Legislature of the State of Mississippi Your petitioner Johan Perret would respectfully state that he is a free mulatto living in the county of Kemper—that he is the grand son of a white woman, and was born in the State of North Carolina and county of Anson. That when a Small boy, he was apprenticed by the Court of Common Pleas and Quarter Sessions of Anson County to the Rev. Charles Hailey and to remain an apprentice until he became of the age of twenty one years. That in 1844 he came to the State of Mississippi and county of Kemper, and has remained with him Since that *time.* That your petitioner is now twenty three years old, Your petitioner would most respectfully State that he is an invalid and has been so for two years and that he is dropsical. that he is unable in consequence of ill health to leave the State and that he is unwilling to or that he would vastly prefer going into Slavery. Than to be compelled to leave. That the Rev Charles Haily [*sic*] has been to him a Kind Master and friend, that he is unable to purchase him even if your petitioner was of any value Your petitioner prays your Honorable body, to pass an act permitting him to go into slavery, and that The Rev. Charles Hailey be permitted to appear before the Police Court of Kemper County and there give his consent to become his master without having to pay any Stipulated price for the reason that Said Haily is unable to buy him and the further reason that your petitioner does not in truth think that he is of any value and in duty bound your petitioner will ever pray—

[signed] Johan Perret

SOURCE: Petition of Johan Perret to the Mississippi Legislature, ca. 1859, Records of the Legislature, Petitions and Memorials, 1850–59, RG 47, MDAH. No act was passed. PAR #11085921.

148. Citizens of Maury County to Tennessee Assembly, 1859

Maury County Tenn Nov 14t 1859

To the General Assembly of the State of Tennessee Now Sitting,

We your petitioners and Citizens of Maury County would suggest that we have for several years discovered a fearful evil and difficulty fastening upon our body politic, that if not ~~Arested~~ Arrested and a stop put to, will be obliged to end in fatal consequences, And ruinous to the Citizens & slave holders of the Country,

We Mean the traffic & Sale of Ardent Spirits to the Slaves, We know of no other Vice or dissipation in our Community half so ruinous as this liquor traffic with Slaves, it has become verry profitable & a money making business. The penalty for transgressing the present law is but little *terror* compared to the gain they are making in the traffic, they can make money enough to pay all the fines & a handsome profit too, Cannot the law making power fix such penalties upon the transgressors of the law as will put a stop to the liquor traffic with the Slaves, the present law with its penalties does no good

It is Verry hard, it Can not be done, a Slave holder Cannot Controle his Slaves & take Care of them While they Can Steal & Sell and obtain liquor When they please, & get drunk, it prepares them to Commit Crimes they Would not otherwise do. In the present condition of affairs if the law does not restrain & stop the traffic bad consequences May result between the traffickers & the slave holders, ~~V~~ We think the law making power should enact such a law with such penalties as will put a Stop to Such a Course of Conduct as are now going on Amongst us. We your petitioners Ask your Honourable body for such relief as they have in their power to give and that a law be passed—

That it shall not be lawful for any person or persons to Sell give or loan ~~to~~ any intoxicating liquors to any Slave or Slaves without a permit in the genuine hand writing of the Owner or Owners or there [*sic*] agents, or those having controle of Said Slave or Slaves

That it shall Not be lawful for any person the owner of a Grocery or having Spirituous liquors in there possession to permit any person white or black bond or free to sell give or loan any intoxicating liquors to any Slave or Slaves without a permit in the genuine hand Writing of the Owner or Owners or those having immediate Controle of Said Slaves or Slaves

Any one found Guilty of any of the above offences shall be guilty of Felony & be Confined in the Jail & penitentiary ~~ary~~ house for a term not less than *1* & not more than *3* years

We are fully of Opinion the passage of the above law would put a Stop to the liquor traffic with the Slaves—

	Names	Names
[signed]	Nimrod Porter	Wm Perry Jr
	P, W, B, Thomas	J S Martin

D,J, Estes	Wm Watkins
John Estes	Bob, N, Moore
Jesse S Harris	R. H. Hill
	[98 additional signatures]

SOURCE: Petition of Citizens of Maury County to the Tennessee General Assembly, 14 November 1859, Legislative Petitions, #27-1859, reel 20, TSLA. Granted.[1] PAR #11485901.

1. The law made the sale of liquor to a slave a misdemeanor punishable by a fine of not less than five or more than ten dollars. *The Code of Tennessee, Enacted by the General Assembly of 1857–8* (Nashville: E. G. Eastman, 1858), 517.

149. Grand Jury of Hays County to Texas Legislature, 1859

The State of Texas
Hays County
November 30th 1859

To the Honorable Senate and House of Representatives of the State of Texas now in Session:

The undersigned, Grand Jurors, of the County aforesaid, Now in Session, Would Most respectfully Solicit your particular attention and ask the passage of an act, of the present Legislature to forbid Negro Slaves the *right* to hold in their own name and for their own use, as property, Horses, Cattle, Land and Stock of every description; as we see daily the baneful influence and effects on the Slave population. as in duty bound We will ever pray[1]

[signed]	J. C. Watkins, Foreman	}	James L. Malone
	James M. Malone	}	C, R, Perry
	Jno. H. Cock	}	J P. Hallford
	James Harris	}	D. L. Lindsay
	William L. Malone	}	John Mayes
			[10 additional signatures]

SOURCE: Petition of the Grand Jury of Hays County to the Texas Senate and House of Representatives, 30 November 1859, Records of the Legislature, Memorials and Petitions, RG 100, TSL-AD. PAR #11585904.

1. Five years later, on 26 May 1864, the assembly passed a law making it unlawful for any slaveowner to permit slaves "any pretended ownership or control, in his or her own right, over any horses, cattle, sheep or hogs, within this State." H. P. N. Gammel, comp., *The Laws of Texas, 1822–1897,* 5 vols. (Austin: Gammel Book, 1898), 5:762–63.

150. W. E. Price, Walker County, to Texas Legislature, 1859

to the Sinate and House of Representitives of th State of Texas in session at Austin December 1859
yor petitioner W E Price of Walker county Respectfully Represent to you hounerable Body that he had a Cirtain negro man (Cuggoe) absconded from his Servis in th state of Alabama on or about the year 1835 and that your petioner Came across him in Texas in th year 1856 and Regained posesion of said negro But that one Jame Davis of Polk County did inveigh and Conspire With said negro Cuggoe and filed his petion to th District Court of that County praying th Court to Decree him to Be A free man on th grounds that he th negro Was in Texas under the Mexacan government Which is holy contrary to th constitution of th Republic of Texas and as there is many other negroes here Before th Declaration of Independance of Republic of Texas and to Save much trouble and Litigation your petitioner prays th pasage of A Law in Absolution that all persons of colar that was Slaves Before they came to Texas Eather By absconding or Runing away from th legal owners and Came to Texas Before th Declaration of Independance of Texas shall Be Delivered up to th Legal owners With Damage on satisfacttaroy proof that such negro Was Realy A Slave Before he came to Texas and that his Being in Texas Before th Independance shall not Be so Construed as to give him his freedom

And your petitioner as Well for him Self as others Will In duty Bound Eaver pray

[signed] W, E, Price

SOURCE: Petition of W. E. Price to the Texas Senate and House of Representatives, 14 December 1859, Records of the Legislature, Memorials and Petitions, RG 100, TSL-AD. Rejected. PAR #11585903.

151. H. L. Houze et al., Enterprise, to Mississippi Legislature, 1859

Enterprise Miss Dec 16th/59

To the Honerable the Sennate and House of Representatives of the State of Miss in General Assembly Convened

The Undersigned being appointed a Committee, as herein afterwards Explained—beg leaf to State the following facts and then ask such relief in the premises as your honerable body may deem just and Equitable, (to wit, Sometime in the summer of 1858 a Certain Negro fellow Called Peter belonging to Dr E A Miller (of Wayne County in this state) ~~and~~ was in the Employ of the Rail

Road Company at the time near this place did on one Sabbath day waylay the road or private path and Caught and by force violated the person of a beautiful young Lady by Committing *a Rape*, The Said Boy was Caught the same day and on the next day was brought to this City for trial He was Regularly tried by a Magistrates Court & Jury in the presence of the young Lady and her parents and found guilty of the Crime Charged and was fully Committed for trial at the next term of the Court

In view of the delay and the unsafty of the County Jail; and in the presence of Weeping Innocence Prostrated beneath such odious violence,—the injured one in her weakness looking up as it were, to the Manly hearts and strong arms of those around her Crying for vengance; under these Circumstances the appeal was too strong too great to be refused—the perpetrator was taken, by about 50 of our citizens and hung the same night—,The next day there was a large meeting held to consider the matter: at which time resolutions were unanimously passed ratifying what had been done and at the same time appointed the undersigned a special Committe to petition the Legislature to grant the same relief to Dr *Miller* as he would have been Entitled to from the state had his Negro been hung by due process of Law, (as he undoubtedly would have been)

The Said Negro was valued by Competent judges in due form at Fourteen hundred dollars (1400$)

We feel (and we doubt not but your honerable body will agree with us) that the security of our wives and Daughters, Demand in all such cases prompt and Summary punnishment—the public sense of all our people approve it; The State is not a looser thereby; you have precedent for your guide; from all these Considerations your petitioners beg that you will pass an act for the relief of Dr Miller and appropriate what the state allows in cases where the regular action of the Law takes the Life of a Negro slave; and your petitioners as in duty bound will ever pray

[signed] H, L, Houze
W, B, Smith
Committee

L B Moody
J. M. Hand
R. S. Wier

SOURCE: Petition of H. L. Houze et al. to the Senate and House of Representatives of Mississippi, 16 December 1859, Records of the Legislature, Petitions and Memorials, 1860, RG 47, MDAH. Rejected. PAR #11085901.

152. James Rose et al., Charleston, to South Carolina Assembly, ca. 1860

To the Honble
The President and Members
of the
Senate of South Carolina

The petition of the undersigned citizens of Charleston respectfully Sheweth, That they have seen with regret in the papers, the draught of a bill proposing to drive our free coloured people from the State under the heaviest penalties.

Your petitioners can find no reason for such severity, on the contrary, they believe the project one of wrong and injustice to a class of our inhabitants who ought to be objects of our care and protection.

We know many among them who command the respect of all respectable men, many who are good citizens, patterns of industry, sobriety, and irreproachable conduct, There can be no better proof of this than the fact that they hold property in the City of Charleston to the value of more than half a million of Dollars.

Their labour is indispensable to us in this neighbourhood. They are the only workmen who will, or can, take employment in the Country during the summer. We cannot build or repair a house in that season without the aid of the coloured carpenter or bricklayer.

But we put their claim to protection on a higher ground. In their humble station they are equitably entitled to the rights which the laws of their native place have secured to them. These may be properly called vested rights, which neither justice, nor humanity, nor Christian charity can wantonly assail

We are the strong and they the feeble. Let us not begin now for the first time in our history to subject ourselves to the charge of oppressing the weak and unresisting

If there are evil persons among them as there are all classes let the laws punish those who deserve punishment. But let us ref[us]e to involve innocent and guilty, virtuous and vicious, industrious and idle, in one indiscriminate ruin. There are individuals among them to whom the safety of the community may be confidently intrusted. They are sincere friends, why alienate them however humble

Your petitioners respectfully solicit the attention of your Honorable body to these objections to the proposed bill, and as in duty bound will ever pray.

[signed]	James Rose	John Harleston
	Wm J. Grayson	E N Fuller
	Benj Huger	Rev. Lucien O. Lance
	Oney Harleston	J, J Cohen
	William Harleston	Lewis F. Robertson
		[119 additional signatures]

SOURCE: Petition of James Rose et al. to the South Carolina General Assembly, ca. 1860, Records of the General Assembly, #2801, SCDAH. Granted.[1] PAR #11386004.

1. In 1860, the Charleston foundry owner James M. Eason, a secessionist recently elected to the assembly, introduced a bill to prohibit free persons of color from entering into contracts for "any mechanical pursuits." Other legislators proposed that beginning 1 January 1862 free blacks remaining in the state be sold as slaves. Neither bill became law, however, partly because free people of color secured the support of prominent Charleston whites. Michael P. Johnson and James L. Roark, *Black Masters: A Free Family of Color in the Old South* (New York: W. W. Norton, 1984), 266, 276–80.

153. Citizens of Currituck County to North Carolina Assembly, ca. 1860

North Carolina.

To the Senate & House of Commons ~

Your Memorialists, citizens of Currituck County, respectfully petition your honorable bodies to take immediate steps to relieve the people of this State of the free negro population, which has always been a nuisance, and now become an element of great danger. Scattered over the State, having at all times free communication with the slaves, the free negroes furnish a ready and safe medium for the diffusion of incendiary doctrines which we have abundant reason to believe have, especially of late, been instilled with the minds of the slaves, and they thereby rendered insubordinate and ripe for any wicked enterprise to which they may be instigated by northern emissaries. The minds of our people have for several years past been directed to this source of danger, but recent events have produced a deep and settled conviction of the necessity of guarding against it, either by expelling the free negroes, or reducing them all to the condition of slavery. Your memorialists are [convinced] with no qualms as to the right of the Legislature either to expel them from the State, or to reduce them to a condition to slavery.

Disfranchised in this State by the convention of 1835, the Supreme Court of the United States, the highest judicial tribunal in our country, by a late decision has decided that they are not citizens under the constitution; and it must be admitted that here, the only rights to which they are entitled are strictly & solely legal, and therefore subject to revision or change by act of the Genl Assembly—Whatever diversity of opinion, however, may be entertained in reference to this question, it strikes your Petitioners that there is one view of the subject that cannot fail to impress the mind of every good citizen; all must admit that the present is a time of great danger; such in fact as never before endangered the peace & safety of the Southern States, and threatened the institution of slavery; it is unnecessary to enter into any statement of facts to prove the truth of this declaration; what is the first duty of the people of North Carolina? Surely, to provide all necessary means to ward off the threatened danger—Your Memorialists, firmly believing the removal of the free negroes from the State, or their reduction to the ~~same~~ condition of the slave population, one of the *necessary means,* hold that the plain right of self defense would justify such action on their part through their Legislature, and that such legislation at this time would meet the approving voice of the whole body of the Southern people & challenge the approbation of all others throughout the country who properly appreciate our position & respect our rights. But your Memorialists do not design submitting any argument upon the subject to your honorable bodies, either as to the right or the expediency of the policy they recommend; nor do they propose to advise any particular plan for the accomplishment of the object in view, being content to leave the matter to your own good judgement, guided as they believe it will be by sound patriotism and a just sense of your representative duties—They cannot refrain, however, from suggesting that according to their own judgements the wisest and most judicious policy would be to provide for the removal of all such as might choose to go to the Northern States, within a certain fixed time, and to authorise the several county courts to sell as slaves all such as remained after the expiration of the time named in the act; and believing that sound policy requires that all proper means should be resorted to to strengthen the institution of slavery by increasing the number of slave holding citizens and otherwise, Your Memorialists would recommend, in case the above policy be adopted, that the right of purchase should be confined to those citizens of the state who are not already owners of slaves; that no one person should be allowed to become the purchaser of more than one, except in the case of mothers and small children, that all negroes so purchased shall be exempt from execution for debt, and not transferable by sale and purchase for a term of   years.

Trusting that your honorable bodies will give to this subject that serious attention which its importance entitles it to, your petitioners will ever pray &c

[no signatures]

SOURCE: Petition of Citizens of Currituck County to the North Carolina General Assembly, ca. 1860, Records of the General Assembly, Session Records, Petitions, November 1860–February 1861, box 8, NCDAH. Rejected.[1] PAR #11286002.

1. The issue of forcing free blacks to leave the state or become slaves had been debated for several years. In November 1858, one bill was introduced in the North Carolina House and another in the Senate recommending that free persons of color "select their own masters and become slaves." Neither bill, however, became law. John Hope Franklin, *The Free Negro in North Carolina, 1790–1860* (1943; reprint, Chapel Hill: University of North Carolina Press, 1995), 214–16.

154. Citizens of Frederick, Jefferson, and Clarke Counties to Virginia Assembly, 1860

A MEMORIAL
PRAYING AN ACT
TO EXEMPT A LIMITED AMOUNT OF SLAVE PROPERTY
FROM PROCESS FOR DEBT.

To the Honorable Senate and House of Delegates of Virginia:

The undersigned, citizens of Frederick, Jefferson and Clarke counties, respectfully represent your honorable body that it is highly desirable for the perpetuation of the present social relations of Virginia, for the maintenance of peace within her borders, and for a community of interest amongst all her citizens, that the institution of negro slavery should be fostered by such Legislative Acts as may be calculated to bring the ownership of negro property within the means of the Poor as well as of the Rich; and believing that nothing will promote this end more effectually than to exempt a limited amount of such property from all legal process for debt, your Petitioners pray the passage of a law guarantying to every family now possessed of, or who may hereafter be possessed of a negro or negroes, the right to the enjoyment of property in said negroes to the value of one good slave free from all Judgments, Executions and Liens of every kind, except where such Liens already exist. Your Petitioners believe that under such a law many mechanics and laboring men generally would purchase one servant to wait on their families, and thus that the strong bonds of a common interest would be added to the social feeling which impels the citizens of Virginia to resist alike invasion from without and treason at home.

All which is respectfully submitted.

NAMES	RESIDENCES
Nathl B Meade =	White Post Va
I Mc K Kennerly	Clarke Co "
David Meade Sn	" "
David Meade jr	" "
E W Massey	"
G Mason	"
Geo B Shumate	"
George Gardner	"
Jonas P Bell	"
Dan B Richards	"
[55 additional signatures]	

SOURCE: Petition of Citizens of Frederick, Jefferson, and Clarke counties to the Virginia

Senate and House of Delegates, 1860, Legislative Petitions, Frederick County, VSA. No act was passed.[1] PAR #11686014.

1. Rather than respond to the above request, the assembly in 1860–61 placed a $1.20 capitation tax on slaves over twelve years of age, instituted a license fee of $10.00 for those seeking to buy or sell slaves for profit, and established a 0.05 percent income tax on slave traders. June Purcell Guild, comp., *Black Laws of Virginia: A Summary of the Legislative Acts of Virginia concerning Negroes from the Earliest Times to the Present* (Richmond: Whittet and Shepperson, 1936; reprint, New York: Negro Universities Press, 1969), 140; *Acts of the General Assembly of the State of Virginia, Passed in 1861* (Richmond: William F. Ritchie, 1861), 4.

155. P. A. L. Smith et al., Fauquier County, to Virginia Assembly, 1860

To the General Assembly of Virginia

The petition of the undersigned citizens, residents or property owners of the County of Fauquier & State of Virginia, respectfully represent:

That the maintenance of the institution of negro slavery, with the due subordination of slaves to masters, and generally of the inferior black to the dominant white class, as heretofore existing in Virginia, is all important to the well being and interest of the Commonwealth and of every considerable and useful class of our population. That the great and most operative causes of the corrupting of the habits and morals of slaves, and of infusing into their minds discontent and the spirit of insubordination, and consequently of producing discomfort and unhappiness to themselves, and loss or injury to their masters and to all honest and law-abiding citizens, are to be found in two existing and wide spread evils, viz: 1st The shops or other places for the unlicensed selling of intoxicating liquors to slaves, or carrying on with them other illegal traffic, including generally the receiving of stolen goods; and 2d. The intercourse with slaves (and also with free negroes) of persons, whether vagrants, or temporary sojourners, who in many cases, are voluntary agents or hired emmissaries of Northern associations, or individuals, laboring to destroy slavery in the Southern States, by instigating desertion or conspiracy and insurrection and which persons, generally as itinerants, and mostly, also, as tramping vagrants, and all of them coming from the Northern States, are spread through Virginia, and probably have operated in every county thereof, in some one or other of the various characters of avowed individual beggars, or solicitors for subscriptions to Northern publications, or contributions to some professed public, or pious works, or pedlers (generally without legal license to sell) and even, in some cases, as teachers, religious agents, and preachers of the Gospel! That whenever, through either of these two different means for corrupting slaves, pillaging property, and inducing insubordination, immorality and crime, slaves are thus operated upon by white persons, no matter to what extent, or how frequently, there can rarely be obtained any legal evidence of the facts, because negroes only are privy to such offences, and the evidence of negroes, under our present law, is not admissible against a white person, even though such person may be universally reputed to be a receiver of stolen goods, or a Northern Abolition emissary and conspirator, inviting slaves to desertion, or to revolt or massacre. Therefore both of these dangerous and infamous classes of offenders are almost ent[i]rely safe from prosecution and conviction, and may securely pursue their iniquitous courses.

Therefore, we pray of your honorable body that such new measures of prevention and punishment may be enacted as will make operative the existing legal prohibitions of the offences of Vagrancy, unlicensed dealing with slaves, and pedling; and also by extending stringent repression, and certain and sufficient penalties to all other professed pursuits of itinerant strangers, having neither sufficient vouchers of good character and objects, nor license, nor visible means for support by honest labour. Aiming only to present, in general terms, the exi[s]ting evils, and to pray for relief in general, we do not presume to prescribe *special* or precise remedies; but submit to the wisdom and discretion of the Legislature the devising and adoption of such enactments as will afford sufficient remedies for the great and growing evils and dangers under consideration

[signed]	P A L Smith	Thos R, Foster
	Edwd Turner	J. W. Patterson
	E P. Clark, M D	Richd N Johnson
	Wm L. Sutton	Jno Owens
	Jas W. Foster	William Garrison
		[55 additional signatures]

SOURCE: Petition of P. A. L. Smith et al. to the Virginia General Assembly, 10 January 1860, Legislative Petitions, Fauquier County, VSA. Granted.[1] PAR #11686007.

1. In 1860, the assembly passed laws to prohibit free persons of color from selling, and slaves from buying or selling, "ardent spirits." It also enacted a statute increasing the penalty for helping a slave escape to twenty years in the penitentiary. June Purcell Guild, comp., *Black Laws of Virginia: A Summary of the Legislative Acts of Virginia concerning Negroes from the Earliest Times to the Present* (Richmond: Whittet and Shepperson, 1936; reprint, New York: Negro Universities Press, 1969), 91, 121, 169.

156. Ann Archie, Marshall County, to Mississippi Legislature, 1860

Marshall Co. Miss—
January 12, 1860
To the Honourable Legislature of the State of Mississippi,

Your petitioner Ann Archie, a free woman of colour, aged about twenty two, in behalf of herself & infant child Julia now residing in the county of Marshall

& State of Mississippi ~~begs leave to state,~~ requests your honourable body to pass an act to empower her & her child to become slaves of Andrew H. Caldwell of said state & county, with whom your petitioner has long been acquainted & with whom she would prefer to live together with her offspring as slaves, to being compelled to emigrate to another state ~~or to be sold to the highest bidder.~~ She therefore prays your honourable body to pass such a law as will secure her object & permit her & her child to remain in the state of Mississippi as the property of said Andrew H Caldwell.

my
Ann X Archie
mark

In behalf of herself & child
Test
James Lester
J R J Creighton
Thos J Hudson

I read ov[e]r this paper to the woman above named, and explained it to her, and she acknowledged to me that she executed it, with a full understanding of its object and purpose.

Jany 16 1860
Alex: M Clayton

SOURCE: Petition of Ann Archie to the Mississippi Legislature, 16 January 1860, Records of the Legislature, Petitions and Memorials, 1860, RG 47, MDAH. No act was passed. PAR #11086007.

157. Walker Fitch, Augusta County, to Virginia Assembly, 1861

To The Honorable The General Assembly of The State of Virginia

The petition of Walker Fitch respectfully represents unto your Honorable Body that he is a Free Man of Color over the age of twenty one years & a resident of the County of Augusta—That he is tired of his condition of Freedom and is desirous of choosing a Master & changing his condition to that of Slavery.—That he chooses as his Master Michael G. Harman Esqr. of said County who is the own[er] of your petitioners Wife, and he prays your Honorable Body to pass a Law authorizing his enslavement to Mr. Harman. And as in duty bound he will ever pray &c.

his
Walker X Fitch
mark

Augusta County towit:

Walker Fitch a Free Man of Color, whose name is signed to the above writing, personally appeared this day before me a Notary Public for said County & acknowledged his said signature to be his free & voluntary act, & being duly sworn declares that his said application is made without collusion & freely, with full Knowledge of the effect of his application if granted, & I do farther certify that I explained fully to the said Walker Fitch the effect of his said Application before he affixed his signature to the same.

Given under my hand this 7th day of January 1861

[signed] H. M. Bell N.P.

The undersigned do hereby certify that they were present at the foregoing examination of Walker Fitch who is now in Custody in the jail of Augusta County on a charge of forgery & are Witnesses of his signature to the above petition, and after conversing freely with said Walker Fitch & Explaining fully to him the effect of his application, they are perfectly satisfied that the application is made of his free & voluntary consent & wish & that there is no collusion. And they recommend to your Honorable Body to pass a law in accordance with the petition. Witness our hands this 7th day of January 1861.

[signed] G M Cochran
A J Garber
Wm D Anderson
Thos J Michie
H. H. Peck

The undersigned to whom reference is made in the petition of Walker Fitch has examined the said petition. He is the owner of the Wife and children of said Walker & has had him in his employment for several years, & is willing to accept said Walker as his slave upon equitable terms, if it shall please the General Assembly to grant his petition.

[signed] M G Harman

SOURCE: Petition of Walker Fitch to the Virginia General Assembly, 7 January 1861, Legislative Petitions, Augusta County, VSA. No act was passed.[1] PAR #11686102.

1. A few months later, on 28 March 1861, the Virginia General Assembly passed "An ACT for the Voluntary Enslavement of Free Negroes, without Compensation to the Commonwealth." The law stated that free blacks could choose a master or mistress, apply to the circuit court in the county where they had resided for twelve months, and state their case as to why they wanted to become slaves. Their argument had to be made in the presence of a lawyer for the commonwealth "so that no injustice is done to the applicant." *Acts of the General Assembly of the State of Virginia, Passed in 1861* (Richmond: William F. Ritchie, 1861), 52–53.

158. W. T. Smith et al., Marshall, to Texas Assembly, 1861

Marshall Texas January 17th 1861

To the Honorable's E A. Blanch, Eli T Craig, E. H Baxter, & George W. Whitmore

Gents

We the undersigned Petitioners respectfully Wish and request you to endeaver to get a bill passed by the Legislature of Texas to prevent the competition and encouragement of Negro Mechanick as we think that it is not just or right to give Slaves the advantages or liberties that they are now endeavering to take or get to put down White Workmen whose daily living is made by the sweat of their brow in their industrious pursuits. And men too, who have been reared upon Southern Soil and who have always been With the South and all her institutions

But we do most Solemnly object to being put in Competition With Negro Mechanicks who are to rival us in the obtaining of Contracts for the Construction of Houses Churches and other Buildings—or any other of the Mechanical Branches that are taking by contract

We would therefore appeal to you as your fellow Citizens and Constituents to remedy this one feature that is now if let a lone to be greatly to the disadvantage and draw back of our Bright Lone Star State—

We Say Negroes forever but Negroes in their Places (Viz: in Corn & Cotton Fields) And if there are those who have Negro Mechanicks to do their own work let them! have them, but we do not want to be equalized with them by allowing them to go at large contracting for Jobs of work upon their own account or on account of those who pretend to be their agents, or to be made the competitors of Negros in this a true Southern State—

We think that a law might be passed to confine them to the hire of Some Workman or undertaker [of contracts] whose duty it will be to keep them in their places and under proper control Without the owner or Master being at all injured

[signed]	W T Smith	W, A, Salmon
	C, W, Slater	James R. Fyffe
	L A Henderson	Phil Brown
	G, M, Stevens	J H VanHook
	J C. Curtis	W Mills Johnson
		[22 additional signatures]

SOURCE: Petition of W. T. Smith et al. to E. A. Blanch, Eli T. Craig, E. H. Baxter, and George W. Whitmore, 17 January 1861, Records of the Legislature, Memorials and Petitions, RG 100, TSL-AD. No act was passed. PAR #11586101.

159. John Kelker, Frederick Kelker, and Cecil Kelker, Santa Rosa County, to Florida Assembly, 1861

To the Honorable General Assembly
of the State of Florida

The petitioner of the undersigned, John Kelker, Frederick Kelker, and Cecil Kelker, inhabitants of Santa Rosa County, Respectfuly showeth that theay are free persons of color, natives of West Florida, and all born anterior to the treaty of session with Spain.[1] Except the last named who, was not born before, is the Daughter of Parents, Subjects of Spain, and Residents of West Florida at the date of the treaty, that theay have been continously in Florida at all times, and have conducted themselves at all times as peaceable, Sober, and industrious persons abiding the laws and performing all the duties imposed by the laws, that at the last Session of your Honorable Body an act was passed releiving and exempting certain persons therein named being persons of color, of the city of Pensacola, from the restriction and penalties imposed upon them and Persons of their class by Several laws of the State of Florida reciting as the reason of the act, that theay were Subjects of the King of Spain anterior to the date of the treaty of session with that nation.

Your petitioners being embraced by the Spirit and reason of the act mentioned beg to be relieved from its penalties and restr[ic]tions by a Special act of your Honorable body including the children of the Said John and cecil all of whom seven in number, being minors, and Your petitioners will ever pray

his
[signed] John X Kelker
mark

his
Frederick X Kelker
mark

his
Cecil X Kelker
mark

Milton Fla
September 18 1861

When I went to Pensacola to reside, which was in 1832 the Kelker family resided in the vecinity of Pensacola and were mentioned as old Spanish Subjects the Petitioners John & Frederick Kelker were of that family and have resided continuously in the county up to the Present

[signed] Geo. Walker

I James E. Simpson do hereby certify that I have known Fred and John Kelker from the Year A D 1821 and that they have lived in the State of Florida ever since that time. Witness my hand & Seal Oct 11 1861

[signed] James E. Simpson S S

SOURCE: Petition of John Kelker et al. to the Florida General Assembly, 18 September 1861, Records of the Nineteenth Century Florida State Legislature, FSA; Testimonial, George Walker, 18 September, 1861, ibid.; Certificate, James E. Simpson, 11 October 1861, ibid. Granted.[2] PAR #10586101.

1. In the Adams-Onis Treaty of 22 February 1819, Spain ceded Florida to the United States; and after its ratification, Florida became a U.S. territory in July 1821.

2. *The Acts and Resolutions Adopted by the General Assembly of Florida, at Its Eleventh Session, Begun and Held at the Capitol, in the City of Tallahassee, on Monday, November 18, 1861* (Tallahassee: Office of the Floridian and Journal, 1862), 50.

160. Citizens of Union County to North Carolina Assembly, 1864

To the honorable the Genl. Assembly of the State of North Carolina

The undersigned petitioners, Citizens of Union County, respectfully represent and sheweth to your honorable body that our said County of Union although as patriotic as any in the State, having furnished as many Soldiers to fight our battles, as any other in the State of the same population, that none has surpassed her, in privations, sacrifices and hardships in defence of our common country, Yet Union is comparatively a poor County, the Slave population being much less than many Counties, who have furnished no more, if as many Soldiers as our County—

Your petitioners further shew, that where the labouring class consists chiefly of White Men, and where those White men are mainly in the Army as in the case with this County, leaves but few to make support, for the thousands of Women and Children and old men that are left behind—and is exceedingly difficult with every means employed, that we have at command to keep our Soldiers families from Starvation, besides involving our County in debt, to such an amount as may well result in bankruptcy and ruin—this County is Situated between Anson and Mecklenburburgh [*sic*], ~~Counties, both~~ either of which Counties own upwards of Six thousand Slaves, whilst Union has only about two thousand, and yet this County has furnished as many Soldiers if not more men for the battle field than either of those Counties, and this comparison will also apply to many other Counties of the State, and in this way shew the unequal bearing of this War, and how much more oppressive it is upon the poor than the rich—which matter we pray your honorable body duly to consider, and remedy to the extent of your power,

Your petitioners furthermore shew to your body, that our said County, in addition to the help received from the State, have already contracted a debt of upwards of Fifty Six thousand Dollars $56,000, for the purchase of provisions ~~for the purchase of provisions~~ for the support of the indigent families of our Soldiers, and at this time have but little meat & Bread provided wherewith to feed those families the balance of the year, and we are left no alternative but to greatly increase the indebtedness of the County, or to leave the families of our brave and patriotic Soldiers (to [ink smear] of them) to suffer and starve for bread—

Therefore we the undersigned petitioners pray your honorable body, to grant as such relief, and give us such assistance in the premises as you may have the power to do, either to assume our debt, in part or [ink smear] the whole, to allow us a greater portion of the appropropriation [*sic*] from the State than has been allowed us, or such other help and assistance in the premises, as in the Wisdom and humanity of your honorable body, you may think proper and right, and as in duty bound we will ever pray &c

May 1864

[signed]	D.A. Covington	Julius A. Belk
	F.S. Wiatt	Aaron [Hairtell?]
	J. E. Irby Clk County Court	J F Richardson
	C.W. Richardson	Jacob Long
	J. C. Helms	William Long
		[38 additional signatures]

SOURCE: Petition of Citizens of Union County to the North Carolina General Assembly, 27 May 1864, Records of the General Assembly, Session Records, NCDAH. No act was passed. PAR #11286401.

BIBLIOGRAPHY

The Acts and Resolutions Adopted by the General Assembly of Florida, at Its Eleventh Session, Begun and Held at the Capitol, in the City of Tallahassee, on Monday, November 18, 1861. Tallahassee: Office of the Floridian and Journal, 1862.

Acts and Resolutions of the General Assembly, of the State of South-Carolina, Passed in December, 1800. Columbia: Daniel and J. J. Faust, 1801.

Acts and Resolutions of the General Assembly of the State of South-Carolina. Passed in December, 1817. Columbia: Daniel and J. J. Faust, 1818.

Acts and Resolutions of the General Assembly of the State of South-Carolina, Passed in December, 1820. Columbia: D. Faust, 1821.

Acts and Resolutions of the General Assembly of the State of South-Carolina, Passed in December, 1822. Columbia: Daniel Faust, 1823.

Acts and Resolutions of the General Assembly of the State of South-Carolina, Passed in December, 1823. Columbia: D. and J. M. Faust, 1824.

Acts and Resolutions of the General Assembly of the State of South Carolina, Passed in December, 1825. Columbia: D. and J. M. Faust, 1826.

Acts and Resolutions of the General Assembly of the State of South Carolina, Passed in December, 1828. Columbia: D. and J. M. Faust, 1829.

Acts and Resolutions of the General Assembly of the State of South Carolina, Passed in December, 1829. Columbia: D. and J. M. Faust, 1830.

Acts and Resolutions of the General Assembly, of the State of South Carolina, Passed in December, 1834. Columbia: E. F. Branthwaite, 1834.

Acts of the General Assembly of the State of South-Carolina, from February, 1791, to December, 1794, Both Inclusive. Vol. 1. Columbia: D. and J. J. Faust, 1808.

Acts of the General Assembly of the State of South Carolina, Passed in December, 1842. Columbia: A. H. Pemberton, 1843.

Acts of the General Assembly of the State of South-Carolina, Passed in December, 1845. Columbia: A. G. Summer, 1846.

Acts of the General Assembly of the State of Virginia, Passed in 1861. Richmond: William F. Ritchie, 1861.

Acts of the General Assembly of Virginia, Passed at the Session of 1834–35, Commencing 1 December, 1834, and Ending 12 March, 1835. Richmond: Samuel Shepherd, 1835.

[Acts] of the State of Mississippi, Passed by the General Assembly, at their Third Session, Which Commenced the Third of January, and Ended the Twelfth of February, 1820 in the City of Natchez. Natchez: Richard C. Langdon, 1820.

Acts Passed at a General Assembly of the Commonwealth of Virginia, Begun and Held at the Capitol, in the City of Richmond, on Monday the Fifth Day of December, in the Year of Our Lord One Thousand Eight Hundred and Eight. . . . Richmond: Samuel Pleasants Jr., 1809.

Acts Passed at a General Assembly of the Commonwealth of Virginia, Begun and Held at the Capitol, in the City of Richmond, on Monday, the Fifth Day of December, in the Year of Our Lord, One Thousand Eight Hundred and Thirty-one. . . . Richmond: Thomas Ritchie, 1831.

Acts Passed at a General Assembly of the Commonwealth of Virginia, Begun and Held at the Capitol in the City of Richmond, on Monday the Fourth Day of December, in the Year of Our Lord, One Thousand Eight Hundred and Fifteen. Richmond: Thomas Ritchie, 1816.

Acts Passed at a General Assembly of the Commonwealth of Virginia: Begun and Held at the Capitol, in the City of Richmond, on Monday, the Fourth Day of December, One Thousand Seven Hundred and Ninety-Seven. Richmond: Augustine Davis, 1798.

Acts Passed at a General Assembly of the Commonwealth of Virginia, Begun and Held at the Capitol in the City of Richmond, on Monday the Second Day of December, in the Year of Our Lord, One Thousand Eight Hundred and Eleven. . . . Richmond: Samuel Pleasants, 1812.

Acts Passed at a General Assembly of the Commonwealth of Virginia, Begun and Held at the Capitol in the City of Richmond, on Monday, the Third Day of December, One Thousand Eight Hundred and Four. Richmond: Samuel Pleasants Jr., 180[5].

Acts Passed at a General Assembly of the Commonwealth of Virginia, Begun and Held at the Capitol, in the City of Richmond, on Tuesday, the Tenth Day of November, One Thousand Seven Hundred and Ninety-Five. Richmond: Augustine Davis, 1796.

Acts Passed at the Eighth Annual Session of the General Assembly of the State of Alabama, Begun and Held in the Town of Tuscaloosa, on the Third Monday in November, One Thousand Eight Hundred and Twenty-Six. Tuscaloosa: Grantland and Robinson, 1827.

Acts Passed at the First Session of the Fourth General Assembly of the State of Tennessee, Begun and Held at Knoxville, on Monday the Twenty-First Day of September, One Thousand Eight Hundred and One. Knoxville: George Roulstone, 1801.

Acts Passed at the First Session of the Third General Assembly State of Tennessee, Begun and Held at Knoxville, on Monday the Sixteenth Day of September, One Thousand Seven Hundred and Ninety Nine. Knoxville: Roulstone and Wilson, 1799.

Acts Passed at the First Session of the Twenty-Third General Assembly of the State of Tennessee. 1839–40. Nashville: J. Geo. Harris, 1840.

Acts Passed at the General Assembly of the State of North Carolina, at the Session of 1830–31. Raleigh: Lawrence and Lemay, 1831.

[Acts Passed at the] General Assembly of the State of Tennessee, Begun and Held at Nashville. . . . Nashville: T. S. Bradford, 181[3].

Acts Passed at the Second Session of the Eighth General Assembly of the Mississippi Territory Begun and Held at the Town of Washington, on the Seventh Day of November, One Thousand Eight Hundred and Fourteen. Natchez: P. Isler and McCurdy, 1814.

Acts Passed at the Second Session of the Fourteenth General Assembly of the State of Tennessee. Knoxville: G. Wilson and Heiskell and Brown, 1822.

Acts Passed at the Thirteenth Annual Session of the General Assembly of the State of Alabama,

Begun and Held in the Town of Tuscaloosa, on the Third Monday in November, One Thousand Eight Hundred and Thirty-One. Tuscaloosa: Wiley, McGuire and Henry, 1832.

Acts Passed by the General Assembly of the State of North Carolina, at the Session of 1831–32. Raleigh: Lawrence and Lemay, 1832.

Acts Passed by the General Assembly of the State of North Carolina, at the Session of 1834–35. Raleigh: Philo White, 1835.

Alexander, Adele Logan. *Ambiguous Lives: Free Women of Color in Rural Georgia, 1789–1879.* Fayetteville: University of Arkansas Press, 1991.

Aptheker, Herbert. *American Negro Slave Revolts.* New York: Columbia University Press, 1943.

Ayers, Edward L. *Vengeance and Justice: Crime and Punishment in the Nineteenth Century South.* New York: Oxford University Press, 1984.

Bailey, David Thomas. "A Divided Prism: Two Sources of Black Testimony on Slavery." *Journal of Southern History* 46 (August 1980): 381–404.

Bamman, Gale W., and Debbie W. Spero, eds. *Tennessee Divorces, 1797–1858; Taken from 750 Legislative Petitions and Acts.* Nashville: Gale Bamman, 1985.

Bassett, John Spencer. *Slavery in the State of North Carolina.* Johns Hopkins University Studies in Historical and Political Science, vol. 17. Baltimore: Johns Hopkins University Press, 1899.

Berlin, Ira. *Slaves without Masters: The Free Negro in the Antebellum South.* New York: Pantheon Books, 1974.

Berlin, Ira, Leslie S. Rowland, Barbara J. Fields, Thavolia Glymph, Steven F. Miller, Joseph Reidy, and Julie Saville, eds. *Freedom: A Documentary History of Emancipation, 1861–1867.* New York: Cambridge University Press, 1982–.

Blassingame, John W. *The Slave Community: Plantation Life in the Antebellum South.* New York: Oxford University Press, 1972.

Bogger, Tommy L. *Free Blacks in Norfolk, Virginia, 1790–1860: The Darker Side of Freedom.* Charlottesville: University Press of Virginia, 1997.

Burn, W. L. *Emancipation and Apprenticeship in the British West Indies.* London: Jonathan Cape, 1937.

Campbell, John. "Work, Pregnancy, and Infant Mortality among Southern Slaves." *Journal of Interdisciplinary History* 14 (Spring 1984): 793–812.

Catterall, Helen T., ed. *Judicial Cases concerning American Slavery and the Negro.* 5 vols. Washington, D.C.: W. F. Roberts, 1932. Reprint, New York: Octagon Books, 1968.

Clark, Elizabeth. "Matrimonial Bonds: Slavery and Divorce in Nineteenth-Century America." *Law and History Review* 8 (Spring 1990): 25–54.

The Code of Tennessee, Enacted by the General Assembly of 1857–8. Nashville: E. G. Eastman, 1858.

A Collection of All Such Acts of the General Assembly of Virginia, of a Public and Permanent Nature, as Are Now in Force. Richmond: Samuel Pleasants Jr. and Henry Pace, 1803.

A Collection of All Such Acts of the General Assembly of Virginia, of a Public and Permanent Nature, as Are Now in Force. Richmond: Samuel Pleasants, 1814.

A Collection of All Such Acts of the General Assembly of Virginia of a Public and Permanent Nature as Have Passed since the Session of 1801. Richmond: Samuel Pleasants Jr., 1808.

A Compilation of the Statutes of Tennessee, of a General and Permanent Nature, from the Commencement of the Government to the Present Time. Nashville: James Smith, 1836.

Cox, Edward L. *Free Coloreds in the Slave Societies of St. Kitts and Grenada, 1763–1833.* Knoxville: University of Tennessee Press, 1984.

Curry, Leonard. *The Free Black in Urban America, 1800–1850: The Shadow of the Dream.* Chicago: University of Chicago Press, 1981.

Cushing, John D., comp. *The First Laws of the State of North Carolina.* 2 vols. Wilmington, Del.: Michael Glazier, 1984.

Digest of the Laws of Virginia, Which Are of a Permanent Character and General Operation; Illustrated by Judicial Decisions. Richmond: Smith and Palmer, 1841.

Ellison, Mary. "Resistance to Oppression: Black Women's Response to Slavery in the United States." *Slavery and Abolition* 4 (March 1983): 56–63.

Fede, Andrew. "Legitimized Violent Slave Abuse in the American South, 1619–1865: A Case Study of Laws and Social Change in Six Southern States." *American Journal of Legal History* 29 (April 1985): 93–150.

Fifth Annual Report of the Library Board of the Virginia State Library. Richmond: Davis Bottom, 1908.

Fifth Census; or, Enumeration of the Inhabitants of the United States, 1830. Washington, D.C.: Duff Green, 1832.

Finkelman, Paul, ed. adviser. *State Slavery Statutes.* Frederick, Md.: University Publications of America, 1989. Microfiche edition.

———. *State Slavery Statutes: Guide to the Microfiche Collection.* Frederick, Md.: University Publications of America, 1989.

———, ed. *Women and the Family in a Slave Society.* New York: Garland, 1989.

Fish, Cheryl. "Voices of Restless (Dis)continuity: The Significance of Travel for Free Black Women in the Antebellum Americas." *Women's Studies* 26 (October 1997): 475–95.

Fitchett, E. Horace. "The Origin and Growth of the Free Negro Population of Charleston, South Carolina." *Journal of Negro History* 26 (October 1941): 421–37.

Fox-Genovese, Elizabeth. *Within the Plantation Household: Black and White Women of the Old South.* Chapel Hill: University of North Carolina Press, 1988.

Franklin, John Hope. *The Free Negro in North Carolina, 1790–1860.* 1943. Reprint, Chapel Hill: University of North Carolina Press, 1995.

Gammel, H. P. N., comp. *The Laws of Texas, 1822–1897.* 5 vols. Austin: Gammel Book, 1898.

Goodstein, Anita Shafer. "Black History on the Nashville Frontier, 1780–1810." *Tennessee Historical Quarterly* 30 (Winter 1979): 401–20.

———. *Nashville, 1780–1860: From Frontier to City.* Gainesville: University of Florida Press, 1989.

Guild, June Purcell, comp. *Black Laws of Virginia: A Summary of the Legislative Acts of Virginia concerning Negroes from the Earliest Times to the Present.* Richmond: Whittet and Shepperson, 1936. Reprint, New York: Negro Universities Press, 1969.

Gutman, Herbert. *The Black Family in Slavery and Freedom, 1750–1925.* New York: Pantheon Books, 1976.

Haggard, J. Villasana. *Handbook for Translators of Spanish Historical Documents.* Austin: University of Texas Press, 1941.

Hartgrove, W. B. "The Story of Maria Louise Moore and Fannie M. Richards." *Journal of Negro History* 1 (January 1916): 23–33.

Haskel, Daniel, and J. Calvin Smith. *A Complete Descriptive and Statistical Gazetteer of the United States.* New York: Sherman and Smith, 1847.

Hine, Darlene Clark, and David Barry Gaspar, eds. *More Than Chattel: Black Women and Slavery in the Americas.* Bloomington: Indiana University Press, 1996.

Hogan, William Ransom, and Edwin Adams Davis, eds. *William Johnson's Natchez: The Ante-Bellum Diary of a Free Negro.* Baton Rouge: Louisiana State University Press, 1951.

Humphreys, Rena, and Mamie Owen, comps., *Index of the Mississippi Session Acts, 1817–1865.* Jackson: Tucker Printing House, 1937.

Hurd, John Codman. *The Law of Freedom and Bondage in the United States.* 2 vols. Boston: Little, Brown, 1858–62. Reprint, New York: Negro Universities Press, 1968.

Jackson, Luther Porter. *Free Negro Labor and Property Holding in Virginia, 1830–1860.* Washington, D.C.: American Historical Association, 1942.

Jennings, Thelma. "'Us Colored Women Had to Go through a Plenty': Sexual Exploitation of African-American Slave Women." *Journal of Women's History* 1 (Winter 1990): 45–74.

Johnson, Guion Griffis. *Ante-Bellum North Carolina: A Social History.* Chapel Hill: University of North Carolina Press, 1937.

Johnson, Michael P., and James L. Roark. *Black Masters: A Free Family of Color in the Old South.* New York: W. W. Norton, 1984.

Johnson, Whittington B. "Free African-American Women in Savannah, 1800–1860: Affluence and Autonomy amid Adversity." *Georgia Historical Quarterly* 76 (Summer 1992): 260–83.

Johnston, James Hugo. "Race Relations in Virginia and Miscegenation in the South, 1776–1860." Ph.D. diss., University of Chicago, 1937.

——. *Race Relations in Virginia and Miscegenation in the South, 1776–1860.* Amherst: University of Massachusetts Press, 1970.

Journal of the House of Representatives of the State of Tennessee at the Twenty-Fifth General Assembly, Held at Nashville, on Monday the 25 Day of October, 1843. Knoxville: E. G. Eastman and L. Gifford, 1844.

Journal of the Senate of the State of Tennessee at the Twenty-Fifth General Assembly, Held at Nashville. Knoxville: E. G. Eastman and L. Gifford, 1844.

King, Wilma. *Stolen Childhood: Slave Youth in Nineteenth-Century America.* Bloomington: Indiana University Press, 1995.

Koger, Larry. *Black Slaveowners: Free Black Slave Masters in South Carolina, 1790–1860.* Jefferson, N.C.: McFarland, 1985. Reprint, Columbia: University of South Carolina Press, 1995.

Kolchin, Peter. *American Slavery, 1619–1877.* New York: Hill and Wang, 1993.

Laws of North-Carolina. At a General Assembly, Begun and Held at the City of Raleigh, on Monday the Nineteenth Day of November, in the Year of Our Lord One Thousand Eight Hundred and Ten, and in the Thirty-Fifth Year of the Independence of This State. N.p., 1811.

Laws of North-Carolina. At a General Assembly, Begun and Held at the City of Raleigh, on Monday the Nineteenth Day of November, in the Year of Our Lord One Thousand Seven Hundred and Ninety-Eight, and of the Independence of the United States of America the Twenty-Third: It Being First Session of This Assembly. N.p., 1799.

Laws of North-Carolina. At a General Assembly, Begun and Held at the City of Raleigh, on the Thirteenth Day of December, in the Year of Our Lord One Thousand Seven Hundred and Ninety-Four, and in the Nineteenth Year of the Independence of the Said State: Being the First Session of the Said Assembly. N.p., 1795.

Laws of North-Carolina. At a General Assembly, Begun and Held at Raleigh, on the Twentieth Day of November, in the Year of Our Lord One Thousand Seven Hundred and Ninety-Seven, in the Twenty-Second Year of the Independence of the Said State: Being the First Session of the Said Assembly. N.p., 1798.

Laws of the Republic of Texas, Passed at the Session of the Fifth Congress. Houston: Telegraph Power, 1841.

Laws of the Republic of Texas, Passed at the Session of the Fourth Congress. Houston: Telegraph Power, 1840.

Laws of the State of Delaware, Passed at a Session of the General Assembly, Commenced and Held at Dover, on Tuesday the Fifth Day of January, in the Year of Our Lord, One Thousand Eight Hundred and Forty-Nine. Dover: S. Kimmey, 1849.

Laws of the State of Delaware, Passed at a Session of the General Assembly, Commenced and Held at Dover, on Tuesday the Second Day of January, in the Year of Our Lord, One Thousand Eight Hundred and Twenty Seven. Dover: J. Robertson, 1827.

Laws of the State of Delaware, Passed at a Session of the General Assembly, Commenced and Held at Dover, on Tuesday the Seventh Day of January, in the Year of Our Lord, One Thousand Eight Hundred and Fifty-One. Wilmington: Johnson, Chandler and Harker, 1851.

Laws of the State of Delaware, Passed at a Session of the General Assembly, Commenced and Held at Dover, on Tuesday the Third Day of January, in the Year of Our Lord, One Thousand Eight Hundred and Thirty-Seven. Dover: Samuel Kimmey, 1837.

Laws of the State of Delaware [Passed at a Session of the General Assembly in 1825]. Dover: n.p., [1826].

Laws of the State of Delaware [Passed at a Session of the General Assembly in 1832]. Dover: n.p., [1833].

Laws of the State of Mississippi. N.p., [1822].

Laws of the State of Mississippi. N.p., [1823].

Laws of the State of Mississippi. N.p., 182[4].

Laws of the State of Mississippi, Passed at a Regular Session of the Mississippi Legislature, Held in the City of Jackson, January, February, and March, 1852. Jackson: Palmer and Pickett, 1852.

Laws of the State of Mississippi, Passed at the Regular Session of the Mississippi Legislature, Held in the City of Jackson January, February, and March 1850. Jackson: Fall and Marshall, 1850.

Laws of the State of Mississippi, Passed at the Seventeenth Session of the General Assembly, Held in the Town of Jackson. Jackson: George R. Fall, 1834.

Laws of the State of Mississippi, Passed at the Sixteenth Session of the General Assembly, Held in the Town of Jackson. Jackson: Peter Isler, 1833.

Laws of the State of Missouri, Passed at the First Session of the Fourteenth General Assembly, Begun and Held at the City of Jefferson, on Monday, the Sixteenth Day of November, Eighteen Hundred and Forty-Six. . . . Jefferson: James Lusk, 1847.

The Laws of the State of North-Carolina, Enacted in the Year 1821. Raleigh: Thomas Henderson, 1822.

Laws of the State of North Carolina, Passed by the General Assembly, at the Session of 1846–47. Raleigh: Thomas J. Lemay, 1847.

The Laws of the State of North-Carolina Passed in 1802. N.p., 180[2].

Lebsock, Suzanne. *The Free Women of Petersburg: Status and Culture in a Southern Town, 1784–1860.* New York: W. W. Norton, 1984.

Leslie, Kent Anderson. *Woman of Color, Daughter of Privilege: Amanda America Dickson, 1849–1893.* Athens: University of Georgia Press, 1995.

Malone, Ann Patton. *Sweet Chariot: Slave Family and Household Structure in Nineteenth-Century Louisiana.* Chapel Hill: University of North Carolina Press, 1992.

McMillen, Sally G. *Southern Women: Black and White in the Old South.* Arlington Heights, Ill.: Harlan Davidson, 1992.

Morris, Thomas D. *Southern Slavery and the Law, 1619–1860.* Chapel Hill: University of North Carolina Press, 1996.

New Handbook of Texas. 6 vols. Austin: Texas State Historical Association, 1996.

Newton, Lewis W., and Herbert P. Gambrell. *Texas Yesterday and Today.* Dallas: Turner, 1949.

Phillips, Christopher. *Freedom's Port: The African American Community of Baltimore, 1790–1860.* Urbana: University of Illinois Press, 1997.

Phillips, Ulrich B. *American Negro Slavery: A Survey of the Supply, Employment and Control of Negro Labor as Determined by the Plantation Regime.* New York: D. Appleton, 1918.

———. *Life and Labor in the Old South.* Boston: Little, Brown, 1929.

———, ed. *Documentary History of American Industrial Society.* 2 vols. Cleveland: Arthur H. Clark, 1910.

Private Acts Passed at the First Session of the Twentieth General Assembly of the State of Tennessee. 1833. Nashville: Allen A. Hall and F. S. Heiskell, 1833.

Private Acts Passed at the Stated Session of the Nineteenth General Assembly of the State of Tennessee. 1831. Nashville: Allen A. Hall and Frederick S. Heiskell, 1832.

Public Acts of the State of Tennessee, Passed at the First Session of the Thirty-Second General Assembly, for the Years 1857–8. Nashville: G. C. Torbett, 1858.

Public Acts Passed at the First Session of the Twentieth General Assembly of the State of Tennessee. 1833. Nashville: Allen A. Hall and F. S. Heiskell, 1833.

Public Acts Passed at the Stated Session of the Nineteenth General Assembly of the State of Tennessee. 1831. Nashville: Allen A. Hall and F. S. Heiskell, 1832.

Rawick, George P., ed. *The American Slave: A Composite Autobiography.* 39 vols. Westport, Conn.: Greenwood, 1972–79.

Ripley, C. Peter, Jeffery S. Rossbach, Roy E. Finkenbine, Fiona E. Spiers, Paul A. Cimbala, Michael F. Hembree, and Donald Yacovone, eds. *The Black Abolitionist Papers.* 5 vols. Chapel Hill: University of North Carolina Press, 1985–92.

Rogers, George. "Slavery in South Carolina." In *Dictionary of Afro-American Slavery,* edited by Randall M. Miller and John David Smith, 699–706. New York: Greenwood, 1988.

Russell, John H. *The Free Negro in Virginia, 1619–1865.* Baltimore: Johns Hopkins University Press, 1913.

Schafer, Judith Kelleher. "'Open and Notorious Concubinage': The Emancipation of Slave Mistresses by Will and the Supreme Court in Antebellum Louisiana." *Louisiana History* 27 (Spring 1987): 165–82.

———. *Slavery, the Civil Law, and the Supreme Court of Louisiana.* Baton Rouge: Louisiana State University Press, 1994.

Schomburgk, Robert H. *The History of Barbados Comprising a Geographical and Statistical Description of the Island.* London: Longman, Brown, Green and Longman's, 1848. Reprint, London: Frank Cass, 1971.

Schwalm, Leslie A. *A Hard Fight for We: Women's Transition from Slavery to Freedom in South Carolina.* Urbana: University of Illinois Press, 1997.

Schwarz, Philip J. *Slave Laws in Virginia.* Athens: University of Georgia Press, 1996.

———. *Twice Condemned: Slaves and the Criminal Laws of Virginia, 1705–1865.* Baton Rouge: Louisiana State University Press, 1988.

Schweninger, Loren. "Doctor Jack: A Slave Physician on the Tennessee Frontier." *Tennessee Historical Quarterly* 57 (Spring/Summer 1998): 36–41.

———. *A Guide to the Microfilm Edition of Race, Slavery, and Free Blacks: Series 1, Petitions to Southern Legislatures, 1777–1867.* Bethesda, Md.: University Publications of America, 1999.

———. "John Carruthers Stanly and the Anomaly of Black Slaveholding." *North Carolina Historical Review* 67 (April 1990): 159–92.

———. "Property Owning Free African-American Women in the South, 1800–1870." *Journal of Women's History* 1 (Winter 1990): 13–44.

———. *Race, Slavery, and Free Blacks: Series 1, Petitions to Southern Legislatures, 1777–1867.* Bethesda, Md.: University Publications of America, 1998. Microfilm edition.

Shammas, Carole. "Black Women's Work and the Evolution of Plantation Society in Virginia." *Labor History* 26 (Winter 1985): 5–28.

Sobel, Robert, and John Raimo, eds. *Biographical Directory of the Governors of the United States, 1789–1978.* 4 vols. Westport, Conn.: Meckler Books, 1978.

Stampp, Kenneth. *The Peculiar Institution: Slavery in the Ante-Bellum South.* New York: Alfred P. Knopf, 1956.

Statute Laws of the State of Tennessee, of a General Character; Passed since the Compilation of the Statutes by Caruthers and Nicholson, in 1836. Nashville: J. G. Shepard, 1846.

The Statute Laws of the State of Tennessee, of a Public and General Nature. Knoxville: F. S. Heiskell, 1831.

The Statutes at Large of South Carolina. Columbia: A. S. Johnston, 1840.

The Statutes at Large of South Carolina. Columbia: T. S. Piggot, 1858.

Supplement to the Revised Code of the Laws of Virginia: Being a Collection of All the Acts of the General Assembly of a Public and Permanent Nature, Passed since the Year 1819. Richmond: Samuel Shepherd, 1833.

Syndor, Charles. "The Free Negro in Mississippi before the Civil War." *American Historical Review* 32 (July 1927): 769–88.

Thorpe, Francis Newton, comp. and ed. *The Federal and State Constitutions Colonial Charters, and Other Organic Laws of the States, Territories, and Colonies.* 6 vols. Washington, D.C.: Government Printing Office, 1909.

Tushnet, Mark. *The American Law of Slavery, 1810–1860: Considerations of Humanity and Interest.* Princeton, N.J.: Princeton University Press, 1981.

Wahl, Jenny Bourne. "The Bondsman's Burden: An Economic Analysis of the Jurisprudence of Slaves and Common Carriers." *Journal of Economic History* 53 (September 1993): 495–526.

Weiner, Marli F. *Mistresses and Slaves: Plantation Women in South Carolina, 1830–1880.* Urbana: University of Illinois Press, 1998.

White, Deborah Gray. *Ar'n't I a Woman? Female Slaves in the Plantation South.* New York: W. W. Norton, 1985.

———. "Female Slaves: Sex Roles and Status in the Antebellum Plantation South." *Journal of Family History* 9 (Fall 1983): 248–61.

Wikramanayake, Marina. *A World in Shadow: The Free Black in Antebellum South Carolina.* Columbia: University of South Carolina Press, 1973.

Wood, Betty. *Women's Work, Men's Work: The Informal Slave Economies of Low Country Georgia.* Athens: University of Georgia Press, 1995.

Wood, Peter. *Black Majority: Negroes in Colonial South Carolina from 1670 through the Stono Rebellion.* New York: W. W. Norton, 1974.

Wright, James. *The Free Negro in Maryland, 1634–1860.* New York: Columbia University Press, 1921.

INDEX

LOREN SCHWENINGER has written and edited numerous scholarly articles and books on African American history, including *Black Property Owners in the South, 1790–1915* and *Runaway Slaves: Rebels on the Plantation* (with John Hope Franklin). In 1991, he was a Senior Fulbright Lecturer at the University of Genoa, Italy. He is currently a professor of history and the director of the Race and Slavery Petitions Project at the University of North Carolina at Greensboro. The decade-long project is underwritten by the National Historical Publications and Records Commission, the National Endowment for the Humanities, and the Charles Stewart Mott Foundation.

Typeset in 10.5/12.5 Minion
with Fenice display
Designed by Copenhaver Cumpston
Composed by Celia Shapland
for the University of Illinois Press
Manufactured by Thomson-Shore, Inc.

University of Illinois Press
1325 South Oak Street
Champaign, IL 61820-6903
www.press.uillinois.edu